Reflections of a Citizen Teacher

Literacy, Democracy, and the Forgotten Students of Addison High

Todd DeStigter

University of Illinois at Chicago

National Council of Teachers of English
1111 W. Kenyon Road, Urbana, Illinois 61801-1096

Staff Editor: Tom Tiller
Interior Design: Jenny Jensen Greenleaf
Cover Design: Carlton Bruett

NCTE Stock Number: 29714-3050

It is the policy of NCTE in its journals and other publications to provide a forum for the open discussion of ideas concerning the content and the teach-ing of English and the language arts. Publicity accorded to any particular point of view does not imply endorsement by the Executive Committee, the Board of Directors, or the membership at large, except in announcements of policy, where such endorsement is clearly specified.

Grateful acknowledgment is made for permission to reprint the song lyrics at the opening of Chapter 5: "Dirty Blvd.," words and music by Lou Reed, © 1988, 1989 METAL MACHINE MUSIC. All rights controlled and ad-ministered by SCREEN GEMS–EMI MUSIC INC. All rights reserved. In-ternational copyright secured. Used by permission.

Library of Congress Cataloging-in-Publication Data

DeStigter, Todd, 1961–
    Reflections of a citizen teacher: literacy, democracy, and the
    forgotten students of Addison High/Todd DeStigter.
        p. cm.
    Includes bibliographical references and index.
    ISBN 0-8141-2971-4 (pbk.)
        1. Hispanic Americans—Education (Secondary)—Michigan—
    Addison—Case Studies. 2. Hispanic American students—Michigan—
    Addison—Social conditions—Case studies. 3. Literacy—Social
    aspects—Michigan—Addison—Case studies. 4. Educational anthro-
    pology—Michigan—Addison—Case studies. 5. DeStigter, Todd,
    1961– I. Title.
    LC2675.A33 D47 2001
    373.1829'68073—dc21
                                                                    00-064604

This book is dedicated to the memory of my mother,
Carole Jean Schultze DeStigter.

CONTENTS

ACKNOWLEDGMENTS

In some ways, writing a book can be a lonely enterprise: the years of reading and research, the countless hours watching a cursor blink back from a computer screen. However, despite the periods of isolation, this project has provided an opportunity for me to enjoy many supportive and enriching relationships with people and organizations that deserve my sincere thanks for their contributions to this work.

This book would not have been possible without generous and consistent financial assistance from the University of Michigan's English Department, School of Education, Joint Ph.D. Program in English and Education, and Rackham School of Graduate Studies, and from the University of Illinois at Chicago Institute for the Humanities. Each provided resources in the form of fellowships, travel grants, and summer stipends that enabled me to continue my reading and writing.

To Hedy and the late Charles Feit, I express my thanks for allowing me to live in their apartment in Santiago, Chile. Because of their hospitality, I made friends I will never forget, went places I never thought I'd go, and learned Spanish well enough to engage in the conversations recorded and discussed in this book.

To my friends in the Michigan English and Education Program I owe thanks for their friendship and counsel. Randall Roorda, Andrew Halevy, Debbie Mintor, and Renee Moreno each made important contributions to my understandings of literacy, teaching, and the consequences of my research. I wish especially to acknowledge Aaron Schutz, now at the University of Wisconsin, Milwaukee, whose agile intellect and creative scholarship kept me asking new questions and seeing things in ways I hadn't before.

I also wish to thank Anne Ruggles Gere for her interest in and support of this project. From my first year as a graduate student, Anne treated me like a trusted colleague, and the faith she showed in the integrity of my decisions was a great source of encouragement. Martin Packer, too, deserves my gratitude for introducing me to the theory and practice of educational ethnography and for providing advice and direction during our weekly coffee shop meetings during the first years of this project. I am grateful as well to my UIC colleague David Schaafsma and to Cathy Fleischer for their thorough, thoughtful responses to earlier versions of this manuscript and for their ongoing guidance in helping me understand and articulate the democratic, ethical mandates of literacy education. I also thank NCTE editors Michael Greer, Zarina Hock, and Tom Tiller for their support of this book and for shepherding it to publication.

I am especially indebted to my mentor and friend Jay Robinson for his careful readings of several drafts of this work and for the conversation we've been sharing for the past ten years. Jay's lifetime of passionate scholarship and unrelenting commitment to exploring ways in which language might help make this a more humane world has represented, for me, the best of university pedagogy. I have never known anyone whose intellectual energies are more infused with and motivated by a profound love for others.

My thanks are also due to the teachers and staff of Addison High who welcomed me as a colleague and friend. Though I must use pseudonyms, Beth Rienstra, Laura Vedder, and Alice Martinez (you know who you are) are among the finest teachers I have ever had the privilege of working with. I am also thankful to the students whose words and experiences are documented in these pages and who have enriched my life in more ways than I could ever name. These young people have astounded me with their courage and resilience, their love of life, and their gift to me of friendship.

To Susan Forest, without whose companionship and technical support this book would not have come together, I am and will always be deeply grateful. Finally, I thank my family, and especially my daughter Kaitlin, for their willingness to listen to all the stories about my friends in Addison.

FOREWORD

VICTOR VILLANUEVA
Washington State University

*A*fter first reading Mike Rose, we spoke, and we said that the story in Lives on the Boundary *was rich, very much like the stories of people of color. And there was kind of a nod among us, we teachers and scholars of color who had managed to congregate. One says, "Heck (or something to that effect), for one, we don't get no white mentors.*

Todd DeStigter suggests a new era, a time of mentors rather than social workers.

When Todd DeStigter wrote *Reflections of a Citizen Teacher* he was working in Ann Arbor. It's important, because he is able to play out the contrasts between the school where he worked and the one where he performed his research—a research we need to know about as the demographics of the country shift. Now he's at the University of Illinois in Chicago. That pleases me. Because as you will read in the pages that follow, Todd DeStigter knows Latinos y Latinas, knows us in our variety, in our multiplicity. He meets us, we Latinos and Latinas, talks with us, respects us. And in his telling, you learn about us in our multiplicity, at least to some degree, some degree more.

Latino multiplicity[1] —

A thousand years before the first Europeans arrived on Puerto Rico, the native peoples of the mainland and the lesser Antilles migrated to Puerto Rico, where they could live in relative peace, able to fish and live off the fresh vegetation—pineapple and varieties of tuber that have no name in English. We don't know the names of the first inhabitants of Puerto Rico. Our history is the history told by the Europeans, who, conferring their values on the land, took the language of the local imperial lords. We only

know the names given the first Puerto Ricans by their first colo-
nizers, the first to raid them, the first to enslave them, the ones
the Europeans honored by naming the region after them. These
first colonizers were the peoples of Carib. And they named the
people of that island Arawak, *and the culture of the Arawak was*
called Taino. *And their island was named* Boriquén.

Then came Columbus. . . . And then Ponce deLeón. And
then the priests. And we don't really know what happened when
they spoke, what transpired between the priests of Spain and the
Boricua Arawakas of Taino Ways. So, to the analogous[2]

The scene is Peru. It's the end of the fifteenth century.
Father Valverde, a Franciscan, is speaking to the Incan phi-
losopher-rhetorician about the ways of the world. The
Franciscan intends to be instructive, an attempt to raise the
indigenous from its ignorance. The Incan doesn't recognize
the developmental mindset and enters into dialectical inter-
play. Having heard of how things work according to Father
Valverde, the Incan responds:

You listed five preeminent men whom I ought to know.
The first is God, three and one, which are four, whom
you call the creator of the universe. Is he perhaps our
Pachacámac and Viracocha? The second claims to be the
father of all men, on whom they piled their sins. The
third you call Jesus Christ, the only one not to cast sins
on that first man, but he was killed. The fourth you call
pope. The fifth, Carlos, according to you, is the most
powerful monarch of the universe and supreme over all.
However, you affirm this without taking account of other
monarchs. But if this Carlos is prince and lord of all the
world, why does he need the pope to grant him conces-
sions and donations to make war on us and usurp our
kingdoms? And if he needs the pope, then is not the pope
the greater lord and most powerful prince of all the world,
instead of Carlos? Also you say that I am obliged to pay
tribute to Carlos and not to others, but since you give no
reason for this tribute, I feel no obligation to pay it. If it
is right to give tribute and service at all, it ought to be
given to God, the man who was Father of all, then to

Jesus Christ who never piled on his sins, and finally to the pope. . . . But if I ought not give tribute to this man, even less ought I give it to Carlos, who was never lord of these regions and whom I have never seen.
The record of this meeting at Atahualpa notes that,
The Spaniards, unable to endure this prolixity of argumentation, jumped from their seats and attacked the Indians and grabbed hold of their gold and silver jewels and precious stones.
And when the slaves of Puerto Rico rebelled, slaves from Africa were brought in, and the Boricuas ran inland, away from the fortressed walls of El Morro, and the rebels acquiesced to the Spanish while trading with Dutch and English, French and Italian pirates who would find other ways to enter the island. This subversion became jaibería *[a strategy that remains for Puerto Ricans, a resignation to power relations without a relinquishing of power, really]. And I understand Angel Rama, when he says that it is in the Caribbean that "the plural manifestations of the entire universe insert themselves."[3] My mother's name is Italian (the line is never lost in the Spanish tradition, my mother becoming María Socorro Cotto deVillanueva, and my becoming Víctor Villanueva y Cotto until I was Americanized as Victor Villanueva, Jr.). My mother's name: Italian. The memory of that first Italian? Lost.*

Centuries later, I am Puerto Rican—a product of the first migrations of Puerto Ricans to New York in the late 1940s, though my mother arrived through what was euphemistically called "indentured servitude," what others called "white slavery," as if somehow more barbaric than the slavery of Asians and of Africans. And I assimilate. And I don't . But I know how to seem to be—jaibería—and the memory provided by stories told. Memory does hunger. And it's fed through the stories told.
Professor DeStigter has stories to tell. And along the way he turns to Dewey and others who he sees as in some way agreeing with Dewey in explaining the political and educational realities for the multiple Latinos, Latinas, and others of color. And with Dewey and those others Professor DeStigter discusses how we might approach the difficulties of the proto-bilingual, mainly, in

an overwhelmingly assimilationist world—with more of an understanding of us, we Latinos and Latinas, than I tend to see,
with a clear understanding of teachers in public high schools, the
veteran white teachers with good hearts and many years at the
job, those who become "realists," the middle-class teachers of
color, those who had known poverty, those who might not have,
and with an understanding of the community and its folks of
color. This is a rich text. One could be tempted to read the narrative, the stories, and bypass the theory and research woven within
the narrative. But the narrative demands a careful read, a critical
read. Professor DeStigter invites it. Only through a thorough read
through the citizen students will we find our ways to becoming
sound citizen teachers.

Notes

1. The following will appear in "*Cuentos de mi Historia:* An Art of
Memory" by Victor Villanueva, in *Scholarly Writing Combinations:
Personal, Professional, Pedagogical,* edited by Deborah Holdstein and
David Bleich (New York: Modern Language Association, in press).

2. Although this internal quote is contained in the reference cited in
note one, the source material can be found in "On The Rhetoric and
Precedents of Racism," *College Composition and Communication,* June
1999, 645–661, by Victor Villanueva.

3. In Pamela María Smorkaloff's *Cuban Writers On and Off the Island:
Contemporary Narrative Fiction* (p. vii), 1999, New York: Twayne.

CHAPTER ONE

Introduction: Unfamiliar Territory

*The point, then, without doubt, is to change the world.
But how?*

Ross Chambers, *Room for Maneuver:
Reading the Oppositional in Narrative*

Unfamiliar Territory

It is a long way from Ann Arbor to Addison, Michigan, almost an hour even if the roads are clear of snow. But on a December morning in 1992, as my Honda crawled through the fog at 35 m.p.h. behind a Ford pickup, I knew the trip would take even longer than I had expected. A few years earlier, at ten past eight in the morning, I would have been in a classroom at Ohio State University, sipping coffee at the feet of the eminent rhetorician Edward P. J. Corbett. I would have been marveling at how he could recite from memory entire paragraphs from Richard Whately's *Elements of Rhetoric,* or scribbling in my notebook his explanations of the nuances of Aristotle's original Greek that are lost in even the best translations. I might also have been considering the project due the following week in my composition theory course, the one in which I was evaluating the responses instructors had written on the essays of students I had never met. In any case, I would have been thinking about rhetoric and how to be a better English teacher.

That day, though, my gloved hand gripping the steering wheel, I was on my way to Addison High School to meet with Maria Alvarez,[1] a guidance counselor who had been referred to me by a friend who worked as a language arts coordinator in a neighboring school district. When Alvarez and I had spoken over the telephone a couple of weeks earlier, she confirmed that a large part of her job was to work with the school's Latino students, many of whose families had come seeking work in the area's fields or small industries. My plan was to gain access to these students' classrooms, to study their literacy practices, and then to use my background as a writer and teacher to improve, in whatever way I could, their experiences and opportunities within what I knew to be a predominantly White environment. As I left my university world of fashionable coffee shops and the stately silence of the graduate school reading room, I listened to the instructional tape in my car: "En qué clase de concurso participó Alberto, un concurso de inglés o un concurso de matemáticas?" I knew that I must think in Spanish again, that I must cross *la frontera* into another world that was, in many ways, far away from my own.

I couldn't see much, my headlights only making the mist glow a lighter shade of gray, so I leaned forward and squinted, downshifted to third gear, and followed the red taillights ahead of me. The steam from the mug of coffee resting on the dashboard clouded the windshield as I read the directions I had received over the phone and scrawled between the lines of a form that urged me to renew my subscription to *College English*. The truck's lights glowed brighter, and I braked as we approached a stop sign. On the gravel alongside the two-lane blacktop, his shoulders stooping under the weight of a heavy green overcoat, stood an old man wearing large rubber boots, with clouds of warm breath rising from beneath his orange hunting cap. He waved to the Ford as it rolled to a stop. I edged to the intersection, smiled and waved, but he just stared at the stranger in the unfamiliar foreign car.

Along the pavement's crumbling edge, signs warned me to "Pass With Care," and as I coaxed a bit more speed from the Honda, we swayed with the contours of the road that had settled into the earth and that sidestepped, sometimes by just a few feet, the pale and listing barns that struggled to remain standing as hay pushed through the cracks in their walls. Some of these structures had given up and collapsed, like old horses too tired to pull a plow through another row. Others, though, loomed strong and straight, their bright paint smooth, doors open, framing the silhouettes of gigantic farm machinery. By and by the fog began to thin. Beyond the ditches stretched a landscape of frozen corn-fields, the rich and generous topsoil left by Lake Erie centuries ago now resting beneath a white blanket of snow patterned by the tracks of snowmobiles and the stubble of cut corn stalks. About fifty yards from the road, three horses huddled, heads down, near an old tractor that sulked among the tall weeds that had been far enough beneath its rusted frame to have escaped last fall's mowing. Someone had thrown a green plastic tarp over the engine compartment, and an upside-down bucket was perched atop its vertical exhaust pipe, like a tilted head regarding me curiously at the end of an outstretched neck.

I passed several large houses, stout, mostly white, their wide front porches ornamented by delicately carved wood. The smaller homes seemed deferent by comparison, a few partially stripped of the siding that normally covers silver sheets of insulation material, and several cluttered with what I considered to be too many cars—up to six crowded into a single driveway. In one yard sat a tan Buick LeSabre, its vinyl top peeling like weathered paint, the handmade sign propped in a window inviting passersby to "Make Offer."

The tape in my dashboard stereo congratulated me for having "very successfully completed" another Spanish lesson and clicked to a stop. I tuned to my favorite Detroit station for the morning sports news but shut it off, unable to hear the scores through the static. To pass the time, I practiced describing things out loud in Spanish, taking my cues from whatever sped by (here and throughout the text, quoted English words will be italicized when they were in fact spoken in Spanish): *"I am very far from any town or city, and because there is no broadcast station nearby, my radio isn't working well." "All the houses have white tanks that contain natural gas for heating them." "Many of the houses have American flags out front. The flags are not moving because there is no wind." "I see a factory that makes some things from* . . . silicone." *"This afternoon, I need to change the oil in my car."* Eventually I reached the sign that welcomed me to Addison. *"Welcome to Addison." "The houses are closer* . . . to each other *now."* I passed a movie theater, a couple of convenience stores, and a tiny brick building its faded sign advertised as "Maureen's Styling Shoppe."

Addison High is an expansive two-story brick structure that sprawls on about twelve acres of former farmland, its main entrance separated from the street by about two hundred yards of what in the spring and summer is a neatly trimmed lawn. Facing the street are two signs that pronounce this to be a "Drug-Free" and "Weapon-Free" zone. The school's four main corridors form a square around a courtyard, and from the west side of the building extends a long hallway leading to the gymnasium and locker rooms. The amount of space the school occupies is not an accident, I was later told by an elderly man who had lived in Addison almost all his life: "I remember when they were trying to decide where to put the new school; this was back in the '50s. A lot of folks wanted to put it farther east, nearer the center of town, but some people were pressuring the Board to move it farther west, away from the sections of town where a lot of the Mexicans had moved in." About halfway between the street and the school, a concrete walk is interrupted by a replica of the Liberty Bell, recognizable by the crack in its side, surrounded by four tall poles, each supporting an American flag.

Only a few minutes late, I turned into the school parking lot and coasted over the speed bumps and into a space marked "Reserved for faculty." I looked into the rearview mirror. My skin looked unusually pale, the result of the Michigan winters that kept me huddled inside with my books and my Macintosh. I straightened my tie, rubbed a smudge and some dust off my good shoes, and headed up the long walk to the main entrance. As I approached the Liberty Bell, I saw that it rested on a concrete platform encircled by wooden benches that are, up close, dry and cracked, one of them marred by a hole burned into it. Two teenage girls who were standing nearby, their hands stuffed into the pockets of their winter coats, told me that the flagpoles represent the four grades (nine through twelve) at the high school.

"Are you students here?" I asked.

"No, not any more," one of them said. "About a year ago I quit."

I continued to the entrance and, once inside, wandered for a few minutes until a tall boy wearing a Detroit Tigers baseball cap directed me to the counseling office.

"Go back the way you came, hang a right at the first hall-way, and just keep going."

Alvarez graciously dismissed my apologies by mentioning that the fog had delayed the buses, too. As she offered me a seat in her office, I asked about the photographs tacked to her bulletin board of two young men in military uniforms. "My sons," she said. "I'm a Marine mom." We chatted for a few minutes, then Alvarez focused on the point of my visit.

"So, why do you want to work with Latino students?" she asked.

I began by explaining that my reasons were partly personal, that as a boy growing up in a West Michigan farming community, I had spent several summers pulling weeds out of local onion fields for $1.25 per hour. Even for sprightly kids of thirteen, it was grueling work. We crawled between rows that stretched for hundreds of yards through black soil that drew the summer heat down around us like a canvas. One year, the boss decided to save money on herbicide, and as a result the weeds grew faster and thicker than ever before, choking the onions and leading him to add a family of migrant workers to our crew. I remember their arrival. These were the "migrants," as we locals called them, the families from Texas and Mexico who drove into town each spring in heavily loaded vans and station wagons. In our adolescent eyes, the migrants were workers of legendary abilities, the John Henrys of the onion fields, only instead of driving steel, they pulled weeds. Whole families worked side by side—fathers and mothers, teenagers, children as young as three or four who carried water and even pulled some of the smaller weeds. The migrants lived in shacks behind the main barn, about seventy yards from the "big house" where the boss lived, and they spent their evenings chatting in lawn chairs set outside or watching little league baseball games at the city park. Though my earnings went to pay for luxuries like bicycles and baseball cards, the migrants used their wages for food and clothing. I remembered, too, that though these families had children of all ages, the migrants often arrived in town before my friends and I had been dismissed for summer vacation, and they remained working several weeks after we had returned to school.

After my summers in the onion fields, I didn't think much about the migrants until I took my first high school English teaching job in Los Angeles, where many of my neighbors were *illegales*. In the building next door, six men lived together in a well-kept two-bedroom apartment. They worked harder than anyone I've ever known—long hours at car washes and restaurant kitchens. On Sunday afternoons we played soccer together and then drank beers on my apartment balcony. It was then that they would show me photos of their wives and children back in Mexico.

Though these acquaintances with Latino workers were more or less accidental, I told Alvarez that my interest in working at Addison High also related more directly to my interests in literacy and teaching. I said that as an educator, I thought it important to be responsive to studies which document the rapid rise of the number of Latino people in the United States. From 1980 to late 1989, the total U.S. population increased by about 9 percent (from 228 million to 248 million). In contrast, the Latino population grew about 40 percent (from 14.4 million to 20.1 million), a rate over four times faster than the rest of the U.S. population (Valencia, 1991b).[2] While Latinos in 1993 made up about 8 percent of the total U.S. population, demographers estimate that in approximately the year 2005, that figure will have risen to more than 13 percent, and Latinos will surpass African Americans as this country's largest ethnic minority group. By 2050, Latinos are expected to number about 55 million people, nearly one fifth of the U.S. population (Secada et al., 1998).

As might be expected, this demographic shift is anticipated to occur in school-aged children as well. Examining long-term projections from 1982 to the year 2020, Pallas, Natriello, and McDill (1988) note that among the U.S. population from newborns to age 17, the number of White youngsters is expected to decline by over 6 million (13 percent) during this period. The number of Latino children, however, will more than triple—increasing from 6 million in 1982 (9 percent of the national youth population) to 19 million in 2020, when they will make up 25 percent of the country's youth population. Put another way, Pallas et al. point out that almost three of four children in the U.S. in 1982 were White; in 2020, only about one in two will be White. In 1982, about one in every ten children in the U.S. was Latino;

by 2020, that ratio will change to about one in every four (Pallas et al., 1988, p. 22, cited in Valencia, 1991b, p. 19).

Reflecting the overall rise in the number of Latino students in the U.S., the number of so-called "language-minority" (LM) students is also growing rapidly, and most of these students are native speakers of Spanish (Nieto, 1992).[3] In 1991, the number of LM students in U.S. public schools was over 2.3 million, representing 5.5 percent of the total student population (Fleischman & Hopstock, 1993, p. 6). This number is an increase of almost a million since 1984. Moreover, it is expected that by the year 2020, the number of children speaking a primary language other than English will more than double to almost 6 million (Natriello, McDill, & Pallas, 1990, p. 55). In addition to their limited English proficiency, LM students face further educational challenges. Fleischman and Hopstock (1993), for instance, report that 38 percent of LM students in the average school have very limited literacy skills in their native language (p. 6). As a result of these and other difficulties, 27 percent of LM students in the average high school are assigned to grade levels at least two years lower than age/grade norms, compared to 11 percent of all students.

I stressed to Alvarez what I suspected she already knew— that as the number of Latino students in the U.S. grows, so does the importance of addressing their needs as people whose cultures and language abilities have not sufficiently been attended to by our schools' traditional curricula or teaching methods. I knew this omission had produced serious consequences, as the dropout rate among Latino students is two to three times the rate for European Americans or African Americans (Secada, 1998). I added that I was especially interested in Addison as my research site because most of the studies on Latino students focus on schools either in urban areas (Carger, 1996; Romo & Falbo, 1996) or in regions like Texas, Florida, and California that have high concentrations of Latino residents (Foley, 1990; Valdés, 1996). I had reasoned that a study conducted in Addison would contribute to the relatively lean body of information available concerning Latino students in northern rural settings, where they constitute a relatively small percentage of the overall student population.

As Alvarez and I continued our chat, I also mentioned that I was eager to spend time in and around Addison High because during my six years as a high school teacher, I had grown to realize that it no longer made sense to me to think of reading and writing as "neutral" technologies or discrete practices occurring in hermetically sealed classrooms. Rather, I had begun to understand literacies as events, activities, the playing out of social roles that take on meaning in the sociocultural contexts in which they occur. Though I didn't say so there in Alvarez's office, I was thinking of Brian Street's (1984) admonition that "the skills and concepts that accompany literacy acquisition, in whatever form, do not stem in some automatic way from the inherent qualities of literacy . . . but are aspects of a specific ideology" (p. 1). Because of what Street calls "the ideological and therefore culturally embedded nature" of literacy practices, reading and writing are best understood as they take place within specific situations that are inscribed by social institutions, which include but are not limited to educational ones (p. 3). Such a model, it seemed to me, required a revised conception of my work as a literacy teacher, an expansion from a concern with individual readers and writers in isolated classrooms toward a broader attentiveness not only to how students, in interaction with others, develop identities as literate persons but also how they negotiate sociocultural forces like race, gender, and social class, which are integral aspects of the contexts where these negotiations occur (Hynds, 1997, p. 11). In other words—and this I did say to Alvarez—I wanted to better understand the causes and consequences of students' reading and writing, and to do that I had to observe and participate in these activities within their broadly defined contexts. Ultimately, I said, I hoped that by writing about the teachers and students of Addison High I could contribute to important conversations concerning the particular educational needs of Latino students in predominantly White school settings.

Alvarez then asked me exactly what I wanted to do at Addison High. I confessed that at that point I didn't really know, that I needed to observe for a while, to talk to teachers and students, to see what issues arose, and to find out how my training and experience as an English teacher might be useful.

"Well," Alvarez said, "if you're willing to work for free, there's plenty to do right here." She explained that despite the fact that Latinos constitute nearly 16 percent of a total Addison High population of more than 1,300 students, budget constraints had made it difficult for the school to implement measures needed to address the special needs of language-minority students. In fact, she said, the Addison school district did not actually offer bilingual instruction. Rather, the district employed only one full-time English as a Second Language (ESL) teacher, who spent her days traveling from building to building, attempting to help those students who were most at risk. Though Alvarez conceded that the number of students in the Addison High ESL class was fairly small—usually no more than ten per semester—she added that because the ESL teacher was in the high school only one period per day, the LM students were left to fend for themselves, with no organized training in English, no content-area instruction or materials in their native languages, and almost no recourse but to assimilate on their own as best they could.

Alvarez reached into a desk drawer and pulled out a sheet of calculations.

"Look," she said. "We've got pretty serious problems among Hispanic students even if they do speak English." She passed me the paper, which documented that at that point in the 1992–93 school year, 40 of Addison's 320 seniors were Latino.[4] Only 11 of these 40 students had the 2.5 GPA generally thought necessary to go to college. Three had a 3.0 or above, with the highest at 3.6. Alvarez noted, however, that this student was the son of a White woman and a Chicano father who divorced when the boy was two years old. The mother remarried, this time to a White man. "Essentially," Alvarez said, "the kid's been raised in a White family. The problem gets worse, though," she continued, "when you keep in mind that of the 30 to 40 kids who fail the U.S. history course each year, the one required for graduation, almost half of them are Hispanic, even those who speak fluent English." She shrugged her shoulders and shook her head. "These kids just don't have the study habits they need to get by."

I wondered to myself whether Alvarez might be simplifying things a bit, whether the academic struggles of Addison's Latino students might be due less to their allegedly poor study habits than to what and how they were taught and, more generally, to an educational environment that was insufficiently responsive to their needs. In short, I wondered whether Latino students' study habits were more of a symptom than a cause of the troubles they experienced at school.

Alvarez became more enthusiastic, however, when I confirmed that I was willing to tutor students for no pay. "We really need someone here when the ESL teachers aren't in the building," she said. "You'll be just like a new staff member. How would you like to help tutor Rosa?"

"Who's Rosa?"

Alvarez told me the abridged version of Rosa's story. Rosa, her mother, and her six siblings came to the U.S. mainland from Puerto Rico nearly three years before, and they had lived in Pennsylvania and Wisconsin before settling in Michigan. Rosa was seventeen, but she didn't have enough credits to qualify as a second-semester first-year student.

"Why not?" I asked.

Alvarez punched a few keys on her computer, and Rosa's attendance record lit up the screen. At a glance, I estimated that there were about twenty T's (for "truant") behind Rosa's name. According to school policy, Alvarez said, students forfeit course credit when their number of truancies climbs above ten. Alvarez explained that a lot of the T's should probably be A's (meaning "absent"—the parent had called school), but until the previous week, Rosa's family hadn't had a phone. Just as well, the counselor said. Rosa rarely talked—very shy. Alvarez called down to the principal's office for permission for me to accompany Rosa to class. As she hung up the phone, she smiled. "He says that if you can get Rosa to come to school, he'll give you two Ph.D.'s. Would you like to meet her?"

Shy Rosa had been waiting in the reception area. She wore jeans decorated with silver chains, a white shirt, and a black leather jacket. I stood as we were introduced.

"Rosa, this is Mr. Destrickski."

"DeStigter."

"*Hello*," she said, staring at the floor.

"He's interested in helping you and some of the other Spanish-speaking students."

Rosa managed a slight smile. *"I don't understand."*

"He's interested in helping you and some of the other Spanish-speaking students. Okay?"

"Okay."

I asked Rosa, first in English and then in my feeble Spanish, how she would feel about my attending classes with her a couple of times per week and helping her understand her assignments.

"Fine. I've had tutors before," she said.

We talked a bit more, and I learned that Rosa's most difficult classes were math, geography, and English. We shook hands, wished each other a "Merry Christmas," and said good-bye until next semester. I thanked Alvarez and walked outside to my car. Tucked behind the windshield wiper was a parking ticket.

I managed to get a "substitute teacher" parking permit to hang from my rearview mirror, one of the many adjustments I made as I continued to drive twice each week to Addison High for what would turn out to be a three-year study focusing on a small number of Addison High's language-minority students, the school itself, and the community it serves. But despite the many hours I spent in Addison, even at the conclusion of this project, when I sat face to face with Manuel, a fifteen-year-old migrant worker from the *barrio* of Brownsville, Texas, it was impossible to ignore the *frontera* between us. His hands alone—the tomato-field dirt worked under the skin, the gang insignia tattooed in the loose flesh where the forefinger meets the thumb—testified to the distance separating his life, his *cultura,* from mine. Nonetheless, *Reflections of a Citizen Teacher* is a story of using reading and writing to try to understand and then to narrow such distances, all in an attempt to help change the world into a more humane and just place than it is now.

Evolving Perspectives of a Citizen Teacher

As my conversation with Alvarez reveals, my interest in the education of Latino and language-minority students stems from a combination of my own personal history and the evidence of their increasing numbers in our nation's schools, as well as from indications that Latino adolescents often face academic challenges that non-Latino students do not. Similarly, my ways of thinking and talking about the experiences of the young people introduced in this book are the result of my attempts to connect the day-to-day work of teachers to the broader social contexts within which that work takes place. This way of understanding schools represents an effort to shift points of view from the general to the specific and back again, and to see how particular instances of teaching and learning either promote or resist larger cultural and political trends and priorities. Like the observations and reflections of all teachers, this approach is also shaped by the values that we educators bring to our work, those ideals which provide the outline of a vision by which we may assess whether or not schools are contributing to a progression toward the kind of society we desire. In short, I'm talking about a conceptualization of teaching as part of a larger sociopolitical and ethical project.

For my part, the project to which I am most committed at present is democracy. Why democracy? Permit me to offer a partial answer to that question by repeating a question posed by John Dewey (1938/1963): "Can we find any reason that does not ultimately come down to the belief that democratic social arrangements promote a better quality of human experience, one which is more widely accessible and enjoyed, than do non-democratic and anti-democratic forms of social life?" (p. 34). Though more specific reasons for this commitment, and for my understanding of democracy, will, I hope, become clear throughout this book, for now let me say briefly that, following Dewey, I am using *democracy* to refer to a way of interacting with others by which all people have the desire, ability, and opportunity to participate in shaping their individual and collective lives. Put another way, I understand democracy to be a process of associated living in which individuals participate in deciding what their world should be like, in acting to pursue these aims, and in sharing equitably in the consequences of that action. For an educator to play a part in promoting democracy thus defined, I believe it is crucial that she or he regard the contexts of school and society as overlapping, interactive, and mutually influential. This kind of complex observational and analytical perspective, when infused with a desire to advance the ideals of democracy, come together in a disposition which I will call that of a "citizen teacher."

In many ways, my conception of the citizen teacher reflects the priorities and analytical methods of educators and theorists who advocate what is commonly called "critical pedagogy." As Peter McLaren (1995) has summarized, proponents of critical pedagogy "are united in their attempts to empower the powerless to transform social inequalities and injustices" (p. 29). While the citizen teacher shares these overall goals, his or her specific way of pursuing them is by expanding and strengthening institutions and human relations that support participatory democracy. Also, although critical pedagogy tends to stress a Marxist interpretation of the politics and power relations that influence schools, citizen teachers will supplement this framework with an emphasis on cultural influences and on poststructuralist notions of identity that go beyond class-based analyses. Further, while Amy Gutmann (1999) has described democratic education as that which preserves "the intellectual and social foundations of democratic deliberations" (p. 14), the citizen teacher is interested not only in how the opportunities to participate in such deliberations depend on rational discourse and the influences of power and authority, but also in how the equitable distribution of such authority relies in part on local, affective relations among diverse people. As I imagine it, then, a citizen teacher is a person invigorated by hope, a person who believes and acts on the notion that democratic education can further social justice and the release of individual human potential. This hope is tempered, however, by the citizen teacher's honest recognition of the stark differences between the way she or he would like the world to be and the way it really is.

Indeed, as an aspiring citizen teacher, I confess that when I consider the challenges to democracy either in the localized settings of schools or in the broader public spheres of U.S. society, I feel a mild but incessant form of anxiety that smolders in me like a low-grade fever. As a citizen of the United States, I worry about what I see as the degradation of democracy in our nation's public policy and civic life. I worry, for instance, about the growing separation in this country between the rich and the poor, about the appalling fact that one in every four of the nation's children lives in poverty, about the most recent statistics showing that more than 44 million Americans are without health insurance. I worry, too, that progressive attempts to address these and other disparities will continue to be hindered by the exclusion of certain voices from public debates due to the concentration and influence of money in the political process.

As a teacher, I find some reprieve from these concerns in my work, especially when I recall the many positive things that schools do. Schools provide a place where young people can learn about the world beyond their immediate experience, where they can discover and develop their gifts and interests. Guided by committed, creative teachers, students in schools may also acquire the skills, knowledge, and credentials necessary for certain types of higher education and careers, as well as foster enriching relationships with peers and adult mentors. At the same time, however, despite these and many other benefits, it is sobering to acknowledge the aspects of schooling that run counter to the participatory ideals of democracy. I am thinking, now, in Kozol's (1991) phrase, of the "savage inequalities" in resources between wealthy and poor school districts and in the attendant experiences of students and teachers in these settings. I am thinking, too, of the alarming rise in the frequency of and weight given to standardized tests that measure "knowledge" divorced from any kind of social or ethical context. These concerns extend to the subjection of schooling to market forces through the introduction of choice plans, to the commodification of students by viewing them as human capital to meet corporate needs, and to the deep academic trenches assigned to students as part of tracking systems that prepare young people for life on predetermined strata of society.

From the perspective of a citizen teacher, these two sets of concerns—the sociopolitical and the educational—merge into one, as schools are recognized to simultaneously reflect and contribute to the inequities of the broader society. To be sure, as I've noted, schools do many good things, but they also play a part in defining and determining the world's winners and losers. And while educators can be gratified to know that our work serves some students well, it seems to me that—as citizen teachers—we are also compelled to think hard about the fate of those students whose needs we often attend to less successfully. As Cornel West (1999) reminds us, such considerations are among the obligations of living in a democratic society:

> Democracy always raises a fundamental question: What is the role of the most disadvantaged in relation to the public interest? It is similar in some ways to the biblical question: What are you to do with the least of these? If we do not want to live in a democracy, we are not obliged to raise that question. In fact, the aristocracy does not address that question at all. Chekov wrote in a play, "The Czar's police, they don't give a damn about raising that question. That's not the kind of society they are." But within a democratic society that question must be continually raised and pushed. (p. 9)

In their efforts to explore possible answers to this and related questions, citizen teachers will, it seems to me, necessarily discover new ways of understanding what goes on in their classrooms. Over long periods of time, they will observe their students and themselves closely, and from these observations will arise insights according to which they may assess their own and others' assumptions and theories about teaching and learning. These citizen teachers will, in other words, develop the reflective inquisitiveness of a teacher-researcher—a professional sensibility which, as Cathy Fleischer (1995) has noted, underscores the relationship between the activities within classrooms and the conditions beyond them:

> By first looking critically at their particular experiences as teachers in particular classrooms, and by then reflecting on recurring themes in those particular experiences in order to make sense of the complex world that exists in their classrooms, teacher-researchers prepare themselves to create worthwhile learning environments, to develop purposeful curricula, to devise productive methods of teaching. Such practice is what Paulo Freire calls "praxis": critical reflection and action that changes conditions of being in the world. (p. 14)

As citizen teachers exercise this kind of critical reflection in their daily work, they may find useful analytical frameworks which are drawn from anthropology and sociology and which have helped me to make sense of what I have observed in and around Addison High. Though some of these frameworks are by now familiar, they are potentially helpful to teachers with current, democratic concerns in that they highlight the dialogic relationship between the activities of individuals in localized settings and the larger sociocultural structures within which these activities are inscribed.

One such framework is "social reproduction" theory, which introduces a Marxist perspective to analyses of education by calling attention to the ways in which schools contribute to the maintenance of social class differences (Bowles & Gintis, 1976). This process is made possible, in part, by the dominant classes' reproducing the cultural forms that ensure their own privileged place in society. As Pierre Bourdieu (1979) has argued, schools play a particularly important role in legitimating and reproducing certain forms of knowledge, ways of speaking, and ways of relating to the world that capitalize on the type of familiarity and skills that only certain students have received from their family backgrounds and class situations. Thus, as institutions that at once reflect and mediate what Bourdieu calls "dominant cultural capital," schools help ensure generational continuity of the cultural (and, hence, the socioeconomic and political) privilege held by the dominant classes in capitalist societies.

Applying this interpretive framework to my reading of Addison High, I began to understand the school culture, its history, and the ongoing practices of its teachers and administrators as reproducing the ideological privilege that places Latino students on the margins of the Addison High community. More specifically, because pedagogical actions are embedded in a system subjected to the effects of dominant class ideologies, I came to recognize some of the complex ways in which language teaching—as an inseparable aspect of culture—mediates social relations at Addison High, including those relations that result in the continued domination of some groups over others. From this perspective, reading and writing activities in the Addison High curriculum, when restricted to filling in blanks on worksheets or answering questions at the end of textbook chapters, illustrate how the school's officially sanctioned literacy practices are just one part of the larger symbolic discourse the school uses to reinforce the marginal status of its LM Latino students.

Such outcomes appear less inevitable in light of revisions to and departures from social reproduction theory that set forth a view of culture as being actively and diversely constructed in localized contexts. Paul Willis (1981a), for instance, has argued that social reproduction encounters resistance in the form of what he calls "cultural production"—the process of self-formation within the working class itself which underscores the agency emanating from small groups and thereby challenges the values of dominant culture (p. 58). Further, feminist and postmodernist scholars have challenged the "grand narrative" tendencies of social reproduction by demonstrating that individuals dismantle and reconfigure competing cultural systems in the process of fashioning shifting and multiple identities in different settings and for different purposes (Abu-Lughod, 1991; Clifford, 1986; Hemmings, 1996; Vasquez, Pease-Alvarez, & Shannon, 1994). In the well-known story of her own evolving identity, for instance, Gloria Anzaldúa (1987) writes, "Cradled in one culture, sandwiched between two cultures, straddling all three cultures and their value systems, *la mestiza* undergoes a struggle of flesh, a struggle of borders. . . . The coming together of two self-consistent but habitually incompatible frames of reference causes *un choque*, a cultural collision" (p. 78). In such circumstances, Dorinne Kondo (1990) has noted, people "forge their lives in the midst of ambivalences and contradictions, using the idioms at their disposal" (p. 302, cited in Eisenhart, p. 20).

If, as these writers contend, culture is not a shared and coherent value system, but a fractured, porous, and contested terrain, then the notion of identity emerges with democratizing potential. For from an analytical perspective that is attentive to individuals' evolving identities, broad sociocultural forces may be seen as influencing but not ultimately defining who people are or completely determining what they are capable of thinking and doing. Nonetheless, the diverse ways in which students draw upon and revise sociocultural influence as they construct situational identities are not always consistent with democratic ideals. Alejandro, for instance, is a Mexican American who speaks

English fluently, earns straight A's, and works hard to advance the interests of Latino students at Addison High. Rosa, in contrast, a Puerto Rican student who speaks almost no English and who has attended school only intermittently, has fewer choices in decisions that shape her experiences at school. This is not to say that students like Alejandro and Rosa do not share a collective Latino identity or that this identity is unimportant. Far from it, as we shall see. Rather, it is to stress that these and other students are "Latino" in unique ways and with varying consequences in terms of their ability to participate meaningfully in the activities of their school and community.

Despite the possible benefits to citizen teachers of noting how students' active construction of identity goes beyond the simple comparative stance implicit in social reproduction theory, several writers in the past few years have objected to what they see as academe's obsession with so-called "identity politics." For instance, Todd Gitlin (1995) and Michael Tomasky (1996) have called for restoring social class as the foundation of cultural critics' analytical vocabulary, arguing that class is a unifying category that transcends identity and enables real work to be done in the interests of social justice. In response, scholars like Nancy Fraser (1997) and Robin Kelley (1997) contend that the attempted erasure of race and gender in favor of a class-based politics betrays an assumption that class struggle can be separated from the historical contexts of its making. Fraser and Kelley argue convincingly that class is lived through identities forged in large part from race and gender, adding that calls for a rejection of allegedly stagnating identity politics in favor of class solidarity ignore the fact that identity has always profoundly shaped labor movements and has been the motivation for class solidarity. As Kelley summarizes, "social movements rooted in race and gender do not necessarily elide or ignore class, but rather are often the ground upon which class conflicts are enacted" (p. 202).

Whether they come from the trailers and bungalows on Addison's east side or from the multilevel mansions on the western edge of town, whether their parents pick tomatoes in the outlying fields or perform surgery at the local hospital, the students of Addison High demonstrate in their daily lives the inseparability of their class and ethnic identities. With few exceptions, Addison's Latino students are poor, and their self-identification as "Mexicans" is infused with a consciousness of their families' histories of laboring in the area's fields and factories. Although these students at times express a tentative identification between themselves and working class Whites, Latino students at Addison High seem to know well that there are material consequences of being "Mexican." Moreover, as these students demonstrate who they are to themselves and others, they make clear that to be "Mexican," to not "act White," is to avoid dressing, talking, and acting like the "rich kids." Given the correlation between these students' ethnicity and their social class, a citizen teacher concerned with how his or her work might help rectify socioeconomic inequities cannot dismiss the question of how these inequities have been historically drawn and are currently maintained along ethnic lines.

By sketching this overview of some of the principal ways in which people have assessed various sites of social interaction (including schools), I have not tried to offer a thorough account of the analytical repertoire of educational researchers and other cultural critics. Rather, in addition to providing a glimpse of how I have made sense of what I saw and heard at Addison High, my aim has been to suggest the remarkably broad range of phenomena that citizen teachers must consider as relevant to their work. From national, even global economic and political structures to the most subtle comments and gestures of individual students and teachers in small-town classrooms, there is very little that doesn't matter, very little that doesn't become meaningful when drawn into the citizen teacher's interpretive horizon. In short, citizen teachers have a lot to think about. And as we consider the daunting, even baffling complexities of teaching and learning, it is crucial, I think, that we look for help in lending to these considerations a coherence that enables us to act in ways that further a democratic vision. As I've already hinted, after searching for a long time, I know of no better place to find such help than in the collective work of John Dewey. I say this for at least two reasons.

First, Dewey's intellectual reach is sufficiently vast to encompass and unify what I see as the more specified frameworks of contemporary cultural criticism, which tend to focus alternatively on either the constraining power of social structures or the creative potential of human agency. By anticipating and bringing together these diverse analytical perspectives, Dewey affords a broad yet nuanced view of the mechanisms by which individuals both construct and are constructed by the social universe in which they live. Decades before the popularization of social reproduction theory in educational research, for instance, Dewey (1916/1985) recognized the relationship between schooling and the maintenance of class differences: "The present industrial constitution of society," he wrote, "is full of inequities. It is the aim of progressive education to take part in correcting unfair privilege and unfair deprivation, not to perpetuate them" (pp. 119–120). Also, providing an antecedent to more recent discussions of shifting, multiple, or so-called "hybrid" identities, Dewey (1929/1962) pointed out that what he calls a person's "individuality," though drawn in part from existing sociocultural conditions and traditions, "is impossible to develop . . . by an all-encompassing system or program" (p. 167). Rather, Dewey argues, individuality is "at first spontaneous and unshaped" and is then "continually made and remade" as it is expressed "in changing conditions and varied forms" (p. 168). Moreover, Dewey weighed in on an earlier version of the current debate concerning whether society's problems and possible solutions to them should be understood in exclusively socioeconomic terms. According to Dewey (1939), social analysis that attempts to explain events and frame policies solely in terms of economic conditions is "pre-scientific" in that such analysis assumes a preordained kind of truth, a "monolithic theory of social action and causation [that] tends to have a ready-made answer for problems that present themselves." Because it excludes from its frame of reference important factors such as cultural influences and human affect, Dewey contends, this kind of narrowly Marxist analysis "prevents any critical examination and discrimination of the particular facts involved in the actual problem" (p. 100).

My point here is not to imply that scholarship since Dewey is redundant or superfluous, but to provide evidence of the ways in which Dewey invites a wide range of concerned and critical voices into a single conversation. As I suggested above, it is only by participating in such a conversation that citizen teachers prepare themselves to ask hard questions about the conditions under which literacy and schooling might play a role in enabling people to exercise a greater range of choices in their lives. The more I think about the experiences of Latino students at Addison High, the harder (and less honest) it gets to make any essentializing statements about the liberating power of human agency in localized contexts or the constraining force of expansive social structures. Rather, as Dewey helps us see, these and other dynamics are interactive, and they get played out differently in different sites and with different results.

In addition to the ways in which Dewey lends a measure of coherence to the complexities of social analysis, there is a second reason why I believe he provides a useful model for the citizen teacher, and that is his unwavering commitment to democracy. As we shall see more thoroughly in this book's upcoming chapters, Dewey's ideal of democracy (1916/1985; 1927/1988) is one in which "full and free" communication allows people to identify their common interests, to act together in pursuit of these interests, and then to share in the results of their collective activity. This ideal is not limited to (though it certainly includes) the workings of government; rather, it extends to and transforms all areas of life. Thus, whether Dewey is talking specifically about the United States' involvement in global conflicts, the struggles of organized labor, the management of schools, or the intimacies of human relationships, he is really talking about democracy. It is the leitmotif of all his writings, the glue that binds together the massive volumes of his life's work. However, even to some of his contemporaries, Dewey's relentless allegiance to democracy is blinded by optimism, failing to account for either people's "distorted" perception of the "real world" (Lippmann, 1922/1965) or the "predatory self interest" that characterizes political conflict (Niebuhr, 1941). As I read Dewey, though, he is fully aware of the imperfections of America's democratic experiment. He recognizes that democracy is not a blissful state or condition to be achieved once and for all, but an arduous process, a struggle that must be continually revised and defended in ways responsive to present circumstances. But despite democracy's problems, Dewey

(1927/1988) is unequivocal in his opinion of how to solve them: "The cure for the ailments of democracy," he once wrote, "is more democracy" (p. 354).

Clearly, Dewey's notion of democratic life is one which enlists the participation of all members of a society, regardless of their social position or vocation. Nonetheless, because what Dewey (1916/1985) calls the "habits" of democratic thought and conduct are learned, he often places special emphasis on the work of teachers to develop in young people the capacities and sensibilities that contribute to the creation and maintenance of democratic communities. Though Dewey (1922/1988) regrets that schools too often foster "a systematic, almost deliberate, avoidance of the spirit of criticism in dealing with history, politics, and economics," he also imagines a day when "teachers become sufficiently courageous and emancipated to insist that education means the creation of a discriminating mind." At such time, teachers will devote themselves to cultivating in themselves and their students "the habit of suspended judgment, of . . . discussion rather than bias, [and of] inquiry rather than conventional idealizations." When this happens, Dewey anticipates, schools will become "the dangerous outposts of a humane civilization" and "begin to be supremely interesting places" (pp. 331–334; see also Westbrook, p. 313).

So far, I have described a "citizen teacher" as someone who understands her or his localized teaching practices as part of a broader project to promote democracy. In doing so, I have made the fundamental assumption that most people reading this will actually want to be a citizen teacher, if they don't consider themselves one already. But rather than pass over this assumption and move on, I think we educators would do well to confront it by asking ourselves an important question: Do we really want to live democratically? The question may seem rhetorical, but I don't mean it to be. For if by "living democratically" we mean something like creating conditions in which all people are able to participate meaningfully in the decisions that affect their lives, such a prospect may be as threatening to some as it is promising to others. In order to answer this question, it seems to me that we first have to come to terms with our understandings of the tangible consequences of democracy. Is, on one hand, the struggle for decent food and clothing, for sound, safe housing, for an enriching education, and for access to medical care a zero-sum game in which one person's gain is another's loss? Or, on the other, if democracy leads to a more equitable distribution of these and other resources, would such changes be a victory for all people, a setting aside of our baser tendencies of narrowly conceived self-interest—a way, to use Freire's words, for all people to become "more fully human"? In my view, the citizen teacher will tend to think the latter—that we are healthier and happier, as individuals and as a society, both in body and spirit, when we act on the belief that the interests of others are also our own.

If we educators do indeed decide that the humanizing effects of democracy are worth the time and energy we devote to our careers, then our task as citizen teachers becomes one of finding ways to demonstrate what we value. I have said that democracy is predicated on participation, and it is through such participation in our local communities and in the broader public sphere that a commitment to democracy becomes consequential. This kind of participation presumes the ability and the opportunity to act with others toward common goals, but it also requires motivation to do so, motivation which, I believe, arises from a sense of responsibility for the well-being of people other than ourselves. Though this responsibility may at times feel like a burden, I think it best to attempt to view it as a gift to be managed and used wisely. German theologian Dietrich Bonhoeffer (1955/1971) taught that the worst thing respectable people can do is to refuse to be responsible for the world, to simply stop caring. The consequence of such a choice is to continue the trends I mentioned earlier toward the concentration of power and the resulting loss of choices people have to direct their lives. Aleksandr Solzhenitsyn, who knew well that people's forsaking this responsibility is a prelude to tyranny, wrote that "[Hu]mankind's sole salvation lies in everyone making everything his business" (1980, p. 17). In taking on such responsibility, in "making everything [our] business," I'm not talking about exercising a paternalistic benevolence based on the supposed authority derived from our expertise as educators. Dewey (1941/1988a) addressed this issue when he wrote that a common "vice" of people who (like citizen teachers) seek to promote the social welfare is that they attempt to do

so "in ways which fail to engage the active interest and cooperation of others." This cooperation, Dewey tells us, "must be the
root principle of the morals of democracy" (p. 276). Further,
when I say that the citizen teacher must be responsible, I do not
mean "responsible" in its more cautious connotation. For the
responsibility enacted by a citizen teacher is not about playing it
safe; it is not about doing what is expected or sanctioned. On the
contrary, responsibility as I am writing of it is about taking risks.
It is about attempting the unfamiliar, succeeding in some instances,
perhaps failing in others, and then using the knowledge gained
from these experiences to better equip ourselves to try again.

As readers may have surmised by now, my conception of the
citizen teacher is a deliberate allusion to the "citizen soldier,"
that person who fought in defense of democratic ideals in the
American Revolution, the "commoner" who played a small role
in what became a far-reaching, decidedly uncommon project that
changed the world. Like citizen teachers, citizen soldiers saw as
part of their identities as citizens the obligation to struggle in the
interests of a democratic vision, however imperfectly that vision
was reflected in reality. There is, however, a significant difference
between the citizen soldier and the citizen teacher. While citizen
soldiers temporarily set aside their daily tasks and walked away
from the plow, the loom, or the anvil to join in the struggle for
democracy, citizen teachers, in contrast, enter into and remain
engaged in this struggle directly through their work. To be sure,
we citizen teachers may seek to promote democracy in a variety
of ways; we may write letters to public officials, join neighborhood organizations, or vote. Mostly, though, our participation
in fostering democracy occurs when we take up our books and
our chalk, when we prepare our lessons and develop curricula,
and—most importantly—when we model the democratic habits
of critical intelligence and cooperation in our daily encounters
with our colleagues and students.

As anyone who has tried to do this knows, such participation is not easy or uncomplicated, for the undemocratic conditions that Dewey (1929/1962) described seventy years ago are
no less true today: "The ideal of equality of opportunity and
freedom for all has not become the wellspring of a new intellectual consciousness; it is not the vital source of any distinctive and

shared philosophy. It directs our politics only spasmodically, and while it has generously provided schools it does not control their aims or methods" (p. 17). Stephen Fishman (Fishman & McCarthy, 1998) has noted that, given the imposing scope of such challenges, it is easy to despair, to view the strategies Dewey sets forth as unfeasible in that they seem to demand a large-scale revision of public policy or a revolutionary change in American values (p. 5). Still, though Dewey's aims are ambitious, his methods are practical, for he urges us to pause, to take stock of the conditions around us, and to ask ourselves this: "How are we to employ the means at our disposal so as to form an equitable and just society?" (1929/1969, p. 17). In my view, Dewey's question implies an invitation to a patient, deliberate working-out of democracy in a manner that he admits must be "slow," "piece-meal," and pursued "one step at a time" (1916/1985, p. 137). By thinking of our daily work as part of this ongoing process, we may also come to realize that while we can do only little as individual citizen teachers, as a citizenry of educators committed to democracy we can do much in our collective pursuit of the kind of society that Dewey envisioned.

Analytical Reading and "Creative" Writing

In the previous section, among the points I've emphasized is the importance of citizen teachers' understanding their work as situated within sociocultural settings that extend well beyond classroom walls. In Addison, I attempted to bring this kind of understanding to my encounters with Latino students and their teachers. That is, I recognized early on that in order to grasp precisely why Latino students often struggle with their schoolwork, why they tend to drop out in disproportionate numbers, and—more generally—why being Latino matters at Addison High, I needed to observe and interpret these students' experiences at school within the complex arrays of historical and social forces that constitute the contexts of their education. In my search for models of how I might do this, I found ethnographies of education to be especially useful, for ethnographic research is characterized most basically by long-term participant observation and by "thick" descriptions (Geertz, 1973) of specific events and artifacts within the cultural contexts that lend them meaning. These methods, it seemed to me, would be an effective way of understanding the connections between students' day-to-day experiences in school and the many factors, both within Addison High and beyond it, that shape these experiences. As readers will soon discover, however, my work in Addison also took on characteristics of a case study in that I came to focus on a small number of students whose achievements and struggles would, in my estimation, be of particular interest to citizen teachers.

As I just mentioned, ethnography is characterized in part by long-term participant observation in a given research site. In my case, this participation primarily took the form of my acting as a tutor and teacher aid in several Addison High classrooms. By taking on this role, I not only gained access to places that are normally off-limits to anyone who is not either an Addison student or staff member, but I also took a small step toward justifying my presence in these sites by being at least somewhat useful. The class I attended most consistently was second-period ESL, where my activities ranged from observing to assisting students either individually or in small groups as directed by their teachers. For the rest of the school day, I continued to act as a tutor by going to content-area classes with various ESL students. Which classes I attended was often determined by the number of ESL students in a given section. If, for instance, several of these students were scheduled to be together during a certain period, I would attend that class in order to provide help to the largest possible number of students. At other times, however, I would accompany a single ESL student to a class in which he or she was having particular trouble understanding and completing the assigned work. My role as a tutor also included meeting with ESL students during their study halls or at lunchtime to work on specific assignments, usually ones that were due within the next day or two. I also frequently translated homework or tests, acted as an interpreter in conversations with teachers who spoke no Spanish, and served as an informal advocate for ESL students by asking their teachers for alternatives to or extensions on particularly difficult assignments.

While most of my time at Addison High was spent in classrooms or other sites where I did my best to help ESL students with their schoolwork, my participation among these students was not limited to activities directed by strictly academic concerns. Rather, I also attended dozens of extracurricular gatherings such as student organization meetings, all-school assemblies, and sporting events. This participation extended beyond the high school to include visits to the homes of several Latino students, where I enjoyed the opportunity to meet and talk with their siblings and parents. Although these diverse forms of participation in no way afford a comprehensive view of the complex experiences of Addison's Latino students, my hope was that by acting with and observing them in several different situations, I would be able to gain at least a somewhat more complete sense of the contexts that influence their literacy practices in school.

Just as my participation in the lives of Addison's Latino students occurred in a variety of settings in which I played different roles, my methods of gathering data took several forms. The most important of these was the taking of detailed handwritten notes, which I transferred from a composition booklet to computer files at the end of each day. These notes included descriptions of classroom settings and activities, comments by teachers and students, and whatever reflections or analyses occurred to me at the time I wrote them. I also made extensive use of a miniature audiocassette recorder. Equipped each morning with freshly recharged batteries, a stash of blank tapes in my backpack, and the consent of students and teachers who were present, I recorded a considerable number of conversations, including whole-class sessions, discussions that took place in classrooms or hallways between periods, and group or individual interviews. At times, these interviews were impromptu and informal, as when I would be chatting with a student or teacher and the conversation unexpectedly turned to issues related to my research interests. More often, though, these interviews were formal in that they were prearranged and followed an open-ended format in which the discussion, though at times moving into areas I did not anticipate, was guided by a series of research questions I had prepared in advance (McCracken, 1988; Schatzman & Strauss, 1973). After reviewing these audiotapes, I transcribed the conversations and comments that, in my view, are relevant to this study. Finally, in addition to note taking and audio recording, my data collection included the gathering of written artifacts such as homework assignments, samples of student writing, bulletins issued by school administrators, and documents I discovered in the archives of the Addison School Board, at the city's public library, and at the county historical society.

My analysis of these data has been guided by the general approach of qualitative research to define analytical categories during the process of research and then to seek to discover patterns of interrelationship among them (McCracken, 1988, p. 16). More specifically, my way of making sense of Latino students' experiences at Addison High has followed an approximation of the "constant comparison" method described by Glaser and Strauss (1967), which involves constructing tentative analytical categories as they arise from observations, coding data as they may be relevant to these categories, and comparing new data to those which have been previously collected. As I've already mentioned, when I entered Addison High I had some kind of unspecified idea that I wanted to study Latino students' literacy practices. However, what emerged from my work there and in conjunction with my own reading and thinking at the time was not so much a focus on reading and writing per se, but a sense of the importance of understanding Latino students' literacies in the sociocultural and relational contexts in which they occur. Thus, though readers will see students reading and writing on just about every page of this book, my analyses focus on the conditions shaping these practices and on the ways these conditions either promote or hinder democratic aims.

By now I hope it is at least somewhat clear how I "read" Addison High and the activities of the people who occupy it. From these readings, I attempted to gain an understanding not only of why Addison Latino students so often endured troubles at school, but also of how I might use my belief in reading and writing as potentially empowering activities to help create opportunities for these students and their teachers to make their literate experiences more democratically inclusive and productive. Toward that end, I have organized this text so as to preserve the narrative of my developing understandings of the realities I observed in Addison and of what I came to believe might be an appropriate response to them.

Chapter 2, "The Strangers," focuses on a student named Rosa, with whom I worked during my first semester in Addison. Through an account of our attending a day of classes together, I offer an initial glimpse of the struggles she encountered on a daily basis. I then move to contextualize Rosa's difficulties at school by discussing statistical evidence of the high dropout rates among Latino students in the U.S. and by arguing that the marginalization Rosa experienced at school was a reflection of the class and ethnic divisions of the city in which she lives. To provide this context, I draw upon the extensive literature available on the attrition rates of Latino students nationwide, written histories of Addison, and a tour of the city given to me after school by three boys I met in Rosa's geography class.

Chapter 3, "(Mis)Understanding Failure," explores the complex causes of Rosa's inability to pass any of her classes. I argue that educators must resist the temptation of assuming that language difference is the only barrier Latino students face in attempting to adapt to an unfamiliar environment. In Rosa's case, her difficulties in school resulted not only from her inability to speak English but also from factors like the distracting behavior of peers in lower-track classes, the specialized language used in academic disciplines, and the inconsistency of her education since moving to the U.S. Moreover, I describe the candid frustration of Alvarez, Addison High's Latina counselor, who—despite her considerable effort and good will—was ultimately unable to persuade Rosa to attend school consistently. At the end of this chapter, I draw on Dewey's notion of the "continuity of experience" to suggest that Rosa's "failure" was the result of at least three things: her teachers' being unresponsive to her specific needs as a learner; the alienation she felt at the margins of the school community; and the fact that her definition of "success" differed from that set forth by Addison High.

Chapter 4, "Structured Exclusion," introduces two additional language-minority students—Angela and Claudia—whose exasperating experiences in English-only content-area classes may be seen as the result of a school structure that fails to provide LM students with the instruction they need in order to be ensured equal educational access. I argue that part of this structure, which I contrast with Dewey's depictions of democratic communities, are coping strategies used by LM students like copying homework and cheating on tests. Though these practices are not officially sanctioned by the school, I argue that they are, nonetheless, tacitly condoned as a part of Addison High's sociocultural structure that enables school personnel to avoid providing students like Angela and Claudia with the educational opportunities they need and deserve. As an additional aspect of this structure, I discuss the history of Addison's bilingual program and of judicial decisions and legislative actions that have left vague the legal obligations that schools have to their non-English-speaking students.

In contrast to Chapter 4's focus on the ways in which social structures often hinder democratizing agency, in Chapter 5, "Agency, Individuality, and the Politics of Fear," I emphasize the decisions individual teachers make that either resist or reinforce the constraints within which they think and work. Drawing from classroom observations and from a conversation among Angela's teachers, I refer to Dewey's notion of socially responsive "individuality" to demonstrate that some of Addison's teachers find ways of accommodating LM students despite the circumstances that make it difficult for them to do so, while others choose to abdicate these professional and ethical responsibilities. By analyzing comments from an interview with an Addison history teacher, I further argue that this neglect is rooted in an ideology that legitimates "functional" and "cultural" literacy over "critical" literacy and that deems bilingual education (and, hence, the students served by it) as a threat to allegedly "American" values.

Chapter 6, "Identity, Resistance, and the Production of Persons," draws primarily on the work of Willis, Bourdieu, and Antonio Gramsci to highlight the role of the culture of Addison High in maintaining undemocratic divisions among students, divisions that fall mainly along lines of ethnicity and social class. I argue that what it means to be a "Mexican" at Addison High is created by symbolic markers that, while establishing a strong sense of Latino identity, also frequently lead to these students' exclusion from the benefits of mainstream culture. At the same time, however, I show that these identities do not fit neatly into "mainstream/marginalized" categories. Rather, they are compli-cated by relationships among Latino and African American stu-dents and by differences among Latino students in social class.

Having discussed some of the symbolically created and main-tained ethnic and class divisions at Addison High, I devote Chapter 7, "The *Tesoros* Literacy Project: An Experiment in Democratic Communities," to describing a collaborative literacy project I initiated in response to what I saw as the marginalization and alienation endured by Addison's Latino and poor White students. Once each week for ten weeks, ESL students and White counter-parts came together to read Spanish- and English-language texts, to write essays, poems, and stories, and to respond to each other's work. All activities were centered on the notion that students should value the *tesoros,* the treasures, of their own lives. Be-cause the *Tesoros* project provided students with opportunities to share common experiences while retaining distinct identities, I argue that the project may serve as a model and a metaphor for the negotiations that are required—and the democratic agency that is possible—when diverse people engage in community-form-ing praxis.

In Chapter 8, "Good Deeds: A Citizen Teacher's Reflections on Usefulness," I highlight and reflect upon the challenges of engaging in cross-cultural educational projects of the type I was attempting among Addison's Latino students. Citing myself as an example, I suggest that despite the intention teachers and re-searchers may have to be useful to their students and "subjects," epistemological uncertainty and unequal power relations often threaten to turn educators' aspirations for usefulness into acts of exploitation. However, citing Dewey's discussion of the proper role of the social scientist and Jay Robinson's notion of "critical empathy," I suggest that productive relationships between diverse peoples are possible if such people can establish with each other empathic connections which become the bases for mutual influ-ence and collective action.

Finally, in the Epilogue, I recount a return visit to Addison two years after I completed the initial study and moved away. Some of the students, we shall see, are successfully pursuing ca-reers and futures they have chosen for themselves. Others, how-ever, dream of alternatives to their present lives but find their circumstances difficult to change, in part because of their limited options after having dropped out of Addison High. To see these students in the early years of adulthood attests, I think, not only to their remarkable intelligence, determination, and courage, but also to the obligation of schools to nurture these gifts by responding more attentively than they often do to such students' needs.

As I have previously indicated and as this summary confirms, this book is essentially a narrative, an account of people playing out certain kinds of social roles, literate and otherwise, that is told as a story. As such, it joins several works (Clifford & Marcus, 1986; Clough, 1992; Cohen, 1993; Tierney, 1993; Wolf, 1992) in drawing attention to the notion that trying to understand and work with others is inevitably a way of *representing* others, one kind of construction among many possible kinds. Educational ethnographies are, in this view and as Clifford Geertz (1973) said of all anthropological writings, "fictions . . . in the sense that they are something made" (p. 15). This is not to say that my account of Latino students at Addison High is merely the product of my imagination; though "made," it is not completely "made-up." Like all teacher-researchers who aim to be responsible about their work, I have tried to be circumspect in my methods by, for instance, identifying issues as I perceive them to have arisen out of specific contexts, seeking multiple interpretations of events and practices, and citing interviews and student writings in an attempt to at least minimize my own mediation of these voices. However, despite these efforts to allow the reader a kind of interpretive agency that is independent of my own, whatever information I offer is being filtered through my White middle-class sociocultural lens and thus is colored by ways of perceiving the world with which I am familiar. In short, readers can't fully see around my point of view. What is ultimately recorded here, then, is a representation of "the way things really are," when in fact they are the ways things are to me.

As writers like Ruth Behar (1993) and Eva Hoffman (1989) have argued, the potential for abuse in such a project is substantial. For insofar as writing about people is a way of creating them for readers, my construction of the Latino "others" at Addison High raises the possibility that I will unfairly judge them against my own partial understanding of the world and exploit our un-equal power relationship in self-serving ways. Indeed, Lois Weis (1995) has noted that "this process of 'othering' is key to under-standing relations of domination and subordination, historically and currently" (p. 18). Echoing this warning, Renato Rosaldo (1989) writes of the "lone ethnographer who rides off into the sunset in search of natives" (p. 30), a journey from which he returns home to write an account that objectifies his subjects and their lives. In my case, these potential dangers are heightened by limited Spanish fluency, which Vasquez, Pease-Alvarez, and Shannon (1994) have rightly claimed increases the likelihood that researchers will commit serious errors about the meanings im-plicit in a group's language and culture (p. 3). In light of these cautions, I may be the wrong person to write this book, which may be, at worst, almost a parody of the "quest" genre, with me missing a pith helmet, khaki shorts, and a rifle, but wielding none-theless the imperialistic sensibilities of an invader bent on impos-ing my own way of living and seeing on others.

Despite these very real hazards, I have pursued this project in what for me is unfamiliar territory because of the need to dis-seminate information regarding the quality and availability of education for Latino and other language-minority students in this country. While acknowledging the dangers of this kind of trans-lation, Eisenhart (1997) writes of the importance of such efforts:

> For educational researchers in particular, it is one thing to be careful about interpretations and generalizations; it is quite an-other to disengage from collecting data that might contribute to improving education. Policy makers and other decision makers will not stop trying to frame the experience of "others" in dis-course or making plans that affect "others," while postmodernists deconstruct old accounts. (p. 40)

As Eisenhart suggests, educational researchers, in presuming to translate the experience of "others," must walk a line between, on one hand, being sufficiently self-conscious of the fact that they are composing others according to their own views, and, on the other hand, reporting to readers the conditions and consequences of marginalized students' schooling. By telling *Reflections of a Citizen Teacher* as a story, I have tried to approach such a balance. For while I do describe apparently "real" goings-on in and around Addison High, my choice of narration highlights my central interpretive role and the fact that such descriptions are inevitably my own best guesses as to what was important, what things meant in the contexts in which they occurred, and what is useful for readers to know. Because this is so conspicuously a story told by me, this narrative form is intended in part as a challenge to the veracity of my own perspective, an invitation for readers to evaluate my account in light of their informed views and experiences. While writing in this way may not afford readers an unobstructed view, it may at least prompt some people to look over my shoulder a bit and try to see things for themselves.

In assessing my story in terms of their personal experiences and in connecting it meaningfully with their own teaching lives, it is likely that most readers of this book will struggle along sociocultural and linguistic borders similar to the ones I have attempted to cross in Addison. For although the number of Latino students in the U.S. is growing, the ranks of teachers who share their ethnicity and language is not. Emily Feistritzer (1986) has reported that in 1986 only 2 percent of the teachers in U.S. public schools were Latino. More recently, commenting on a National Education Association poll showing that 87 percent of its members are White, NEA executive director Robert Chase said that the failure to attract and keep minority teachers threatens to deny minority students the role models they need to succeed in school. Unfortunately, the small number of ethnic minority teachers is unlikely to increase any time soon. Drawing on a 1990 study, Linda Darling-Hammond (1995) has noted that between 1975 and 1988, the number of Latino and American Indian candidates receiving bachelor's degrees in education dropped by 40 percent, and the number of such candidates awarded education master's degrees plummeted by nearly two-thirds (p. 180). This growing shortage of Latino teachers presents serious problems in that it works against the need for a multicultural teaching force as schools are becoming more and more culturally diverse. As Valencia (1991b) has argued, Latino teachers are needed not only to serve as role models for Latino students, but also to deliver bilingual education and to help promote racial/ethnic understanding among all students (p. 14).

The urgency of addressing these students' needs is heightened by the scarcity of bilingual teachers, regardless of their ethnicity. According to Fleischman and Hopstock (1993), while there are more than 360,000 teachers providing instruction to LM students in the U.S., only 10 percent of these are credentialed bilingual teachers. Moreover, while some schools serve large numbers of Latino LM students and are thus likely to have some sort of bilingual education program in place, it is more common that LM students represent a small proportion of a school's overall student population. Fleischman and Hopstock report that 20 percent of schools with any LM students served four or fewer such students. Also, while the mean number of LM students in schools that had such students was seventy-six, the median number was twenty-one. In other words, most of the schools that do have LM students serve a relatively small number of them (Fleischman & Hopstock, p. 3).

Taken together, these statistics suggest that it is becoming increasingly untenable to consider the education of Latino and/or LM students to be the responsibility solely of Latino and bilingual teachers. Given the growing gap between the number of Latino students and the number of Latino teachers in U.S. schools, it is crucial that all teachers prepare themselves to teach these students well—even if this preparation cannot, in most cases, be based upon Spanish fluency, shared cultural heritage, or formal professional specialization. Indeed, the fact that a large and growing number of Latino LM students constitute the public we are called to serve creates a situation in which White, monolingual English-speaking teachers—even those with years of experience—are among an association of novices in an educational system where cultural and linguistic border crossings are almost inevitable. As the ensuing pages reveal, I have struggled in such attempts. Readers will see me candidly confused, occasionally frustrated, and making decisions that now seem ill-advised, even dim-witted. Thus, this book should not be read as a model of how to work with Latino students. Rather, I present it as an example of one White teacher's attempt to do so in spite of his own limitations, a story which raises issues that are likely to recur in the careers of this generation and the coming generations of teachers, and an opportunity for all educators to reflect on how they might negotiate their relationships with ethnic- and language-minority students usefully and ethically.

Though most of my "conclusions" remain open or ambiguous, I can say, based on my experiences in Addison, two things of which I am reasonably certain and which I hope come through in this book. First, if, as citizen teachers, we continually strive to understand the specific ways in which our localized classroom work operates dialectically with broader sociocultural forces, then we increase the likelihood that we will be able to shape—rather than merely accept—our worlds. Second, our attempts at democratizing agency are most likely to be humane and productive when they are motivated and informed by empathetic relationships with others. Such relationships are not in themselves sufficient to dismantle the powerful structures that hinder students' being able to make meaningful decisions about their futures, but they are a necessary way for teachers and other people who hold positions of relative power to better understand and then to work in the interests of disenfranchised students. I hope that in the pages that follow, readers may find these notions illustrated (and complicated) in ways that will be useful as they seek to be attentive to those young people who, in our schools, tend to be forgotten.

CHAPTER TWO

The Strangers

> *Our worst crime is abandoning the children. Many things we need can wait. The child cannot. Right now is the time bones are being formed, blood is being made, and senses are being developed. To this child, we cannot answer "tomorrow."*
>
> GABRIELA MISTRAL, *Readings for Women*

A Day with Rosa

The Addison High counseling office is a wide and welcoming place. Its expansive reception area is dotted with pyramids made of broad carpeted steps, where students can sit and talk as they wait for appointments in the adjacent offices. The room's posters and displays suggest to students how they might spend life after graduation. By far the most prominent display is the one set up by the armed forces, which I later learned send recruiters to the school several times each month. I sat on the first step of one of the carpet pyramids and studied the display looming on the top platform. A soldier, his face camouflaged by green and black grease paint, stared back. "Be All You Can Be," read the caption beneath. Stacks of brochures in the rack below the poster explained how. A few feet away, shelves lined with the catalogues of scores of colleges and universities lay beneath strings of colorful pennants from many of these same schools. It was the first week after the winter break, and I was there to meet Rosa.

During the holiday break, I had had the chance to review some specifics regarding the struggles of Latino students in our nation's schools. Although Señora Alvarez had cited poor study habits as the reason for poor performance by Latino students, the statistics I had seen revealed disturbing trends that suggested larger, more complex causes. Among these figures are those indicating that Latino students are more likely to drop out of school than are students of other ethnic groups. According to a 1992 Department of Education report, dropout rates fell between 1972 and 1991 from 12.3 percent to 8.9 percent for Whites and from 21.3 percent to 13.6 percent for African Americans (McMillen, 1993). Among Latino students, however, this rate increased from 34.3 percent to 35.3 percent. Additional data show that although Latino students made up only 11.2 percent of the 1992 high school population, they accounted for 30 percent of all dropouts. Compounding this problem is the fact that Latino adults are less likely to complete high school later in life. While the number of twenty-eight-year-olds who had not completed high school in 1992 was 9.2 percent of Whites and 12.5 percent of African Americans, for Latinos that figure was 36.8 percent (McMillen, p. 169). Moreover, Latino students who leave school have lower education levels than their White or African American counterparts: just over one-half of Latino dropouts, compared with one-third of White dropouts and one-fourth of African American dropouts, have less than a tenth-grade education (McMillen, p. 127). Consistent with these national trends, Latino students in grades 9–12 in Michigan drop out at rates three to four times higher than the rest of the student population. Further, according to a 1986 Michigan Department of Education report, the K–12 Latino dropout rate is as high as 55 percent, making it the highest in Michigan of all identifiable racial/ethnic groups, with the exception of American Indians (Michigan Department of Education, pp. 1, 11).

As I later discovered from an annual report prepared by the Addison High administration, the overall average dropout rate at Addison High between 1992 and 1994 was allegedly 8.2 percent, with a retention rate of 91.8 percent. These numbers, however, are misleading due to flawed logic in their calculation.[1] In contrast, a local college administrator undertook a statistically sound close study of the dropout rate at Addison by comparing the number of students enrolled as first-year students with the number of those who graduated four years later (after adjusting for those who moved in and out of the district).[2] This more reliable approach suggests that the average overall Addison High dropout rate between 1990 and 1994 was actually 28 percent.[3] Although the Addison High administration does not keep official statistics on dropout rates by race/ethnicity, the same college administrator extended his study to focus on Latino students. With the help of an Addison High staff member, he painstakingly reviewed student enrollment records and contacted members of Addison's Latino community to find out whether students who had left Addison High over a five-year period had transferred to other schools (as the official version claims) or had stopped attending school altogether. Based on these efforts, he calculated an average Latino-student dropout rate of 49 percent, with an additional 6 percent of these students not graduating with their class but still enrolled in school.

As Rosa walked into the reception area, Alvarez emerged from her office to reacquaint us, and as the bell rang calling us to first period, the counselor sent Rosa and me off with a cheerful "Have a good day." We made our way through the crowded hallways, Rosa walking a step ahead, appearing a bit embarrassed to be shadowed by a thirty-year-old stranger. I tried to strike up a conversation in Spanish.

"*What did you get for Christmas?*"

"*A sweater and some tapes,*" she said. I waited to tell her about my new toaster, but she didn't ask.

First Period: Geography

Mr. Harry Morton is a jovial social studies teacher and wrestling coach who uses an old golf club as a map pointer and talks much more loudly than he needs to. Having received a memo in his mailbox from Alvarez warning of my arrival, he welcomed me with a firm handshake and escorted me to a desk behind Rosa's, asking the boy already there to move to an empty seat on the far side of the room. I had just settled into my chair when, across the aisle, a thin girl with big eyes and short hair finished saying something to a friend and turned to face me.

"Nice tie," she said. "Are you a student teacher or something?"

"Not really. I'm just here to help Rosa." I moved my desk

alongside Rosa, who lifted her hand to cover her eyes and slouched in her seat.

On the wall, among the requisite maps of a social studies room, was a large sheet of white paper—about three by four feet—with the heading "Mission Statement of the Addison Public Schools." This document, I learned from Morton, was the result of nearly two years of work by faculty and administrators who had met during free periods and after school to draft a comprehensive list of "learning outcomes"—goals, articulated by department, that specify what the school hopes to accomplish by the time each student graduates. The statement, printed in bold letters, read as follows: "The mission of the Addison School District is to provide learning outcomes which challenge each student to achieve academic excellence, foster social participation, and promote development of self-esteem, all in preparation for becoming a contributing citizen in a world environment."

Maneuvering among the rows of desks, Morton explained that the worksheet packets he was handing out were worth one hundred points each and were due on the days of tests, which were also worth one hundred points.

"The point here," Morton paused to announce, "is that if you're conscientious and do the homework, you have a good chance of passing the class regardless of how you do on the tests." While Morton was still talking, I whispered this information to Rosa, drawing looks from several students for doing what would normally draw threats of a detention. Rosa shifted her weight and slid lower in her chair. Morton then began an introductory lecture on the political and physical geography of Latin America, in which he included everything from Tierra del Fuego to Mexico and the Spanish-speaking islands of the Caribbean. His voice was quick and animated as his golf club scanned the Amazon rain forest and the Andes Mountains on maps projected onto a screen at the front of the room. He pointed to borders and bodies of water, explained the climate of various regions, and tossed in anecdotes describing aspects of the cultures of selected countries. The students, including Rosa and a brown-skinned boy across the room wearing a cap decorated in front with a Mexican flag, listened quietly.

Copies of these maps, Morton explained, could be found in the homework packets and were to be labeled with the cities, countries, and other items listed on the back of each sheet. I leaned over and translated the instructions to Rosa, who suggested that we go to the library and work so as not to disturb the class.

"*Well, Rosa,*" I said, "*I think it would be better for us to stay here so that you can listen and practice your English.*" Rosa sighed, took a pencil from her purse, and wrote her name at the top of the first page in the packet. Every minute or so, I continued to lean over and whisper the gist of Morton's lecture, but eventually Rosa seemed to lose interest and began doing the homework the teacher had said was to give her hope of passing the class. Rosa was able to find the correct chapter in the textbook, but then wrote the characteristics of the Brazilian economy in the worksheet box labeled "Physical Geography." When I pointed out the error, Rosa faintly said, "*Thank you.*"

As Rosa copied the appropriate lists from her book onto the worksheets, I tried to follow Morton's lecture, which somehow led to his telling a story about a Norwegian exchange student who had attended Addison High the previous year. This boy, according to Morton, was a "fine student," a "great success," who had worked very hard to learn English and was a star 800-meter runner for the track team. A student raised his hand.

"I wonder how you'd teach someone like that English."

Morton replied that the best way is to immerse the person in an English-speaking environment. I translated this to Rosa and asked if she'd found that to be true. She raised her eyebrows and shrugged her shoulders. "*I don't know,*" she said.

I wondered whether Morton's answer might be true for some people, like those who have the status and confidence that come along with doing well in school, being an exceptional athlete, or having the money to choose to study abroad for a year. But then I thought of Rosa, of her dozens of absences, of the fact that I had yet to see her speak to another student. I thought about how easy it would be to fall into a cycle of finding it difficult to connect with people because of shyness and/or an inability to speak their language, which would result in further lack of exposure to that language, which would result in even more withdrawal, and so on.

As the period drew to a close, Morton announced that the following week there would be a quiz on the maps distributed that day. I told Rosa about the *prueba*. She nodded and continued to draw on her notebook: hearts and a name I couldn't read.

"Who's that?" I asked. Rosa answered without looking at me.

"A boy in Puerto Rico." She had also drawn a face that looked like an alien as depicted in television shows like *The X-Files*—thin-limbed with a long face and large, glistening eyes. The English major in me loved the irony; the teacher in me was troubled that it may have been, in some ways, a self-portrait. By and by, I gave up on translating Morton's lecture, which jumped from class trips to Asian food in Detroit to finding a McDonald's in the Swiss Alps. Rosa told me where the next class was, but I did not walk with her, sensing that she preferred not to have me tagging along through the hallways.

Second Period: English as a Second Language (ESL)

Several days earlier, I had spoken over the telephone with each of Addison High's new ESL instructors: Alice Martinez, a certified ESL teacher, and Fran Soto, a part-time aide. As the first regular ESL teachers to work in the Addison system in several years, both Martinez and Soto had spoken passionately about the district's need for bilingual instructors and were eager to begin this, their first semester on the job. Martinez had been born in San Antonio and had moved to Addison when she was very young. Soto, born and raised in Mexico, had moved to Brownsville, and then to Addison after marrying. This experience of having been uprooted and transplanted to Addison—this process of having had to adjust to a new environment and language—was something Martinez saw as crucial to the work she was about to begin.

"It's not just the language," she told me. "These kids need someone who understands what they're going through." She then shared with me a story of her first day in kindergarten: "The teacher was going down the list of students, and when she got to my name, she didn't know how to pronounce it. She hesitated, fumbled a few times, and then said, 'Well, we'll just call you Alice.' From that point on, everybody has called me Alice. They put it on the official school roll. All the kids, everybody, even my mother and my family, eventually called me Alice. I was only five, but I'll never forget it. It was the day they took my name away from me."

I arrived in the ESL classroom as the teachers were unpacking bags filled with books and papers. Martinez introduced me to the six students as they filed into the room: Vinita and Alex, Lebanese siblings whose first language was Arabic; a Mexicana named Elizabeth; a Chicana named Julie; Miguel, who had arrived from Guatemala two years ago; and Rosa. Martinez then took the time to have each of the students tell a bit about themselves, "In English if you can," she said. Vinita and Alex managed to explain that they had just moved from Detroit, where their family had lived with an uncle. Miguel was staying with his aunt while his parents were visiting a sick relative in Texas. Julie, speaking English without a Spanish-language accent, said that she wanted to be a cosmetologist when she graduated. With Soto translating, Elizabeth said that she missed her friends in Mexico. Rosa, too, spoke Spanish.

"My name is Rosa, and I'm from Puerto Rico."

"What else can you tell us?" Soto encouraged.

"I have six brothers and sisters."

"Rosita," Martinez said, "can you say that in English?" Rosa looked down at her hands. Martinez continued.

"Rosita, how do you say 'six' in English?"

"Six."

"Very good, *very good*, Rosa. Six children in the family, *like the six we have in our little family, this class.* Okay, Todd, your turn."

I told them my name, that I had been born and raised in a small town in western Michigan, and that though I had been a high school teacher for six years, I was now a student interested in learning about their experiences at school.

Martinez then distributed a sheet with dozens of small sketches of people involved in various activities, such as running, sewing, playing soccer, and riding a bicycle. Working in pairs, the students were to write as many verbs as they could that explained the drawings, which, as Martinez explained, the class would then use in a collaborative story. She repeated the instructions in Spanish. Vinita and Alex formed one pair; Julie moved her seat next to Elizabeth's. Martinez rested her hand on Miguel's shoulder.

"Mi'jo, I want you to work with Rosa," she said.

As the students settled into their task, I moved to a seat near Miguel and Rosa. Miguel spoke first.

"What do you think this one is?" he asked.

Rosa crossed her legs and shrugged. *"She's cooking?"*

"I think so," he said, and wrote "cook" beneath the drawing. Rosa leaned over to check the spelling and wrote the word on her paper.

As the students worked, I noticed the difference in the general condition of the two classrooms I had seen so far that day. Whereas Morton's room was decorated with colorful posters and maps, many of them drawn by students, the ESL room seemed cavernous and abandoned. The desks were in five rows, each with seven desks that faced a chalkboard extending nearly the entire length of the front wall. Centered at the front of the room was a large desk, which seemed to belong to no one; at least no one seemed to be responsible for its appearance, for the top was strewn with piles (not stacks) of accounting books, file folders, loose papers, and bits of chalk. Like the rest of the room's furniture, this desk was not just cluttered; it was dirty (a distinction my mother used to make): the finger I ran along the desk top came up dusty. A small table in the right front of the room held cardboard boxes containing papers dated five months before, coverless dictionaries, and several Styrofoam cups. Shadeless windows glared on the left wall, and on the cinder blocks between these windows several long marks scarred the paint. Trash littered the insides of the desks: a used facial tissue, broken pencils, and Kit Kat and Snickers wrappers.

Because Martinez was in the high school only one period per day, this space was not one she was at liberty to decorate and supply as she would have liked. Rather, this was a room designated for business classes. An adding machine and several copies of a textbook entitled *An Introduction to Accounting* rested on the big desk. On the front chalkboard were scribbled what to me were opaque phrases like "Name of annual dividend" and "Factors of supply and demand," as well as several math problems calculating the effects of such factors. On the floor between the fourth and fifth rows of desks was a strip of electrical outlets used to supply power to the adding machines for an accounting class, and a faded poster advertising scholarships to various business programs hung on the bulletin board to the right of the door that led to the hallway. Taped to the wall in the back right corner of the room, beneath an American flag, was a brochure for Davenport College (a business school in Grand Rapids). The air smelled musty, like a grandparent's attic but without the pleasant memories.

Other than the teachers and students themselves, the only evidence that this was an ESL classroom was the list of vocabulary words Martinez solicited from the students and wrote on the chalkboard bolted to the right wall. At the top of this list she had scrawled the word "SAVE!"

The ESL classroom's back wall was made of glass from about three feet above the floor to the ceiling and extending the wall's entire length. On the other side of this large window was a narrow room used to store outdated and unused office equipment. Beyond this storage space, through yet another wall of glass, was a computer lab fully equipped with twenty IBM PC's, the screens glowing a vibrant blue in contrast to the ESL class's gray floors and pale yellow walls. From behind the two glass partitions, Martinez and her students could watch the computers as they might have window-shopped at Saks.

In this setting, Martinez and Soto circulated among their students, offering advice, answering questions in both English and Spanish. The teachers seemed to know just what their students could understand in English and challenged individuals according to their abilities. However, what struck me most about Martinez's and Soto's teaching was their demanding yet gentle demeanor. While insisting that students remain focused on their work and that they speak English whenever possible during classroom exercises, these teachers also were quick with their praise, encouragement, and demonstration of their affection for their students. This was, it appeared to me, an affinity born from empathy, and even though this was only my first day in the ESL classroom, Martinez shared with me a candid example of what she seemed to view as the struggle she and her students faced together.

She told me that a couple of days before, the computer class had been supervised for a day by a substitute teacher who had a reputation for being unable to control her students. The regular computer teacher, Mr. Dautermann, fearing that his students would somehow damage the PC's in the lab while he was gone, gave instructions that the substitute conduct class in the ESL room. Rather than having the ESL students simply move into the lab for the day, Dautermann insisted that they not be allowed near his expensive and fragile machines. Thus displaced, the ESL class was forced to meet in the narrow and dusty storage area between the two classrooms. Mimicking what she perceived to be Dautermann's attitude, Martinez said that her "little brown-skinned kids" decided to relocate to the cafeteria, which even as early as second period is expansive and noisy, with people setting up tables and shining the food counters. Martinez recalled that the ESL students were upset with what they saw as a flagrantly racist incident. "You have rights. You're just as much a teacher as they are," Martinez said they had told her. She added that in theory, of course, her students were right, but that in reality there was little that she, a first-year teacher of Latinos, could say to resist a White computer teacher with thirty years of seniority. Martinez had grown angry as she told the story: "No offense, Todd, but the Anglo students walk in here and get whatever they need, but not my kids."

After I heard Martinez's story, the appearance of the "ESL" room seemed to take on meaning that it hadn't carried before. The more I looked around the room, the more I sensed that this space conveyed what I believed to be the clear and consistent message that those students huddled over their worksheets really didn't matter, that they were second-class citizens who did not have the right to participate fully in the opportunities available in this school community of alleged equal opportunity. For although other students passed through the room each day as they attended one of their many classes, that fact that this had been designated as the ESL room suggested to me that of all places in the school, this should have been the one sanctuary where the ESL students felt that their lives and what they had to say were genuinely important. Sadly, despite the efforts of Martinez and Soto, what they were likely to "hear" from this site was quite the contrary. No posters celebrated the students' heritages and home-lands, no shelves contained books in their native languages, and no bulletin boards held work which told the stories of the students' lives in the United States and around the world. To the contrary, it seemed that the ESL students were intruders in a place designed for others—that though they were there, they didn't truly belong. This room was the educational equivalent of a vacant lot, a ghetto neglected by the community's more affluent and influential members, the "margin" we read about in our professional literature.

Third Period: Math

Ms. Dolgan taught Transitional Math, the department's most basic course, from a bunker formed by her desk and a large lab table at the front of the room. That day, behind this barricade, coming no closer than about eight feet from even the first row of students, she was discussing the concept of prime numbers. Dolgan explained that any prime number "X" only has two factors: "X" and 1.

"What's the letter for?" Rosa whispered.

"It can mean any number," I said.

Rosa looked at me from beneath crinkled eyebrows. To illustrate what are not prime numbers, Dolgan asked the class what factors could be divided into 24. Receiving no response, she answered her own question.

"Well, 1 of course. What about 2?"

A boy spoke up, "Yeah, that would work."

Dolgan continued. "How about three?"

"Yup," another student called out. As the class generated the list of factors, "4, 6, 8—no, not 8, no, wait, yeah—12," Rosa waited to copy the numbers in her notes until Dolgan had written them on the board. This hesitation concerned me, making me suspect that she did not understand what I learned from the boy behind me was review for her classmates.

"Rosa, do you understand what Ms. Dolgan's doing?" I asked in English. "Do you know what a 'factor' is?" Rosa gave me a puzzled look. I repeated my questions in Spanish.

"I think so," she said. Unconvinced, I wrote "8" in my notebook.

"*Can you tell me what are the factors of 8?*" Rosa did not say anything. "*What numbers can be divided into 8?*" Rosa looked at the number on the page for several seconds.

"*I don't know,*" she said. We took it a number at a time. I was encouraged when she said that 1 and 2 would both work, but when she also guessed 3, I suspected this would take some time. Dolgan announced that there would be a quiz on factoring and identifying prime numbers in two days.

Fourth Period: Science

A substitute was in charge of the class that day, so a student walked on the counter and reached up to open a window. Even after the bell rang, several students strolled around the room, talking to friends. A boy grabbed the cap from the head of a friend, who threw a pencil at the thief, hitting me in the shoulder. "Sorry, sir!" the boy said. "I was aiming at that kid in the blue shirt."

The teacher, who looked a bit haggard even though it was still only about 10:45 A.M., announced the assignment: Working individually, students were to read two sections in the textbook on electrical circuits and answer the questions on a worksheet, which was to be collected at the end of the hour. We had about forty minutes. Rosa and I turned to the appropriate pages—nine in all. I pointed to the first paragraph and asked Rosa to read. She stared at the page for a moment, then shook her head.

"*I don't understand.*" Seeing little chance of reading the entire assignment and completing the worksheet in the allotted time, I scanned the pages and suggested to Rosa that we begin the worksheet, with me trying to explain things as best I could as we went along.

"*That would be good,*" she said. "*I failed this class last semester. The homework is very hard.*"

Until that point in the day, I had been fairly pleased with my ability to communicate with Rosa. My lack of Spanish fluency had been a concern for me, for though I had recently attended some university review sessions designed for graduate students who needed to pass their language exams, my last Spanish class had been in undergraduate school, twelve years before. Nonetheless, I had practiced, and the first three periods of the day had been manageable. Summarizing and translating the language of even a basic science text, however, was an entirely different project. I struggled to convey concepts of circuitry, current, and resistance, finally relying heavily on metaphors and sketches. Rosa copied the diagrams I drew, asked pertinent questions, and was able to explain to me in her own words the answers she wrote on the worksheet. We nearly finished the assignment, but the bell rang with two questions to go. Rosa said, *"That's good,"* walked to the front of the room, and handed the worksheet to the teacher.

Fifth Period: English

Mr. Robbins's lesson was on expository paragraphs. There are three types, he said: those that define, those that explain a process, and those that give reasons. Examples of each could be found in the textbook. As I had already seen a couple of other times that day, the class was chaotic—students talking loudly while Robbins tried to discuss the notion of a topic sentence. A boy sitting across the aisle told me that "this is a bad class." With the students occupied by their own conversations, Robbins asked and answered his own questions. The assignment, due the next day, was to write three expository paragraphs, one of each type. Students were to fold a sheet of paper in half, do their "prewriting" on the top half, and their "writing" on the bottom half. Three pages, three unrelated paragraphs.

Rosa asked that we begin with a paragraph of definition, so I asked her to suggest a topic.

"I don't have any ideas," she said. I remembered that she had spoken to me of her uncle, so I encouraged her to define what a "good uncle" is. I asked her questions about what he does.

"He helps around the house," she said.

"How? What exactly does he do?"

"Helps with homework, translating. He plays with my brothers."

"What games do they play?"

"Basketball and soccer."

"How else does he help?"

"He washes dishes and cooks."
"What are your favorite foods that he cooks?"
"Rice, beans."

In English, I wrote in sentence form the details Rosa had provided; I asked her to read them to me, and then she copied what I had written onto her paper. While most of the students finished the assignment during class, Rosa and I completed just one paragraph.

LUNCH

Although the Addison High teachers' lounge is located adjacent to the cafeteria, a piece of paper taped over the small window on the door keeps students from seeing what's going on inside. When I entered the room with my backpack over my shoulder and my tape recorder in hand, a few eyes regarded me with suspicion but quickly returned to the brown bags and Tupperware containers scattered across the linoleum tables. Most of the teachers were seated at a long table that ran nearly the length of the room, while a group of men gathered at a round table, discussing the professional football playoffs. Harry Morton waved me over to the group of football fans and introduced me to the others.

"This is Todd. He's going to be around helping one of our Hispanic kids."

"That's great," a man said. "Who you working with?"

I told him. "Oh, Rosa," he said. "I had her in my class last semester. She misses a lot of school."

"Yeah, I heard," I said. The man continued. "You know, I didn't hear her speak until the very end of the term. One day I was handing back assignments, and she said 'Thank you.' Before then, I didn't even know what her voice sounded like."

"She doesn't talk in my class either," Morton added. "I wish I could help her, but I don't speak Spanish—well, I can say 'taco' and 'enchilada,' but that's about it."

I ate my sandwich, pretzels, and apple and drank my coffee, listening to a conversation that wandered from sports to the weather to the teacher union's labor negotiations with the school board. By the time the bell rang, the coffee had left a stale taste in my mouth, so I slipped in a piece of gum as I made my way out into the hallway.

Sixth Period: Study Hall

I had arranged to meet Rosa in the library, and as I navigated through the security turnstile, I spotted her waiting at a table near the back. I paused to introduce myself and state my business to the librarian, a short, thin woman with glasses, who welcomed me and then asked, "So you're another tutor?"

"I guess so," I said.

"I've seen Rosa in here last year with other tutors—students, I think, from Addison College. Well, good luck."

As I pulled up a chair beside Rosa, she asked, *"Do you have gum?"*

"Yes. Do you want some?"

"No," she said, *"You're not allowed to chew gum here."* I threw the gum in a nearby trash can and asked Rosa what she'd like to work on. *Geography.* She already had out on the table the textbook and the worksheets Morton had passed out during first period.

"Okay, let's try to read some of this," I suggested. *"Do you think you can understand these sentences?"*

Rosa shrugged. *"I don't know."*

"Well, let's try." In English, Rosa read the first of several paragraphs about different geographical regions of Brazil. *"Can you tell me, in general, what that paragraph said?"*

"No, I don't understand it." I sat for a moment, wondering what to do next. I thought of beginning a list of vocabulary words from the text that she could study on her own. I thought of trying to find a geography book printed in Spanish. I looked at the clock and thought of Morton's admonition to keep up with the homework.

"Okay, this first paragraph says that there are many different regions of Brazil. . . ." We skimmed through the assigned reading, with me translating the general information, pausing to point out the specifics that Rosa needed to copy onto various boxes and blanks on the worksheet. By the end of the period, we

had finished two sections of the worksheet—about half the assignment.

Seventh Period: Introduction to Computers

When I arrived, the second-floor computer lab was already filled with students seated in front of the twenty-six Macintosh "Classics" that had been brand-new the previous September. Students glanced from workbooks to screens, inputting information and printing documents, and then scurried to a sheet of paper taped to a wall that listed the sequence of upcoming assignments. Rosa had taken, and failed, this course last semester. While she retrieved a file from the hard drive, the teacher, Mr. Pearson, showed me a printout of the assignments students had completed over the course of the previous term. Beside the list of names, small numbers indicated the assignments completed and the points awarded for each. The totals were impressive: Just about all the students had completed all their work, with Rosa being the exception. Beside her name were three numbers—points, Pearson explained, for having completed introductory lessons on basic skills like "clicking" and "dragging." The rest of Rosa's numbers, about twenty in all, were zeros.

"After the first couple of weeks," Pearson said, "she didn't finish any of the assignments. Even if she had," he continued, pointing to the column marked "attendance," "she would have lost credit for being over the ten-absence limit." According to Mr. Pearson's chart, Rosa had missed thirty-six of the school year's first ninety days.

I found a chair and set it next to Rosa, who, in spite of not having mastered the skills taught the semester before, was trying to get through the most recent assignment: a spreadsheet that required students to arrange sales and purchase information for a fictitious auto parts company. With each click of the mouse, the computer "beeped," indicating an error. Pearson was occupied with another student, so I tapped the kid next to me.

"Excuse me, do you know how to do this?" The boy leaned over and looked at Rosa's screen.

"Oh, yeah. I did that a couple of days ago. Here." He clicked and scrolled with impressive speed. "There. Now it's all set up.

All you gotta do is type in those numbers. Don't forget to hit 'Return' after each one." After I relayed the information to Rosa, she began slowly transferring the data, leaving me with time to review the workbook. There, printed clearly in plain English, were the instructions Rosa needed to complete the assignment on her own.

Eighth Period: Child Development

Beth Reinstra stood in the hallway outside her classroom, greeting passersby and everyone who walked into her room. Several students paused to chat, one boy giving Reinstra a "high five" as he walked through the door. I waited until she finished asking a student about his performance in a basketball game the previous night and shook her hand.

"Oh, yes, Ms. Alvarez sent me a note about you. Glad to meet you. I'm really glad you're here. I don't speak a word of Spanish, and Rosa seems very shy."

Reinstra began the class with a review of the students' names and by asking each of them to repeat the individual goals they had set for themselves at the beginning of the semester. The first wanted to graduate from high school; another, noticeably pregnant, wanted to have a healthy baby; a third, his head resting on the table in front of him, wanted to sleep. Reinstra introduced me to the class, explaining that I was going to help Rosa, who, confronted by the extra attention, slouched a little bit lower in her seat as she had in geography.

"Rosa," Reinstra asked. "Where are you from?" I translated, and Rosa spoke quietly:

"Puerto Rico."

A loud voice echoed from across the room: "I'm from Puerto Rico, too!"

Her name was Daniela. Reinstra asked Daniela if she could speak Spanish. "I spoke Spanish before I knew how to speak English; that's all we speak at home." Reinstra seemed relieved.

"Well, when Todd's not here, maybe you can fill in and help Rosa."

"No problem," Daniela said. Rosa shielded her eyes with her left hand and drew circles on her notebook.

Reinstra walked over and stood next to Rosa. "Rosa, the other day I don't think we heard what your goal is." Rosa looked at me.

"*Your goal,*" I said.

"*I don't know—to pass this class.*"

"She wants to pass your class," I said to the teacher. Reinstra nodded.

"That sounds like a pretty good goal to me," she said.

Reinstra's assignment for the day was to cut out magazine pictures that illustrate characteristics the class members wished to foster in their own children. Rosa wrinkled her nose.

"*I don't want to,*" she said. For the second time that day, I didn't know what to do, for, in this case, Rosa's resistance was not merely a matter of her not understanding English. Speculating that Rosa had finally had enough of being shadowed by a conspicuous stranger, and not wanting to let the opportunity with Daniela slip away, I called her over and asked her to explain the assignment and discuss it with Rosa. Daniela carried her books to our table, sat next to Rosa, and asked her what part of Puerto Rico she was from. Rosa told her but then looked away. Daniela, however, persisted, explaining to Rosa how her family moved to the States when she was very young and how every couple of years they return to the island to visit relatives.

"*Do you think you'll ever go back?*" Daniela asked. Rosa said that she hoped so, that she missed her friends and grandparents very much, but that such a trip was difficult because of the expensive airfares. The conversation was one-sided, as Daniela spoke volumes in effortless Spanish while Rosa continued to keep her eyes fixed on the cover of her notebook, usually replying in single words and never asking Daniela any questions.

Eventually, Rosa relented to Daniela's energy and began flipping through the magazines looking for pictures. Even as she worked, though, she told me she didn't like this class, that she'd rather be in "*computers.*" I wondered what made the computer lab, a class in which she didn't complete an assignment all last semester, more attractive than this.

"*I don't know; I just don't like this teacher.*" Was it that there she could isolate herself with the screen and not interact with people, whereas here she had little or no excuse not to converse with others? Isolation, I supposed, was easier with computers. Here Rosa had a teacher who seemed to be willing to make an extra effort to include her in the activities of the class and a peer who could be her liaison with the rest of the students—just what she needed, I thought. That Rosa had clipped only two pictures by the end of the period and had stopped talking to Daniela didn't make sense to me at the time.

As I drove home to Ann Arbor at the end of the school day, I worried about Rosa and all that she would be expected to do before I returned the following week. I thought of the geography book she couldn't read and the packet of worksheets that would most likely remain incomplete. I thought of her struggles to do even the basic division Ms. Dolgan assumed she knew. Would Rosa be able to keep up in her science class? Would she get the help she mentioned her uncle sometimes found time to give her when he came home from work? Or would I arrive next week to find her still puzzling over electrical circuits while her classmates had moved to the next chapter? Would Mr. Robbins give Rosa credit for the one paragraph she had completed in English class? Even if he did, what about the next time he asked her to write in a foreign language? And then there was the computer class. Never mind that Rosa had not learned the skills that had been introduced during first semester; she would have, Mr. Pearson had said, a "fresh start" this term. But she was already behind, and likely to be more so by the time I returned to ask the boy next to us for help. Child Development had been modestly encouraging, but given Rosa's dislike for this class, I wondered whether even Reinstra's attentiveness and Daniela's charisma would be enough to offset the disheartening effects of the rest of Rosa's school day.

Although it occurred to me that it would take a while to assess just how much English Rosa did or did not know, it was clear that one of the principal causes of Rosa's difficulties in school was that she often had little idea what was going on. We had made enough progress for me to suspect that most of what Rosa had been asked to do was not beyond her ken, that she was not "slow" in the sense that a learning disability kept her from understanding features of the Brazilian economy or how to record the monthly expenditures of an auto parts store. Nonetheless, in every class I had attended that day, the teachers' instructions and the assigned readings had been met with the same response: *"I don't understand."*

The fog had burned off beneath the afternoon sun, but even though I now had no trouble seeing the road and the fields, many things about Rosa's situation at school remained unclear to me—things that led me to say, with Rosa, "I don't understand." I had little doubt that Rosa's inability to speak English presented some challenges for her teachers. But it seemed to me that this challenge could be met in one of two ways: Either Rosa's teachers could despair about the fact that it was difficult for them to communicate with her and leave it entirely up to Rosa to overcome her lack of English fluency and whatever other "deficiencies" she was presumed to have, or these educators could accept Rosa as one of the students they were called upon to teach and then work toward meeting her needs by drawing upon the knowledge, abilities, and experiences she brought to their classes and by seeking to make her learning relevant to her life outside of school (Poplin & Weeres, 1992; Sleeter & Grant, 1991). This second option, though in some ways inconvenient, was not impossible. Research has shown the positive effects on language-minority (LM) students' performance of instruction that incorporates attention to linguistic and cultural differences, as well as the differences that accompany social class (Abi-Nader, 1993; Lucas, Henze, & Donato, 1990; Moll & Diaz, 1987). Such attention might take the form of ensuring that LM students are exposed to a rich and demanding curriculum in a language they understand, that they are challenged by high expectations, and that their parents are welcomed and encouraged to participate in the life of the school (Lucas et al.; Moll, 1992). More specifically, in, for instance, an English class, teaching methods that signal an appreciation for students' languages and cultures might include having students record oral histories of family members, conduct peer interviews, and write for interactive journals (Nieto, 1994).

Given the fact that such options existed for creating a better learning environment for Rosa than what she currently experienced, I wondered about several things I had observed that day: Why was there no one in the school to help Rosa learn her content-area subjects in her native language as she grew more comfortable with English? Why had none of the teachers offered Rosa corresponding texts in Spanish? Why had no one explored alternative ways of assessing Rosa's progress? Why had no one other than Reinstra arranged for her to receive help from some of Addison's dozens of bilingual students? I remembered the hand that shielded Rosa's eyes, and I decided that if I were in her shoes, uprooted from my home, taken away from my friends and extended family, I, like she was, would be "shy." In fact, I began to wonder not so much why Rosa missed so many classes, but why she came to school at all.

The City of Addison: A Tour and Brief History

It is difficult to say what led to the mutual interest that evolved between Roger and me. For weeks we sat across the aisle from each other in the back of first-period geography, where, when I wasn't helping Rosa, he told me several times that he couldn't understand my interest in a class that bored him senseless. While I watched, listened, and scribbled in my notebook, Roger would often turn up the collar of his camouflaged jacket, pull the bill of his Dallas Mavericks baseball cap down over his eyes, and, arms folded, slouch into a nap. A White student with pale skin, curly dark hair, and sharp, uneven teeth, he was, as the social studies teacher and wrestling coach Harry Morton described him, a "problem" in class. I had seen him kicked out of the room twice, once for repeatedly talking out of turn, once for telling the teacher to go to hell. By and by, though, Roger and I began to talk, and during these conversations I learned that he worked nearly every day after school on a dairy farm, that the scar on his cheek was the result of his having driven a snowmobile into a barbed wire fence, and that he and his family were, in his words, "country— we like to listen to Garth Brooks, Randy Travis, stuff like that." Sometimes, my questions for Roger focused on school: who his favorite teacher was and why, which classes he found most difficult, the names of the student cliques that gathered in the hallways and cafeteria. At other times, I asked him about the community in which Addison High is situated.

Having been in Addison now for several weeks, I had gained a general familiarity with the city and the surrounding Huron

County—fragments, mostly, from conversations with teachers and students, written histories of the area, and errands I had run around town during lunch period. Addison, located about sixty miles from Detroit and with a population of about 20,000, is supported by an economic base of agriculture and small industry that had attracted migrant workers, primarily from Texas and Mexico. These people now formed the base of Addison's Latino population, which, at about 16 percent, is the second largest per capita in Michigan. One day as I quizzed Roger on details of the geography and demography of Addison, he seemed to tire of my questions.

"Look," he said. "If you want to know about the town, why don't I just show you around after school. I ain't working today, so I got time."

I had convinced two brothers, Esteban and Juan, Latinos recently arrived from South Texas, to accompany Roger and me on the tour. The four of us met in the school lobby a few minutes after the final bell and headed out to my car.

"Hey, Todd," Esteban said. "You got a low rider? That's what I want—a '62 Impala, just to cruise around in." Roger called "shotgun," and I apologized to the brothers for not having a car with a bigger back seat. Before we left the parking lot, all three were smoking Marlboros.

"Todd, you want one?" Esteban held a cigarette in front my face. I hesitated, remembering my plans to go jogging as soon as I returned to Ann Arbor. "No thanks," I said. I put a cassette by the Mexican pop group Maná into my dashboard tape player and, handing my notebook to Roger, explained that he was in charge of recording what we saw while I drove.

"What. I don't know what the fuck to put in here."

"Just write down what I tell you," I said. "Words, phrases. I'll remember the rest when I get home tonight." I slid a fresh tape into my minicassette player, pushed "record," and wedged it between the front seats. As we pulled away from the school, Juan and Esteban sang along with the music: *"Like a bird would like to be able to fly without wings, like a fish would like to be able to swim without water, I'd like to be able to live without you. But I can't; I feel as though I'm dying; I'm drowning without your love."* The music was slow and sad, and the boys sang better than I expected—in tune and not straining too much on the high notes.

"This music reminds me of the clubs we used to go to in Texas," Esteban said between drags of his cigarette. "We would go there and they'd play this music. There were lots of really sweet girls there." I had first met Esteban in January, when he showed up in the geography class a few weeks into the term. At age seventeen, he was two years older than his brother, with callused hands and powerful build. He had quickly earned a reputation among the students as an accomplished artist. One day as the class worked on a group project, I strolled over to talk to him and found him putting the finishing touches on a striking drawing of a woman he identified as his girlfriend, Nancy. Esteban confessed that he missed her very much, and that if he had the $160 for a bus ticket, he'd have made plans to return to Texas to be with her during spring break. Juan, a bit heavier than Esteban, his face appearing slightly swollen, had impressed me as a hardworking student from the times we had worked on math homework together during his study hall. He had asked many questions during these tutoring sessions, especially about adding and subtracting negative numbers, and had carefully recorded each step of the calculations, refusing merely to write the answers that were listed in the back of the textbook.

I asked Roger to make a note of the small but neatly kept houses that extend along the streets in the neighborhood immediately to the east of the high school. The driveways were cleared of snow, with the clean, even edges made by gasoline-powered snow blowers.

"Why did you move here to Addison?"

"Hey, Todd," Esteban said, "you better speak English or Roger won't understand what the hell you're saying. Well, we were working in Virginia, but we came here to work in the fields." Esteban continued, explaining that they had worked from August through October harvesting tomatoes and pumpkins. "We worked the tomatoes for about a month, but only about two to five hours a day. When we were picking pumpkins, though, we worked about ten hours a day. It was pretty good money; we were making five dollars an hour." While their families had resolved to remain in Addison for a year because they didn't have

the money to return to Texas, they planned to go south in No-
vember of that year and to return again in April to help with the
spring planting.

My guides were chain smoking and giving me directions as
we made our way through the streets of Addison. After a few
minutes we crossed M-62, a state highway that widens from two
to four lanes and is called "Main Street" as it bisects the town—
Addison's version of the "tracks" some folks live on the wrong
side of. Mike, an Addison High graduate and a student in one of
my courses at the university, had explained in an interview how
the town is divided racially and economically by this very tangible line:

MIKE: Well, it's like Main Street [M-62] goes through town, if
you're going south, to the right of it, that would be the
West Side, that would be the wealthier side of town. The
East Side is the more poor sections of town.

TODD: Can you describe a bit more about how the West Side is
different from the East Side?

MIKE: Bigger houses, my mom's boss one time was a dentist,
and he lived on the West Side, on Stephen Street, which,
if you had money, I mean lots of money in Addison, you
were on Stephen Street or these little boulevards out
through there, and these houses are just very luxurious. I
mean, with the pillars in the front and the upkeep is very
nice, nice big lawns. And then on the East Side, I mean,
the houses are right next to each other, the lawns are
small, you know, not kept up as much. There's more
factories and businesses out towards the East Side; on
the West Side as you go out there's more farms. So, the
one side's more "inner city" whereas the other side is
like a city but then it spreads out. It's more relaxed.

Mike's description confirmed what I had heard from some of
the Addison students, who had described the East Side as "trashy,"
"run down," with "houses about to fall over," and populated by
"welfare people." Charlie, who sat near Roger and me in geography class, had described this area even more dramatically. A
thin White boy with black hair combed in a tall pompadour,
long sideburns, and an obsessive fascination with Elvis Presley,

Charlie had leaned toward me, his elbows resting on the table between us.

"Watch out for the East Side," he had said. "It can be a terrible place." Then Charlie's eyes had grown wider, and he had lowered his voice, almost to a whisper. "In 1956, the year that Elvis hit it big at the Suncoast Record Studio in Tupelo, Mississippi, a guy was murdered under the Center Street Bridge. Stabbed fifteen times. He was going to play football at Michigan, but he never made it."

But if the East Side of Addison is characterized by its dilapidated housing, equally remarkable is the impressive presence of industry. Roger pointed out a large dairy processing plant consisting of red brick buildings and tall blue holding tanks.

"Make a note," I said. "'Dairy plant.' How tall do you think those tanks are?"

Roger looked up from the page. "I'd say about forty feet." He recorded the figure in my notebook.

"Take a left," Juan said. "That's a Mexican party store there on the corner. Lots of Mexicans buy their booze there."

Appearing on the right was a Ford plant that extends for three blocks, which Roger explained makes parts like bumpers for pickup trucks. The plant is Addison's second largest factory, employing over 1,000 people in 1989 at an annual payroll of nearly $42 million. I turned right as directed, and a state correctional facility came into view. Two prisoners were sweeping the driveway. I turned to Roger.

"Make a note of those prisoners."

"Got it," he said. I'd never seen him write a word in class, but by the time we passed a factory that makes convertible automobile tops, Roger had begun to fill the pages of my notebook without prompts from me.

"Okay, now check this out," Roger pointed. "They make cupboards for your kitchen in there." The DeHaan Industries Addison plant, one of eleven nationwide, sprawled to our left, enclosing more than 400,000 square feet. Founded by a World War II veteran in 1946, the corporation has earned a local reputation for philanthropy, as its owners have contributed generously to the construction of churches and Christian schools and colleges. According to the curator of the Huron County Historical Society, DeHaan Industries' vice president of finance and treasurer "believes that the same principles of hard work, honesty, and Christian concern the DeHaans have applied in their personal lives have been central to the success of DeHaan Industries."[4]

Immediately beyond the plant, Roger ordered, "Turn here." We made a left into the Royal Mobile Home Court, a series of small side streets lined by rusting trailers. I had heard of this place; it had been described by a few Addison High students as the site of "a lot of drugs," and "where the Mexicans hang out." The edges of the street were dotted with old pickup trucks. A Ford Pinto was up on blocks, its front wheels removed and lying on the asphalt.

"This is a pretty nasty place, lots of drug deals and a shooting every once in while," Roger explained, making a note about a screen door torn from its hinges. "My girlfriend used to live in that trailer right there. One time her dad came over—he lived in the one there—and started giving me shit, like I'm no good and shit like that. I finally got sick of it and went up to him like I was going to kick his ass. They had to pull us apart and stuff. Another time there was these three big Mexican girls who were hassling a friend of mine. I went over there and one of their boyfriends was there. I chased him down this street—yeah, this one right here—with a metal pipe, but then when I got into my truck to take off, they started grabbing at me. I had to, like, kick at them to get away. It was crazy."

We left the trailer park, turned right onto Ontario Street, and drove through a neighborhood of small houses huddled close together, their siding in need of paint, their porches sagging. Most of the cars were badly corroded; the luckier ones had primer spots on the fenders. Mike had told me about Ontario Street: "It's the street you don't want to go down if you don't know nobody. When I first moved there, I heard the stories about Ontario Street, like, that's not the area you want to go to. It's just known for its drugs. I mean, people have seen a lot of crack deals and stuff like that. A lot of gangs. From what I've heard it's spreading out more around that area. Always lots of fights."

A small African American girl wearing a pink coat, the white fur around the hood framing her face, rode a tricycle on the sidewalk. She paused to watch us go by.

"Where do you guys live?" I asked Juan and Esteban, glancing in my rearview mirror. Juan glanced to his right and answered quietly.

"Over that way a few blocks." Esteban flipped the tape in my recorder.

We made a left onto Maple Street, heading west back toward the M-62 dividing line. As we crossed the highway, we passed between the two courthouses which seemed to form a gateway that reminded me of the INS checkpoint separating the destitution of Tijuana and the affluence of San Diego. On the left of this passageway stood Addison's old courthouse. A striking architectural landmark, this Romanesque-style Victorian structure, built between 1884 and 1886, boasts classical columns, terra-cotta reliefs, and a frieze of colored tiles. On the right, the new building, sacrificing elegance for utility, is an efficient glass and steel box. The homes just beyond the courthouses are small and well-kept and grow larger with each block. By the time Roger instructed me to turn right, the houses were massive, reclining about fifty yards from the street, their bulk made graceful by slender white colonnades and foreign luxury cars parked in circular driveways. Roger made a note: "Country club down that road. It's kind of rich there."

It was time to head back. We made our way back across town and pulled onto Esteban and Juan's street, a narrow one-way alley on the East Side. I got out of the car and thanked the boys for their time.

"That's okay," Esteban said. "This time of year we don't do anything after school anyway. Just watch T.V."

On the way to Roger's house, I asked him about his family.

"My mom and dad usually go there on weekends," he said as we passed a country-western dance club. He wrote the name of the bar in my notebook. "I usually hang out with my girlfriend. She dropped out of school to take care of our daughter."

"Oh, yeah? What's your daughter's name?"

"Melissa. When my girlfriend's mom comes home from work

at about one, she goes to her job. She was working at McDonald's, but she hated that. Her boss was an asshole. Now she's a cashier at the mini-mart just before you get to River Road."

"I have a daughter, too," I said. "She's ten. I can hardly believe it. She lives with my ex-wife in Cleveland, but I go pick her up and bring her to Ann Arbor every other weekend. Long drive."

Roger smiled. His gums were dark red. "Yup, they're a lot of work. The farm that I work at is out that way." He pointed to our left. "I told my boss that I'd like to get to be a veterinarian. He said if I did I could take care of his cows."

As we pulled into Roger's driveway, I bottomed out the car in a pot hole. I thanked Roger for his help.

"Aw, I'm glad to do it. My girlfriend will be happy that I made it home coherent. Usually when I go out after school, I come back pretty fucked up. I'm a party animal, man. I can party with the best of 'em. I'll see you next week at school."

"So long," I said. I backed out of the driveway, tuned my radio to NPR, and headed north for home.

My tour guides represent a new generation of workers in Addison and the surrounding Huron County. Since the first White settlers began to arrive in the 1820s, the history of the area has been marked by spurts of growth followed by periods of consolidation—with the constant productive influence of agriculture made possible by the flat and fertile land the area's early Irish and German settlers cleared and drained. Growth was encouraged by the construction of a railroad connecting Addison and Toledo, Ohio, in 1836. This was the first railroad in America west of Schenectady, New York, eventually establishing Addison as an important link between Chicago and the East. But in recent years, the types of agricultural jobs Roger dreams of are dwindling. While farming in Huron County remains a significant economic force, this segment of the economy fell from 4.6 percent of the county's earnings in 1971 to 2.7 percent in 1981 (Community Problem-Solving Committee Report, 1992, p. 6).

A more powerful sector of the Huron County economy is manufacturing, which first grew sharply in the latter portion of the nineteenth century, when the area became the nation's leading producer of wire fencing, using the railroads to ship its products. In the twentieth century, while the area never became a producer of cars like Dearborn or Flint, it was and continues to be home to a number of companies manufacturing parts for automobiles. The area's industrial capacity again grew significantly in the 1930s, when Huron County became a center for the manufacture of refrigeration and air-conditioning equipment and components. Today, the refrigeration company in a neighboring town remains the largest employer in the county, with over 2,000 workers on the payroll. This industrial growth has been prosperous for a segment of Addison's population. The city has a thriving and newly renovated downtown area. Turn-of-the-century Victorian homes add grace and elegance to the city's historical district, and Addison boasts a small symphony orchestra and the third oldest continuously operating opera house in the United States.

Despite this prosperity, fluctuations in industrial production in recent years have led to a sense of underlying instability in the area. Huron County unemployment was 14.5 percent in 1980, peaked in 1982 at 18.1 percent, and fell to 7.2 percent in 1989. Although area employment has increased in recent years, it has done so primarily in the service sector, where many people are underemployed or working at minimum-wage jobs. According to the most recent statistics available, the service sector accounts for a slight majority share (51 percent) of Addison's total employment. Relatively well-paying manufacturing jobs, however, declined from roughly 50 percent of all employment in 1981 to 36 percent in 1994 (Bureau of the Census, 1994). Reductions in the availability of industrial jobs have resulted from the closing or downgrading of several important local employers such as the Anderson Spring Division, which made seats for automobiles and employed over 800 workers but closed in 1982. According to Tom, an Addison High security guard, Great Lakes Chain and Cable, an important employer in the automobile industry, downsized its workforce in the 1980s from over 1,000 to about 200 before closing its Addison operations completely in 1992 and moving to less expensive labor markets in Arkansas. In the 1980s the Ottawa Furniture Company also joined the migration of companies to the South. The loss of about 2,000 jobs at these three companies—in addition to the loss of another 1,000 jobs at Addison's Ford facility—made the 1980s a very difficult time.

Tom, who uses his security employment to supplement his job in a small local factory in order to put his three daughters through college, explained: "It used to be that you could just go from one job to another. You can't do that anymore."

Tom's story was corroborated by a conversation I later had in a local coffee shop called the Pit Stop. The booths and tables being full, I had found a spot at the counter, where an elderly man wearing a Cat Diesel cap and a black jacket sat to my right. Between sips from his mug of coffee, the man told me that he had moved to Addison in 1952, when "there were a lot of good jobs." Soon, though, layoffs and union breaking become a recurring theme of his story. The man explained that companies would hire people to work for $14 an hour and then "come out with a take it or leave it" offer of $7 and a discontinuation of benefits. If the union refused, the company would either hire new employees or move the plant out of state. After the company he worked for moved to Indiana in 1982, he drove a truck for a canoe manufacturer until his retirement a few years ago. He spoke with a sense of pride of the "long hauls" to Maine and Missouri. Last year the canoe company went bankrupt. "Yep, there were lots of jobs here in the '40s and '50s," he said as he finished his coffee and stood up to leave. "Not so many now."

The general picture of Huron County, then, is of a working-class region extremely vulnerable to economic trends and characterized by below-average income. In the city of Addison, the 1989 median household income was $24,788 compared to a state level of $31,020 (21 percent lower). Moreover, in the same year, more than 25 percent of the city's 1,925 families with children under 18 were living below the poverty line.[5]

Despite the hard times brought on by shifting economic winds, a prominent role in the development that has occurred in Addison and the surrounding area has been played by Latino laborers, who arrived in two primary waves to meet employment demands of prosperous business ventures. The first Latino workers arrived in 1919, when the Continental Sugar Company recruited workers for the area's sugar beet fields to replace the labor force that had previously come from Eastern Europe but had been interrupted by World War I. In 1940, responding to the labor demands of wartime industrial production, the second wave of

Latino workers arrived. This was the first time Latinos were hired for such jobs, and it was these men and women who stayed in large numbers; their children and grandchildren now form the base of Addison's Latino population. This second wave of immigrants, arriving from Texas and Mexico, created housing shortages so acute that manufacturers sought to solve the problem by billeting many Latino families in barns at the county fairgrounds. As a local historian has noted, "The quarters here were crowded, poorly ventilated, and generally unattractive."[6] An Addison Latina resident who recalls living in these quarters as a girl said that "people there lived like horses." As I had learned from my tour, the situation hadn't improved nearly as much as one would hope. Nonetheless, Latino immigrants have continued to move to Huron County, with their numbers increasing 20.6 percent between 1980 and 1990 (Bureau of the Census, 1990).

But if Latino workers have been used in the past to satisfy periodic labor demands, more recent competition for jobs in the manufacturing sector has led to tension between working-class Whites and Latino immigrants. The man with the Cat Diesel cap had told me that he worked most of his adult life in an office furniture plant, which "back in the '60s" received a lucrative government contract to supply thousands of offices with desks, chairs, and file cabinets. The situation grew complicated, however, when someone the man described as a "government civil rights worker" came to town and notified the company that it would lose the contract unless it agreed to lay off Whites with greater seniority before more recently hired Chicanos to achieve a more racially balanced work force. Rather than either forfeit the contract or comply with this requirement, the plant managers decided to cut back to a four-day work week for everyone, which meant that all employees kept their jobs, but with a 20 percent pay cut. Tom, the Addison security guard, had also implied that vying for employment contributed to racial tension in Huron County: "With all the immigrants moving to the area, there's more and more people going after the same jobs."

In Addison, where so much of the quality of life is tied directly to small industry, the struggle for sustained employment is one that Latino residents are clearly losing. In 1989, the median income for Addison Latino families was $19,942, compared to

$29,910 for Whites, with more than 30 percent of Latino families living below the poverty line (compared with 15.2 percent of Whites). Of Latino families with children under 18 years old, the percentage of those living below the poverty line was 37 percent. Moreover, the percentage of Latino individuals living below the poverty line was 33.8, compared with 18.1 percent of Whites. Latino households receiving some type of public assistance income constituted 27 percent of all Latino households, compared to 12 percent for Whites. Even this meager security, however, is threatened by the current political climate. General Assistance was one of the numerous cuts in welfare during Michigan Governor John Engler's first year in office as he erased a $1.8 billion state budget deficit. Programs to pay utility bills were cut 42 percent. A general program to help poor people with emergency situations was slashed 72 percent. In all, $315.5 million, or 13 percent of state welfare spending, was cut from the Department of Social Services budget during Engler's first year in office—a trend he has since continued.[7]

Mirrored in scores of communities throughout the country, the bleak economic situation of many of Addison's Latino residents is both commonplace and ironic. Encouraged by corporate recruiters' promises of a better life, immigrants from Texas and Mexico came to the area and were exploited for their labor as they helped build the wealth of the community, only to be shut out from the prosperity their work made possible. Since the first years of this century, Latino workers and their families have, to a large extent, remained "outsiders," sufficient to fill a position in a sugar beet field or on an assembly line, but kept from sharing in the affluence that abounds on the city's West Side.

Ideally, as members of the public that Addison High School is entrusted to serve, Latino students might find substantial hope for improving their lot through education. However, as integral parts of our communities, schools are both implicated and invested in the ideologies and life circumstances those communities establish and perpetuate. Indeed, Addison High does more than reflect the city's dominant discourses and desires; it constitutes a dimension of the structures that reproduce the values and privileges of existing elites, actively sustaining divisions among people that—in the case of Addison and so many other communities—fall in large part along racial lines. Addison as a community has relegated its Latino residents to its lowest socioeconomic level; Addison as a school district helps maintain this condition by jettisoning nearly half of its Latino students.[8]

In order to reverse this trend, Addison High would have to live up to its stated democratic mission—the one I had seen displayed on Morton's bulletin board—and "challenge *each* student to achieve academic excellence" (emphasis added) by creating circumstances in which students like Rosa could succeed; it would have to "foster social participation" by respecting Latino students as valuable agents in the school community; it would have to "promote development of self-esteem" by being attentive to the complexity of Latino students' particular needs and by including and celebrating their cultures in the curriculum. In short, Addison High would have to struggle against the trends of the larger community that hinder the ideals of freedom of choice and equality of opportunity. It would have to engage in an institutional effort to create conditions wherein Rosa could participate meaningfully in the activities of the school community and in the decisions that affect her life. It would have to become, in other words, what Peter McLaren (1995) has called a "counterpublic sphere," a democratic space dedicated to understanding, critiquing, and striving to rectify the types of injustices chronicled in the city's history and current census data (p. 33). Harriet Romo (1996) has argued that schools can work toward achieving these ambitious aims through measures such as school leadership that makes immigrant and migrant students a priority, instruction based on such students' previous educational experience, outreach and communication in parents' home language, and staff development to help teachers and other staff members serve language-minority students more effectively. Though I was hoping to find evidence of something resembling these measures in subsequent visits to Addison High, my further experience attending classes with Rosa and my growing sense of the many causes of her difficulties in school soon made me see that such measures had not yet been taken.

CHAPTER THREE

(Mis)Understanding Failure

Through all my experiences with people struggling to learn, the one thing that strikes me most is the ease with which we misperceive failed performance and the degree to which this misperception both reflects and reinforces the social order.

MIKE ROSE, *Lives on the Boundary*

More than Words

Based on my first day of attending classes with Rosa, I had concluded what common sense had suggested from the beginning—that among the reasons for her difficulties in school was her lack of English fluency. Without my tagging along to offer labor-intensive (and what appeared to be humiliating) tutoring, she had been unable to follow lectures and instructions, read her textbooks, or ask for help. Rosa's teachers had themselves expressed feelings of helplessness and frustration at their inability to communicate with Rosa and were worried about her prospects for the new semester.

Our concern for Rosa's difficulties with English were not completely groundless, for data indicate that limited English-speaking ability among Latino students hinders their chances for success in school. For instance, in a study of nearly 18,000 Latino and White high school seniors, Fernandez and Nielsen (1980) concluded that "as the student's self-judged proficiency in English increased, so did their educational aspirations, achievement test scores, and propensity not to be over-aged for a high school senior student" (as cited in Durán, 1987, p. 39). Further data on language use show that the dropout rate of 32 percent for Latino students who speak Spanish at home is nearly three times the overall student dropout rate, and two times the rate for those who speak English "very well" or do not report using Spanish at home (McMillen, 1993, p. 84). In sum, these data indicate that dropout rates tend to increase as English language ability declines—from 17 percent among Latino students who speak English "very well" to 83 percent among those who report no ability to speak English (McMillen, p. 84).

However, to find a correlation between the ability to speak English and the likelihood of succeeding in school is not to demonstrate that a lack of English fluency is the sole (or, as I will argue, even the primary) cause of Latino students' dropping out. If this were the case, the solution would be simple enough: immerse Spanish-speaking students in an all-English environment until they master the second language, and then mainstream them into regular classes, assuming they are destined for success on the school's terms. In fact, the situation is not quite so simple. I do not wish to imply here that English fluency is unimportant in Addison High or any other public school in the United States. However, according to a 1986 study in Michigan, fewer than 4 percent of the Latino students who dropped out of school said that they did so because they "had trouble with English" (Michigan State Board of Education, p. 32).[1] This figure suggests that educators and policy makers tend to oversimplify the complex issues surrounding the education of Latino students, especially those like Rosa who speak little English, and to assume that language is their only barrier. As Vasquez, Pease-Alvarez, and Shannon (1994) have argued, schools, driven by an overriding concern to assimilate students into the American mainstream by teaching them English, have generally failed to provide an optimal learning environment for language-minority (LM) students:

> English-language and basic-skills acquisition are viewed as the most important educational goals for this student population, with devastating results. Students with minimal or no knowledge of English are deprived of learning experiences in which they can use their native languages to express themselves fully. To aggravate matters, when children's teachers are not proficient in their students' native languages, they are not in a position to adequately judge the children's abilities because they fail to rec-

ognize the range of skills the children are manifesting as they converse in their native languages. Meaningful and relevant activities that entail the use of information and skills are rarely the focal point of instruction in classrooms of language minority students. (p. 149)

But if factors other than a lack of English fluency are the source of language-minority students' problems at school, these factors are often not apparent to those of us who are native English speakers and whose cultures are usually the dominant ones mediated by the school. Although as well-intended educators we may care deeply about students and about establishing relationships with them that might better situate us to learn ways we can work to improve their lives, we must look beyond solutions like the one articulated to me concerning Rosa in the teachers' lounge by Mr. Morton: "She's just gotta learn English. I can't help her if I can't talk to her." Again, I am not saying that if Rosa remains in the United States she won't in many ways benefit from speaking English. Nonetheless, if we citizen teachers are to address the problems of Latino students' alienation and attrition, and, by extension, their lack of opportunity to participate in the collective activities that affect their lives, then we need to understand that language is only one of the daily obstacles they face as they walk through our hallways and sit in our classrooms. As I continued my semester with Rosa, the forms these obstacles sometimes take came into view.

A Difficult Language Made More So

Although nearly all of the teachers I met at Addison High were capable and committed educators who were cordial in their interactions with Latino students, many of these same teachers harbored an underlying suspicion of students who did not speak English. In the hallways, after class, even during a chance meeting in a local restaurant, faculty members admitted to me that they thought such students sometimes exaggerated their inability to understand English, that they used language as a ruse to avoid doing their assigned work. One day as we talked in her classroom during lunch, Ms. Dolgan, the math teacher, mentioned that some of the other Latino students had told her that, at least in gym class, Rosa "understands more than she lets on," implying that Rosa used her "alleged" limited knowledge of English as a way to avoid activities she preferred not to participate in. I admitted to Dolgan that I had seen a bit of evidence that on its surface would appear to support her suspicion. In geography class just that morning, Mr. Morton had instructed the students to turn to a particular page in the textbook, and before I could say *"two hundred forty-four"* in Spanish, Rosa was there. At other times I had watched Rosa correctly retrieve a particular worksheet from her notebook, collect materials from the front of the room to work on a science project, and even reply when Alice Martinez, Rosa's ESL teacher, had asked her, in English, how she was doing. "Fine," Rosa had said.

However, I pointed out to Dolgan that although these could be taken as signs that Rosa did indeed understand some English, this apparent "evidence" was actually Rosa's either imitating her classmates or displaying a knowledge of English at only its most basic level. In science class, when Rosa saw other students carrying test tubes and beakers back to their desks, she did the same. When she turned to the correct page or responded to a simple greeting, she was using skills one learns in the first few weeks of a foreign language course. Nonetheless, as anyone who has tried to learn a second language knows, there is a difference between recognizing numbers or responding to simple, predictable conversations and trying to navigate through the specialized vocabulary of the academic disciplines.

In his well-known study of twelve hundred Canadian immigrants in grades five, seven, and nine, Jim Cummins (1981) found that while these children typically took two to three years to reach proficiency in basic second-language communicative skills, students being schooled only in a second language required five to seven years to reach the level of native speakers in those context-reduced, cognitively demanding language tasks needed for school (see also Collier, 1989; McLaughlin, 1992). Similarly, Mary Sue Ammon (1987) cautions educators against mistaking students' general word recognition in talking and listening for an ability to process these words in new and written contexts. As Ammon explains, nonverbal speech cues facilitate sentence analysis, and she also points out that spatial, temporal, and personal references are more concrete and sentence structures less complex in most conversations than they are in written discourse (p. 73). In other words, these researchers assert that a second-language learner typically finds it much easier to chat face-to-face with someone about common subjects than to read a textbook about unfamiliar course content.

From the perspective of a citizen teacher, there is considerable danger in underestimating the amount of time LM students need in order to attain the fluency called for in second-language classrooms, for it is only by achieving such fluency that LM students are able to participate fully in the life of a school. Unable to speak the specialized English related to content-area course topics, unable to understand lectures and instructions, these students are barred from the knowledge they need if they are to gain the obvious benefit of passing their classes or purposefully choosing their actions as informed citizens both within and outside of school. At least as important, however, is the fact that by being unable to contribute to classroom conversations, by having to just sit there in silence, such students are divorced from the collective intellectual activity of their teachers and peers. Disconnected from such activity, these students are in danger of learning habits of passivity and helplessness that are poison to the participatory ideals of democracy.

This difficulty in mastering specialized academic language was evident in my own interactions with Rosa. With our situation aggravated by my own limitations in speaking Spanish, it once took me an entire study hall period to explain to Rosa the distinctions between velocity, speed, and acceleration. Similar problems arose with math (multiples, factors, decimals) and English (plot, subordinate clause, alliteration). Again, it was not that Rosa recognized no English. I had seen her, for instance, accommodate a White classmate who had asked in English to borrow a pen. And when she once told me that she had lost something I couldn't quite understand, she clarified in English that she was missing an "earring." Nonetheless, these and several other English words and expressions that Rosa had shown she knew were those that had proven useful in her immediate experience, not the key terms that are printed in bold letters in high school textbooks. Martinez once expressed her frustration with teachers' assuming a fluency Rosa and other Latino students did not have in this way: "They hear these kids speaking a few words in English in the cafeteria, and right away they think there's no language problem. Well, I've got news for them: they're wrong."

But even if Rosa had been familiar with the specific languages of academic content areas, her difficulties in understanding English were often compounded by classroom environments clouded by cyclones of noise and visual distractions. Addison High offers three courses of study: Vocational Training, General Education, and College Preparatory. I had learned from conversations with teachers and from classroom observations that the higher track classes were generally filled with White students from Addison's wealthier families. These students had spoken to me of their participation in extracurricular groups such as the football team, the drama club, and the yearbook staff. They had told me of their plans to attend schools like Michigan, Wisconsin, Dartmouth, or Oberlin. Casually but carefully dressed in $50 Champion sweatshirts, Nike sneakers, and expensive, custom-fitted wool baseball caps, Addison's college-bound students had impressed me with their incisive and focused class discussions of topics such as the Bill of Rights and Milton's characterization of Satan in *Paradise Lost*.

In contrast, Rosa and Addison's other LM Latino students were generally relegated to classes in either the vocational or general tracks. Here the kids wore sneakers decorated with insignias I did not recognize and inexpensive caps made of cotton with adjustable plastic straps in the back. The frequent presence of Latino students in lower-track courses is not an exclusive characteristic of Addison High. On the contrary, research has shown that through "ability grouping" at the elementary level and through "tracking" in secondary schools, Latino students nationwide are present in disproportional percentages in lower-track classes and are thus often exposed only to "low status knowledge" characterized by unchallenging, rote learning rather than the analytical and creative "high status knowledge" that is a prerequisite for college admission (Oakes, 1985; Valencia, 1991a).

This common practice of "tracking" is supported by ideological norms in our society about what constitutes "intelligence" and how "ability" is genetically distributed among individuals. That is, we tend to think of intelligence and ability as fixed, innate traits—"things" that are located in people from birth. We do not, in other words, understand intelligence or ability as characteristics that are defined according to norms that are specific to a particular culture and/or class; nor do we tend to think of these traits as constructed according to the opportunities available to learn ways of thinking and acting that dominant groups are in a position to declare as valuable. In sum, we tend to think that a child is naturally "gifted" (or not), and this assumption, when coupled with our American affinity for individualism, justifies placing her or him in an accelerated (or remedial) educational program.

Among the problems of this culturally insensitive ability grouping is the fact that the effects of being placed in low-achieving tracks (and labeled early in life as a "loser") can be devastating for students, especially those from ethnic- and language-minority groups. For instance, John Goodlad (1985) found that first- or second-grade children who are lower-tracked by their teachers' judgments of their reading and math abilities, or by testing, are likely to remain in the lower tracks for the rest of their schooling. In addition, he found that poor and ethnic-minority children are more likely to be relegated to lower tracks than are their White counterparts. Viewing the issue of tracking from a different perspective, Hugh Mehan and Irene Villanueva (1992) found that when Latino and African American students were removed from their lower-track classes and placed in college prep courses with high-achieving students, these minority students benefited in a number of ways, including higher college enrollment. These and other studies (Lucas, Henze, & Donato, 1990; Romo & Falbo, 1996; Valdés, 1996) strongly suggest that a rigorous academic curriculum, especially one that is linguistically accessible to language-minority students, serves the educational and social interests of such students more effectively than do remedial or compensatory programs (Nieto, 1994, p. 409). Sadly, entrenched as Rosa was in the lowest of Addison High's academic tracks, she had little hope of being meaningfully challenged to realize her potential.

Beyond what I observed to be the low intellectual expectations of these courses, an additional feature of them that created difficulties for Rosa was that their frequently chaotic atmosphere made it all the more challenging for her to understand what was expected of her. For most of the school day, Mr. Robbins was a fine teacher and adept at keeping his students "on task." In the lower-track class in which Rosa was enrolled, however, he experienced unusually severe problems with classroom management. On a fairly typical day, for instance, though students were supposed to have been taking turns reading aloud from the textbook, most were engaged in conversations of their own, often with friends several rows away. Two boys sat on the backs of their chairs, while the girl in front of me pulled up the hood of her sweatshirt and rested her head on her desk. Another girl stood up and walked across the room, sat next to a friend, and returned to her seat only after finishing a conversation lasting several minutes, despite having been told three times by Robbins to "quiet down." To be heard over the noise, Robbins spoke rapidly and loudly, making words Rosa might have known individually blur together in a cacophony of background noise further obscured by slang. It was as though Rosa was caught in a cross fire of words that rushed by in random bursts. As Robbins began a brief lecture on foreshadowing, Rosa took cover, closing her textbook and then her eyes.

After class, when all but a few of the students had left, I walked up to Robbins to explain that because Rosa could not read the short story he had assigned, neither had she been able to answer the questions he had collected as homework. I added that, despite his careful preparation of the day's lesson, the distractions around us had made it difficult for Rosa and me to make much progress in class.

"Yeah, I can see how that would be tough for her," he said. He then rolled his eyes and smiled. "These days," he said, "anyone going into teaching is either crazy or soon will be."

I nodded. "Yeah, they're a lively class," I said. I slung my backpack over my shoulder and headed into the hallway, remembering some of those exhausting, difficult days I had had as a high school teacher and wondering how much Robbins's own struggles affected Rosa's performance in school. In that particular class, the teacher was, himself, barely surviving; how could he maintain an environment in which a supposedly shy Latino student who didn't understand English might have even the hope of success?

Education Gaps: What Rosa Didn't Know and Why

Predictably, Rosa's difficulties with English continued to be a source of frustration. Because my schedule at the University that semester enabled me to attend classes with Rosa only one day each week, Rosa struggled without the consistent tutoring that might have enabled her to learn in her native language, and she thus fell further and further behind in her schoolwork. By the eighth week of the term, her teachers' record books, like Mr. Pearson's computerized list, showed a series of blanks behind Rosa's name.

In spite of these persisting problems, our days together left me at times with a guarded optimism, as we were able to make some small progress. It had become our routine to do most of our work in the library, where, at a corner table, we could talk without disturbing the rest of the class or embarrassing Rosa. Here we completed tasks like labeling a geography map, writing brief responses to a poem assigned in English class, or filling in blanks on a science worksheet with answers that could be found almost verbatim in the textbook.

What I soon realized, however, was that the work Rosa was able to do was limited to that which required little prior content-area knowledge or foundational skills other than a basic ability to read and write, or, in math, to add and subtract. Lucas et al. (1990) have noted that because of the strained economic and political circumstances in the countries and regions they've left, many students "have had interrupted schooling, and thus come unprepared not only in English, but also in content knowledge, basic study skills, and knowledge of school culture" (p. 316). Such was the case for Rosa.

This lack of educational foundation could not, in my view, be traced to what Rosa had told me about the schooling she had received in Puerto Rico. Although, according to Rosa, her school *"was small, with three rooms that were made of metal,"* its curriculum, she explained, was similar to that of schools in the continental United States: *"We studied math, geography, and history—just like here."* Thus, although Rosa's descriptions of her education in Puerto Rico suggest an environment different from that of Addison's elementary and middle schools, her account did not point to any deficiencies in the instruction she received there. Rather, the more serious cause of Rosa's not being prepared for her Addison High classes seemed to be her inconsistent attendance since moving north. After leaving Puerto Rico, Rosa's family had lived first in Chicago and then in two Wisconsin cities and a town in Western Pennsylvania. Rosa made clear that she didn't enjoy the schools in these places any more than she did in Addison. *"I didn't like those schools, either,"* she said. *"Nobody spoke Spanish."* Rosa also told me that during this time, her attendance had been sporadic, due both to the family's moving from city to city and to periodic visits to Puerto Rico. That being the case, during the two and one-half years between Rosa's leaving Puerto Rico and her arrival in Michigan, she had had no sustained schooling. Due in part to these family circumstances, Rosa had not had the chance to acquire the educational foundation that her teachers expected and that the work they assigned required.

"It is imperative," Ms. Dolgan called out one day over the din of student voices, "that the sample test on positive and negative numbers be finished by the end of the class period."

I sighed and looked at Rosa. Though I had made some suggestions to Dolgan concerning how I thought Rosa might benefit from revised assignments and alternative forms of assessment that were more attuned to Rosa's prior schooling and difficulties with English, no such arrangements had been made. As usual, Rosa and I packed up our books and went to the library, settling in at our favorite table in the corner. Dolgan had told me that her math class had been working with positive and negative numbers for about a week now, but Rosa said that for her the lessons hadn't been much help. *"I don't understand what she says, and nobody else in my class speaks Spanish,"* she said. When I asked to see the homework Rosa had done since last week, she pulled from her notebook a sheet of paper on which she had copied the answers to the odd-numbered exercises printed in the back of the textbook. The test was to be given the next day, and it was clear to me that Rosa had a lot to learn in twenty-four hours if she were to have any hope of earning a passing grade.

"Okay, Rosa, the first thing you need to know is that numbers greater than zero are called 'positive numbers,' those less than zero, 'negative.'" Rosa nodded and took a pencil from her purse. I pulled a sheet of paper from the recycling bin and drew a number line extending from negative ten on the left to positive ten on the right. *"You can see how to add and subtract numbers by drawing arrows above this line. Let's do two plus two."* I put my pen above the two and drew an arrow two spaces to the right, ending above four. *"Now you try it; two plus three."* Rosa began at the two, moved her pencil three spaces to the right.

"Like this? Five?"

"That's it," I said. *"Now we're going to try something a little more difficult."* For the next several minutes, I first modeled and then asked Rosa to do a variety of problems. I drew an arrow illustrating negative three minus two; she did negative two minus four. I drew negative five plus ten; she successfully followed with negative four plus eleven. When I did one minus negative two, drawing the arrow two spaces to the right, Rosa looked up and frowned. *"Don't worry; it's not that hard. Subtracting a negative number is like adding a positive."* After I did several more examples, it was Rosa's turn: negative five minus negative two. Rosa began at negative five, paused, and then drew an arrow two spaces to the right: negative three. After working through several more examples and reminding Rosa of the basic rules when she seemed confused, I wrote out ten problems of various kinds—adding negatives to positives, subtracting negatives from negatives, and so on—that could be done with the visual aid of our number line. Leaning over the paper as she worked, sometimes chewing the eraser end of her pencil, Rosa spent the rest of the period working through these problems. She finished as the bell rang. Nine of the ten were correct. The sole mistake she corrected after I asked her to check it again.

Rosa smiled more broadly than I had ever seen and made a suggestion that surprised me: *"We should show this to the teacher."* We hurried out of the library and into the hallway crowded with students on their way to lunch. Rosa had done it,

I thought as I sidestepped a group of boys. By hearing explanations of the concepts in a language she understood, by working from her existing knowledge of addition and subtraction, she had learned a basic but potentially confusing process that is one of the foundations of the Trans Math class. Now, we needed to continue to build gradually on what Rosa had learned. We needed to postpone tomorrow's test, sit down with Dolgan and lay out a schedule that advanced in steps that would challenge Rosa but not bewilder her. We needed to give her a chance for more practice, for more of the success that seemed to propel her around the corner and down the corridor toward Dolgan's classroom. When we arrived at the door, we found it locked, the lights turned off inside. Rosa stood there with her paper in her hand as I tried to think of something to say.

"*I'll take this to her mailbox in the office,*" I said as she handed it to me.

"*Thanks. I'll see you after lunch,*" she mumbled and walked away. I went to the office and slid Rosa's work into Dolgan's mailbox, along with a note explaining what we had done that period in the library and suggesting that Rosa be given additional practice in lieu of the test. The next week when I returned to Addison and spoke with Dolgan, she said she was pleased that we had "accomplished something" but that Rosa had, "unfortunately," still failed the test. "It was pretty much just blank," Dolgan said.

Handing in homework with only the odd-numbered problems "answered," leaving tests blank except for her name at the top of the first page, Rosa continued to fail Trans Math, science, English, and geography in the weeks that followed. She worked hard during our brief weekly sessions, but the more time I spent with Rosa, the clearer it became that even if her lessons had been conducted in Spanish, it was unrealistic for her teachers to expect her to do what they required in the time allowed. Rosa was encountering concepts that were cumulative and interdisciplinary, concepts that required the preparation of years of instruction and internalization. With disheartening regularity, I observed that Rosa was simply not prepared for the work demanded by the Addison High curriculum. We couldn't complete science worksheets because of Rosa's inability to do the basic division needed to calculate speed as a rate of kilometers per hour. For a Trans Math assignment, I explained to Rosa that supplementary angles must equal 180 degrees. *"If angle A is 88 degrees, and angles A and B are supplementary, how many degrees in angle B?"* Rosa concentrated and subtracted 88 from 180: 108. These and many other instances made it seem that whatever we tried, the ghost of an inconsistent academic past brooded over our shoulders.

Not having been a full-time student for so long, not having consistently rehearsed the literacies required in classrooms, and not having grown accustomed to the routine of attending school on a daily basis, Rosa continued to struggle not only with her schoolwork, but also with her attendance. Señora Alvarez, the school counselor, had warned me of Rosa's truancies since arriving in Addison, and things hadn't improved since I had begun working with Rosa at the beginning of the semester. One morning as I waited for Rosa in the counseling office, I had the chance to ask Beth Reinstra, the Child Development teacher, how Rosa was doing in her class. Reinstra said she had noticed some improvement in Rosa's work after having insisted that Daniela—Reinstra's bilingual student—help Rosa each day.

"I can get her to do a few things with Daniela's help," she said. "But the problem, Todd, is that she's never here." Alvarez, who had seen us talking through her open office door, joined the conversation.

"Rosa comes on Thursdays, when you're here, but take a look at what's happening the rest of the week." Alvarez handed me a printout of Rosa's second-semester attendance. I counted the number of "T's" (for "truant"). Her total thus far was nineteen, meaning that she had already almost doubled the number of absences allowed before forfeiting course credit. Though it was only the beginning of March, Rosa had already failed all of her classes.

The Location of Failure

Standing in that counseling office after an early morning drive through the snow, I felt a disheartening futility concerning this whole project. The hundreds of miles on the road, the hours spent struggling through chaotic classrooms and stacks of homework, the pages of field notes I had already written and saved on my computer back in Ann Arbor. What possible use did any of my work as a tutor and researcher have? What was, after all, the point of all these efforts if they did not in some way help Rosa be more "successful" in school? At the University, I could in large part determine what happened in my classrooms. I could revise assignments and extend paper deadlines; I could meet with students for conferences in my office and shape course requirements to meet their needs and interests. Perhaps more importantly, my students shared with me the assumption that earning a high grade in a composition class and becoming conversant in the discourse of the University were pursuits that would yield tangible rewards and that, therefore, deserved a place high on our list of priorities. But here in Addison, I felt that I had little control over what teachers would continue to require of Rosa or whether or not she decided to show up for school. That growing sense of help-lessness fueled a frustration that I am not proud to confess.

When Rosa arrived about twenty minutes before the begin-ning of second period, I asked to talk to her in a seminar room adjacent to the counseling office waiting area.

"Rosa, I just found out that you haven't been coming to school. Do you know that you already have been absent so many times that you've lost credit for the semester?"

Rosa looked at her notebook. *"Yes, I know,"* she said. I didn't let up.

"I'm really frustrated that you haven't been here more often. How can I help you if you don't show up? Why don't you come to school?"

"I don't like school," Rosa said. *"And I've been sick."*

Rosa and I made it through the day in more or less typical fashion, but I continued to be troubled by what I saw as "her" failure to come to school. Again, though it's professionally and personally humbling to say so, my reaction that morning to Rosa's absences suggests that my own White, middle-class, culturally based notions of "individual responsibility" and "the value of an education" had kept me from completely letting go of the sim-plistic conclusion that Rosa herself was the cause of whatever difficulties she was having at Addison High. However, by and by, as I thought hard about what I had seen of Rosa's classroom experiences since the beginning of the term, it became clearer to me that the assumptions about schooling that to me seemed so self-evident did not ring true in Rosa's experience. In my case, going to school and doing what I was supposed to do had landed me high school teaching jobs and a place in the graduate program of a pretty respectable university. For Rosa, going to school meant setting herself up for failure. Seen from this perspective, the notions that I had tried to suppress but that had come out in my earlier conversation with Rosa were similar to those that prompted what I saw as the Addison teachers' indifference to Rosa's struggles, their reluctance to obtain and use materials in Spanish, and their refusal to consider alternative methods of assessment. To uncover such assumptions and their practical consequences is, I think, to begin to understand Rosa's attendance problem more as a *symptom* of ideologically driven and unresponsive teaching than as a *cause* of her continuing to fail nearly all of her classes.

This tendency to "locate" failure in the student is a move that some researchers have suggested is made easier by the common practice of designating certain students as "at-risk." As Ronda and Valencia (1994) have argued, the designation of "at-risk" is based on the model of "deficit thinking" that has been one of the major paradigms used in trying to understand the low academic achievement of some students, particularly those from low-socioeconomic and ethnic-minority groups. Ronda and Valencia contend that "at-risk" has thus become a person-centered explanation of school failure. It is a construct preoccupied with describing supposed cognitive and motivational deficiencies in students, particularly alleged shortcomings rooted in their familial and economic backgrounds, and it pays little attention to how schools are institutionally implicated in the ways that exclude students from learning (Ronda & Valencia, pp. 366–367).

At Addison High, this understanding of "deficits" located within students was made manifest not only in teachers' practices with their LM students but also in a survey conducted by the director of the community's "Upward Bound" program, which is designed to help students become the first in their families to enter college. The survey asked faculty and counselors at a local college and at Addison High what they considered to be the "top ten predictors of college failure." The results are as follows:

1. Weak study and critical thinking skills

2. Poor time management skills

3. Ineffective reading, writing, and math skills

4. An inability to apply effective test-taking strategies

5. Weak communication skills and need to define their educational priorities

6. Lack of high school preparation that addresses conflict management/resolution

7. An inability to accept diversity

8. Inappropriately used drugs and alcohol

9. Lack of access to necessary supplies (i.e., calculator, computer) and insufficient funds to access higher education

10. Entered the employment cycle (which is necessary for survival) and thereby experienced further hindrance and interference with academic success

Clearly, most of these predictors focus on individuals' traits and downplay whatever effect the school might have on "student" failure. While numbers 6, 9, and 10 imply that causes of students' difficulties may lie either in the school's curriculum or in students' economic situations, the other factors cited seem to place the "defect" in the students' intellect or character, suggesting that when trying to explain the failure of Rosa and other "unsuccessful" students, the Addison High faculty and staff were looking not at themselves and their school, but at the students and their upbringing. One way to understand why these teachers and administrators located students' failure as they did is to view school personnel collectively as an unresponsive and oppressive institution. However, if we think of schools not only as institutions constructed to serve the interests of the powerful but also as being made up of people acting as individuals, we take, I think, a step toward a more complete understanding of why some students "succeed" while others do not—an understanding that includes an awareness of what Dewey (1916/1985; 1927/1988; 1929/1962) describes as the interactive relationship between the individual and society, and of the importance of citizen teachers' acting distinctively to promote democracy within the communities they occupy.

At Addison High, among the specific mechanisms that perpetuate the notion that students and their families are the location of failure are the miscommunications between the school and its Latino families. Recalling her first years in the area, a woman from Mexico with three sons in the Addison system told me of her reluctance to contact teachers and counselors when her children were having troubles at school:

> *I didn't do anything. I had a lot of problems. I didn't speak any English, and I thought, How am I going to do anything if I can't communicate with them? I didn't have much communication with the school because I was afraid because I didn't understand them. I want to go to school in order to learn English perfectly, a hundred percent, because I want to understand perfectly what my children's teachers say to me and what's happening and what they're doing in school. Because before I wanted to talk to them, to find things out, but I couldn't.*

Recent ethnographic studies (Carger, 1996; Romo & Falbo, 1996; Valdés, 1996) have confirmed that this fervent belief in the value of education and a strong commitment to encourage their children's schooling is common among Latino parents. Also common, however, are the difficulties these parents experience in their attempts to work with schools in their children's interests. Although some of these difficulties are the result of language barriers between parents and school personnel (Delgado-Gaitan, 1988, 1990), Valdés (1996) points out that such situations are further complicated by the fact that schools and families tend to make assumptions about each other that result in frustration and a lack of effective collective efforts to improve students' experiences at school. According to Valdés, the schools she studied expected a "standard" family whose members were educated, who were familiar with how schools worked, and who viewed their role as complementing the teachers' role in developing children's academic abilities. Valdés further notes that when children came to school without certain skills—skills that their families in good faith believed the teachers should teach—school personnel assumed parental indifference, troubled homes, and little interest in education (p. 167). On the other hand, Valdés also writes that while the parents clearly valued education, they were often hindered in their attempts to participate in their children's schooling by difficult socioeconomic circumstances and by a lack of clarity concerning what schools expected of them (p. 176).

In Rosa's case, this lack of cooperation between the home and the school was evident in the tensions that grew between Rosa's mother and the counselor Sra. Alvarez. In some ways this conflict is ironic in that, for many years, Alvarez has consistently been an attentive, even affectionate, advocate for Addison's Latino students, as well as the primary contact person at school for Addison's Spanish-speaking parents. Nonetheless, at various times during my semester with Rosa, Alvarez shared stories with me that suggested that she and Rosa's mother disagreed concerning what roles the school and the family were obligated to play in Rosa's education. These disagreements, I think, provide an example of how the background and sociocultural assumptions of school employees can lead them to place the blame for failure on students and their families rather than on the school's (lack of) response to their educational and social needs.

One morning I arrived at the counseling office, where I was to meet Rosa, but instead found Alvarez waiting for me to apologize for the fact that, because the previous school day had been canceled due to snow, she had not called Rosa to remind her that I was going to be there that day. The result was that Rosa had failed to show up for school. When Alvarez had called Rosa's home for an explanation, Rosa explained that her brother had worn her sneakers that morning, so she had nothing to put on her feet.

Alvarez motioned for me to follow her into her office. Once inside, with the door safely closed, she said that while she was talking to Rosa that morning, she could hear Rosa's mother "yelling like crazy" in the background—what about, Alvarez was unsure. Alvarez explained that this was hardly the first time a phone call from school had angered Rosa's mother, who, according to Alvarez, "gets very angry" at attempts by teachers and counselors to reach her, even if those calls are made in Spanish. "She can be a hostile person," Alvarez said. "I don't think she's encouraging her daughter to get an education at all."

Apparently, this tension between Alvarez and Rosa's mother had been building for quite some time but had become especially hostile in recent days. Alvarez told of how Rosa's mother had come to school the previous week, demanded a conference, and complained that, rather than helping her daughter, the school was badgering her family without addressing the issues she saw as problematic, one of these being that teachers continued to mark Rosa "absent" even though she suffered from toothaches that kept her in pain and at home. This conversation, Alvarez said, had been "very heated," with "voices raised." I mentioned that Rosa had told me that her family could afford little dental care in Puerto Rico and that even after a root canal about a year ago, her teeth still needed a considerable amount of work.

"I know that, and I can appreciate it," Alvarez said. "But what bothers me is that the mother expects the school to do everything for them, not just arranging for dental care but also contacting all kinds of social service agencies." The usually even-tempered counselor was clearly angry, adding that although Rosa may indeed have had trouble with her teeth, there had been days when she had called in sick due to a toothache and then had been seen, in her words, "roaming the streets" later in the day.

Alvarez claimed that she had done her best to be accommodating to the family in many ways. She had arranged for school bus drivers to alter their routes so that Rosa and three school-age siblings—who attended different buildings within the Addison system—could ride the bus together. Last year, she had negotiated funds from the district office and hired a tutor to be with Rosa in the morning and then supplemented that help with the assistance of a Spanish major from Addison College to cover the afternoons.

"It was a huge investment for one kid, but even then she didn't show up for school. What is my role here?" Alvarez finally asked in exasperation. "Because I speak Spanish I'm expected to be a social worker. We can do just so much, but eventually they have to help themselves."

Alvarez's comments suggest, I think, that the lack of connection and cooperation between Latino families and school staff cannot be defined only along ethnic and/or linguistic lines, as they tend to be drawn in most educational contexts. For in addition to the cultural differences arising from Alvarez's Mexican heritage and the Puerto Rican origin of Rosa's mother, class distinctions separated these women as well. As Romo and Falbo (1996) have pointed out in describing the schools they studied, these socioeconomic differences can be consequential in that even Latino school personnel often expect and encourage Latino students to accept and adapt to the academic and behavioral standards that emanate from the White American culture of the school:

> Even if some of the teachers, for example, were of Hispanic origin, they were often too far removed from the cultures of working-class or low-income Mexican-origin families. Because of the educational levels required to be a teacher, librarian, counselor, or school administrator, it was almost inevitable that these school staff were oriented toward meeting middle-class needs by expressing middle-class values. (p. 191)

Unlike Rosa's mother, who had lived a life that continued to be destabilized by poverty, Alvarez's experience is one that had come to be attuned to the middle-class orientation that Romo and Falbo describe. Not long after my first meeting with Alvarez, she had shown me photos in her office of her father and her siblings, who had recently met in Texas for a family reunion. What she said as she described the photos offers a glimpse of a personal history that had helped form values that are similar to those of the institution where she works:

"When I was a girl in Texas," Alvarez said, "we were very poor. We didn't own a car, and we had to rent our house. But my father, in spite of all the male chauvinist things he can say sometimes, was determined that his daughters were going to go to college, even though especially in those days Latino girls were just supposed to get married and have kids." Alvarez pointed out the individual people in the photo. "This is my oldest sister. She went to college and started teaching; then she helped put her [Alvarez pointed again], my other sister, through college. And when she graduated and started working, it was her turn to put me through college. Our father had a vision for us, and that was that we were all going to get an education."

This vision eventually led to Alvarez and her husband's establishing themselves in Addison over thirty years ago. In addition to Alvarez's salary from Addison High, her husband's income as a respected small businessman is steady, and they have comfortably raised four children in Addison, all of whom have—according to their mother—"always thought of themselves as Americans."

Although my repeated attempts to arrange a meeting with Rosa's mother to hear her story were unsuccessful, what I was able to gather from Rosa (and later, her siblings) demonstrate the vast differences in the ways individual Latina women negotiate what anthropologist Pierrette Hondagneu-Sotelo (1994) calls the "gendered transitions" that accompany attempts to reinvent oneself as a Latina in modern U.S. society. Though Hondagneu-Sotelo writes specifically of Mexican migrants living in California, her analytical framework is useful, I think, in underscoring the distinctions between individuals that schools and many other social institutions tend to conflate in the generic category of "Latina." Hondagneu-Sotelo argues that in order to understand migration to the U.S. and the changes it brings about in people, one must understand it as a both a macro and micro phenomenon. That is, Hondagneu-Sotelo acknowledges the importance of a broader, "macro" perspective: The functions that labor migrations have played (and continue to play) in the development and maintenance of modern capitalism in the United States are an integral part of her discussion. However, she also maintains that conspicuously absent from the macrostructural perspective is any sense of human agency or subjectivity. She writes that immigrants, rather than being portrayed as human beings, "are portrayed as homogeneous, nondifferentiated subjects responding mechanically and uniformly to the same set of structural forces" (p. 6). As a corrective of what she takes to be this limited view, Hondagneu-Sotelo emphasizes the immediate context of family and community relations that shape how different people will respond to the pressures exerted by broad social, economic, and political structures. Specifically, she argues that unique and shifting gender relations *within* families circumscribe migration options and decisions. Thus, the cultural legacies experienced by individual women, she writes, "are *selectively* reproduced and rearranged through migration and resettlement in the new society. Family and community relationships, the maturation of the immigrant community, and the ways these intersect with the local economy form a constellation that reconstructs gender relations" (p. 32, italics added).

By emphasizing that such transformations are the result of a dialectical interaction between broad sociocultural forces and the localized relationships that people like Rosa's mother and Alvarez have experienced in their families and communities, Hondagneu-Sotelo helps us see how individuals' histories, dispositions, and economic circumstances can vary greatly from person to person despite assumed cultural similarities. As we have seen, Alvarez's socioeconomic status, as well as her long-term residency in Addison, have given rise to relatively "mainstream" views that complicate her ability to work effectively with Rosa's mother toward improving Rosa's experiences in school. Again, I wish to emphasize that during my time in Addison, I developed a great respect for Alvarez and her advocacy on behalf of the school's Latino students. She is fiercely proud of her Mexican heritage, and for decades she has acted as the primary liaison between Addison High and its Latino families. Nonetheless, as someone who had acclimated to the community, she seemed to expect Rosa and her family to do the same, and when they did not, Alvarez located the source of Rosa's failure in her background and home life.

Being Alone

Rosa is shy. Alvarez had warned me of that, and I saw little during my days at Addison High to suggest otherwise. When we had the opportunity to work together in the library, I had gotten into the habit of asking her questions that couldn't be answered in a simple "yes" or "no" just to get her to talk to me. However, to avoid classroom situations which Rosa told me *"embarrassed"* her, I now rarely moved my chair alongside Rosa's when the teacher was leading a lesson, choosing instead to remain seated behind her and translate only specific instructions to assignments and tests. One morning in particular, I could tell by the pained look on Rosa's face when I walked into Mr. Morton's geography class that she was not pleased to see me: her left hand, in what had become a familiar gesture, moved to her forehead, shielding her eyes. Not knowing quite what to do, I managed a *"How are you?"* Rosa shook her head and mumbled something I couldn't understand.

"What?"

Rosa repeated herself, but still I couldn't make out what she was saying.

"I'm sorry, I can't hear you."

She turned to face me and sighed. *"My head hurts,"* she said.

Morton explained the assignment—to label a series of geographical and political maps of Eastern Europe—and gave the class the remaining twenty minutes to begin. After a few minutes of working together with Rosa, filling in such landmarks as the Pindus Mountains and the Sava River, I was satisfied she could do the assignment on her own, but ten minutes later, when she told me she was "finished," I checked and found that she had completed only about half of the items on the list. I figured that Rosa probably didn't much care about the Sava river.

"Yugoslavia," I explained, *"means 'all Slavs.'"*

"Hm," Rosa said.

Morton came over to tell me that as of that day, Rosa still had not taken the previous week's quiz on countries and capitals of Western Europe and that—in addition to the absences that had caused her to fail the term—she had missed seven days in the past two weeks. It was odd how we had this conversation about Rosa, speaking of her in the third person, while she was sitting right there. I looked at Rosa, her hand over her eyes, and thought of the words of Ralph Ellison (1952/1989): "I am an invisible man. . . . I am invisible, understand, simply because people refuse to see me" (p. 3).

Considering the extent to which Rosa seemed isolated from her teachers and the other students, it became clearer to me that Rosa's "shyness" was not an essential trait, like her height or her eye color. Rather, it was, I think, the result of alienation caused in large part by her inability to speak to most of her peers and by the despair brought on by relentless failure. There in Morton's geography room, I again wondered why Rosa came to school at all. Legally, she was old enough to drop out. From what I could see, she showed little understanding of or interest in her studies; at school, she had no friends. This social isolation, I suspected from some reading I had recently done, was likely to have ongoing academic consequences for Rosa, since the ways in which students interact with classmates has been shown to have a significant relationship to growing proficiency in a second language (Strong, 1983). But in Rosa's case, what need was being met by her continued presence at school? Did she feel that as long as she just showed up she had at least the chance of getting an education? Was Addison High merely a place for her to have contact with people who were more or less her own age, even if that contact was almost completely limited to physical proximity? I asked Rosa these questions, then and at other times, but she never seemed to feel like talking about it, at least not to me.

I met Rosa in the library later that day to continue with her geography homework. Instead, we wound up talking about Rosa's dislike of school.

"I liked school in Puerto Rico" Rosa said. *"But here I don't understand anything."* She admitted that she attended school only because her mom forced her to. Alvarez, Rosa said, wouldn't let her go to adult night school, which was attended by Rosa's older sister Maria and where, Rosa said, *"the teacher speaks Spanish."* Though Rosa claimed not to know why Alvarez "wouldn't let her" go to night school, the counselor later told me the school district had a policy that forbade paying the $60 per semester for students under 18—who could be in the high school—to transfer to the evening adult education program. This $60 was more than Rosa's family could afford. Part of what attracted Rosa to night school was that, with a bilingual teacher, the language barrier would ostensibly have been removed, but I also suspected that the security of being with her sister would have been a welcome change from the social solitude she endured at Addison High.

That solitude was relieved briefly that semester when Pedro, who had been Rosa's neighbor in Puerto Rico, moved to Addison. A handsome and outgoing boy, Pedro rode the bus to school with Rosa and was in her math and science classes. There, I sat in the back of the room and watched. They came into class together, talked and laughed loudly, wrote on each other's folders, and passed each other notes. Fully bilingual, Pedro translated for Rosa, helped her with her homework, and ate lunch with her in the cafeteria. Dolgan, the math teacher, noted that "all of a sudden she started handing in all her homework." At every opportunity, Pedro and Rosa were together, friends. Even though Rosa knew she had lost semester credit, she came to school every day during those two weeks that Pedro's family remained in Addison, but when Rosa's companion abruptly moved to Cleveland, her attendance again fell off drastically. Rosa showed me a letter she received a couple of weeks after Pedro had left. She let me read it, then held it with both hands.

"I miss him," she said, staring at the envelope. *"It was nice when he was here, but now I don't know anybody who speaks Spanish."*

The anxiety of being alone continued to erode Rosa's sporadic attendance. One afternoon during lunch period I wandered through Addison High's "student lobby," an entryway and informal gathering place that faces south and has large windows extending from the floor to the second-floor ceiling. Even in the winter, the constant exposure to sunlight creates a greenhouse effect, making the room uncomfortably warm. A few students, mostly alone, lingered on the benches, and, as I passed by, a boy looked up from his bag of chips. Light brown hair fell over his forehead; I noticed he had unusually large feet.

"So, how's it going," I asked.

"Not bad."

"School treating you all right?"

"I guess so," he said. As the boy and I chatted, Rosa entered the lobby and placed a call from the pay phone under the stairs leading to the second floor. Though I continued to talk to the boy with the bag of chips, I couldn't help overhearing. Rosa was speaking with her mother, and what I heard most clearly was a repeated request to come home: *"But my stomach hurts, and I'm really tired."* From the look on her face and the exasperation in her voice, I could tell her pleas had been unsuccessful. As Rosa placed the phone back in its cradle, gave me a small wave, and left the lobby, I thought about the corrosive physical consequences of processing emotions like loneliness and desperation. It occurred to me then that although most of Addison High's 1,300 students viewed "success" in terms of good grades or a spot on the football team, for Rosa a successful day was one in which she stayed home and avoided the stomach pains and headaches that came with feeling very much alone.

I tried to help Rosa feel like she belonged at Addison High, to be—despite the brevity of my weekly visits—her companion. I tried to strengthen the personal connection between us, to establish a relationship I suspected would be the important beginning of any effort to keep Rosa in school. She began to teach me more and more Spanish, shaking her head and chuckling at the many words and phrases I didn't know. One afternoon in the library we postponed our work on a science worksheet and instead spent our time together paging through a world atlas. We found Puerto Rico, and Rosa showed me her hometown, Guayama. She told me that she lived near the beach, where her family and neighbors had enjoyed cookouts and swimming in the ocean. It was clear to me that in spite of the poverty that forced her family to move north, Rosa had been very happy there. I then showed Rosa where my hometown is, and the rest of the period we shared stories about growing up in our respective neighborhoods. It was instances like these which I now think may have been among the most important aspects of my time in Addison that semester, for by listening to each other's stories, we began, I think, a kind of dialogue that enabled Rosa to connect that normally alienating space called Addison High with the life she had lived and what she seemed to value most: her friends, her extended family, and her home. During these conversations characterized by the democratic principle of mutual learning, conversations in which I ceased to be only the "Anglo" tutor bringing knowledge from my privileged position as a high school and university teacher, I began to understand further that the academic "success" I had assumed was best for Rosa could be achieved only at the cost of an alienation that Rosa was unwilling to pay.

Still, as much as I like to remember moments such as these, when I'm candid with myself I have to admit I never knew Rosa very well. I still don't. Even now, I have so many questions—questions about her interests, peers, and teachers, questions about what she thought might be useful for her in school, questions about what she hoped her life would be like. As I mentioned earlier, it's not that I didn't ask these questions. Rather, I think it's because I never gave Rosa a good reason to answer them. And so the response I did get was almost always the same: *"No sé"*—or silence.

It's not altogether surprising to me that Rosa and I never fully established one of those close relationships that teachers sometimes make with their students. At least part of what kept us from doing so was my meager Spanish. Beyond language alone, however, I was never able to cross the broader cultural differences that separated us. For although Rosa and I were both "outsiders" at Addison High, her alienation was much different from my own. In the months since I had first arrived, I had made friendly acquaintances among the students and staff. I called the teachers by their first names as we ate lunch together in the faculty lounge; I exchanged greetings with familiar faces in the corridors. As a teacher and native speaker of English, I found Addison High to be an environment that suited me well, an institution constructed upon and operated by principles consistent with my small town, middle-class background. Moreover, at the end of the day, I got into my car and drove away, back to the self-validating context of Ann Arbor. I came and went at will with no personal risk. Rosa, on the other hand, was bound to circumstances over which she could exercise little control. She could not speak the school's language or complete her assignments. She could not make the friends she desperately needed. She could only stay home. As a White teacher, I represented not only a history of oppression based on ethnicity and social class, but also the specific forms of these relations as they are played out in schools. For Rosa, to have accepted me would have been to accept a world in which she had little value. Thus, though I have stated, in essence, that I was never able to build a bridge traversing the gulf that separated me from Rosa, it is perhaps better said that she had the good sense not to cross it.

In addition to these racial and socioeconomic differences between Rosa and me, the reality of power relations based largely on gender dynamics gave Rosa further reason to keep her distance. Lois Weis (1995) has argued that in order to understand relations of domination and subordination, it is important to highlight the extent to which "othering" includes a sexual naming and marking (p. 18). As Weis shows through discourse analyses of conversations with high school students, one of the ways in which some White males write themselves as "pure" (that is, as having socially acceptable sexual and moral standards) is to define and elaborate their identity in opposition to women of color, who are seen by such males as, in Weis's words, "disgusting and beyond the boundaries of what constitutes an acceptable heterosexual object" (p. 23). Though I will stop short of using such strong language to describe my perceptions of Rosa, it's difficult to rule out the possibility that at least part of my efforts to change her into a "good" Addison High student may have been rooted in the kind of genderized constructions Weis describes. For Rosa's part, despite my efforts to affirm her as a person and to help her exercise greater control over her life by furthering her education, insofar as the relationship between us was inevitably influenced by this pervasive discourse of disdain, she had some reason to doubt that I would regard her, a Puerto Rican woman, as something other than an object.

Given my growing realization that I was unlikely to be much use in keeping Rosa from feeling alone in school, I hoped that such relationships might be forged with other Spanish-speaking students in Martinez's ESL class. If she could build friendships with these peers who understood not only her language but also, to some extent, her experiences of being an "other" in a strange place, I thought that such affective connections might lead her to attend school more consistently. My optimism was largely the result of what I had noticed to be the atmosphere of acceptance and mutual assistance that Martinez had created and nurtured among her LM students. Though Rosa and her ESL classmates frequently received the message that they did not belong at Addison High, during second period they enjoyed a respite from the troubles they encountered throughout the rest of the school day. Here, they could express themselves and vent their frustrations in their native languages. It was a space of understanding and empathy where the teacher listened carefully and offered words of encouragement, a space where students shared their lives in ways I had not seen in other Addison classrooms.

Among the strategies Martinez used to establish these bonds was to ask the students to write in their journals about personal issues and experiences. One day, the assignment was to describe— in English, if possible—things that made them happy. After about twenty minutes, Miguel shared what he had written. We learned that he was happy when he celebrated his birthday with his family, "but the best was my health." He was less decisive about the Michigan snow: "I just don't liked, and I liked, I just don't know." He then read that his parents were still visiting relatives in Texas, having left him to live temporarily with his aunt and uncle. "I love my parents I wish they come back sooner but at same time to they stay a little longer more time in Texas. Because I was the only one male kid, they let me do whatever I wanted to do." Miguel added that he was proud that he had failed no classes the previous semester and that his mother works hard. He also wrote about his friends: "We share our problems and help each other like to copy each other's homework."

Elizabeth, who had moved to the area from Mexico about eight months before and was also living with an aunt and uncle, wrote specifically of Addison High:

> I like to come to school because I learn more what I know. My parents let me to come here for learn English language, and I can get a good careers. I'm happy when I came to the school, because, I have relationship with other persons. I'm happy to be here in this class, because I learn more English and have more communication. This class I enjoy. I was sad when I moved here but it's hard for me to live without my parents, but I want to be somebody in the life, for to help them.[2]

That Rosa had written in Spanish didn't bother Martinez. Several times during the semester, I had seen Rosa working with Soto to translate her words into English, but Martinez usually was content to have Rosa do her assignments in her native language. Rosa, in a barely audible voice, read that what made her happy was to receive letters from her grandparents. She added that she loved her mom and respected her stepfather. I was surprised when she mentioned school: *"I feel very good about being in school. I'm going to come every day. I'm not going to go home because I'm feeling a little bad. I came to school because Sra. Alvarez told me not to fail."* Though, as I've mentioned, Rosa had already failed her classes due to absences, I was moved by what seemed like an earnest attempt to please her teachers.

When my turn came, I took a picture of my daughter, Kaitlin, from my wallet and passed it around. At Martinez's request, I spoke English as I explained that what made me happy was the time Kaitlin and I were able to spend together on alternate weekends. It didn't much matter to me, I said, whether we went to university hockey games, shot pool at the campus union, or just stayed home and watched TV. Arranged in a circle, we in the ESL class then talked more about what we had written, asking questions of each other that might provide ideas for revisions. Rosa sat silent, withdrawn from the other class members even though the conversation was in Spanish. She rested her head on her desk. *"My head hurts,"* she whispered to me. I noticed after about three or four minutes that I and the others were ignoring Rosa. It was very easy to do.

As I periodically glanced over at Rosa, watching her drift along the periphery of the conversation, I wondered and worried about the cumulative consequences of her being essentially forgotten in her content-area class and now, increasingly, in ESL. Later, I thought about these consequences in terms of Dewey's (1938/1963) notion of the "continuity of experience," which he defines as follows: "The principal of continuity of experience means that every experience both takes up something from those which have gone before and modifies in some way the quality of those which come after" (p. 38). Dewey points out that the central problem of education is to select for learners the kind of present experiences that live fruitfully and creatively in other experiences. This ongoing progression of intellectual and moral development, this series of experiences that, ideally, prepares people for democratizing action in subsequent experiences, is what Dewey calls "growth" (1938/1963, p. 36; 1916/1985, pp. 46–58). Because, according to Dewey, experience occurs in the interaction between what goes on "inside a person" and the "objective conditions" of his or her environment, teachers have a responsibility to create a context of teaching and learning that leads to growth. Dewey (1938/1963) puts it this way:

A primary responsibility of educators is that they not only be aware of the general principle of the shaping of actual experience by environing conditions, but that they also recognize in the concrete what surroundings are conducive to experiences that lead to growth. Above all, they should know how to utilize the surroundings, physical and social, that exist so as to extract from them all that they have to contribute to building up of experiences that are worthwhile. (p. 40)

Dewey stresses that in making decisions about how best to create "worthwhile" experiences, educators must consider "the needs and capacities of the individuals who are learning at a given time" (p. 44). Failure to account for the unique "powers and purposes" of the learner, Dewey tells us, is what leads to the flawed notion that certain educational subjects or methods are intrinsically beneficial. Dewey is clear on this point: "There is no such thing as educational value in the abstract" (p. 46).

While considering the continuity of Rosa's experiences at Addison High, it became increasingly clear to me that while activities like factoring whole numbers, calculating the acceleration of falling objects, or writing expository paragraphs in English were appropriate for many of Rosa's classmates, they were not, as I had seen, valuable to her. To be sure, many of the factors influencing Rosa's experiences at school lay outside her teachers' sphere of influence. The residual effects of her family's poverty, her history of inconsistent school attendance, and her loss of the companionship of her relatives and friends in Puerto Rico were all among the things that affected her experiences at Addison High. Moreover, I thought about the difficulties that would be involved in her teachers' attempts to offer the special time and attention Rosa required as they also struggled to meet the needs of the scores of students who passed through their classrooms each day. Clearly, there were things about Rosa and their jobs that her teachers could not control.

Nonetheless, I remained convinced that this fact did not absolve them from the obligation to attempt to create positive educational experiences for Rosa as best they could by manipulating those factors in their classrooms over which they did exercise some measure of influence. Sadly, in the absence of such efforts, Rosa was not learning much math or geography or science. But neither was she learning things that, in my view, are of particular interest to citizen teachers. She was not learning what her gifts and interests are or how she might develop these potentials through activities she recognized as relevant to her past, present, and future life. Nor was she learning how she could bring these distinctive gifts and interests to her participation in the associated activity of her school community.

Viewed another way, however, students may be said to be learning a great deal even when it seems that we educators aren't teaching them well. In Rosa's case, because of the continuity of her particular experiences at Addison High, what she *was* "learning" was that the school had no significant obligation to her and that she didn't count as being among those our democratic ideals compel us to provide with a meaningful education. And while Rosa learned that the school had little to offer her, she "learned" as well that she had virtually nothing of value to offer the community of her classmates and teachers. That is, she "learned" that she was incapable, perhaps even unworthy, of making even a modest contribution to the collective social and intellectual work that she saw going on around her every day she came to school. Given the destructive power of such lessons, I feared the extent to which they would continue to influence Rosa's participation not only at Addison High, but also in the public spheres that lie beyond it. Indeed, Rosa had learned that she had very few options for participating at school, and so the ones she exercised were to lay her head on her desk or to stay at home.

I waited at the counseling office at the beginning of the school day, but when Rosa didn't show up, I asked Sharon, the secretary, for the information card listing Rosa's home phone number; there were several. The first number—listed as Rosa's home—had been disconnected. With the second number I reached a man who described himself as a friend of Rosa's family but said he had not had any contact with them for months. The third number had also been disconnected.

Sharon couldn't tell me anything about Rosa's whereabouts, and Alvarez was out of town that day, so I walked down to the attendance office. There, from a woman I had never met, I learned that during the second week of April, Rosa had officially dropped out of Addison High. I stood there in silence for a moment, not knowing what to do. I thought seriously of just going home. I decided to stay, though, because I had told Martinez I would attend a party we had been planning for weeks in the second-period ESL class. I thought of getting Rosa's address from the office and driving over to her house to try to convince her to stay. I realized, however, as I sat on a bench in the student lobby, that such a visit would be pointless. Rosa had lost credit long ago. She was at home with her mother and young siblings. Though, according to the school, she had failed and dropped out, at least now she was no longer alone.

In the ESL room I told Martinez what I had learned. She took a deep breath and let it out slowly. "Looks like we lost another one," she said.

Without Rosa, we began to prepare for the party. For months we had huddled together in the middle of this cavernous and degenerating accounting classroom. We had pushed aside the desks we didn't need, preferring instead to sit close in a circle and share the table space needed to write. Our journals had told stories in English, Spanish, and Arabic of what we had done yesterday, or five years ago, or what we hoped to do five years from now. Often, we had exchanged these journals and responded to each other's work, encouraging each other to tell us more about things we found especially interesting. Some of the things we wanted to say in our stories were difficult to express in English, so we struggled together to find just the right words.

I knew a lot about each of the class members, for we also had frequently shared pictures of each other's homes and families. I had seen a photo of Miguel's grandmother standing on the dirt floor of her Guatemalan kitchen; I knew the faces of Elizabeth's friends back in Mexico; I had seen pictures of Vinita dancing at her cousin's wedding reception in Lebanon; I knew that two weeks ago Julie and her brother had gone to the Pontiac Silverdome to see the "monster trucks." My "classmates," in turn, had seen photos of Kaitlin and of my sister and me shooting baskets in the driveway of my dad's house in Hudsonville. They knew that my sister lived in Chicago and that her boyfriend's name was Ned.

But today we were having a fiesta. Martinez had brought in a brightly colored and beautifully woven Mexican *mantel*, which we spread across three desks we had pushed together. On this makeshift table we laid food that celebrated our diversity and invited participation in each other's histories. Enchiladas, chicken mole, tortillas, fried vegetables from Lebanon, a Dutch pastry called bonket (a sweet and flaky crust wrapped around almond paste), and soda brought by Miguel, who had refused to cook. Alex plugged a tape player into one of the outlets intended for an adding machine, and we listened to pop music from Mexico and Palestine as Vinita taught us her favorite Lebanese folk dance. Several students in Mr. Dautermann's computer lab turned around to see what all the excitement was about.

Guests were welcome: Julie's mother and baby brother, Elizabeth's uncle and older sister, two administrators from the district offices who introduced themselves as Diane and Karen, a social studies teacher with a free period, and a few students who had wandered in from the hallway. As we ate and talked, it occurred to me that there is something about food that many Americans underestimate. To many of us, it is something to be bought and consumed so that we can get on with more important things. We have little understanding of what a Vietnamese high school classmate of mine once called "the intimacy of bread." But at our party, each dish came with a story, and we listened and learned of the families that enjoyed these foods and of the people who had taught us to prepare them. To be heard over the music from Alex's tape player, members of just about all the strata that made up Addison's school district leaned toward each other and talked, genuinely interested in what others were saying. As I got up to refill my Dixie cup with Mountain Dew, I looked over the room and saw that, for just this one period, the system had broken down—that some of the people at Addison High had found a way of talking and being together despite the schedules and titles and languages and cultural differences that usually kept them apart.

With only about ten minutes left in the period, Rosa appeared at the door with a dish in her hand. Weeks ago, she had volunteered to bring the rice, and so she had. We talked. These days, she was cleaning rooms at a local motel. Rosa liked her job; her co-workers, she said, spoke Spanish. Then she thanked me for trying to help her.

"It was my pleasure," I said.

With the end of the hour approaching, we packed up our leftovers, unplugged the tape player, and prepared to return to our routine for the rest of the day. Rosa said goodbye; the ESL students disappeared into the White stream that flowed through the hallway; Diane and Karen hurried off to a meeting; and Martinez worried that she was going to be late for an appointment with a student at the middle school.

"Don't worry," I told her. "I'll clean up." I wiped the linoleum desks with a paper towel and returned them to the rows in which we had found them. On my way out of the room, as I turned out the lights, I looked over my shoulder and was disappointed to see that everything was back in its proper place.

CHAPTER FOUR

Structured Exclusion

Bilingual education done well gives excellent results; bilingual education done badly gives poor results, just as one would expect.

LILY WONG FILLMORE, "Against Our Best Interest: The Attempt to Sabotage Bilingual Education"

Familiar Surroundings

It felt good to walk the halls of Addison High again, to maneuver through the between-class traffic and nod to familiar faces after having been away for so long. After Rosa had dropped out, though I had continued to come out to the school until summer vacation, it was clear to me that I needed to improve my Spanish enough to keep my conversations with non-English-speaking students from grinding to a halt when I requested that they repeat themselves *"más lentamente"* for the second and third time. My solution was to spend the fall semester living in a friend's apartment and studying in Santiago, Chile, a city of five million where, by and by, I came to feel at home. I walked for hours through the crowded streets, read the newspaper in cafés, did my homework in public parks—anything to avoid being alone, anything to find an opportunity to practice the unfamiliar language. Along with a bit more Spanish, I came to know which buses to take, how to avoid being cheated by cab drivers, and how to stand on the metro without stumbling as the car slowed unevenly into a station. I found restaurants where paint peeled from the walls but where a bottle of wine cost less than a Coke and where for the price of a Big Mac and fries you could eat an empanada the size of a cigar box or a plate full of shellfish that had been pulled from the Pacific that morning. Fellow students at the language institute I attended eventually became friends who invited me into their homes. I played *ajedréz* (chess) with a ten-year-old; I attended birthday parties and family barbecues, even a funeral.

While in South America, I often thought about how my experiences of being away from home were different from Rosa's. Her limited English skills, her dark skin and hair, and her status as a Puerto Rican in Addison were liabilities that marked her as an object of neglect, even denigration. For my part, in contrast, though the sights and sounds of Santiago were new to me, they were often familiar and affirming: blonde models stared down with blue eyes from billboards advertising Revlon products, and friends asked me to translate the lyrics from CDs they had recently bought by bands like R.E.M. and Pearl Jam. Equipped as I was with the benefits of being a North American with a university education, fellowship money, and a U.S. passport riding like a badge in the breast pocket of my Banana Republic shirt, when I stumbled through a sentence in Spanish, Chileans would chuckle, graciously correct me, and encourage me to try again. In short, for social, cultural, and economic reasons, my and Rosa's being "foreigners" had completely different consequences. Rosa's difference brought her ostracism; mine brought me opportunity.

As much as I enjoyed my time in Chile, after I returned to Michigan there was a side of Santiago I did not miss, a side that had little to do with minor hazards like dangling from the running board of an overcrowded bus or inconveniences like having to check my backpack every time I entered a grocery store. For in Santiago I had felt not only the local hospitality and the immense beauty of the Andes but also the subtle yet pervasive sense that what I took to be human rights were tenuous, that they were not rights at all but privileges subject to the whim of a ubiquitous *jefe.* Just a block from my institute stood the governmental palace where, twenty-five years earlier, President Salvador Allende had locked himself in a second-floor office and shot himself in the head as General Pinochet's tanks bombarded the building from the adjacent plaza. I had seen police on street corners cradling "Uzi" machine guns, traffic cops who threw a man into the trunk of their patrol car and slammed the lid shut, and, through clouds of tear gas during a protest on the anniversary of the 1973 coup, an armored riot-control vehicle equipped with a water canon spraying fluid laced with chemicals that induced vomiting and diarrhea for several days. The next morning I learned from the newspaper that a young man had died after having been run over by one of these vehicles and that another demonstrator had been killed by a police bullet through the neck.

Back home I savored the freedom that to me had always seemed a part of the North American landscape. Nonetheless, despite the allure of this vision our nation has of itself, my experiences with Rosa had confirmed that our alleged liberty, our justice, is not necessarily available, as our pledge suggests, "for all." More specifically, as a part of that vision, while we hope that our schools will function as sites of inclusion and opportunity, what they too often do is perpetuate some people's political and economic disenfranchisement. In an ethnically diverse school district like Addison, one might expect to find a great many human and financial resources devoted to celebrating Latino cultures and to addressing the specific needs of students whose native language is Spanish. I had found instead that only a few members of the Addison faculty and administration viewed limited-English-proficient students as a priority.

I diverged from the stream of students in the hallway and turned into the ESL room to find Alice Martinez and Fran Soto hunched over their planning book. When I cleared my throat, they turned and smiled.

"Todd! There you are. How have you been? It's been so long. Tell us about your trip. So much has happened. My son and his wife had another baby. . . ."

I understood much more clearly than before their easy and intimate words, having learned them in contexts that for me had been immediate and meaningful. And in between hugs of welcome I promised to bring with me on my next visit the photos I had taken of friends and mountains during my trip. I had known where to find the ESL class that morning only because I had called Martinez a few days earlier. Though the class was meeting in a different room from last year, it was again a space on loan, this time from a history and U.S. government teacher. This new class consisted of only four students: Sunny, from Lebanon; Daniel, an exchange student from Brazil; and two Latina students I hadn't met before, Claudia and Angela. Martinez introduced Claudia as Rosa's sister, and I immediately saw the resemblance in her narrow face and high cheekbones. As we moved our desks into a circle, I asked Claudia what her sister had been doing since she had left school.

"Not much," Claudia said. *"She gets up late and spends a lot of time sitting on the couch at home watching television."*

Though I learned later from Martinez that Claudia had an attendance record that rivaled her sister's in the number of truancies, as the class period went on the differences between the two siblings became clear. While Rosa had been very quiet, eyes down, mouth closed, Claudia, in response to her ESL teachers' attentiveness, smiled broadly and often, speaking readily in both Spanish and an accented but fluent English. She was affectionate and demonstrative with her teachers. Rosa's hands had often remained still in her lap; Claudia's reached out and rested on Soto's and Martinez's arms and shoulders. In everything I saw that first day, she was eager to please. When Martinez announced a writing assignment, Claudia jumped to her feet. *"I'll get the journals,"* she said. Claudia took a short stack of spiral notebooks from a corner shelf and distributed them to her classmates. When she lingered a bit too long at Daniel's desk, Martinez broke in.

"Mi'ja, sit down."

"Oh, Ms. Martinez, you love me too much," Claudia said.

"That's right, which is why I want you to get to work." Martinez rested her hand on Claudia's shoulder as the girl passed by on the way to her seat. Claudia's journal was decorated with a large Minnie Mouse sticker and the names of several boys. On the inside cover she had taped a laminated "Certificate of Participation" from the middle school choir. Martinez and Soto called the class's attention to the document, saying that Claudia should keep it in her cumulative school portfolio. Claudia smiled, apparently enjoying the attention for a moment, but she quickly urged the class to resume the lesson begun the previous day.

"C'mon, Ms. Martinez. We gotta finish our stories about the pictures before we can take the quiz."

Angela, who had arrived in Addison halfway through the previous semester from Matamoros, Mexico, and who was suffering from what Martinez described as a severe case of homesickness, watched Claudia and Martinez in silence from her desk, her round face, dark skin, and broad nose indicating her Native Mexican heritage. She wore stonewashed jeans, a sweater studded with red and yellow rhinestones the size of quarters, and a large white bow in her hair. In a later interview, Angela described to me some of the details of her family and educational history:

> *When I was a little girl in Matamoros, my mom worked in a factory, and she had to leave us alone to go work. After that, when I was about five, I would go with my grandmother to sell clothes or food, or we'd go do errands in the neighborhood. At that time, my godfather made bread in his house, and my grandparents had started to do that, too. We would sell the bread and donuts they made. And so we sold that and corn and snow cones to make money.*

Angela's memories of her schooling in Mexico are generally unfavorable. She said that her classes *"weren't very good because the teachers didn't really care about the students"* and that she and her siblings sometimes had confrontations with their peers:

> *At school I remember my three brothers, they would get mad at people when they'd say bad things to them. Sometimes when we were there, there were some gangs, and the kids in a gang were trying to fight with my brothers all the time. And one time I couldn't find one of my brothers at school, so I went to look for him, and the kids, the kids in the gang, had him on the floor and they were hitting him, so I had to fight with those kids. And it was bad because the principal called my mom, and so I got punished; I got grounded for the weekend.*

Despite these problems, Angela said that she *"did pretty well in school"* and that she stayed there long enough to complete *primaria* (elementary school through the sixth grade). At age thirteen, however, Angela was a year or two older than most of her fellow graduates, her schooling having been interrupted from time to time by the need for her to help support her family. Angela explained that after finishing *primaria*, she was awarded a partial scholarship to study at a *segundaria* (middle school) but that she had to pass up this opportunity *"because we still had to pay for classes and books and uniforms, and we didn't have the money because my mom was the only one who was working."* Angela then attended *"beauty school"* for a while, but she withdrew from that program when, at age fifteen, she moved to the United States.

Angela made clear to me that her family's immigration to Michigan was not initially intended to be permanent and that they could afford this move only with financial assistance from relatives:

> We came to the United States because my older brother came here first, but then he got sick; he had problems with his ear. So he sent us some money so we could come here. We were just going to come here for a visit. I don't think we even locked the door of our house, but we stayed. And when we got here we had two or three people to help us out. My brother and an uncle and my aunt and a grandmother.

Upon arriving in the Addison area, Angela attended high school in a neighboring district for three months. In that school, however, Angela explained that *"they didn't help me. They didn't have an ESL class. I got some help from my cousins there, but they were really embarrassed to help me, so then someone told me that I could get more help in Addison, so we moved here. And the people here, like Mrs. Martinez, they help me a lot more."*

Despite her generous words for Martinez, Angela was having serious troubles at Addison High, for though she spoke almost no English and had attended only *"beauty school"* in the two years since graduating from *primaria* in Mexico, in Addison she had been placed in a regular first-year-student schedule with no academic support save what Martinez could offer during a single period. Predictably, Angela could not complete her schoolwork, and, with the exception of ESL, she had failed all of her first-semester classes.

As Angela and her ESL classmates worked through an exercise, Martinez wrote two sentences on the chalkboard and asked Angela to combine them: "Carlos is a boy." "The boy is tall." Angela stared at the board and did not say anything for a moment.

"I don't know." She talked into her hand, like Rosa used to do. When Martinez translated the sentences, Angela answered immediately.

"Carlos is a tall boy."

Martinez had just finished guiding the students through a few more pairs of sentences when the history teacher whose room the ESL class was borrowing strolled through the door. Dressed smartly in a white shirt, sweater vest, and colorful tie, he nodded and smiled as we looked up from our journals. He then sat down at a computer behind his desk at the front of the room and inserted a disk into the drive. Martinez shrugged and returned her attention to her students, explaining the instructions for a quiz they were about to take. She talked a bit louder than usual, her voice adjusting to the sputtering whine of the history teacher's dot-matrix printer.

The noise seemed an echo from last year, reminding me of my exasperation at feeling that Rosa did not matter and that nobody—except a few of the people in this room—missed her now that she was gone. The *prueba* required the students to complete sentences with vocabulary words they had taken from magazine pictures: "The girl is playing with the _____." (The photo was of a girl and a basketball.) "The boy is cutting the _____ with the _____. " (A boy cut a piece of paper with a pair of scissors.) Because the quiz focused specifically on the vocabulary omitted from the sentences, Soto, Martinez, and I helped the students with the rest of the words. For Angela, I translated "playing" and "cutting." This and other work done with the ESL students was, as I had learned the previous year, extremely labor-intensive, requiring almost constant one-on-one contact between instructors and students, as well as adaptation to the different paces at which the students worked. Martinez, who had written a separate quiz for Daniel, leaned over and whispered in Claudia's ear:

"Come on, *Mi'ja*, think. I know you know this one." When Claudia, who had never learned to read or write in either English or Spanish, answered, Martinez wrote the girl's response on the paper. Soto had arranged her seat in the aisle between David and Sunny, moving her attention back and forth like she was watching a tennis match.

When everyone had finished the quiz, Claudia gathered the papers and handed them to Soto. We moved the desks back into rows, glanced at the clock, and waited out the last few minutes of the period. I asked Angela how she liked school. She quietly admitted *"not much"* and said that she wanted to return to Matamoros. She added that she spent much of her time at home trying to stay in touch with her Mexican friends by writing them long letters, one of which she pulled from the inside pocket of her notebook and showed to me. I held the four pages of Angela's letter for a moment, silently acknowledging a literacy that would not have been evident from what I had witnessed that day in class. I told her that I hoped her friends wrote back; she assured me they did. I then strolled over to one of the history teacher's bulletin boards and studied a poster published by *Newsweek* magazine. Over a world map, the caption read: "The whole world is watching fifty countries guilty of persistent human rights violations." The guilty countries—among them China, Peru, and Mexico—were shaded red. The United States was a light and pleasant shade of tan—what is often called flesh color. The history teacher's printer advanced to another page.

In establishing and maintaining the priority it will place on the education of its Latino students, Addison High, like other social institutions, is involved in a complex process hinging on at least two types of factors that may be assessed in light of Dewey's conception of democratic communities: institutional structure and individual agency. First, as institutions, schools are characterized by structures that shape the activities of individuals within them. When I use the word "structures," I am referring most basically to a complex network of material realities, ideologies, policies, and practices that work together either to enable people to think and live as they choose or to constrain them from doing so. These structures include the school's administrative hierarchy, its curriculum, the pedagogical methods of its teachers, its physical layout, and even its daily schedule. For instance, because the structure of Addison High allows for only one ESL class to be taught each day, the learning opportunities of individual students with special language needs are strictly limited.

Placed in a larger context, the structure of the school is intimately and ideologically tied to the community it serves: the historical, demographic, economic, and ethnic characteristics of Addison are important in defining the positions people occupy in particular institutional settings within this community. These relationships are, in turn, influenced by structures on the state, national, and international levels, structures that include, for example, U.S. economic and immigration policies and the history of European and American colonialism. Thus, I use both the singular *structure* and the plural *structures* as a deliberate way of emphasizing that what I call a "structure" is neither discrete nor static, but a system of interrelated realities that operate within— and at the same time are composed of—other structures. Several insightful and influential ethnographies of schooling (Eckert, 1989; Willis, 1981b) have relied upon this sort of structural analysis, focusing in particular on how schools situated within capitalistic societies reproduce socioeconomic class relations.

These structures that constrain (or enable, depending on your point of view) what can happen in the world do not appear immediately or by accident; rather, they evolve and survive because people have made and continue to make decisions about what those structures will be and how they will operate. Thus, as crucial as structural considerations are in understanding why institutions such as Addison High exist and function as they do, it is equally important to acknowledge a second influence upon Addison High's treatment of its Latino students—the role of individual agency within those structures. Indeed, too often the insights afforded by structural analyses of schooling have come at a substantial cost, for even as we come to understand more clearly how the structures of our society encourage (and sometimes compel) us to believe and behave in prescribed ways, what often gets lost is the sense that breathing, thinking, decision-making people live within these structures. In effect, we erroneously create structuralist "boxes" for people from which there is no escape and within which there is no mobility. This is not to deny that Alice Martinez teaches within the constraints of an inadequate budget and an environment tainted by racial prejudice; it is, however, to acknowledge the possibility of her resistance to those structures and the hope that she may somehow revise them. Moreover, to say simply that certain Addison teachers and administrators have been "programmed" or "shaped" to perpetuate injustice based on race and/or socioeconomic class runs the danger of absolving them from their personal responsibility to struggle against a system that privileges some students over others.

In essence, then, a dialectic is constantly in process between the structures that tend to determine who we are and the agency which presents either possibilities for revising or culpability for maintaining them. This dialectical relationship between structures and agency is, I believe, a useful way to observe and reflect upon the experiences of Latino students at Addison High. Further, I think that such analyses can be effected in new ways that are especially productive for citizen teachers by evaluating interactions between structure and agency according to Dewey's principles of democratic societies. Since this kind of evaluation is my aim in this and the ensuing chapter, it may be helpful to describe a bit more thoroughly than I already have just what Dewey seems to mean when he talks about democratic forms of associated living.

As several writers have noted (Damico, 1978; Detlefsen, 1998; Fishman & McCarthy, 1998; Westbrook, 1991), Dewey (1916/ 1985) asserts that the two criteria characterizing a democratic society are "the extent in which the interests of a group are shared by all its members, and the fullness and freedom with which it interacts with other groups" (p. 105). Dewey's definition further posits democracy as dependent upon circumstances that allow all people to participate "on equal terms" in identifying and working toward their "shared common interest" within a localized community, while at the same time allowing for what he calls the "flexible readjustment of institutions" within groups through productive interaction with other communities (p. 92). As this definition suggests, mere aggregated, collective action does not in and of itself constitute a democratic community. Rather, in Dewey's thought (1927/1988), communal life develops only in contexts in which people consciously and collectively plan, pursue, and share in the consequences of their associated activities: "Wherever there is conjoint activity whose consequences are appreciated as good by all singular persons who take part in it, and where the realization of the good is such as to effect an energetic desire and effort to sustain it in being just because it is a good shared by all, there is in so far a community" (p. 328). This "clear consciousness of communal life" (p. 328) is possible, Dewey contends, only when "the art of full and moving communication" is sufficiently developed to allow people to determine their "genuinely shared interest in the consequences of interdependent activities" (p. 332). In sum, then, Dewey's ideal democratic society is one in which people communicate in ways that enable them to identify common interests that guide collective action, to participate in such action and share in its consequences, and to revise their aims and institutions in response to interaction with other communities.

In this chapter, I will bring this conception of democratic life to a discussion focusing on the sociohistorical structure that determines the type of "bilingual education" that is (un)available to Addison's language-minority (LM) students. Specifically, I will look at what may be called three aspects or components of this structure, which in my view runs contrary to democratic ideals by denying LM students equal access to education: first, I will describe the lack of native-language instruction offered to Spanish-dominant students in content-area classes; second, I will broaden my perspective by exploring the history of district-level decisions that have kept Addison High from implementing a legitimate bilingual program; and third, I will discuss the manipulation of nationwide legislative and judicial actions that has enabled the district to avoid addressing the needs of its LM students. At the same time, I will continually remind readers that the structure denying Addison's LM students a democratizing education is the cumulative result of personal agency in the form of decisions people have made and continue to make in their daily lives.

Taking the "Bilingual" and the "Education" Out of "Bilingual Education"

In Ms. Daniels's third-period science class I counted thirty-two students. Daniels—I guessed her age to be about thirty—assigned me a seat next to Angela and quieted the group with the help of Ms. Palmer, a special education instructor who acted as much as the class's disciplinary enforcer as she did a tutor. Daniels was, according to several of her students, a good teacher: "pretty hard" but "nice," someone who would "explain things to you if you don't get it" and who "wouldn't talk down at you." To look at her room it was apparent, as she told me after class, that she required her students to be "very productive" and that she preferred to assign "a lot of hands-on work." Student-made posters of the periodic table, models of space stations, and drawings of "things in the ocean" hung from the walls and ceiling. When I asked which of the projects was Angela's, Daniels said that Angela hadn't completed any of her required work. "She came here halfway through last semester and failed. I don't know what to do with her," Daniels said.

As the students settled into their seats and began to quiet down, Daniels passed out a science magazine and directed the class to an article on tornadoes. The students took turns reading aloud while I quietly summarized each paragraph for Angela in Spanish. Remembering Rosa's isolation, hoping that my sharing a bit of personal history would help Angela feel at ease, I added— in a whisper—a story of my own:

"Before I was born, a tornado killed twelve people in my hometown. My father used to tell me how he watched through the basement window as the tornado went by. He said it sounded like 'a thousand freight trains.'" I continued, saying that from my parents' backyard a gap was still visible in a line of trees separating two onion fields through which the twister had passed.

Angela replied that she had never seen a tornado but that in Matamoros she had experienced several hurricanes blowing in from the Gulf of Mexico. When the storms hit, she said, she just stayed at home with her family. I looked up; a boy across the aisle was staring at us, the girl in front of him turned sideways in her seat to face us as well.

"Hey," he said quietly. "I seen a funnel cloud once. Me and my dad were coming home from my uncle's house, and we had just . . ."

Ms. Palmer appeared alongside the boy.

"Follow along," she said. Palmer lingered for a moment, then drifted back to her place in the rear corner of the room. Angela stared at her desk and didn't say anything, her dark face now tinged a shade of red. I felt awkward for having caused the disturbance, for having distracted the students by "talking out of turn," and above all for having embarrassed Angela by calling attention to her need for extra help—to the fact that she was different, "deficient." I stopped translating and remained silent as the class finished reading. Daniels announced that answers to the six guide questions at the end of the article were due the next day as homework. Students were allowed to work in pairs, and by the end of the period just about everyone had finished writing. Angela and I had made it to number three, a question about a family that had been the victims of a tornado. Alongside the article was a picture of a mother, a father, and two children standing among a heap of splintered boards and twisted furniture: their home. I wondered whether Angela sensed the irony of her reading of these people's having lost their home when only recently she had lost hers.

The next time I visited Angela's science class, Daniels was absent. In her place a tall man with a thick mustache led the class in a review for the next day's test.

"The fifty multiple-choice questions that will make up the test," he announced, "will be taken from the review sheet which you all have and which I will now give you the answers to." I scribbled his words into my field notebook; the students sat ready, pencils poised, heads lowered, as though they waited for the crack of a starter's pistol. "Number one, circulatory; number two, vein; number three . . ." At first I tried to explain to Angela the meaning of each term, but given the breakneck speed at which the man read, by the time we had reached number seven, it was all I could do to record the answers. Angela sat immobile and watched. "Number sixteen, auricle; seventeen, ventricle; eighteen . . ."

Several students shifted in their seats; others looked up and shook their heads. A girl across the room let out a crusty sigh and said, "Yeah, right." I was impressed by the students' efforts to do what the substitute teacher had asked. They were working hard; they just couldn't keep up. The tall man tried to continue but could no longer ignore the many requests to slow down.

"If you miss something, get the answers from someone else," he said. "Number thirty-three . . ." Finally, a student named Terry had had enough.

"Geez, would you slow down?"

Ms. Palmer glared at him from beside the substitute. "I don't expect the rudeness," she said.

Terry stood up, put one hand on his hip and extended the other, open-palmed, toward the teachers standing behind the lab table. "As a student," Terry began, "I expect my teachers to at least . . ." Palmer interrupted, telling him to leave and pointing toward the door. Terry kept talking. "I expect my teachers to at least talk in a way we can get the answers we need. I mean, if it's important enough for us to know for the exam, it's important enough for us to be able to write down, right?" Though my hand still ached from writing the review sheet answers, it occurred to me that Terry's logic seemed sensible. For a moment Terry and Ms. Palmer stood silently facing each other, motionless, like two gun fighters in a B western movie, each waiting for the other to make the next move. Then, suddenly, Palmer stepped to her right and pushed what is known around Addison High as "the panic button"—a device in each classroom that alerts the office to a disciplinary emergency. Principal Dohm arrived directly and, standing in the doorway, his clipboard under his left arm, looked at Terry.

"Is this the gentleman?" he asked. Palmer nodded, and Terry was escorted from the room.

When Angela asked me what was going on, I told her that Terry had been upset because the teacher had been reading too quickly.

"*I agree,*" she said. I asked Angela whether she wanted me to try to arrange for some other project in lieu of taking the exam. "*I don't know,*" she replied, but by the time we had finished the review sheet, Angela had decided that she preferred to take the exam. The following week Daniels pulled me aside and showed me the results of Angela's test. She had scored thirty-six percent, which was an "F," even with the curve.

Few people would disagree that among the tenets of public education in this country is the idea that all children, regardless of race, sex, religion, or language ability, should have equal access to education. However, one need not look hard to discover that the realities of schooling stray far from this democratic principle. Part of the reason for this discrepancy between the "ideal" and the "real" in students' varying educational experiences stems from confused notions of what constitutes "equality." As the example of Angela's struggle in science class suggests, for students with limited English skills, "equal access" must mean more than merely providing students with the same lectures, assignments, and textbooks. It is true, of course, that everyone in third-period science was given identical review sheets and tests. Nonetheless, because of Angela's inability to understand English, she did not have the same access to Daniels's unit on the human circulatory system as did her English-speaking classmates.

The question of how best to resolve these inequities has led to an ongoing and highly partisan debate in this country regarding the effectiveness of bilingual education, which Sonia Nieto (1992) has broadly defined as "an educational program that involves the use of two languages of instruction at some point in a student's school career" (p. 156). As Carlos Ovando (1990) has noted, this issue has become so thoroughly entangled in language and cultural politics that even purportedly disinterested researchers have often characterized their findings and conclusions in ways that are consistent with their interests (p. 350). In my view, the politicized and polemical nature of this debate results in part from the tendency of people of shared good will but divergent opinion to base their views on competing notions of "common sense." On one hand, it seems obvious to opponents of bilingual education that the best way for LM students to achieve the English fluency necessary for certain kinds of academic and professional success in the U.S. is for them to be immersed in English-only environments, which should include schools. On the other hand, advocates of bilingual education scratch their heads and wonder who can possibly object to the notion that it is both practical and ethical to teach students in a language they understand.

While arguments concerning how best to remove language barriers that thwart schools' announced democratic goals of equitable educational opportunity often come from widely differing ideological positions, the specific teaching measures included under the term "bilingual education" vary considerably and therefore do not necessarily represent an extreme "either-or" choice. According to Nieto (1992), the most common model of bilingual education in the U.S. is called the "transitional bilingual education" approach, in which students receive their content area instruction in their native language while they are learning English as a second language: "As soon as they are thought to be ready to benefit from the monolingual English-language curriculum, they are 'exited' out of the program" (p. 157). Another approach is "maintenance bilingual education," a more comprehensive and long-term model. As in the transitional approach, "maintenance" students receive content-area instruction in their native language while learning English as a second language. The difference, Nieto notes, is that there is generally no limit set on the time students can be in the program. The reasoning here is that the child's native language and culture are worth maintaining not only because they enable students to draw upon prior knowledge for new learning but also because the student's language and culture are assets in their own right and are therefore an appropriate channel for continued learning. As Virginia Collier (1989) has noted, this reasoning is based upon research that has repeatedly shown "that students literate in their native language will be more successful than those whose language is ignored, denied, or replaced" (p. 518). Of particular interest to some researchers has been the positive effect of native-language instruction that focuses on literacy development (Hakuta & Gould, 1987; Hudelson, 1987; Fillmore & Valadez, 1986). These investigators argue, essentially, that a person learns how to read only once, and that literacy skills and concepts learned in a native language provide a "scaffold" for acquiring new knowledge in additional languages.

Nieto has rightly cautioned, however, that part of the problem in relying on bilingual education to effect equal educational access is that the term "bilingual" is often used for practices that do not necessarily address LM students' particular needs or that do so only in limited ways. For example, English as a second language (ESL), the type of class Martinez teaches at Addison High, is, in Nieto's words (1992), "an integral and necessary component of all bilingual programs" (p. 157). Indeed, few advocates of bilingual education deny that, given the reality of English dominance in the U.S., LM students benefit from learning English. Nieto (1992) herself acknowledges that "a primary objective of bilingual education is to have students become proficient and literate in the English language" (p. 156). ESL programs can be especially useful if they take into account theoretical developments regarding second-language learning that suggest that learning a new language is best accomplished under conditions that favor simulating natural communication events over formal instruction of linguistic structures and grammatical rules (Chamot & O'Malley, 1986). However, ESL instruction alone is not bilingual education, and serious difficulties arise when ESL instruction is not accompanied by native-language instruction in students' content-area classes. The experiences of Rosa and Angela, for instance, show that while such students may be in the process of learning English, they are also falling further and further behind in classes like geography, math, and science.

As we have seen, with the exception of Martinez's second-period ESL class, this practice of immersing LM students in monolingual English environments and assuming they will learn English as a means of survival is the primary form of "educating" language-minority students at Addison High. This so-called "immersion" or "sink or swim" approach is allegedly supported by studies showing that evidence of the effectiveness of bilingual education is, at best, inconclusive. James Crawford (1989) has documented that one of the more influential of these studies was conducted by the American Institutes for Research (AIR), which in 1977 published its conclusion that bilingual programs had resulted in "no consistent significant impact" on the education of limited-English-proficient children (p. 87, cited in Ovando, p. 351). Crawford cites a 1981 report by Keith Baker and Adrianna de Kanter as having reached similar conclusions. After examining more than 300 bilingual research studies and identifying only twenty-eight of them to be valid and reliable according to their criteria, Baker and de Kanter determine that these remaining studies are inconclusive and that they do not, therefore, provide a rationale for bilingual education.

More recently, in a meta-analysis of studies on bilingual education, Christine Rossell and Baker (1996) dismissed as methodologically unacceptable those that did not include "a treatment and a control group and a statistical control for pre-treatment differences where groups were not randomly assigned" (p. 7). Based on data from the remaining "acceptable" studies, Rossell and Baker argue that submerging LM students in an all-English environment has been shown to be more effective than transitional bilingual education or ESL instruction in teaching students English and math skills. Specifically, according to the authors, research evidence indicates that, on standardized achievement tests, "transitional bilingual education is better than regular [i.e.: immersion] classroom instruction in only 22 percent of the methodologically acceptable studies when the outcome is reading, 7 percent of the studies when the outcome is language [a test of a student's understanding of grammatical rules], and 9 percent of the studies when the outcome is math" (p. 7).

Bolstered by studies such as these, proponents of native-language restrictions in school settings argue that, far from providing language-minority students with increased opportunities for success, bilingual education actually contributes to their continued subjugation. Herbert Walberg (1989), for instance, has captured the sentiments of many opponents of bilingual education as follows:

> For many immigrant children who are not proficient in English, the problems of second language and academic learning are more acute largely because they come from deprived socioeconomic backgrounds. More than others, these children need maximum exposure to English in school in order to learn it and because they may be deprived of such exposure at home and in their neighborhoods. Because bilingual education deters from the very factors that promote English mastery and other academic accomplishments, it can hardly be held out as their hope. (p. 20)

Promoting alternatives to the immersion approach can be a delicate task in the face of such testimony from scholars, in part because advocates of bilingual education are sometimes suspected not only of political bias but also of self-interest in defending their field and hence their jobs. In Walberg's (1987) view, "Getting information from [researchers and practitioners in bilingual education] is like asking your barber if you need a haircut" (p. 71).

Despite such cynical accusations that bilingual educators place their own interests before those of LM students, a large number of researchers have challenged the notion that LM students are best served by taking the "bilingual" out of bilingual education. Crawford (1989), for instance, argues that large-scale evaluative studies denying the effectiveness of bilingual education—studies like those of the AIR, Baker and de Kanter, and Rossell and Baker—are flawed in at least three ways: First, such studies tend to obscure the striking diversity of bilingual education program design and quality; availability of resources, materials, and trained staff; mix of English and native-language instruction; and students' social and linguistic backgrounds. Second, these evaluations face a series of logistical obstacles—from tracking transient student populations to finding appropriate comparison groups—in judging bilingual education against its alternatives. Finally, Crawford notes, these studies are subject to political pressures in crucial decisions about study design and conclusions (p. 88).

In addition to Crawford's critique of the validity of research that questions the effectiveness of bilingual education, advocates of native-language support in schooling point to a growing number of evaluative studies indicating that bilingual education does indeed produce good results for LM students. In 1987, for instance, a panel of educational researchers commissioned by the U.S. General Accounting Office challenged the anti-bilingual education position, saying that research did indeed show positive effects of transitional bilingual education on students' achievement in English-language competence and in subjects other than English. Similarly, J. David Ramirez (1991) and Nieto (1992) conclude, after surveying large numbers of bilingual programs, that transitional or maintenance programs are more effective than immersion programs not only in teaching LM students content-area knowledge but also in teaching them English. Nieto (1992) adds that an additional benefit of effective bilingual programs is that they may have secondary effects of motivating students not to drop out of school and of avoiding the serious disruptions of family relations when children learn English in school and lose the use of their native language. In sum, Nieto (1992) argues that research reviews indicate that "even if the primary purpose of instruction is to learn English (a debatable position), immersion programs do not seem to work as well. In contrast, the positive effects of bilingual education, from lowering dropout rates to literacy development, have been found time and time again" (pp. 160–161).

More recently, two 1997 studies taking a comprehensive view of the effectiveness of bilingual education conclude that, while no single approach will work for all students in all situations, some form of bilingual education is a promising means of helping LM students overcome educational obstacles (August & Hakuta,

1997). Among the findings of these studies are that primary-language instruction allows LM students to access complex academic instruction earlier than with other approaches, that content presented in the primary language transfers to English as students develop their English language skills, and that primary-language instruction does not impede the acquisition of oral English.

Despite this considerable evidence of the effectiveness of bilingual education, and despite the similar conclusions of several recent ethnographic studies (Carger, 1996; Lucas, Henze, & Donato, 1990; Romo & Falbo, 1996), one could suggest that the disagreement among researchers concerning whether native-language instruction is indeed useful to LM students casts doubt on whether bilingual education can be empirically justified. For my part, however, the recent meta-analyses attesting to the usefulness of high-quality bilingual education programs are compelling because of their comprehensiveness. Moreover, I find ethnographic studies which conclude by advocating bilingual education to be reliable because the qualitative methods of these studies are attentive to the nuances and complexities of LM students' educational experiences. Though researchers like Baker, Rossell, and de Kanter would deem these studies as "methodologically unacceptable," I believe it is their methodology that makes these studies most convincing. In my view, then, it is unfortunate that many LM students in places like Addison High remain immersed in English-speaking content-area classes and are thus shut out of meaningful instruction and learning. Such schools have, in effect, taken the "bilingual" out of "bilingual education." In assessing whether or not language-minority students are being adequately served by our schools, however, it is important to consider not just whether the curriculum is linguistically accessible to LM students but also whether the pedagogical practices and student activities of bilingual programs are indeed legitimate forms of teaching and learning. In other words, we must consider whether schools have removed not just the "bilingual" but also the "education" from "bilingual education."

As Lily Wong Fillmore (1992) has argued, effective bilingual programs must include a level of curricular content that is "consistent with the level offered to all other students in the school" (p. 368). Wong Fillmore's argument is corroborated by Luis Moll

(1988), who, after a six-month study which focused on effective teachers of working-class Latino students, concluded that while there is often a tendency to reduce the curriculum's complexity to match limited-English speakers' levels of English proficiency, teachers in the effective classrooms he studied assumed that "the children were competent and capable and that it was teaching responsibly to provide students with a challenging, innovative, and intellectually rigorous curriculum" (p. 467). In short, Moll argues, these teachers rejected the idea of "watering down" the curriculum as degrading and disrespectful to their students. Similarly, Tamara Lucas, Rosemary Henze, and Ruben Donato (1990), in their study of six successful high schools that serve large numbers of LM Latino students, found that one of the key features of these successful schools is that high expectations of language-minority students are made concrete by steps like "challenging students in class and providing guidance to help them meet the challenge" and "offering advanced and honors bilingual/sheltered classes in content areas" (p. 324). The importance of high teacher expectations is also asserted by Rosa Torruellas (1992) in her discussion of Puerto Rican students in New York City. She summarizes her argument in this way:

> Low teacher expectations with respect to educational achievement compound the problem [of differing linguistic styles], leading to a loss of self-confidence and, ultimately, internalization by students of the belief that they cannot succeed in school. . . . It is essential that schools create an educational environment where success and self-esteem, not failure, is the expectation of our children. (p. 130)

Ironically, in a sense, many Addison High content-area teachers could be said to be following these admonitions to maintain a rigorous curriculum for LM students—one which is comparable to the levels taught to English-speaking classrooms. However, the lessons I had seen LM students struggle through could not be considered "intellectually rigorous" in useful ways because students were excluded from meaningful engagement with the material. In the absence of instruction that legitimately challenges LM students, what passes for bilingual education at Addison High is actually a game which ignores the fact that LM students are not really learning in the sense of being intellectually involved in creating meaning. This "game," I have found, includes strategies LM students have devised to cope with the inability to do their content-area schoolwork—strategies that are illustrated in the following accounts of "doing schoolwork" with Angela and Claudia in science and math classes.

Side by side at the double-seated lab table, Angela and I plodded through an assignment to read a textbook chapter, locate key terms along the way, and then write definitions to these terms on a vocabulary sheet provided by Ms. Daniels. That I had a difficult time translating terms like "hypothesis" didn't really seem to matter, for after a few minutes Angela noticed that the boys in front of us were finding the definitions they needed in the textbook glossary. I tried to continue to explain each concept to Angela, but I could tell by the way she moved to a new item before I could finish explaining the previous one that she was more interested in the immediate task of completing the list than in understanding it. Terms and definitions, both incomprehensible to Angela, thus filled her assignment sheet as I sat by and interjected a few words of general translation from time to time. A few days later Angela was smiling as I entered the classroom. She reached into her notebook and pulled out the assignment sheet. On the top, written in bright green ink, was "100% Excellent!" *"Good, isn't it?"* she asked.

"Yeah, that's wonderful," I said.

In the next period's Transitional Math class, as is common in the lower-track classes where one generally finds Addison's ESL students, the atmosphere as the tardy bell rang was chaotic. As the students settled in, I watched from my seat behind Angela and across the aisle from Claudia as an African American student named Darryl walked from his seat in the front of the room to a thin girl seated at a desk in the back.

"Sally, get the hell out," he said.

"Forget it, Darryl," the girl said. "You've got your own seat." Darryl strolled away and slouched in his assigned seat, but after a few minutes he began drifting among the rows to various empty desks. He tested a chair for a moment, talked to a neighbor or two, then seemed to grow bored and moved to another. After having insisted at least three times that Darryl take his "proper seat and stay put," the teacher, Ms. Bates, told him to leave. As Darryl crossed the front of the room on his way toward the door, he muttered, "Prejudiced," and then, with mouth open wide and lips pulled back to reveal his teeth, he let out a thunderous belch that drew applause from his classmates. Without breaking stride he bowed modestly as he passed into the hallway.

Bates shook her head and asked the students to take out their notes. Angela looked around, took the cue from her classmates, and complied as Bates began to write notes on an overhead projector, her strong voice easily audible over the whir of the machine's tiny fan: "If the quantity y is taken away from the original quantity x, the quantity left is $x - y$." I translated the sentence; Angela looked blankly at me, her mouth hanging open a bit. She was still copying this first point when, having finished three others, Bates asked if there were any questions and turned off the projector. The homework was numbers 1–30, with number 31 as extra credit, to be completed by tomorrow but not before the class took the day's scheduled quiz.

In Bates's math class, Angela, Claudia, and I had become accustomed to the routine of leaving the room to work on quizzes and problem sets. In the science room next door, which was vacant that period, we could talk out loud without disturbing other students and draw giant diagrams on the blackboard with colored chalk—Claudia's favorite. On some days we had only ten minutes, on others as much as a half hour, but whatever the amount of time, for that interval the space was ours to accomplish whatever we could. The two girls and I pushed our desks into a triangle, and Claudia asked about my daughter, Kaitlin.

"She's fine; I'll see her again this weekend."

I took the quizzes Bates had given me from my backpack and read the first question: "What is the difference between an exercise and a problem?" Before I could say anything, Claudia had translated the question to Angela. We looked at each other and shrugged.

"I'll bet we can find the answer in the book." Claudia suggested. I balked, as I had been doing for several weeks now when the girls had wanted to use their textbooks to find answers to their quizzes, a privilege the students back in Bates's class did not

enjoy. Until that point, I had been moderately satisfied with the progress I fancied that Claudia and Angela had been making in math. When we worked through problem sets, we rarely finished, but I was optimistic in that I had seen slight improvement. They could indeed understand how to make their way through at least some of their homework if only we moved at a pace appropriate to what they had learned in their previous schooling. Bolstered by this partial success, I had encouraged the girls to seek help from Spanish-speaking students in study hall and to refrain from copying the answers to the odd-numbered homework exercises listed in the back of the textbook and from "borrowing" entire assignments from Claudia's friends.

What I took to be progress, however, was in fact continued failure for Angela and Claudia. We could work through the first third of a problem set, and while I could be content that Angela seemed to have understood the concept of supplementary angles or that Claudia had shaded in half a circle when I had asked her to illustrate how much "0.5" is, the grade that went into Bates's record book was still an F. What counted to the girls were results. That day, we had a quiz to do, and Claudia was going to finish it by any means necessary. I thought about the empty spaces behind the girls' names in Bates's book; I thought about how Angela—sitting there holding her head with both hands—had missed several years of school; I thought of Rosa's never having passed a class during her years at Addison High. I opened the textbook to the relevant chapter, pointed to the definition of "exercise," and translated it for Angela. Both girls began writing feverishly.

Alone in our science room, I assumed a spot at the chalkboard while the girls sat poised at their desks with their calculators. The task on the rest of the quiz was basic algebra: specifically, finding the value of a variable. I could do this: I had passed Math 109 in undergraduate school. I read the next question: $17 + x = 24$.

"Okay," I said, *"We have to make 'x' alone. So to do that, we subtract 17 from both sides. How do we do that?"* The girls did not move, so I answered the question myself. *"Take 17 from the left side."* I crossed out the 17 in the equation. *"Now, if we take 17 from this side, we have to take it from the other side,*

too." Still the girls just stared at me. *"What's 24 minus 17?"* Claudia and Angela punched the numbers into their calculators.

"Seven," Angela said.

"Good. Write it down for number three." We moved to the next problem—essentially the same process but with different numbers and a "y" instead of an "x." Though the girls couldn't manipulate the numbers, though they hadn't really understood the concept of isolating a variable, I glanced at the clock, saw that we lacked the time for further explanation, and gave them another simple subtraction problem for their calculators: another correct answer for Bates. We continued through the quiz in the same way. I set up the simple, final step, and the girls filled in the answers with help from their calculators. With each problem the charade became easier as I began to realize the perfect logic of this scenario. Ms. Bates—and now I—would pretend to teach Angela and Claudia, and they would pretend to learn. We were simply going through the motions, staging a parody of Addison's Trans Math class. We were, for the time being, actors, clowns in an academic circus, and I had become just frustrated enough to assume my own role and play along. We blitzed through the quiz, recording correct answers for each question, giddy with our "success." By the end of the period, Angela and Claudia were smiling. Though they hadn't learned any algebra, they were about to earn a number in Bates's grade book.

After class I returned to Bates's room, laid the quizzes before her, and confessed what we had done. I emphasized that I had done virtually all the work and that the quizzes were not an accurate reflection of what the girls would be able to accomplish on their own.

"That's okay," Bates said. "At least they're learning something."

I paused, then clarified that Angela and Claudia had done little more than enter numbers into their calculators, that the girls were in no way ready to move on to the next chapter in the textbook. I suggested that we further explain to them some basic algebraic concepts before prematurely attempting anything more complex. Bates seemed not to hear me.

"We're making some progress," she said. "Claudia has even begun to take notes in class."

While I don't deny that Claudia's taking notes may have represented a step forward, what Bates seemed to dismiss was the fact that, because the girls were overwhelmed by the task of grasping new content in an unfamiliar language, their means of doing their schoolwork—both in math and in the science class described earlier—was either to copy answers from a textbook or a friend, or to enlist the help of a "tutor" to supply them with the answers they needed. These methods of taking the "education" out of bilingual education were commonplace, even becoming almost routine—and now, with my complicity—during my days at Addison High. Moreover, I was not the only tutor who provided LM students with comparable "help." The previous semester, Angela's Spanish teacher had arranged for her to be assisted in science class by a bilingual student named Sara, who described her role during tests and quizzes this way: "Oh, tests and quizzes were a hard thing to do. But on the tests, I'd have the book with me, and I'd look in the book." Even Alice Martinez, who often used her time in ESL class to assist LM students with tests and quizzes from content-area classes, explained that it was *her* knowledge and skills (not her students') that were actually being tested: "Every once in a while I find myself doing that with geography, practically taking the test for them. And then I'll go to Mr. Morton [a geography teacher] and ask him, 'Hey, what did I get on that test?'"

What is remarkable here is not so much that students were copying answers or representing other people's work as their own. Delgado-Gaitan (1987), for instance, argues that the Latino students she studied perceived offering assistance to each other while working in a workbook as a logical extension of the cooperative behaviors that were expected at home. However, while some researchers (Carger, 1996; Delgado-Gaitan, 1987) have found that teachers often harshly view this form of cooperation as "cheating," what sets this practice apart as it is effected by Latino students at Addison High is that it is condoned, even encouraged, by the faculty. A White student in Daniels's science class who opened his textbook and began to copy items onto his answer sheet would receive an F and a detention, but that is precisely what constituted a prominent aspect of Sara's and my "tutoring."

This unofficial though tacit approval of such survival methods may be said to constitute a decision that individual Addison

High teachers have made, a decision that upholds the school's structure of "educating" its LM students. In the absence of a bilingual education program that allows students to genuinely learn content-area material in their native languages, students and their teachers must make do with low expectations that transform behavior that would normally earn a disciplinary referral into cause for celebration. This is not to say that Addison teachers and students view this situation as ideal. As I suggested previously, the school's mission statement proclaims a democratic commitment to a meaningful education for all its students. Nonetheless, if we view agency and structures as operating dialectically—that is, with structures to some degree influencing (even controlling) what we do, and with agency, at the same time, contributing to the formation of structures—then we can see that certain practices may eventually and cumulatively be creating structures regardless of whether or not these practices receive "official" sanction in something like a faculty handbook or a school district's mission statement. Indeed, the fact that Addison High does not officially condone cheating does not mean that cheating isn't an integral part of the structure that enables school personnel to avoid providing students like Angela and Claudia with the educational opportunities they deserve and need in order to participate actively in a democratic society.

I trust that individual teachers—and here I include myself—who either help create or are lured into these and similar practices have students' interests in mind, that we see ourselves as doing the best we can given the constraints that make it unlikely that Angela and Claudia will learn math. Student tutors like Sara were rarely available due to rigid scheduling; Trans Math was, as Bates had said, "the most basic" course offered by the math department. In short, Addison High was not set up to handle students who don't speak English well. Faced with these difficulties, I saw myself as having two equally distasteful choices: I could teach to Angela and Claudia's level of academic preparation, which would result in their failing the course, or I could do what I could to help them gain as many points as possible on their assignments and exams, which would result in their pretending to learn. Unfortunately, either option had the same result: Angela and Claudia, submerged for most of the day in an exclusively English-speaking environment, remained without equal access to the education that the school district promises, that the public assumes, and that democratic ideals demand.

A Program's Brief History

I could smell Olivia Valenzuela's classroom well before I arrived, the heavy but agreeable odor of olive oil and onions having drifted through the open door and into the corridor. Her students had left for their next class period, but a pile of used paper plates, empty soda cans, and an electric frying pan remained balanced on a table in the back of the room. "We cooked some Mexican food last hour," she explained. Students' projects and reproductions of pre-Columbian tapestries hung from the walls, piñatas from the overhead light fixtures. On her desk sat a brown clay vase, about ten lopsided inches tall and looking like it had been made in an introductory ceramics class, filled almost to the brim with multicolored wads of chewing gum. Valenzuela must have seen my eyebrows creep upward. "I know it looks disgusting," she said, "but kids don't seem to mind giving up their gum if they can put it in here."

Valenzuela had a long history with Addison Public High. A popular Spanish and sociology teacher, she had been working in the district for nearly thirty years after having graduated from Addison High as the school's first Latina homecoming queen. "I guess you could say I'm kind of an overachiever," she said. "But don't take my good fortune to be similar to most Hispanic students' experience around here. I was lucky; most of these kids are not."

After my experiences with Rosa, and now with Claudia and Angela, Valenzuela's words came as no surprise. I had seen enough of the daily effects of Addison High's departmental and curricular structures to know that these included practices that defined "education" for LM students in ways that were often exclusionary. Moreover, I had found that the history of the Addison schools revealed that these present practices had evolved within a context that betrayed a decades-long pattern of the district's questionable commitment to its Latino students. As early as 1943, for instance, an Addison superintendent had underscored the urgency of providing additional building facilities to accommodate the rapidly growing number of children of Latino agricultural and factory workers who had immigrated to the area: "I would be neglect in my duty if I did not urge the people of this district to start making preparations for the financing of these buildings now," he wrote. Despite this plea, it would be years before the voters of Addison approved such funding. Further, in 1947 a neighboring school district requested that it be annexed by the Addison system in order to combine services that could be responsive to the needs of Mexican and Mexican American children. The Addison school board, however, denied the request, explaining that they themselves were "overwhelmed" by the rapid increase in the number of Latino students in their own district.

Recalling the sociopolitical environment of the time, several now-elderly Latino residents of Addison said that they had had little voice in these decisions, which they claim were made in part to keep immigrant children out of the elementary and middle schools in Addison's affluent neighborhoods. In the words of Señora Garcia, now in her sixties, "If you didn't live on the west side of Addison, but across the tracks, you just didn't have any status." Señor Olivarez, a former Addison student and agricultural laborer, remembers that even in those schools to which Latino students did have access, the reaction of White teachers and peers was often hostile and painful. Olivarez recalls being told to "go back where [he] came from," and he said that affronts to Latino identity approached the bizarre—as when youngsters with "duck tail" hair styles, which were popular among Mexican and Mexican American students at the time, were removed from class and escorted to the local barber shop during school hours. The cumulative effect of such experiences remains powerful in Olivarez's memory:

> At that time the Mexican was down. You didn't belong in school, and they were doing you a favor by educating you, and you'd better know that. We lived in humility all the time we were there. We would come with our heads down. . . . Sometimes I'd even hate being a Mexican. I'd feel that way. I wished I was White. I'd

wish I didn't have to pick tomatoes. I'd wish I lived in a nice big house like my White friends. I'd see myself as inferior; I'd see myself as inferior as hell.

Given this legacy of racial prejudice in the Addison schools, a legacy which, in my view, lingered in the classrooms I visited with Rosa, Angela, and Claudia, I hoped Valenzuela could help me understand how the decisions of administrators in the early years of the district's bilingual education program were precursors of the decisions still being made to perpetuate Addison's failure to provide viable educational opportunities for some of its Latino students. Put another way, I wanted to uncover instances of the agency that had formed the structures I was now observing and working within—structures which, as I was becoming increasingly convinced, hindered some people's participation in the "conjoint activity" of democratic communities as Dewey defines them.

Already in the early 1970s, the Addison public school district indicated in its philosophy statement a commitment to supporting and advancing "the principles of democracy" by ensuring "each person's right to equal educational opportunity." In order to work toward this goal, the statement continues, "Addison education should strive to recognize and respect the need for special academic and administrative measures in schools serving students whose native language is one other than English. These students should be encouraged and assisted to develop their skills in their native language while they are acquiring proficiency in English." Despite the encouraging and inclusive resonance of these words, at the time they were written Addison's schools made no such accommodations for LM students. In fact, it was not until 1976, in response to a 1974 federal law requiring schools to take "appropriate action" to attend to the needs of LM students, that the district initiated a modest bilingual education program. As Valenzuela clarified, however, while this program was begun in the elementary schools, it wasn't until eight years later that she was hired to extend bilingual instruction to the high school. When she began the high school program in January of 1984, Valenzuela said she "found nothing in place."

For the next three years, Valenzuela taught geography, U.S. history, and study skills to classes she described as "very diverse," including "students who were bilingual, some who could understand Spanish but didn't communicate in it," and also students who were "underachievers, who maybe had reading problems or problems learning in the regular classroom setting." In spite of these classes' being designated as Addison's bilingual program, Valenzuela emphasized that her students "were not necessarily Hispanic" because, as she explained, "if you had all Hispanics, then you were segregating. And so we couldn't do that, so we had to bring some other kids in, kids who were having trouble in other classrooms."

In addition to having monolingual English speakers in bilingual classes, Valenzuela cited several other problems she encountered in those first years. Although her classes were supposed to have been small, with no more than fifteen students, Valenzuela shook her head and laughed as she recalled that "it didn't turn out that way." She also cited difficulties her students faced that were related to their limited English-language ability: "What was hard about it is that these kids had a self-esteem that was pretty shot to begin with, you know? Working with them on self-esteem, teaching them in ways so that it wasn't just a ditto here or a ditto there. We had a lot of hands-on projects." Valenzuela raised her voice slightly as she continued to remember: "And another problem was that I didn't have my own classroom. One classroom I had was that little office across from Mr. Dohm's office, you know the one where the woman works now who does the business? I had to put fifteen kids in that classroom. No ventilation, and the principal we had prior to Mr. Dohm smoked, so we'd often get the smoke coming through. And it was very hot, and we were cramped in there like sardines. And I'm supposed to be teaching these kids. And then another classroom I had was down in the art room. I was supposed to be teaching World Studies. No maps. No globe. But I'm teaching geography. They put up a chalkboard for me, so I had something to write on. But, you know, I didn't have the tools to teach the way they wanted me to teach, so I had to make do."

I asked Valenzuela whether mixing Spanish-speaking LM students with so-called "at-risk" White peers strayed from the original intention of what the bilingual classes were supposed to do. She gave me what seemed like a patient yet weary smile. "I don't think they knew what the classes were supposed to do. I think that the state said that you need to provide bilingual education and this is what they wanted and this is what you may do, Olivia. And, you know, go with it, whatever." As I later found out, it is not unusual to find monolingual English-speaking children who have learning disabilities and/or emotional and behavioral problems in "bilingual" classrooms. Lily Wong Fillmore (1992) claims that this is one of many methods some schools use in their efforts to "sabotage" bilingual education (p. 372).

The situation Valenzuela described continued until 1986, when she was notified that her program would be discontinued due to lack of funds: "After three years they said, 'Well, the money's gone. Too bad.' You know that it takes three years to get a program going, and it seemed like such a waste to me to get it going and then after three years just to quit." Valenzuela was then placed in the middle school to teach English, and her participation in Addison High's bilingual program was limited to intermittent meetings with students during first period: "It really didn't work. It was basically a tutoring class, but it was really hurried. I didn't see the same kids all the time. It was a pullout program; the kids would get pulled out of class to be there."

Confused, I asked, "You said that after '86 the district didn't have money to pay you to stay here in the high school. . . . But my understanding is that there's state money available to school districts to implement some sort of bilingual program that the state mandates, correct?"

"Right. I don't understand the logic of it. All I understood from the Director [of state and federal programs] at that time was that the money was cut, and they couldn't have the program full-time the next year."

I soon learned, however, that the "logic" that escaped Valenzuela became clearer in light of the strategies administrators had been following at the district level which further reinforced and maintained the structure of Addison's "bilingual" program. Almost two years before, when I was still scouting

Addison as a possible research site, the first person associated with the Addison Schools who had been willing to talk to me had been Karen Akers. Akers, an instructional coordinator with the district's office of state and federal programs, described herself as "a teacher," and she had impressed me with her understated but passionate commitment to Addison's LM students. Two days after my meeting with Valenzuela, Akers offered me a seat in her office conference room, brought over two Styrofoam cups filled with 11 a.m. coffee, and spoke with remarkable candor.

Akers explained that in order to understand how the Addison school district had funded "bilingual" education, one must recognize that the money came primarily from two different sources: state funds specifically set aside for bilingual education, and federal Chapter One moneys, which are designated for what Akers called "disadvantaged kids." The state funds, she explained, are provided to assist in "the appropriate education for [LM] students, which is legislated, and it must be provided." Akers underscored her point: "I mean, those kids must have equitable instruction understandable to them, so it's a part of their core program, so it must be provided by the district." As recently as the early 1990s, Akers explained, the state money designated for bilingual education was about $250 per student. Since then, the funds on a per-student basis have been reduced. "What's happening is that there's a certain amount of money that the legislature says is going into bilingual education. They may expand the pot a little, like ten thousand dollars or something, but we're just having more and more students in the state that qualify, so that when it becomes a per capita issue it's less per student. Now it's down to about $183 per kid. . . . It's one of those unfunded mandates that people keep talking about."

I asked how many Addison students had qualified for the state money in each of the last few years. "I'd say between 200 and 240," she said. I did some quick multiplication in my notebook: $183 x 220 = $40,260. That money, she explained, was used for Fran Soto's salary, materials for Alice Martinez's program, and conferences for these two ESL teachers. "As you can see," Akers said, "it's not much."

Faced with shrinking per-student support from the state, the district had, Akers explained, resorted to innovative ways of using federal Chapter One money to assist LM students: "A lot of [LM students] are economically disadvantaged and behind in school, so it's always been a philosophy of ours for those kids to be included in Chapter One. I mean, they have the same needs. They need to learn math; they need to learn English. And a lot of times when we would hire teacher aides with Chapter One money, they'd be bilingual. Now, we have sort of been ahead of the pack on this in that we have wrapped programs together quite a bit, for ten years or so. There's new Chapter One legislation that's just been reauthorized for another five years, and they're asking people to do this kind of stuff. But we have for quite a long time."

While Akers and her colleagues have been resourceful in conflating the bilingual and Chapter One programs in the absence of other sources of adequate funding, Akers acknowledged that this situation is far from ideal. Indeed, at least two possible problems arise. First, though it may be true that some of the LM students' needs are similar to those of "disadvantaged" White students, the challenges faced by limited-English speakers are unique and deserving of specific attention. Second, by relying on Chapter One funding to address the needs of LM students, Addison administrators can too easily dismiss the "problem" of students who do not speak English as already having been attended to. The reality, however, is that beginning with Valenzuela's experience in trying to establish an already overdue bilingual program in the mid-1980s, Addison's record of financial commitment to bilingual education has been spotty at best.

To summarize, although the district established a "bilingual program" in 1976, no such instruction took place at the high school prior to 1984, when Valenzuela began her work, which continued until 1986. For another year, Valenzuela was in the high school just one period per day. In addition, I learned from Akers that between 1986 and 1991 the office of state and federal programs received a federal seed grant to enhance the district's bilingual program, but only at the middle school level. According to Alvarez, the high school counselor, the bilingual assistance available to Addison High students during this time was limited to bilingual tutors who, Alvarez explained, were paid with state money and who either instructed students "in study halls or pulled them out of class." Alvarez recalled only three or four students at any one time receiving such instruction, which lasted no more than half the school day. This practice continued until January 1992, when Martinez and Soto were hired to be the districtwide ESL teachers, spending one period each day in the high school. In Akers's view, the addition of Martinez and Soto was a significant indication of the district's growing sense of obligation to LM students: "We feel good that Alice's position was funded from district money, and so that was a commitment from the district, which is unusual, given its past history."

When one considers this history, the district appears to be ambivalent in its commitment to providing sustained access to education for all its students. It is fair to ask, I think, why the school was late in beginning its efforts to establish a bilingual program, and why—when the district was receiving both federal seed grant funding and per-student allocations from the state— bilingual education was limited in the high school to the inconsistent services of tutors, most of whom were local college students. Moreover, I wonder why the seed grant funds seemed to result in no consistent strategy that carried over to support the present efforts of Martinez and Soto. Though the allocation of district funds to support Martinez's position was an encouraging sign, the Addison school system's collective reluctance to commit its own resources for bilingual education suggests, I think, that the administrators making financial decisions seem to view students like Claudia and Angela as the state or federal government's responsibility rather than their own.

An alternative explanation of the administration's (in)action concerning the district's LM students, however, was expressed to me by Mr. Joseph Benincasa, who, as I had discovered from the minutes of old school board meetings, was assistant to the superintendent and director of instruction at the time Addison's bilingual program was initiated. Long since retired but remembered fondly by the Addison staff members who helped me locate him, Benincasa agreed to meet with me at his home, where he explained the difficulties of introducing bilingual education in Addison, difficulties that ranged from a scarcity of certified bilingual instructors to "resistance or indifference" on the part of the community in general and the teaching staff in particular. By and by, however, it seemed that Benincasa's and the other administrators' disinclination to make bilingual education a high priority in the Addison schools may have been due not just to a chronic lack of local funding or—as I suggested above—an abdication of their responsibility to Latino LM students. Rather, as he reflected with gracious words for the teachers and students with whom he had worked for so many years, Benincasa implied that it was a strong sense of obligation to LM students that was the motivation behind his and his colleagues' decisions in matters that affected such students so profoundly. This obligation included, he said, creating circumstances in which LM students learned English as quickly as possible: "Your obligation is to do the most you can for youngsters. Obviously the school's responsibility is to provide some assistance. As a practical matter, the best way to learn a foreign language is to be immersed. . . . It was simply thought that [immersion] was the best thing for you to become an American. This is the melting pot. That's why that was done."

As we have seen, Benincasa's well-intentioned but, in my view, misguided notion of how best to meet his responsibility to LM students remains strong among contemporary opponents of bilingual education. To be sure, I had learned well in Chile that this immersion approach can in some cases be a highly effective way of learning a foreign language. However, as I suggested earlier, what made that approach work for me was that I was learning Spanish in contexts that were immediately meaningful and relevant to my daily life. I learned (and remembered) the Spanish words for "toothpaste" and "peanut butter," for instance, not because a teacher had included them on a vocabulary list but because I needed to ask someone where these items could be found in the grocery store. Moreover, when I stepped onto the streets of Santiago, I was equipped with the sociocultural and economic capital that enabled me to experience my conversational difficulties as enriching rather than humiliating. In contrast, from what I had seen and heard, the native language of generations of Latino LM students in Addison seemed to be viewed by their educators primarily as a deficiency to be overcome. The failure to recognize such differences in the human contexts of the immersion approach is, I suspect, among the reasons for the individual decisions made by Mr. Benincasa and his successors—decisions which I believe have contributed to the construction and maintenance of an educational structure that denies LM students equal educational opportunity. Whatever reasons lie behind them, the individual decisions I have mentioned here have contributed to the construction and maintenance of an educational structure that denies LM students equal educational opportunity.

To be fair, it is appropriate here to recall that Addison High has recently made the commitment to hire Martinez and Soto to teach English to LM students for one period per day. Nonetheless, as James Lyon (1992), the executive director of the National Center for Bilingual Education, has emphatically pointed out, "No one with an ounce of sense would say that a child who has mastered English, but who has not learned mathematics, history, geography, civics, and the other subjects taught in school was educated or prepared for life in this society" (pp. 364–365). We have seen the cumulative effects of a structure that rarely affords Angela and Claudia (or, earlier, Rosa) the opportunity to receive native-language instruction in content-area classes. We have also explored the district-level decisions that have helped create this structure. At this point, in order to understand more thoroughly why, for instance, Angela should have to sit through a math class conducted in a language she doesn't understand and rely on cheating to gain any sort of academic credit, it is useful to broaden our perspective even further and consider additional factors that have contributed to the structure influencing the education of Addison's Latino students: namely, ambiguous legislative actions and judicial decisions pertaining to the education of non-English-speaking students. As we shall see, although Congress and the United States Supreme Court have taken steps which seem aimed at ensuring equal educational opportunity for LM students, these measures do not specifically mandate that local school districts provide all students with such opportunity.

The Legislation of Neglect

In my conversation with Karen Akers, I asked about laws that I presumed required school districts with a significant number of non-English-speaking students to provide bilingual instruction. Akers pointed out, however, that I was assuming too much: "The law never did say 'bilingual instruction.' It never says that you have to provide these kids with instruction in their native language. It said 'something appropriate.' People can interpret it to mean in their native language, or they can interpret it to mean ESL in English, and that's the trick. I don't think it ever really says 'instruction in their native language,' and that's where the catch is."

Akers's mention of this ambiguity in the wording of government actions regarding the education of LM students echoes what Valenzuela described as the cause of her difficulties in securing district support of her program ten years earlier. I had asked Valenzuela whether scheduling her in the high school just one period each day was a violation of the law. "I would think so," she said. "But here's how they got around it: You have to provide the services, but it doesn't say you have to provide them six periods a day. So even though I was only coming in one hour, they could say, 'Yes we do have some help for these kids.' That way they could justify it if they had to. It was threadbare, but they could."

As Akers and Valenzuela suggested, one of the problems facing LM students is the misperception that civil rights laws have assured all students' access to educational opportunities. This assurance, however, is a myth that is largely based upon three major government actions: the Bilingual Education Act of 1968, the 1974 U.S. Supreme Court ruling on *Lau v. Nichols,* and the Equal Educational Opportunities Act of 1974. Although the "spirit" of these actions is to ensure that schools respond to the needs of language-minority students, the "letter" or form in which they were written does not mandate specific criteria for bilingual education. This lack of clarity, which in my view enables school districts to evade their responsibility to ensure that all students have equal access to an education, contributes to what I have been calling the structure influencing the education of LM students at Addison High.

The Bilingual Education Act (BEA) of 1968 was the first major initiative by the federal government intended to meet the needs of low-income children with limited English-speaking ability. Through the BEA, grants were awarded to local educational agencies, institutions of higher education, and research facilities to develop and operate bilingual education programs and to make efforts to attract and train teachers from non-English-speaking backgrounds (Garcia, 1991, p. 111; Jiménez, 1992; p. 244). However, while it created a competitive grants program to help train teachers and administrators, to finance research on effective teaching methods, and to support educational projects, the BEA did not require school districts to implement programs for LM students. Thus, while it provided resources for districts to develop bilingual programs if they had applied for and were awarded these grants, the BEA did not mandate that schools address the educational needs of LM children.

A similarly well-known but ultimately inconclusive action by a federal organization is the Supreme Court's ruling in *Lau v. Nichols*. While it is known as a landmark in the progress of language-minority students' interests, what I think is most remarkable about the case is the difference between the common public perception of the ruling and what it actually requires. In 1974 Kinney Lau and eighteen hundred other Chinese American children sued the San Francisco Public Schools, claiming that the school district's failure to provide these limited-English-proficient students with language support constituted a denial of equal educational access. In the only decision the Supreme Court has handed down in this area, a unanimous Court ruled that because the district had done nothing to address their lack of English skills, the Chinese-speaking students were being denied their rights to a public education. Justice William O. Douglas delivered the Court's decision, which included the following:

> [T]here is no equality of treatment merely by providing students with the same facilities, textbooks, teachers, and curriculum; for students who do not understand English are effectively foreclosed from any meaningful education. Basic English skills are at the very core of what these public schools teach. Imposition of a requirement that, before a child can effectively participate in the educational program he must already have acquired those basic skills is to make a mockery of public education. We know that those who do not understand English are certain to find their classroom experiences wholly incomprehensible and in no way meaningful. (cited in Jiménez, p. 246)

As decisive as this opinion may sound, it is important to note that while the Court did identify bilingual education as an *option* toward meeting the goal of equitable education, the Court did not order a specific remedy because none had been requested by the plaintiffs. In fact, the Court's decision makes clear that school districts are not *required* to provide LM students with bilingual education in content-area classes. Rather, schools may opt for ESL instruction only or another (unspecified) means of accommodating the non-English-speaking students: "Teaching English to the students of Chinese ancestry who do not speak the language is one choice. Giving instructions to this group in Chinese is another. There may be others" (p. 247).

Part of the Court's failure to prescribe bilingual education in the *Lau* case seems to have been due to the Court's emphasis that schools were responsible for teaching students English as soon as possible. Indeed, among the principal reasons Justice Douglas cites for the *Lau* decision is a section of the California Education Code which declares that "the policy of the state" is to insure "the mastery of English by all pupils in the schools" (*Lau v. Nichols*, p. 251–255). As a further rationale for its decision, the Court quoted a section of a 1970 memo sent by the Office of Civil Rights to school districts with "national-origin minority" enrollments exceeding 5 percent, a memo which suggests an urgency to teach LM students English: "[T]he district must take affirmative steps to rectify the language deficiency in order to open its instructional program to [national-origin minority] students" (p. 254). Finally, while concurring with the decision, Justice Harry Blackmun, joined by Chief Justice Warren Burger, added a significant caveat, which I quote in full because it further underscores the Court's emphasis not on providing native-language instruction in content-area classes, but on insisting that schools with large numbers of LM students are obligated to teach them English:

> Against the possibility that the Court's decision be interpreted too broadly, I stress the fact that the children with whom we are concerned here number about 1,800. This is a very substantial group that is being deprived of any meaningful schooling because the children cannot understand the language of the class-

room. We may only guess as to why they have had no exposure to English in their preschool years. Earlier generations of American ethnic groups have overcome the language barrier by earnest parental endeavor or by the hard fact of being pushed out of the family or community nest and into the realities of broader experience. I merely wish to make plain that when, in another case, we are confronted with very few youngsters, or with just a single child who speaks only German or Polish or Spanish or any language other than English, I would not regard today's decision . . . as conclusive upon the issue whether the statute and the guidelines require the funded school district to provide special instruction. For me, numbers are at the heart of this case and my concurrence is to be understood accordingly. (*Lau v. Nichols*, p. 254–255)

Thus, far from being a mandate for (or even a recommendation of) bilingual education as it is often regarded, the *Lau* decision may be read as an endorsement of linguistic and cultural assimilation that left unresolved the question of what exactly is required of school districts in order to provide equal educational access for language-minority students.

Soon after the *Lau* decision, Congress took a step toward addressing that question by adopting the Equal Educational Opportunities Act (EEOA). As Jiménez (1992) has summarized, the EEOA specifically barred any state from denying equal educational opportunity to an individual on account of race, color, sex, or national origin by "the failure of an educational agency to take appropriate action to overcome language barriers that impede equal participation by its students in its instructional programs" (p. 247). While this move was designed to compel schools to honor the spirit of the *Lau* decision, and while it does require schools to offer programs to meet the needs of their language-minority students, the EEOA failed to specify the exact meaning of "appropriate action" and therefore fails to mandate specific educational treatment.

The point here is that while some legislative and judicial actions have affirmed the importance of instruction that ensures equal educational opportunity for LM students, these measures have not definitively and consistently required schools to provide such instruction. Indeed, varying interpretations of what constitutes compliance with the EEOA have left room for the

Addison School District's equivocal efforts described by Valenzuela and Akers.

I realize that what I have called "equivocal" others would call "flexible." We live in a time when the calls for school "reform" are often taken to mean the freedom for districts—or even individual schools—to do as they see fit. Former Education Secretary William J. Bennett (1988/1992), for example, articulated what remains a popular opinion when he announced the Reagan Administration's commitment to allowing "greater flexibility to local school districts" (cited in Lyon, p. 362). The proposed "reforms," Bennett argued, would "allow local school districts to choose the sort of program, or to design the combination of programs, best suited to their particular needs" (p. 362). Although Bennett's call for less "intrusive federal regulation" is a popular refrain in current American politics, I would caution that the type of "flexibility" Bennett and so many others advocate cannot be assumed to be in all students' best interests. As my research strongly suggests, the Addison school district, left to its own designs and untouched by "intrusive" state and federal regulation, would be content to leave Angela copying answers from the back of her math book.

While I suspect that most Americans would agree that local control of schools is a tradition worth preserving, we must also remember that this was precisely the argument invoked by Governor George Wallace in 1963 when he stood barring the door of the University of Alabama to African Americans. More recently, California voters asserted a claim on control of their own schools by passing the infamous Proposition 187, which, though checked by the courts, sought to bar undocumented workers and their families from state services, including public education. Thus, though the call for flexibility and local control is a popular one, the exercise of such control is not always productive and ethical. Of course, the argument that a proper role of the federal government is to safeguard the right of each student to equal educational access in communities where local structures have failed to do so is neither radical nor new. The *Brown v. Board of Education* decision and other civil rights initiatives, for instance, suggest that throughout this country's history, our nation's collective sense of justice has at times needed prompting from those whom we entrust with positions of leadership. This notion that localism in education must at times be contained is also set forth by Roberto Mangabiera and Cornel West (1998), who argue that schools should not "passively reflect community attitudes," but that they "should examine possibilities of imagination and of life that the surrounding society is unable or unwilling to countenance" (p. 70). Though some might call this "government intrusiveness," I believe that it serves as a reminder that it is sometimes necessary to act at a state and/or national level as part of an effort to change those structures that work against equal educational access in localized settings.

Nonetheless, it is also important to keep in mind that legislation, executive oversight, and court rulings alone cannot revise undemocratic sociopolitical structures: Ironically, as we have seen, though the Bilingual Education Act, the *Lau* decision, and the Equal Educational Opportunities Act seem to have been aimed at contributing to a structure that honors LM students' right to educational opportunity, what these actions actually do is constitute part of the structure that enables school districts to avoid providing LM students with such opportunities. Decisions made in faraway courtrooms or legislative chambers may point us as a society in the right direction, and may even compel reluctant individuals to amend certain forms of injustice. However, as I have pointed out, structures operate in a dialectical relationship with human agency; they not only shape but are shaped by the individuals thinking and acting within them. Therefore, even though efforts to provide Addison's LM students with a meaningful education are constrained by an insistence on English-only content-area classes and by district-level decisions, which in turn are enabled, even if unintentionally, by the rulings of powerful bodies in the federal government, I dare to hope that such a structure may be revised and eventually replaced by another—one constructed by people who believe that students like Angela and Claudia have a right to an education they can understand. This kind of structure, rather than erecting barriers between people based on their social class, gender, ethnicity, or language use, would provide support for the types of communication and human interaction that Dewey contends are essential to a democratic society.

If as citizen teachers we accept the notion that a meaningful education helps people participate in actions with others, and if, with Dewey, we believe that such participation is among the fundamental characteristics of democracy, then it seems to me that we are also acknowledging that all students seeking educational opportunity have, as the American philosopher Nicholas Wolterstorff (1983) has written, a morally legitimate claim that is grounded in the responsibility that human beings have for each other (p. 82). To respond to these obligations individually and collectively, to seek to revise the structures that prevent us from doing so, is not, Wolterstorff argues, an act of generosity, but an imperative based upon the human status of those who are in need. Joel Feinberg (1973) has written similarly of the significance of an understanding of rights as claims imposing obligations:

> A claim-right . . . can be urged, pressed, or rightly demanded against other persons. In appropriate circumstances the right-holder can "urgently, peremptorily, or insistently" call for his rights, or assert them authoritatively, confidently, unabashedly. Rights are not mere gifts or favors, motivated by love or pity, for which gratitude is the sole fitting response. A right is something that can be demanded or insisted upon without embarrassment or shame. When that to which one has a right is not forthcoming, the appropriate reaction is indignation; when it is duly given there is no reason for gratitude, since it is simply one's own or one's due that one received. A world with right-claims is one in which all persons, as actual or potential claimants, are dignified objects of respect, both in their own eyes and in the view of others. No amount of love and compassion, or obedience to higher authority, or noblesse oblige, can substitute for those values. (pp. 58–59)

If we understand equal access to educational opportunity to be a "claim-right" which places on us civil and moral obligations, then we may begin to see that the cost of ignoring our obligations in securing this right for students like Claudia and Angela is to degrade them, ourselves, and our nation's democratic ideals. My hope is that despite the constraints of powerful structures such as those I have discussed in this chapter, educators may accept and embrace this obligation as a foundation of their work as citizen teachers.

CHAPTER FIVE

Agency, Individuality, and the Politics of Fear

We have room for but one language here, and that is the English language; for we intend to see that the crucible turns our people out as Americans, of American nationality, and not as dwellers in a polyglot boarding house; and we have room for but one sole loyalty, and that is loyalty to the American people.

THEODORE ROOSEVELT, "The Children of the Crucible"

Give me your hungry, your tired, your poor,
I'll piss on 'em,
That's what the Statue of Bigotry says.
Your poor huddled masses, let's club 'em to death,
Get it over with and just dump 'em on the boulevard.

LOU REED, "Dirty Boulevard"

In the previous chapter, we saw that the structure of Addison High is intricate and complex, extending far beyond the walls of individual classrooms. We also saw that this structure does not always exhibit the characteristics of democratic communities as Dewey defines them. For in addition to the "official" structure as established by the school board and the laws that (vaguely) regulate it, certain practices—like faculty-sanctioned cheating—have arisen as unofficial yet very real components of a system that fails to provide language-minority (LM) students with access to a meaningful education. We have seen, in other words, that Carla Rodriquez (1989) is correct when she argues that "all those involved in the educational system play complementary roles. . . . In the end, everyone's role is to a very great extent determined by the total working of the institution" (p. 147).

Nonetheless, as I have also suggested, describing the structure of LM student instruction at Addison High offers only a limited view of the challenges faced by these students. Therefore, citizen teachers must also ask how and why this structure functions as it does. To explore these questions is to better understand the dialectical relationship between structure and individual agency as these forces interact to either promote or hinder democratic aims in the daily experiences of students like Claudia and Angela.

While in the previous chapter I focused on the structure influencing LM students' education at Addison High, in the present chapter I will emphasize the role of human agency as it is evident in the behavior of individual teachers. We will see that although some teachers act in ways that resist the undemocratic aspects of the structures within which they work, other members of the Addison faculty reinforce and perpetuate this structure through their tendency to "disown" their Latino students. Frustrated by their inability to communicate with LM students, by the burden of extracurricular and committee work, and by the fact that they are responsible for teaching as many as 140 students each day, these teachers, many of whom are otherwise very gifted educators and gracious people, have essentially made the decision to abdicate their obligation to their LM students. In short, if we continue to ask *why* Angela and Claudia do not have access to education, one answer is that many teachers tend to view them as somebody else's responsibility.

In order to assess forms of teachers' agency in terms of the democratic priorities of citizen teachers, I'll frame my descriptions of such agency with reference to an aspect of Dewey's thought that is not often discussed in the professional literature of educators. I am referring to Dewey's insistence that people's *individual* intellectual and ethical dispositions must be exercised in struggles to bring new and progressive ideas into community life. Given my ongoing concern with ways in which schools might take on the features of Dewey's ideal communities, it may initially seem incongruous to include in my theoretical framework his discussions of the individual, for I think it is safe to say that much of the renewed interest in Dewey in recent years can be attributed to the communitarian impulses of educators seeking an alternative to forms of teaching and learning that so many students find alienating and socially irrelevant. Nonetheless, while there is no denying Dewey's recurring emphasis on the "associated activity" that he argues is essential to vital democratic communities, he also contends that such communities depend upon "individuality," which he defines as "a unique manner of acting in and with a world of objects and persons" (1929/1962, p. 168), a manner that is characterized by persons' bringing their singular intellectual and affective capacities to bear on collective action (1941/1988b). In my view, this notion of individuality affords a way to understand human agency that is especially useful to citizen teachers in that it makes explicit the importance of individuals' actions in fostering democratic forms of social life.

Even while shifting attention to the agency of individual teachers at Addison High, however, I will continue to stress that the "individual" failure to assume ownership of responsibility toward LM students does not occur independently of structural influences. If the scheduling practices of Addison High gave teachers fewer students each day, if departmental grading requirements allowed for more flexibility in assessing LM students, if district administrators provided funding for more bilingual instructors to work with teachers in developing pedagogy appropriate to LM students, I suspect that many teachers would be encouraged to accept the notion that—as the saying goes—they are teaching *students,* not academic subjects. As important as issues like scheduling and class size are to the structure that shapes teachers' actions toward their LM students at Addison High, I will also underscore later in this chapter what I see as a force that occupies an important place in this structure: namely, an ideology which leads some teachers to believe that by refusing to accommodate language-minority students, they are preserving "American values."

Resisting By Responding: The Benefits and Costs of Oppositional Individuality

As I have been arguing, structures can constrain (or enable) but not absolutely determine what people do, and throughout my days at Addison High, I saw examples of individual teachers reaching out to Latino students and teaching them well in spite of the schedules, rules, and policies that hindered the flexibility needed to do so. Ms. Reinstra, the Child Development teacher who monitored Angela's study hall that semester, cajoled a bilingual student to help Angela with her math; Ms. Daniels strayed from her policy and accepted science homework from Angela and Claudia a few days after it was due.

Nowhere, however, was there a more attentive, even compassionate, response to Angela's and Claudia's daily struggles than from Martinez and Soto in second-period ESL. These two teachers, perhaps because of the empathy that came from being Latinas in Addison themselves, took full advantage of the unusually small class and set about doing much more than their institutionally sanctioned task of teaching English. Martinez and Soto knew, as I had learned from working with Rosa the year before, that to serve language-minority students required addressing their affective as well as their academic needs: that during the course of a day characterized by relentless failure and isolation, Claudia and Angela needed a refuge where they were allowed to demonstrate what they *could* do rather than what they could not do.

By now the instructions were familiar: generate a description of the pictures displayed on cards propped against the chalkboard. When Angela's turn came, she hesitated, but Martinez prodded:

"*Okay, mi'ja. Tell me first in Spanish.*" Angela studied the picture of a dark-skinned family smiling in front of a small house.

"*The family looks happy?*" Angela more asked than answered.

"Okay, now how do you say 'the' in English?"

Angela answered quietly.

"*Good. Now, what about 'family'?*"

Angela again answered correctly but needed help with "looks" and "happy." Martinez offered the answers, along with praise to Angela for having gotten as far as she had. "*Okay, Angela, look at their faces, their color. What kind of family do you think they are?*"

"*I don't know.*"

"*Look, make a guess. Are they White?*"

"No."

"What do they look like?"

"Mexicans."

"Good, very good," Martinez said. "Now, they could be from another place, too, right? Like, they could be Puerto Rican, *so can we use 'Latino' instead of 'Mexican'?"* Angela said that that was fine, and Martinez continued. "Now, let's write this out. Claudia, say this together for us in English." Claudia spoke slowly enough for Soto to write her words with a blue marker on a large sheet of paper taped to the chalkboard:

"The Latino family looks happy."

Martinez smiled. *"Good! Angela, give us another sentence, something else. Tell us about your family. Does this picture remind you of your family?"* Angela thought for a moment.

"My family has a big house in Matamoros. It has four rooms and a small yard."

"Claudia, give that to us in English." Claudia translated the sentence orally, after which Soto helped her record her words on the paper. Claudia, Angela, and several classmates continued to take turns, generating and translating sentences prompted by pictures that included a girl playing soccer and vegetables that are often grown and harvested by Latino workers in the fields around Addison. Constantly active, challenged, and successful, these students were responding well to teaching strategies that are effective in all content areas and with students of varying degrees of English fluency—strategies like individualized attention, clear outcomes, clarity in presenting new information, and the careful monitoring of students' progress (Gersten, 1998; Henze & Lucas, 1993). In addition, however, I sensed that at least part of the reason Angela, Claudia, and the others seemed so engaged in Martinez's lesson was that it included practices that are especially important among LM students. As Eugene Garcia (1991) and Barbara Merino (1991) have argued, these practices include using both the students' native language and that which they are learning, developing second-language skills in the context of tasks that refer to students' cultural backgrounds, and respecting the values and norms of their native cultures. Merino (1991) summarizes that second-language teaching environments that promote a high degree of student involvement as well as on-task

behavior are those in which "classroom discourse is contextualized and cultural referents are frequent and given positive value" (p. 140). As I watched Martinez's students continue to flip through and describe the stack of pictures, it occurred to me that it was precisely these kinds of priorities that were being played out that day (and most others) in second-period ESL.

With a few minutes left in the period, Martinez congratulated the students on a job well done and began packing books into her wide canvas bag in preparation for her dash to the middle school. Soto gathered the paper and markers and headed for the storage closet, while Angela and I began to push our desks back into history-class rows. Claudia, however, paused, having spotted a stray card lying face down on a side table. She turned it over and looked at a picture of a gray kitten with a blue bow around its neck.

"C'mon," she said. "We got one more."

"*Mi'ja, the bell's going to ring any minute,*" Martinez said. "*We can finish tomorrow.*"

"Look, we got two minutes. We can do this now," Claudia insisted. Angela rolled her eyes, and I stood still, my desk still askew. Martinez looked at Soto, then at her watch, and then relented. "Okay, *but we have to work fast.*"

Although Claudia's overall attendance record had been getting progressively worse as she had developed the habit of skipping her afternoon classes, in second period ESL she was not only present but reinforcing her role as an enthusiastic class leader. It didn't matter that Claudia could read and write only a few words in either English or Spanish, for Martinez and Soto publicly acknowledged and celebrated Claudia's strengths—most notably, her bilingualism. The people there knew that if they needed something translated, they could read it to Claudia and she could do it. In that class, a place like no other at Addison High, Claudia was given the chance to demonstrate to her teachers, her classmates, and herself that she was a capable student. Put another way, she had the chance to show off a bit.

This class, then, was a refuge, a sanctuary where good things happened—a place where students were not only academically successful but also where people understood what it was like to be in a strange place far from home, where Claudia and Angela could mutter words of frustration and know that not just their language but also their experiences would be understood. Having immigrated to Addison themselves, Martinez and Soto knew what it was like to be isolated by language and culture, and they were determined that at least in this one space Claudia and Angela would feel like they belonged. However, even with the cultural and linguistic background Martinez and Soto shared with their ESL students, these teachers could not have created such an environment without a commitment beyond what was printed in their contracts—without forms of agency that responded to their students' unique academic and affective needs. Martinez and Soto visited their students' homes, knew whose uncle had returned to Mexico or whose brother had just been promoted at work. Martinez's husband sold raffle tickets to his golfing partners in order to help finance an ESL class trip to an amusement park in Ohio during spring break. One day after a class in which Claudia had seemed unusually quiet, even depressed, Martinez told me that Claudia had been "a bit disappointed" from having learned she was not pregnant.

"Isn't that good news?" I asked.

"You've got to remember," Martinez said. "These girls have nothing."

By investing herself so thoroughly in the lives of her students, Martinez went far beyond her institutionally defined role as a teacher. Indeed, Martinez operated from an understanding that I had begun to see from my experiences with Rosa the previous year: to help Addison's LM students succeed in school requires that teachers acknowledge that the contexts in which these students are trying to learn includes challenges that arise from being different and lonely. To be sure, in ESL, Martinez's students studied English, but they did so while nurtured by the emotional support they needed to make it through the day. As we learn from those who teach and conduct research in bilingual settings, such support is an essential foundation for best practices among LM students in both ESL and content-area classes (Fern, Anstrom, & Silcox, 1997; Lara-Alecio & Parker, 1994; Lucas, Henze, & Donato, 1990).

The more time I spent in Martinez's ESL class, the clearer it became to me that the way she interacted with her students was not something that was overtly required of her as a member of the Addison High faculty; rather, it was something she had consciously chosen to do because it was worthy of both her and her students. Of course, Principal Dohm could have forced Martinez's compliance to her contractual obligations to be in the classroom, to give assignments, and to submit grades, but no administrator can compel the kind of commitment she exhibited toward Claudia, Angela, and the others each day during second period. Because of the deliberate, habitual, and humane nature of Martinez's actions, I believe they may be understood as examples of Dewey's notion of individuality.

As I mentioned earlier, Dewey defines "individuality" as a way of "acting in and with" the world. Dewey refines this basic definition, however, by situating individuality in opposition to "individualism," (emphasis added) which is effected through "those activities that make for success in business conducted for personal gain" (1929/1962, p. 90). Driven by narrowly self-serving economic aims, individualism reduces interpersonal relations to exploitation or neglect (1929/1962, p. 18; 1941/1988a, pp. 275–277), and it relies on an ethical indifference that some have called a "negative freedom" *from* responsibility toward others (Berlin, 1969, p. 122; Greene, 1988, pp. 17–18). As Alan Ryan (1995) points out, such individualism—recently revived under the auspices of both neoconservatism and neoliberalism—is "unsatisfying," for it fails to distinguish between individual rights and the neglect of others in need, between civil liberties and the freedom to consume, between legitimate personal aspiration and rapacious greed (p. 33).

In contrast, Dewey's notion of individuality casts freedom as a responsibility and opportunity to act with others in contexts of "definite social relationships and publicly acknowledged functions" (1941/1988b, pp. 224–230). Echoing his description of ideal communities, Dewey (1927/1988) contends that in the process of democratic life, one of the ways individuality emerges is in the extent to which each person participates distinctively in the forming and directing of group activity (pp. 353–354). As Stephen Fishman (1993) has noted, Dewey's metaphor for communities characterized by this kind of distinctive action is that of a well-functioning body, an organic whole whose unique parts complement one another to achieve common ends (pp. 319–320).

However, it is important to note that individuality has even more radical implications than those which follow from defining it as people's acting distinctively toward aims that have been collectively determined. Rather, as Karen Detlefsen (1998) has astutely pointed out, individuality posits the self not merely as the implementer, but also as the *instigator*, of positive social change. Dewey (1941/1988b) puts it this way: "Individual opposition, non-conformity, insubordination may be the sole means by which the existing state can progress" (p. 227). Characteristically, Dewey (1916/1985) is careful to qualify that such innovation does not take place independently of sociohistorical contexts, saying that the role of the individual must be "the redirection or reconstruction of accepted beliefs" (p. 305). Nonetheless, Dewey (1916/1985) argues that, though situated within and drawing from existing social structures, "Every *new* idea, every conception of things differing from that authorized by current belief, must have its origin in an individual" (p. 305, Dewey's italics). This capacity for intellectual variation, for challenging existing knowledge, for critically assessing and revising established beliefs and values, is, in Dewey's view (1916/1985), the domain of the individual, and "indispensable" to social progress (pp. 305–306).

Thus, Dewey's conception of individuality does not imply a separation from society; it does not connote a form of self-reliance that divorces people from dependence on collective arrangements to improve their lives. Rather, individuality is, in sum, the origin of democratizing agency, a source of liberation from the constraining effects of institutions that hinder the cultivation of an experimentalist impulse which brings creativity and imagination to attempts to solve society's problems. In this reading of Dewey, community may be regarded as the medium within which democracy is effected and sustained, while the "continuous readjustment" that Dewey (1916/1985) calls for in social habits begins in the exercise of individuality by people like Alice Martinez. For under Martinez's influence, second-period ESL ventured far from the characteristics of what a class at Addison High typically looks and feels like. That is, ESL was operating differently from how classes were designed to function within the existing structures of the school. Or, to put it in Dewey's terms, Martinez was, by exercising her individuality, "redirecting and reconstructing" education at Addison High. She was revising the role the school had written for her, and she was doing so by accepting her responsibility to respond holistically to the diverse, human needs of her Latino students.

By calling attention to what I see as Martinez's individuality, I am not suggesting that all teachers should try to imitate her exact forms of personal investment in her work. Martinez's life experiences allowed connections with Angela and Claudia that other teachers at Addison High couldn't match, nor should they necessarily have tried to do so. Nonetheless, if Addison's White teachers were unable to provide the type of empathetic care Martinez offered, they might have exercised individuality in other ways. In general, these teachers might have done more to acknowledge that educating LM students was among their professional responsibilities. More specifically, they might have been more active in learning about the many useful strategies that—as we shall soon see—are available to monolingual content-area teachers of LM students. Karen Akers mentioned that she had often attempted to help teachers meet these responsibilities but that most of them had exhibited little interest: "We tried to get classroom teachers to go to [bilingual education] workshops, because at those conferences they're already preaching to the converted, but we didn't get back much of a response. We really have a need for classroom teachers to have this kind of knowledge because the ESL teacher just can't do it all."

I also think many of Addison's teachers could have demonstrated individuality by making greater efforts to know and work cooperatively with Martinez and Soto. This distance between content-area and bilingual teachers, as Nieto (1992) points out, is not unique to Addison High. Nieto explains that one of the many difficulties facing bilingual programs is that the bilingual teachers, especially those from the same linguistic and cultural background as the students, are "often isolated and marginalized in the schools" and tend "to have little interaction with the staff" (p. 167). Reflecting this trend, Martinez had cited her and Soto's anonymity as a problem in Addison ever since she had begun her work at the high school over a year ago: "We're outsiders here, just like these kids. A lot of the teachers here don't even know who we are. A couple of weeks ago I had to go talk to one of the teachers to arrange to translate a test for Claudia, and he was like, 'Oh, you're on the faculty here?'" Similarly, Olivia Valenzuela, recalling her years trying to establish a bilingual education program in the high school, described her experiences in this way: "I was sort of like . . . I felt like the leper of the building."

Despite these and other costs of emerging as "different" in the process of trying to bring about positive change in schools, I tend to think that the kind of individuality effected by Martinez is among the obligations of citizen teachers in all content areas. The exact ways in which teachers enact their individuality will, as is the case with all forms of democratic agency, vary depending on the circumstances. At times an appropriate response to educational injustices will be to speak out at a faculty meeting or to mobilize whatever power we have at our disposal to influence school board, legislative, or judicial decisions. Still, as I watched and listened to Martinez among her students, I saw more clearly that at times we must bring a certain gentleness to our work as citizen teachers. For insofar as a kind word, an encouraging smile, or a patient answer contributes to an environment where young people can learn, even these apparently small gestures become profoundly democratic.

Concentration and the Teachers' Meeting

As difficult as it often was for ESL students and teachers to endure the separation that was the consequence of their "difference" at Addison High, there were times when this isolation seemed like a welcome respite from the rest of the school day. Like ships pulling into port for supplies, Angela and Claudia could enter their second-period classroom and find a sympathetic shoulder and academic success, and though they worked hard in Martinez's class, this was also a time to rest among people who valued and respected who they are before setting out again into an environment where such affirmation was uncertain at best. However, I often felt that among the downsides of this isolation was that Angela's and Claudia's content-area teachers never knew them well, never saw the eagerness that Claudia brought to her learning or the literacy that Angela used to maintain ties to friends in Mexico. My conversations with these teachers revealed that they were unaware of Claudia's and Angela's previous lives and schooling and suggested that to them, these young women were troubled mysteries with inscrutable pasts, faces that corresponded to names followed by an uninterrupted line of blank spaces in a record book. Because they did not know Angela and Claudia as people, I sensed that the Addison faculty also did not know them as learners and that this lack of knowledge sometimes caused teachers to misunderstand Claudia's and Angela's needs and abilities, making it easier for them to dismiss these and other LM students as someone else's responsibility.

The extent to which at least one teacher misjudged Angela's learning potential was illustrated dramatically one morning, which began in ESL class with a game of "Concentration" focusing on English words that had come from a previous discussion of Valentine's Day. Claudia and Angela had set the cards facedown in long rows, and, after having gone around the circle a few times, Angela had seen enough to make her move. The turn before Angela's, I flipped over a card and read the word: "heart," "*corazón.*" I knew I had seen its counterpart before, but my guess failed to produce a match. Angela paused for a moment, then her eyes met those of her opponents seated around the table, like my older brother used to do before he laid down a full house. She then turned over the "heart" card I had just flipped and quickly followed with the second. Next, two more; both read "candy." She scooped up the cards, set them aside, and continued to expose pairs of words the rest of us had long forgotten. Each card snapped confidently as she pressed its corner onto the table. By the time she failed to turn over a matching pair, an impressive stack lay on the desk in front of her. I looked at Soto, and we both raised our eyebrows. Martinez put her arm around Angela's shoulder.

"*I'm so proud of you, mi'ja,*" she said.

Ironically, it was after this class period that Martinez pulled me aside and said that Angela was to be tested the following day for learning disabilities. Ms. Palmer, the special education teacher who served as an aide in science class, had made the referral, suspecting that Angela may be what the district calls EMI (Educable but Mentally Impaired). I could understand why Palmer would have requested the testing; from her point of view, Angela certainly must have seemed "impaired." Just that week in science, Angela and I had struggled to complete worksheets requiring students to fit certain animals (bullfrog, flounder, honeybee, and so on) into categories, matching the animals with various characteristics. As I had learned from our game in ESL, Angela had no inherent inability to match corresponding items, but this particular exercise presented several problems. Most obvious, Angela couldn't read the assignment. In this regard I was less helpful than I would have liked, for I had no idea how to say "flounder" in Spanish, and the term wasn't in my pocket dictionary. Also, Angela didn't have the background knowledge needed to answer many of the questions. She did not, for instance, know that honeybees have six legs. Still, I found it disturbing that while no one seemed willing to spend much time or money to help Angela in her content-area classes, the school was prepared to pay $550 for a test that would essentially have gotten Angela out of her teachers' way. I wondered out loud to Martinez who would really benefit if the test determined that Angela was unfit to participate in mainstream classes; I wondered whether this was just another way for people to consider teaching Angela and say, "It's not my job." Martinez shrugged.

"*Sure it is,*" she said.

The plan to remove Angela from her regular content-area classes is consistent with a larger trend of placing ethnic minority students in special education programs rather than in bilingual courses that are responsive to their real needs and abilities. Nationally, in 1987, 4.4 million public school children, constituting about 11 percent of the school population, were in special education. Mercer (1973) first directed widespread attention to the disproportionate number of minority students in these programs when she found three times more Mexican American students in self-contained classrooms for mildly mentally retarded students than would be expected based on their numbers in the general population of the community she studied. Robert Rueda (1991) argues that much of the cause of minority students' overrepresentation in special education can be traced to federal legislation that in 1975 guaranteed free, appropriate education for all "handicapped" students without regard to degree of impairment. Rueda explains that one of the results of this legislation has been that most students served by the special education system do not fit the traditional stereotype of the more impaired student but are primarily characterized by low academic achievement (p. 255). Because of these revised criteria, and because ethnic and language-minority students generally do not do as well in school as do their White counterparts, minority students end up in special education programs with disproportionate frequency.

Although broadening eligibility requirements for special education represents an opportunity for students challenged with genuine learning disabilities, equating low academic achievement with the need for special education risks mistaking unresponsive teaching practices for minority students' alleged deficiencies. Finn (1984) made precisely this point when he found not only that minority students were overrepresented in classes for the mentally retarded and the emotionally disturbed but also that the highest disproportions occurred in schools where bilingual programs were either small or non-existent. Cummins, too, has argued (1984) that language-minority students' apparent learning handicaps are often "pedagogically induced" in that they arise as a result of low-level, decontextualized teaching divorced from students' cultural and linguistic frames of reference.

I don't believe that Palmer's request that Angela be tested for learning disabilities was motivated by ill will. To the contrary, Palmer is a credentialed, capable special education teacher who is well liked by most of Addison's Latino students, several of whom told me that she often provided them with encouragement and extra help in their classes. Given the fact that no bilingual assistance (except what modest help I could offer) was available to Angela in her non-ESL classes, Palmer's recommendation may be read as an attempt to have Angela placed in a small setting where she could at least receive more individualized attention than she could ever hope to get in a room with thirty other students. Angela was failing almost all her classes, and Palmer was pursuing what she saw as the only recourse available. Regardless of Palmer's intention, however, the possibility that Angela would soon spend most of her school day in a special education class-room was troubling for several reasons. First and foremost, Angela didn't want to be removed from her regular classes. Despite her lack of English fluency, she told me, "*I have some new friends in my classes. They speak Spanish and they help me sometimes.*" Indeed, in an environment where she was unable to speak with most of her classmates, these important social connections would be jeopardized if she were isolated in a special education group that was self-contained for most of the day. Palmer's recommendation was also disconcerting in that it represented a serious misrepresentation of Angela's academic abilities. From what Angela had told me about her success in Mexican schools and from what I had observed of her work in ESL class, she had demonstrated that she is a bright and hardworking student. Though it seems almost too obvious to say so, Angela's problem was not one of intelligence or motivation, but that she didn't understand English and had not been in school consistently for several years. Martinez put it well, I thought, when she said of Angela, "That girl's no more learning disabled than I am." To be sure, for some students Addison's special education classes offered a valuable alternative to the school's standard curriculum and teaching methods, but the program's instructors, who were not trained in bilingual education or able to speak Spanish, could not provide the kind of help that Angela needed. Finally, the more I thought of Palmer's suspicion that Angela was "EMI," the more troubled I became with what seemed to be the tendency to associate a lack of English fluency with a mental or emotional handicap. Rueda (1991) writes that educators often conflate these characteristics because "special education has been dominated by a paradigm that concentrates on within-child dysfunction to the exclusion of cultural and linguistic factors. . . . This model, which has its roots in the medical treatment of severe and often organic disabilities, continues to exert its influence in spite of the fact that the population served now consists mainly of children with diverse cultural and linguistic backgrounds" (p. 265–266). As Rueda's words suggest, the history of special education makes it likely that minority students enrolled in these programs will be viewed not merely as linguistically and culturally different from their mainstream counterparts, but as inherently deficient. I worried that, if placed in a special education setting in which nonmainstream cultures and languages are viewed as a liability to be overcome or at least controlled, Angela would take on this label of deficiency, not just in others' eyes, but eventually in her own as well.

Though Martinez convinced Principal Dohm to postpone Angela's "EMI" testing indefinitely, the fact that it had even been arranged was, in my view, troubling. That worry, along with my concern that Angela was again in danger of failing nearly all her classes, finally gave me the nerve I needed to ask Angela's teachers to meet to discuss possible strategies for her success in school. And so I slid notes into faculty mailboxes, requesting that Angela's teachers gather after school in the office of Sra. Alvarez, the guidance counselor. Despite the snow drifting outside, the small room was cramped and warm. Present were Alvarez, Martinez, Ms. Bates, and Mr. Pearson, the computer teacher. Though I had delivered the notices a week before and had placed a reminder in each teacher's mailbox that morning, Angela's geography, science, and typing teachers had failed to show up. I leaned over and opened the window a crack, letting in a small stream of gray, late-winter wind, and pulled my feet farther under my chair to avoid bumping Pearson's briefcase.

As we waited a few extra minutes for the meeting to begin, Bates asked me what I knew concerning a disturbance earlier that day in her classroom. I told her I hadn't seen anything, that I had been busy helping Angela and Claudia with their notes, but the truth was that I had watched Darryl throw an ink pen that had sailed across the room and into the window with a loud smack. We gave up on the no-shows and decided to begin.

Before turning to the transcript of this meeting—an account that will reveal what I see as some of the misperceptions that Addison teachers brought to their work with native Spanish speakers—I feel compelled to preface it by stating that, in my view, this conversation suggests that the Addison High faculty members were not openly or consciously hostile to their LM students. I confess that in my discussions of Addison LM students' lack of equal educational opportunity, I have raised serious questions concerning the opinions and actions of several of these students' teachers. I don't apologize for that, and I will continue to do so when referring to the following transcript, for I think such ex-

amples need to be documented and disseminated in public forums as the first step of positive change. At the same time, I hope
my comments will not be read as an attempt to vilify the people
in this story. Though we will see that teachers like Bates and
Pearson may be operating from assumptions that have been re-
futed by research or that are contrary to some of my opinions,
this transcript suggests what I have learned from several conversations with teachers on other occasions: there is reason to believe they are people who, as Karen Akers put it, "are trying to
do right by these kids."

The conversation at the teachers' meeting highlights a large
number of issues related to the education of LM students, several
of which I have already raised, and far more than can be discussed here in detail. Therefore, rather than attempting a line-
by-line analysis, I have included only parts of the discussion in
the body of this chapter. However, because this meeting offers
rich and representative examples of the assumptions made by
many teachers at Addison, and because such conversations are
open to multiple readings, I have included the complete transcript in the Appendix. In my analysis here, the numbers appearing in parentheses correspond to line numbers in the complete
transcript. This analysis will focus on sections of the transcript
that are particularly relevant to the present discussion: namely,
those that illustrate assumptions or attitudes that cause teachers
to transfer responsibility for their language-minority students to
someone else. In other words, I will show that although these
teachers are not lacking in concern, even compassion, for their
LM students, their comments provide clues as to why members
of Addison's faculty sometimes say in regard to teaching these
students, "It's not my job."

ALVAREZ: Maybe we should hear from each of you as to where
            you think she's at and also from Ms. Martinez in
            terms of her reading ability. You've tested her and
            you have an idea about where she is and maybe start
            from that point and see what we can do to help her.
            We just heard from Mrs. Schaffer [Angela's typing
            teacher, to whom Martinez had spoken earlier in the
            day], and she said that she was doing a whole lot
            better this semester; she's really opened up, she's

really trying harder, and she doesn't seem to think that there will be a problem with second semester.

PEARSON: So she was here first semester?

ALVAREZ: Yeah.

BATES: I think she understands a lot.

MARTINEZ: Well, yeah, but I don't think she reads much, though. She doesn't understand that much—enough to get by but a lot of it will just go right over her head. She'll pick out a word here or there but then she doesn't really understand what's it's about. Like, I talk in English to her as much as possible. You know, like, "What did you do last night?" and a lot of the time she really can't understand.

TODD: Yeah, and I know from personal experience in trying to learn Spanish that that's a very dangerous thing to do because you can generally figure out what the conversation is about, but it's very easy—because you don't want to feel stupid—to make the next step and assume you're following the conversation when you're really not. I remember times when I thought I knew what was going on and it turned out I had barely a clue.

ALVAREZ: [To Martinez] Do you know how much education she had prior to coming here?

MARTINEZ: She went to the sixth grade. In Mexico, that was as far as she got. And then when she came here they put her in the ninth grade. But I guess she had to pay in Mexico and couldn't afford it.

ALVAREZ: And she's living with . . .

MARTINEZ: Her mother and step-father. And two older brothers and an older girl.

PEARSON: And it's all Spanish?

MARTINEZ: And it's all Spanish. I try to get her to watch some television to practice her English in some way, but her mother does not speak any English and her father a little bit. Her brothers, too, just a bit.

PEARSON: That's two strikes right there on us.

MARTINEZ: Also, she does not socialize other than church, and that's all Spanish. She goes to the Spanish church, and all Spanish functions.

BATES: Okay, well then what *can* we do for her? She doesn't go to the movies; she doesn't hang out with friends.

PEARSON: If I was going to go to Mexico, going to try and be submerged, I think that I would learn the language. But if she's coming here with no intention of being immersed in English, it's like we're beating our head against the wall.

Predictably, among the teachers' major concerns is Angela's limited English proficiency. Though no one goes so far as to deny overtly that Angela faces at least some sort of language barrier, Bates claims that Angela understands "a lot" of English (11), a notion which—when Martinez mentions that Angela had passed driver's education with the help of an interpreter—Bates later repeats: "If she can pass driver's ed. she's capable. We have a lot of kids who can't pass the driver's ed" (84). Bates's comments contain, I think, an implied accusation that Angela was deliberately misleading her teachers into thinking she didn't understand English so she could get by without doing her work. As I noted earlier, this suspicion was common among the Addison High faculty.

As Martinez and I caution, however, one should not confuse recognizing fragments of a conversation with a thorough understanding of its concepts or details (12–24). Indeed, Karen Akers had confirmed that suspicions like those articulated by Bates were partly the result of ignorance among the Addison High faculty of the difficulties of second-language acquisition: "People really have a misconception of how long it takes to learn a language; they want it to happen within six months. I had a call from a neighboring district a couple of weeks ago. A kid had been here a year, and the woman on the phone was all upset because he'd been here a year and wasn't at grade level. Here you have this eight-year-old kid sitting in the class, and they think he's going to learn English just because you tell them to. Stuff like that just makes me laugh."

As Akers's comments suggest, a comprehensive strategy for accommodating LM students would need to ensure that these students receive native-language instruction until such time as they are able to prosper in English-only classrooms. However, as

I mentioned in my discussion of Rosa, research indicates that educators tend to underestimate the amount of time it takes LM students to achieve the fluency they need in second-language classrooms (Cummins, 1981), and that educators mistake LM students' general word recognition in talking and listening for an ability to process these words in new and written contexts (Ammon, 1987). Unaware of studies on language acquisition, and suspicious that LM students often conceal English fluency, some Addison teachers seem to view an unwillingness to accommodate second-language learners not as neglecting their professional obligations, but as showing the good sense to avoid being duped by lazy students.

Even if Angela's teachers had appreciated the time required to learn a new language, their comments suggest that they still would have denied that the school bears a responsibility for (or an interest in) helping students through this process. By arguing that the Spanish spoken in Angela's home constitutes "two strikes" against the staff (35) and that unless Angela intends to learn English, her teachers are "beating [their] head[s] against the wall" (42–44), Pearson makes clear his belief that it is families, not teachers, who must accept the primary onus of teaching students the school's dominant language. Further, Pearson later expresses reservations concerning any sort of ESL instruction at Addison High that might hinder Angela's assimilation to the local environment. For when Martinez points out that Angela was able to pass driver's education course only with Soto's translating for her, Pearson asks, "Aren't we validating the wrong response by you being there all the time?" (86). According to Pearson's logic, if it is desirable that Angela learn English, and if one learns English by practice, then Angela would be best served by being immersed in an English-only environment. Pearson's urgency that Angela learn English as soon as possible reflects what Moll (1992) has noted as a trend among monolingual teachers of LM students, and that is to place English acquisition as the highest priority in the schooling of such children, often at the expense of granting sufficient attention to other learning goals. In this view, it would seem that if a teacher had any responsibility at all to LM students, it would be to ensure that they hear nothing but English.

But if Angela's teachers misjudged her English proficiency and suggested questionable measures to improve it, Bates provides evidence that teachers have also overestimated Angela's preparation in content-area classes. As we have seen from previous anecdotes, the supposedly "universal language" of mathematics had not erased Angela's difficulties in Bates's class. Many hours of observation had shown me that Bates is, generally speaking, a good teacher. Her explanations are straightforward, her expectations fair. Nonetheless, my experiences working one-on-one with Angela suggested that Bates had, as indicated in the following comment from the meeting, misjudged Angela's abilities to meet the requirements in Trans Math (45–55):

> I tested [Angela] when she first came—just her math skills. Because the Transition [Math] book we use was written for the average seventh grader, which would, if she quit in sixth grade, be right where she belongs. But she came in second semester last year, so was at a disadvantage then, which was to be expected. And I couldn't communicate at all with her; she's talked to me a little bit this year, and she's got a few things down. She has the basic skills; that's all you're supposed to need to know: whole numbers, addition, subtraction, multiplication, and division, and if she needs to she can use a calculator. She knows how to run the calculator, not a lot but enough to get by. So she should be able to get by in Transition Math.

I concur with Bates that Angela is capable of basic calculations like addition and division. The problem, however, is that while Bates's textbook does begin with these fundamental skills, it remains at that level for only a few chapters before it advances to much more difficult concepts and procedures. While the final step of more complex problems may have required only a simple calculation, the reasoning needed to get to that final step was often something for which Angela had not been prepared by her previous schooling. Bates, did, of course, offer these explanations to the class, but she did so in a language Angela did not understand. Yet another difficulty for Angela in that particular class was that the textbook was part of a series designed specifically to be more language-centered than most math books. That is, it relied heavily on lengthy written explanations, definitions, and story-problems. While this strategy was supposed to have made the text more "user-friendly," it did so only for students who read English, which, as we know, Angela (and Claudia) did not.

As the teachers' meeting progressed, other suggestions were made that I believe serve as further examples of teachers' misunderstandings of the needs of LM students. In what may be called a "creative" attempt to discover a way to help Angela earn passing grades, Pearson suggests that she take the same class twice in one day: "I'm just wondering with some of these academic classes whether she could take them twice. Take two sessions of it" (172–173). While I admire Pearson's advocating an unorthodox revision of Addison's scheduling policies, mere repetition, as Martinez quickly points out, will not lead to understanding: "No, if she didn't understand it the first time, she's not going to understand it the second time unless somebody's there to translate for her" (177–179). Moreover, to suggest that Angela remain in English-only content-area classes echoes Pearson's earlier comments that he's wary of the whole concept of bilingual instruction. Pearson's ensuing suggestion is that Angela be considered as a candidate for the "study skills class" (188)—an option Martinez dismisses as inappropriate because the class is "for special ed. kids, and [Angela's] not special ed" (189). As I've observed, in these classes the teachers are very attentive in assigning work according to students' specific abilities and in tailoring instruction to accommodate particular needs. Still, all of this instruction is offered in English. While again I give Pearson credit for at least offering options, the notion of moving Angela to the special education class suggests once again that content-area teachers sometimes divert rather than accept the responsibility of having LM students in their classrooms. Further, Pearson's describing Angela's lack of English fluency as a "pretty serious disability" (192) tends to absolve the school of its obligation by implying that Angela is somehow mentally or developmentally "defective." In reality, however, Angela's inability to speak English does not represent a cognitive deficiency any more than Pearson could be called "learning disabled" because he doesn't speak Spanish.

Though the content-area teachers seemed unable to help Angela, Martinez suggests that it may be possible for help to come from using a "buddy system" (195). This option made a great deal of sense to me; Addison High has dozens of fully bilingual students, and in the absence of the district's financial support of a more comprehensive bilingual program, peer tutoring might have provided a low-cost means of offering Angela consistent and coordinated attention both academically and socially (Fern et al., 1997; Lucas, 1996). Bates, however, was skeptical: "We tried that last year, and it really didn't work" (196).

Bates's reference was to Angela's first-semester science class, in which she had been tutored by Sara, a Chicana student fluent in both English and Spanish. According to this arrangement, which Olivia Valenzuela made after Angela had come crying into her room after some geography classmates had made fun of her, Sara was to have accompanied Angela to science class and, in Sara's words, "translate to her and help her do her homework and stuff." As Alvarez points out, however, Sara "decided she didn't want to do it anymore" (111–112), and I discovered in an interview that she had reached this decision for some very good reasons.

Among Sara's concerns was that, because she had never taken that particular science class, she was unprepared to teach Angela the material: "The part that was okay was just translating to her, but I never took that class before and I didn't know what they're talking about myself and then I had to teach her." Though Sara told me she would have liked to review lessons with the teacher as a way to prepare for her tutoring, their schedules did not permit her to do so. Sara also spoke of her frustration with not having had time to complete the assignments. In what sounded very much like the pattern I had fallen into, she described finding definitions or answering questions herself, thus leaving Angela with only the "work" of copying words she didn't understand onto a page. According to Sara, "[Angela] doesn't have anyone at home to help her, so sometimes just to get stuff done I was just doing all the work for her."

Sara's principal complaint, however, was that once she committed to helping Angela, the science teacher and her aide had insisted that she tutor a Lebanese LM student as well. As Sara put it, "The main thing I didn't like was that there was another girl in there, and she sat right next to Angela and she didn't understand anything in English *or* Spanish. And they were trying to get me to help her, too. But I couldn't be helping two people. I was just there for Angela and that's it. And I was like, I can't help the other girl 'cause I can't speak her language. And that's when they got upset with me; they were having a fit." The situation Sara describes results from a small-scaled version of what Fillmore (1992) calls the "close enough" ploy, in which students who need tutoring in a native language are all placed in a room where the majority speak Spanish. The result is that the teacher—as Sara did when she had to tutor both Angela and the Lebanese student at once—reverts to the "common" language: English (p. 372).

Based on her experience with Angela, Sara said that in order for such tutoring to genuinely benefit LM students, several things would have to change. Her first recommendation was one offered by many other experienced teachers of LM students: "They should have teachers in a special room to help her, teachers, like, who have reviewed that stuff and who speak Spanish so they can help her better until she learns English." In other words, Sara argues, Addison High should establish a program of transitional bilingual education. In the meantime, however, Sara saw potential in peer tutoring as long as the student-instructors were properly prepared for the teaching they were being asked to do. In Sara's view, that preparation would require "time . . . to review the book" and the chance to meet with classroom teachers in order to "figure out together" a strategy for teaching the LM students. Because these changes would require a sustained effort on the part of teachers to work collaboratively with student-tutors in ways that might conflict with the present school structure, scheduling priorities might have to be altered to provide student-tutors with a "preparation period" at a time when they can meet with cooperating teachers. Further, as a way of compensating tutors like Sara for their work, the school might have offered them academic credit or an hourly wage.

Fortunately, Sara doesn't view her semester with Angela as having been a total loss. "The good thing is at least I was there helping her and I know how she feels. And she probably feels weird, 'cause I remember what it was like when I was at another school and I didn't know anything." Sara understands that to be in a classroom where one does not know the language makes a person "feel weird," which I think can be taken to mean alienated, alone, incompetent. Nonetheless, Sara also seems to have learned that in order for individual compassion to benefit LM students, it must be accompanied by broader changes that enable such compassion to be channeled in ways that increase the likelihood of LM students' succeeding academically. Despite the problems Sara mentioned, I continue to believe that enlisting Addison's bilingual students as tutors could be an effective and economical way of assisting non-English-speakers. Chesterfield, Chesterfield, Hayes-Latimer, and Chavez (1983) provide evidence of the usefulness of such arrangements by reporting that, among the Spanish-speaking children they studied, interactions with peers in English-dominant classrooms were consistently related to increases in LM student performance (see also Harper & Platt, 1998). Given the potential of peer tutoring, I thought it unfortunate that those attending the teachers' meeting concurred with Bates and discounted such an arrangement as unworkable instead of discussing how it might be improved.

With the peer-tutoring option having been dismissed rather than reassessed, the conversation turned to the subject of trying to find content-area textbooks and other materials in Spanish. As the following section of the transcript suggests, several of Angela's teachers viewed this effort as the responsibility of someone other than the content-area instructor.

TODD: Is it possible to get that math book in Spanish?

BATES: When we had books from the other publisher, we had books in Spanish, but I don't know if this one's available in Spanish. I haven't seen anything to show that it is. This one was written in Chicago, so you'd think it would have a Spanish translation.

MARTINEZ: I'll ask the Chapter One people if we can get that in Spanish.[1]

PEARSON: You know that wouldn't be a bad idea just to order a half a dozen or so, or one of each of those texts if they're available. I don't know if it's available, but there's no harm in asking.

MARTINEZ: You know what else they have? They have a lot of these units on cassette.

TODD: Well, let's call these publishers and find out what they've got.

MARTINEZ: If I knew what they needed, if I could get a list from Mr. Morton, of what he's covering, like oceans, or whatever, I'd see what I could find.

TODD: Okay, Alice, but is that really your job to do that? It seems to me that it's not. It's your job to teach English.

BATES: Whose job is it?

PEARSON: Yeah, [to Martinez] your job is to teach them English as their second language, and that's why I say these sources in Spanish would be really helpful.

MARTINEZ: That's the job of the Chapter One people, to find out alternative methods to teach a student.

BATES: Yeah, not us. When I taught at the middle school, we had these Spanish textbooks, and the Chapter One people got them for us. I never got them.

PEARSON: Well, to tell you the truth, I haven't looked.

Ironically, though Martinez's willingness to locate these materials demonstrates her commitment to her ESL students (228–229), she is at the same time encouraging her colleagues not to consider themselves to be Angela's principal teachers. Moreover, when I wonder out loud whether searching for geography and math materials is among the duties of an ESL teacher, Bates (232) articulates more clearly than anyone the question I've been raising throughout this section: When we think of teaching LM students, whose job is it? The consensus at the meeting seems to be that teaching such students is the task of "the Chapter One people" (221, 236, 239).

In contrast to the teachers' assumption, Akers had made it very clear to me that "Chapter One" funding was intended as "something extra" for students with a wide variety of educational needs, not as the primary resource for LM students. Akers asserted, therefore, that teachers' reliance on Chapter One staff goes beyond what the program was intended to do. Her words go a long way toward summarizing what I am arguing about the tendency of Addison teachers to transfer responsibility for LM students from themselves to someone else:

We're here to be supportive, we've got resources; we've got knowledge; we're here to help teachers make sure that students can be successful where they are. But if a kid's lost his lunch money, that's not my deal. It's frustrating because some of them are very willing to write these kids off as "not my job." When a kid with a wheelchair or a learning disability comes in they think, "Well, that's tough," but they know that it's part of something they need to do. Or with a hearing-impaired kid, they put their machines out and that's kind of a nuisance but they accept it as part of their job. But there's something about a kid who doesn't speak English that people are really willing to say, "That's not my job. That's somebody else's job." If we can somehow transfer that ownership from this [Chapter One] office to the classroom of that student, we'll have accomplished something we've been working on for a long time.[2]

As Akers points out, a crucial step toward creating conditions that improve the likelihood of LM students' success is for content-area teachers to accept their own responsibility for these students' learning. Nieto (1994) echoes these sentiments, arguing that reforming school structures alone will not lead to substantive differences in student achievement unless such changes are accompanied by revisions in how individual educators think about what LM students deserve, what they are capable of achieving, and who is responsible for helping them realize their potential (p. 395). Furthermore, Lucas et al. (1990) have asserted that the most crucial element in Latino students' success in school is that the personal commitments of teachers, administrators, and counselors must come together in a shared belief that all students are able to learn and that all educators play an important role in this process. Emphasizing the importance of collective ownership of responsibility for Latino and LM students' achievement, Lucas and her colleagues note that in the successful schools they studied, "It appeared that all school staff took responsibility for teaching these students. No one expressed the attitude that one group of teachers would 'take care' of LM students and that the others need not worry about them" (p. 330).

Despite admonitions such as these, and despite and the consensus in the Addison teachers' meeting that it would be useful to have content-area materials in Spanish, in the days following the meeting it was I who ended up searching for these books.

After calling several publishers and learning that none of the texts used in Angela's classes were available in Spanish, I finally reached a sales representative who knew my dad and was willing to send me some free copies of science and geography textbooks that dealt with roughly the same material as was found in the Addison High curriculum. I made these calls during lunch period from the teachers' lounge. As I sat with the phone wedged between my cheek and shoulder, Ms. Daniels, Angela's science teacher, sat not ten feet away, eating a sandwich and a bag of Fritos. When I hung up the phone and told her that she should be receiving the Spanish-language text within the week, she smiled, popped a chip into her mouth, and gave me an encouraging "thumbs-up." Though I was glad to help, I hoped that in the future she might choose to make these calls herself.

Among the themes that I think emerge from the teachers' meeting is an affirmation of what I mentioned earlier about the general goodwill of those who agreed to attend. It's likely they had other things to do, and given the fact that it was only I who had extended the invitation, their presence was purely voluntary. At the same time, however, I also believe the meeting suggests that this goodwill was undermined by the teachers' sense of powerlessness, which made them feel unable to be significantly useful to Angela and their other LM students. In an ideal world, such students would have access to a comprehensive program of language development and content-area instruction. They would begin with classes that foster skills both in their native languages and in English, while also learning content-area material in their first language. Gradually, as students gained competency in English, they would be mainstreamed into English-dominant content-area classes with the support of bilingual staff, and this approach would continue until these students were able to participate successfully without native-language assistance (Fueyo, 1997; Harper & Platt, 1998). However, in the overwhelming majority of schools with LM students, these conditions do not exist, and so the responsibility for teaching such students must be taken on by content-area teachers (Fueyo, 1997). As we have seen, these teachers often struggle in their efforts to carefully monitor LM students' learning or to adapt instruction to meet their needs.

Juan Necochea and Zulmara Cline (1993) explain that in situations like these, content-area teachers frequently get drawn into a destructive cycle of self-fulfilling prophecy that is set in motion by the myth that only bilingual teachers can deal effectively with LM students. This myth causes content-area teachers to have low expectations for students and for themselves, which prevents teachers from seeking out and employing alternative strategies and creative approaches with LM students. These teacher behaviors, in turn, result in poor outcomes for LM students, and such outcomes then reinforce the initial myth that content-area teachers cannot teach LM students well (p. 405). As a rule, these teachers do not have competency in their LM students' language, and they do not have formal training in bilingual education. What they do have is approximately thirty other students in each classroom demanding and deserving their time and attention. As the cycle continues to turn, frustration cools to complacency, and neglect becomes commonplace.

What, then, is a citizen teacher to do? How are we to create conditions that promote equal educational opportunity for all students when our cultural, linguistic, and professional histories offer little support of our efforts to do so? To be sure, there are no simple answers to these complex questions, but partial responses do arise in the form of so-called "sheltered content teaching" and in "language-sensitive content teaching." Though similar, these approaches differ in that sheltered content teaching is designed for classes attended exclusively by LM students, while language-sensitive content teaching is considered especially appropriate for mainstream classrooms in which English-learners are mixed with native English-speaking peers (Faltis, 1994; Krashen, 1982). Despite this difference, in both approaches content-area teachers employ strategies aimed at making classroom discourse and instruction more readily comprehensible to LM students. Moreover, in both sheltered content teaching and language-sensitive content teaching, the focus of instruction is not English fluency but the development of skills and the understanding of content-area subject matter (Northcutt & Watson, 1986; Richard-Amato & Snow, 1992). Ideally, the curriculum of these approaches should not differ substantively from that which is taught in "regular" academic courses. Nonetheless, the central tenet of sheltered and language-sensitive content teaching is that the ways in which this curriculum is taught must be flexible and adaptive to a student's English language proficiency and prior educational experiences (Harper & Platt, 1998). As will soon be clear enough, many of the specific ideas associated with these approaches could well be—and often are—applied in the teaching of all students, including those who speak English fluently. However, given the special challenges that people like Angela face in school, the fundamental responsiveness of sheltered and language-sensitive content teaching is, in my view, an especially important feature that teachers such as those who gathered in the after-school meeting must bring to their work.

Though advocates of sheltered and language-sensitive content teaching recommend a wide range of particular classroom strategies and practices, they share the conviction that the effective application of these approaches depends upon teachers' having high expectations of their students (Dwyer, 1998; Harper & Platt, 1998; Henze & Lucas, 1993; Lucas et al., 1990; Moll, 1992). Teacher expectations have a powerful impact on student outcomes; when teachers make high expectations concrete and visible, students benefit from the motivation that comes with the belief that they can successfully accomplish the challenges teachers set before them, as well as those that students discover on their own. It is equally important, however, that teachers have high expectations of themselves. As Necochea & Cline (1993) have noted, "It is likely that the instruction of LM students would be greatly improved if the message sent to monolingual teachers was 'you can do it'" (p. 407). Still, we have seen that it's perilously easy for content-area instructors to succumb to the notion that they can do little to help LM students learn. But teachers must resist this notion. They must be unwilling to accept the apparent inevitability of LM students' failure. From such a defiant perspective, the fact that Rosa and Angela did not pass all or most of their classes at Addison High would be neither acceptable nor immutable. As is the case with LM students, high expectations stir in content-area teachers the motivation they need to learn about and creatively employ those strategies that contribute to LM students' (and their own) success.

Among the ways of conveying these high expectations to LM students is to make clear to them that who they are, and the culture that has shaped their ways of thinking and living, are valuable. While English-speaking White students receive this message constantly through the dominant cultural norms that surround them, it takes a special effort on the part of teachers to send this message to LM students. Advocates of sheltered and language-sensitive content teaching point out that such a message can be strengthened and clarified by incorporating minority students' cultures into their learning and by elucidating the ways in which the skills and knowledge of course content might usefully be applied to their lives outside of school (Lara-Alecio & Parker, 1994). To accomplish this, content-area teachers might highlight examples and illustrations of important events or concepts that reflect LM students' cultures. Teachers might also encourage LM students to speak and write about their past and present experiences. Further, as a way of gaining access to the language and culture of LM students, sheltered and language-sensitive content teachers often refer to the importance of drawing from those "funds of knowledge" which become available when teachers acknowledge the value of using parents and community members as resources in LM students' learning (Fueyo, 1997; Pérez & Guzmán-Torres, 1996). As Gersten (1998) contends, such culturally sensitive teaching strategies not only have directly positive effects on LM students' learning, but they also help break down barriers that often exist between White middle-class teachers and working-class minority students, thereby contributing to the integrity of each student's educational experience (p.22).

As important as it is to bring culturally relevant information to the teaching of LM students, it is also important that teachers take great care in choosing forms of verbal discourse that convey this and other information effectively and that encourage their LM students to use it in critical and complex ways. Verplaetse (1998) found that the monolingual English-speaking teachers she studied were not always successful in this regard, as they unwittingly limited LM students' opportunities to interact verbally in the classroom. Specifically, she found that the teachers issued more directives to and asked proportionately fewer questions of their ESL students than of their students who were proficient in English. She also found that teachers used more high-level cognitive questions with fluent English speakers than with LM students. This discrepancy not only reduced LM students' opportunities for verbal interaction but also hindered their comprehension of content-area material. Verplaetse notes that in resisting this trend, it was crucial that teachers deliberately allow more time for LM students to gather their thoughts and speak during teacher/student interactions. With training and conscious effort, Verplaetse argues, "teachers can adjust their internal clocks to allow for a longer wait time and consequently give LM students more opportunities to respond" (p. 28).

Another verbal strategy that has been found useful for content-area teachers with LM students is what researchers call "modified language input," which basically means adapting spoken language so that it's easier for LM students to understand (Faltis, 1993; Krashen, 1982). Jiménez, Gersten, and Rivera (1996), for instance, identified several discursive options that facilitate content-area teachers' communication with their LM students and arranged these options into three categories: pronunciation (e.g., slower pronunciation, clearer articulations, longer pauses); vocabulary (e.g., using key words frequently, using fewer pronouns, using gestures and visual media to accompany words); and grammar (e.g., using shorter, simpler sentences, using repetition and rephrasing). Affirming at least one of Jiménez's recommendations, Gersten (1998) found that teachers who worked effectively with LM students often used "evocative words" as an explicit focus of their lessons. That is, these teachers selected and used repeatedly a few words that were especially important to the lesson they were conducting. Where appropriate (and discretely, to avoid embarrassing their students), these teachers also used below-grade materials and writing assignments to augment understanding of these concepts. Additionally, using so-called "lesson markers"—verbal cues the teacher uses to let students know where they are in the lesson—has been found to be an effective strategy for increasing comprehensible input for LM students during instruction (Faltis, 1994; Fillmore, 1985). These lesson markers are beneficial in that they provide students with useful information concerning what is expected of them in each phase of the lesson. At the start of instruction, for example, the signal might be "Let's begin," and at the end, "That is all," or "Please put your books away" (Fueyo, 1997, p. 23). I think it's only being honest to concede here that measures such as signaling lesson routines and transitions, repeating key words, or simply speaking more slowly may, in isolation, seem inadequate to the challenge of helping LM students understand what their teachers are saying. Nonetheless, when used collectively and consistently, these strategies have been shown to improve LM students' ability to use what little English they may know to better follow along and participate in content-area classes.

Even if teachers alter the ways they speak with their LM students, however, advocates of sheltered and language-sensitive content teaching point out that teachers who normally depend heavily on oral and written language to convey information to students may need to build into their instruction more diverse, visually oriented media (Faltis, 1993; Henze & Lucas, 1993). Depending on the content area, these media may include books with pictures, magazines, overhead projectors, or movies and videos. As I recall a specific lesson in an Addison High literature class that was especially difficult for Angela, I believe she would have learned a great deal more about life in Elizabethan England from a filmstrip or video than from merely reading an article or book chapter about it. If I may continue indulging my disciplinary bias for a moment, other possibilities for using visual media in language arts classes include showing "comic book" or film versions of stories and novels, or presenting students with maps of narrative settings and posters that convey a literary work's principle themes. Visual media may also be incorporated into assignments for LM students. Again, speaking specifically of language arts classes, such projects might include drawing story lines or pictures of characters, acting out scenes of a play, or illustrating the dominant images of a poem. To most language arts teachers, these and similar methods are not new, and many others can be found in places like the "Teacher to Teacher" section of *English Journal* and in methods texts like Tchudi and Mitchell's *Exploring and Teaching the English Language Arts* (1999) and Wilhelm's *You Gotta BE the Book* (1997). But whatever their source or however they are adapted for LM students, teaching practices that make use of visual media are based on the sound premise that LM students are more likely to understand a concept or narrative embedded in a visual context than one for which they have to rely on a text alone (Henze & Lucas, 1993).

In addition to these specific strategies for supporting LM student instruction, practitioners of sheltered and language-sensitive content teaching emphasize the more general point that for LM students to acquire and improve their skills and knowledge both in English and in content-area class material, they must have diverse opportunities to use these skills and apply this knowledge interactively in all phases of their learning. Such opportunities have been found to arise most often in classrooms where LM students are allowed to work actively and cooperatively with others. As Arreaga-Mayer and Perdomo-Rivera (1996) argue, "Emphasis on whole class or individual seat work limits LM students' opportunities to talk, read aloud, ask or answer questions, and practice their expressive language, all behaviors associated with high language acquisition and academic gains" (p. 252). Thus, in contrast with more individualized modes of instruction, small group activities tend to create opportunities for language use in which LM students are more likely to participate, without competing with the whole class or feeling inadequate or embarrassed by their lack of English fluency (Fueyo, 1997, p. 22). In order to encourage high levels of LM student participation, content-area teachers are encouraged to create a physical environment in the classroom that is conducive to active and cooperative learning processes. This may be done, for instance, by arranging furniture in a way that facilitates collaboration and by establishing learning centers or small-group discussion areas (Fern et al., 1997). Within such a setting, content-area teachers are likely to find it easier to introduce cooperative learning strategies such as group projects, the use of dialog journals, open-notes quizzes, and peer tutoring—all of which have been shown to be especially beneficial to LM students (Arreaga-Mayer and Perdomo-Rivera, 1996; Fern et al., 1997; Fueyo, 1997). Of course, even if teachers work hard to encourage collaboration in these and other ways, there is no guarantee that LM students will not engage in what Brozo (1990) calls "hiding out"—withdrawing from activities, avoiding contact with teachers and peers. Still, efforts to encourage collaboration are nonetheless important, for in settings where students are working together and assisting each other, it is a lot harder for LM students to resist participation in mainstream activities than it is in classrooms where students spend most of their time either listening to the teacher or sitting alone at their desks. Further, in addition to promoting the development of LM students' language skills and content-area knowledge, active and cooperative learning provides a forum in which LM students can simultaneously develop social skills and relationships that are especially important to the democratic priorities of citizen teachers. As Henze and Lucas (1993) point out, if students "are not sitting passively in their seats but are actively involved in seeking information through group and collaborative projects, they must develop skills in solving problems jointly, taking various roles within a group, and negotiating differences" (p. 61).

While sheltered and language-sensitive content teachers offer many instructional strategies such as those I've been describing, these teachers also recommend forms of assessment that have been found to be particularly appropriate for LM students. In general, such forms of assessment are performance-based, aligned with the instructional practices and goals of active learning, and useful in distinguishing between students' language abilities and their understanding of subject matter (Lessow-Hurley, 1996). Tippens and Dana (1992), for instance, have recommended five alternative assessment strategies for use with LM students: (a) concept mapping, in which students identify and write about major concepts and ideas and then explain relationships among them; (b) cooperative learning and group assessment, in which students work with one another to earn their grade; (c) journaling, in which students connect information learned with their own experiences; (d) oral interviews, in which students demonstrate their individual learning through discussions with teachers or peers; and (e) portfolios, in which students collect evidence of their learning and which allow students to present work in their native language or in ways that are not exclusively language bound, such as photographs and videos. Clearly, some of these methods are more effective with students who know at least some English, or they may require the assistance of an ESL colleague or a student fluent in both English and the LM student's first language. But by experimenting with a variety of assessment measures, content-area teachers increase the likelihood that they will gain valuable information about what LM students have learned about course content. This knowledge, in turn, may be applied to the development of strategies for further instruction (Fern et al., 1997).

In the preceding paragraphs, I have offered only a brief sketch of the many options available to content-area teachers who seek to improve the ways they teach their LM students and assess their work. As the meeting with Angela's teachers illustrates, however, educators are often unaware that such strategies even exist, never having encountered them in their initial training or in the course of their careers. In order to help content-area teachers learn more about what they can do to be responsive and useful to their LM students, practitioners and researchers of sheltered and language-sensitive content teaching stress the importance of professional development and collaboration. As Necochea and Cline (1993) point out, this development might take place in workshops that present to teachers a basic knowledge of second-language acquisition and cross-cultural communication, as well as specific models of best practices for serving LM students. However, mere exposure to such information is not enough; rather, content-area teachers must be supported by ongoing staff development and by sustained "team-based" collaboration with their colleagues (Milk, Mercado, and Sapiens, 1992). Margaret Dwyer (1998) has found that one particularly effective form of such collaboration is what she calls the "coaching model," in which teachers with special skills or training in assisting LM students are assigned to work as mentors with content-area teachers. Other "team-based" options include fostering efforts by ESL and content-area teachers to work together to find ways of successfully integrating LM students into mainstream classes, as well as enlisting the support of administrators to provide teachers with regular forums to share useful information and strategies.

Beyond these potential benefits of content-area teacher collaboration, I also think that when teachers make a sustained effort to support each other and share information, they are more likely to exercise the kind of flexibility that is needed to respond to LM students' needs. In several of my conversations with Addison's content-area teachers, among the reasons they cited to explain their reluctance to alter their teaching and assessment for students like Angela was the fact that they were concerned about deviating from what was being done in other sections of the same course or from what was generally expected by "the department." While I appreciate this as a legitimate and collegial sentiment, my sense is that if these teachers had been working closely together, they would have felt more inclined to accept the kinds of "risk-taking" and the "greater tolerance for mistakes" that Necochea and Cline (1993) tell us are essential in designing a wider repertoire of effective practices with LM students (p. 409).

Taken together and adjusted for specific settings and students, the strategies common to sheltered and language-sensitive teaching are means of empowering monolingual content-area teachers to make significant progress in their teaching of LM students. Applying these strategies doesn't require teachers to radically revise their classroom practices at the expense of English-fluent students, nor does it require a huge financial investment. What it does require, however, is a commitment by individual teachers to translate existing research findings and examples of best practices into activities and programs that have positive effects on the daily educational experiences of LM students. In other words, it requires content-area teachers to accept responsibility for their LM students' learning and to demonstrate this acceptance in the forms of agency they enact through the work they do. Or, to put it in yet another way, meeting the challenge of teaching LM students well requires that teachers exercise the "individuality" that, as we have seen, Dewey (1916/1985) insists is the source of the "redirection or reconstruction" of accepted beliefs and practices. This creativity that characterizes individuality, this disregard for the conventional, affords people the flexibility they need to respond ethically and effectively to others in the ever-changing contexts of social relations, whether these contexts be at school or elsewhere. For Dewey (1929/1962) writes that it is impossible to exercise individuality "by an all-encompassing system or program." Rather, he tells us that the definite expression of individuality "is found in changing conditions and varied forms. The selective choice and use of conditions have to be continually made and remade. Since we live in a moving world and change with our interactions in it, every act produces a new perspective that demands a new exercise of preference" (167).

In sum, then, to develop and demonstrate one's individuality is to continually fashion something new, both in the external conditions of experience and in ourselves. For many teachers, to welcome and pursue such changes will be difficult, even threatening. But as Ruth Vinz (1997) has argued, "becoming as a teacher" demands that we "dis-position ourselves" in this way, that we learn to "unknow" what we think our experiences have taught us about teaching and to "not know" with any kind of permanence or certainty how best to negotiate those relationships that are constantly being formed and re-formed within the "alien, nonsensical, sometimes threatening, mostly unpredictable" contexts of classrooms (p. 139). For teachers to embrace and make use of this uncertainty is what Patti Lather (1998) has called "a praxis of not being so sure," an "ontological stammering . . . oriented toward the as-yet-incompletely thinkable conditions and potential of given arrangements" (p. 495). As these teachers seem to know, the individuality Dewey (1926/1989) encourages in people "is not an original possession or gift." Rather, "it is something to be achieved, to be wrought out" (p. 61). This process of developing and exercising one's individuality, this acceptance of the necessity of change even though we cannot fully predict its outcome, affords teachers the creative space they need to respond imaginatively and flexibly to the unique needs of their LM students.

As I have been arguing, the conversation in Sra. Alvarez's office illustrates that when teachers ask, "Whose job is it to teach language-minority students?" too many educators at Addison High—and, I suspect, elsewhere—answer, "Not mine." Often, this denial of responsibility results from misunderstandings about what LM students know and what they need in order to learn more productively. At other times, it results from the balkanization that often develops when people encounter cultural and linguistic difference. But whatever the cause, as Valenzuela had recalled during our conversation, this denial of responsibility was evident even when she began her work at Addison High: "I felt like instead of saying 'I'm a partner with you to help this child,' [the teachers] saw me as an intruder and were not very cooperative. . . . And any time there was a Hispanic kid in trouble, they came to me. '*Your* kids, one of *your* kids,' they'd say. I remember telling the vice principal that not every Hispanic in this building is only *my* kid." When we assess some teachers' sense of their obligations to LM students, it seems that Valenzuela's reminder is as relevant today as it was over a decade ago. Nonetheless, because, as Dewey (1929/1962) tells us, individuality is "not originally given but is created under the influences of associated life" (p. 193), this form of human agency has the potential to revise structures that allow teachers to view LM students as someone else's responsibility, to erase the line between teachers' established notions of their work and those ideas which are sometimes dismissed as alien or different. Thus, individuality readjusts and expands the present, thereby opening possibilities for a new, more democratic future.

Fearing Angela: Ideology and the Politically Incorrect Man

In 1987, members of the Los Angeles teachers' union approved a referendum by more than three to one, calling for the school district to abandon bilingual education (Fillmore, 1992, p. 374). Though no such vote has ever been officially taken at Addison, I suspect that the results would be similar. I say this not because I believe that Addison teachers and administrators consciously seek to neglect their language-minority students; rather, due to vague laws governing bilingual education and teachers' tendency to "disown" their language-minority students, many at Addison High have been able to dismiss the notion that they are responsible for ensuring these students' equal access to educational opportunity.

But while we have noted examples of teachers' agency that result in situations like Angela's sitting uncomprehendingly through a science lecture, the mere act of making such observations does not explain why teachers decide to act as they do. Indeed, in order to understand the bases for these decisions, we must acknowledge once again that the structures within which people live wield a strong (though not absolute) influence over the decisions they make. In other words, we must look for societal influences upon the agency people choose (or are able) to effect, as does Fillmore (1992):

> Looked at objectively, bilingual education does not constitute a big change. It requires neither a radical reorganization nor restructuring of schools. It calls simply for the commonsense practice of teaching LM students at least part of the time in a language they understand. We know that teaching them exclusively in English—while they are still in the process of learning it as a second language—puts them at risk educationally. So why hasn't bilingual education been given a better reception in American schools? Why has it inspired so many acts of subversion? (p. 375)

Fillmore's answer—and I think she is right—is that bilingual education disturbs some "fundamental American prejudices" (p. 368). As Fillmore suggests, in order to reach a more complete understanding of the challenges facing Addison's LM students, we must recognize that the structures constraining them are not only material but also ideological. That is, the material structures we create—like schools—are constituted in part by ideologies that serve as a blueprint for how we construct our worlds. Put another way, ideologies are part of the structures enabling certain people to enjoy a great number of options in their lives while disempowering others. If we acknowledge that ideology is implicated in structures within which people make decisions, we may be better able to recognize the politically charged yet frequently overlooked assumptions and motives upon which those decisions are based. In the context of this chapter, to see the role ideology plays in the structure of Addison High is to enable us to explore how what Fillmore discusses as "fundamental American prejudices" lead some people to view bilingual education as a threat to "American values." In short, recognizing a social structure as ideologically charged helps us further understand *why* LM students are not a priority at Addison High.

In Addison, many of the teachers and administrators I spoke with exemplified those people whom Clara Rodríguez (1989) has described as seeing "a contradiction in arguing for cultural and linguistic retention as well as absorption of the English language and the American culture" (p. 143). Indeed, at Addison, it's not that teachers object to what Rodríguez calls "cultural and linguistic retention" as much as they argue that this retention should not occur at the cost of learning English and (the presumed equivalent) assimilating to a culture supposedly shared by all Americans. Thus, even though nearly all advocates of bilingual education affirm the importance of LM students' learning English, the connections between language and ideology lead some people in Addison to view bilingual education as encouraging ethnic separatism and thereby undermining our national unity. In this view, bilingual education is, quite literally, a threat to "America" as it is ideologically constructed: Angela, instead of being a young woman who doesn't understand her science lessons, becomes a separatist endangering the collective identity and security of the United States.

I first met the politically incorrect man shortly after my arrival at Addison. He had approached me and introduced himself, sympathetically relieving me of my initial lunchtime isolation in the teachers' lounge, where he usually sat at a round table with other male teachers critiquing everything from foreign policy to high school basketball referees. Sometimes as kind of a joke, a woman faculty member would invade the circle, but not very often. To me, as they finished their sandwiches and coffee, the round-table men always looked as though they were about to light up cigars.

Usually, spaces set aside for eating are a refuge for me, a kind of eye in my academic hurricane. By and by, though, the teachers' lounge had became a site of conflict, a place where I grew uncomfortable when some of the teachers made what I heard as reactionary comments on the few occasions when someone—usually Beth Reinstra—raised issues of diversifying the curriculum or altering classroom practices to better accommodate LM students. I made a point of not saying much, opting instead to jot things in my notebook.

One day the lounge conversation centered on an upcoming meeting of a so-called "multicultural committee" of faculty and administrators appointed by the assistant superintendent to explore ways in which the district might be more responsive to the

Addison community's ethnic and linguistic diversity. Reinstra, a committee member, invited me to attend, but euphemistically warned that I'd better plan on observing an "interesting, maybe even spirited" discussion. It was then that one of the teachers seated at the round table announced that he and a few of the other people on the committee were, in his words, the "extreme right," the "silent majority." Everyone listened as he spoke clearly from across the room: "We actually dare say things like, 'We should treat everybody equal' and 'If we implement all these multicultural programs, who's going to pay for them?'" He went on, looking directly at me (and I remember his words pretty accurately): "Oh, at Michigan they even have separate dorms for the Black kids and all sorts of other special privileges, and we already have them here. Imagine if we got on the intercom and announced a scholarship that was to be available only to White males." He went on a bit more, concluding with, "I guess you could say I'm politically incorrect."

I had read Dewey the night before, and I remembered how his definition of "equality" differed from that of the politically incorrect man. According to Dewey (1927/1988), "equality denotes the unhampered share which each individual member of the community has in the *consequences* of associated action" (p. 329). I bit my tongue; it wiggled free. I suggested that the point about equality was one that needed to be made because it raised interesting questions about what it meant to treat everyone equally—whether, by maintaining the status quo, we were being democratic in the Deweyan sense of creating circumstances in which all people could participate in those decisions that affected their lives. I added that not offering LM students instruction in their native languages maintained a very unequal system, and that the consequences of (not) acting to maintain the status quo at Addison High would be a decision that would affect LM Latino students and most of the White students in very different ways. The politically incorrect man gave me a suspicious look; for a second, I thought he was looking at my earring. Mercifully, the bell rang, and Reinstra and I left together. Out in the hall she looked at me, smiled, and shook her head. "Todd," she said, "you've got a gift for pissing people off, you know that?"

As it turned out, though, I hadn't pissed off the politically incorrect man (whom I will call Paul Jones) too much, and later in the hallway between class periods, he seemed eager to explain to me what he had said earlier in the teachers' lounge. Jones said that he had volunteered to serve on the multicultural committee because he feared that otherwise, "people with an agenda" would control the group and that a "small, vocal group claiming to represent the minority would push through proposals that were not necessarily in the best interests of the whole community." Jones pointed out that the Addison population is only 5 percent African American and 17 percent Latino, leaving the remaining 78 percent deserving, in Jones's words, "fair representation."

That day marked the beginning of an ongoing and friendly conversation between Jones and me. His hair flecked with gray, his shoulders stooped slightly forward, his head dipped as though he were afraid of hitting his head on the top of the doorway, Jones became one of the people I looked forward to seeing on my days in Addison. He would lean against a wall, arms folded, and tell me of his childhood in a small Northern Michigan mining town, his move to the southeast part of the state as a newlywed, and the struggles of trying to raise a family on a teacher's salary. I learned, too, that Jones was among the best teachers at Addison High and very popular among students of all ethnic backgrounds. I had seen him stopped in the hallway to be greeted by an African American student who slung his arm over Jones's shoulder and said, "Mr. Jones, 'sup?" On another occasion, a Latino student shook Jones's hand and patted his back, saying, "Hey, Mr. Jones, I saw you and your wife at the game last night. What'd you think?" A small sample of his students described him this way: "Oh, yeah, Mr. Jones. His tests are pretty hard, but he's cool." "He tells really funny stories." One boy known for his thick discipline file offered this critique: "Mr. Jones? He doesn't suck, I guess." Generally, I gathered from these and other students that they were impressed by Jones's energetic classroom demeanor, his clear use of (often amusing) anecdotes to illustrate points of his lectures, and his attentiveness to students' questions and comments.

I believe Paul Jones to be a gifted, hard-working teacher. However, despite Jones's general goodwill, in my view his stance

toward bilingual education contributes to policies that have ad-
verse consequences for students like Angela. Indeed, Jones's resistance to bilingual education is similar to that of most of his
Addison High colleagues, and it is for precisely this reason that
the lack of funds allocated to serving LM students may be more
accurately described as a symptom rather than as a cause of the
absence of bilingual education at Addison High. The point here
is not that Paul Jones isn't a "good person." I happen to think he
is. Rather, what's important is that Jones's views illustrate that
many people's suspicions of bilingual education are rooted in the
assumption that such programs threaten the values and therefore the well-being of our country as they are sustained by an
allegedly unified national identity. These fears became clear to
me during an early morning interview.

Jones sat behind his large desk; I scrunched into a student
seat, dribbling coffee that, fortunately, never reached my tape
recorder. Knowing that I was a consort of Latino students and an
advocate of bilingual education, Paul began with a disclaimer:

"You realize, don't you, that I'm conservative by nature." I
told him not to worry, that I was there to listen to his candid
views based on twenty-four years' experience on the Addison
High staff. I began by asking Jones to reflect on how he thought
the relationship between the school and Addison's Latino students had changed during that time. He thought for a moment,
then spoke:

"Regarding minorities," he said, "I remember a La Raza
movement back in the early and mid-seventies. That was pretty
strong in this area; it's similar in some ways to the more militant
Black movement today—the separatist push. It was a small but
vocal group. You gotta understand it was not the majority of
Latinos in this area, but a small but vocal group that wanted a
separate high school of Spanish-speaking students. Eventually
the thing kind of died out. Since then the Hispanic community in
this area has been fairly quiet. I'm not saying that there's no prejudice really on both sides, that there's not some people who are
prejudiced against Mexicans or there's not some Mexicans who
are more militant about things, but there hasn't been that kind of
pressure. Really, the Hispanic community has been fairly quiet
as a group."

Although I didn't mention it at the time, Jones's use of the word "militant" seemed a bit defensive, almost as though he were fending off an attack against something vitally important, even sacred, by the La Raza movement he claimed had initiated a "separatist push" within the school. So I asked Jones what exactly he meant when he had said that Addison students had been "militant," whether being assertive about their ethnic identities constituted "militancy." He looked at me and paused, folding his hands on the desk in front of him. His answer, though indirect, was very telling:

"Teddy Roosevelt once said that it's okay, in fact it's good, to be proud of your ethnic background, but he said, we've got to stop being hyphenated Americans. And I'm worried about the future of the country in the sense that I think it's good that we study other cultures; I wouldn't be a world history teacher if I didn't. Look around you." I did. Posters of Egypt, Africa, ancient China hung on the walls. Jones continued. "If I see somebody in the history books or I hear of somebody, I always make a point of pointing them out as a hero or somebody who has contributed to history. But at the same time I do think that the most important thing is that we're Americans, not that we're Spanish, not that we're Africans. Again, I think it's nice that we have some ethnic background to look back on, but at the same time, the fact that I'm of German ancestry, that and fifty cents gets me a cup of coffee. You see what I'm getting at?"

Jones leaned forward. I didn't say anything. "In other words, you *make* what you are based on your character, not on the fact of your ethnic background. So that's what I believe. And I don't like excuses being made, and I don't like racism; I don't like people who judge a person based on race. But at the same time I don't want people making excuses using race as an excuse not to succeed. And I see a lot of that. It definitely happens."

I decided to push him a bit.

"Can you talk about what kind of excuses you've heard?"

"I think we all have failures in life, every one of us has their failures, and again I don't want to say there isn't any racism because sometimes I do see it. There's no doubt that there are some Anglos who, for example, if a kid who has a Spanish surname dates a girl who's White that some parents will resent that. I don't deny that. But I've talked about this with my classes that you're going to face that in your lives, but sometimes those things are used as an excuse for every failure you have. Using race as an excuse—and I know it sounds racist, and I really don't mean it as a racist thing—it's enabling. Okay, you're going to face racism; that's a reality of life, until maybe some day we're so multicultural, we're so mixed up, that it doesn't make any difference. But you've got to succeed despite that. You've got to do what you can. And if you sit back and do nothing, you have nobody to blame but yourself. I don't have a great love for the Black Muslims, but I admire them for their beliefs that you've got to stand on your own two feet and do something—which is a very American thing, by the way."

Jones looked a bit tired, but he continued, telling me of his German ancestors who had immigrated to the United States in the early part of the twentieth century and forged a life out of the forests and copper mines of Michigan's upper peninsula. Essentially, he was presenting a familiar argument: namely, to use his words, "My family assimilated and succeeded; why can't people do the same today?"

As Jones finished making his point, I couldn't help thinking of Angela, with her sixth-grade education, and of Claudia, who could barely read or write. The challenges these girls faced required not only individual attention in school but also opportunities not available to these girls because of prejudices in the world outside of Addison High. I had my doubts whether, given the structures of their school and society, Angela and Claudia could (or would even want to) "succeed" by assimilating as Jones's family had done.

When I asked Jones whether he felt the school bore any responsibility to create circumstances that might increase the likelihood of language-minority students' success, he admitted that individual teachers should make some temporary accommodations for LM students, saying they should be allowed to work "under a pass/fail system until second semester." Jones added something I didn't doubt: "So, if students have trouble with the language, I try to be understanding and compassionate." I nodded in agreement, though I recalled that—with the recent exception of Angela in Pearson's computer class—I had never seen an Addison student on a pass/fail system.

Jones stressed, however, what he believed should be the school's primary responsibility and why it should be so: "Well, the school undoubtedly has got to have programs to help the kid learn English. But I will say this at the same time, I'm one person who would strongly be in favor of English being the national language. And I don't say that in a prejudiced way towards Spanish or French or any other language. But I think that if you look at other countries in the world, every country has to have a national language because if you don't you've got serious problems. Even Canada, which is a middle-class democracy, has a serious problem because of language-culture differences. Russia, of course, has terrible problems. India has terrible problems.

"So it is my firm belief that every country in the world needs a language which everybody understands and understands well. When you go to another country, it is your responsibility to learn the language and culture of that country. And I think it is the responsibility of a Hispanic person if they come to the United States and live in the United States to learn English and learn it well. Kids in particular. If you want a future for your children, the only way you're going to get ahead in this society is to speak English and speak it well. I'm not knocking Spanish, and it's nice to have a second language. My grandmother was German, and I wish I had learned German, but to learn German as the language of my ancestors or as a second language, not as my native tongue. So the school's responsibility—particularly in a community where you're going to have a fair number of Hispanics—is maybe to have a teacher to help those kids out in some way, whereby they learn English, or they learn to speak it well."

"Do you mean, then, an arrangement that Addison already has in place? Like the ESL class?"

"Right, that's the type of thing. But at the same time, they've got to try. If I take my kids and I move to Mexico, my kids are going to learn Spanish and learn it darn well to survive in their new society. And that society would expect them to, I might add. So if you come to the United States, don't feed me that line of, 'Well, I want to preserve my Mexican heritage, I want only to speak Spanish, I want to preserve the Mexican culture totally'; in other words, 'I want to make a little Mexico,' because it isn't. If you move here, that's the reality of life. And to survive in this society, if your kids want to do well in this society, they have to speak English; they have to learn the *common culture*—another phrase that I'm sure would get lots of groans in a classroom at the University of Michigan."

"Yeah, probably," I admitted.

"But I still happen to believe in that melting pot. I'm still one of those crazy, weird guys who happens to believe that even though the melting pot is only a theory, never actually happened, it's one of those ideas you strive for because if you don't strive for it, you're never even going to come close to it."

Jones was advancing an argument articulated and widely disseminated by E. D. Hirsch (1987) in his best-selling book *Cultural Literacy: What Every American Needs to Know* and, more recently, in *The Schools We Need and Why We Don't Have Them* (1996). *Cultural Literacy*, especially, though published over a decade ago, sets forth an argument that continues to play a major role in the public discourse concerning American education. As many readers familiar with this text know, Hirsch asserts that the surest way of breaking "the cycle of poverty" is to make students "culturally literate": that is, for schools to break free from what he claims is pedagogy based on Dewey's "content-neutral conception of educational development" in favor of teaching "specific, communally-shared information [by which] students can learn to participate in complex cooperative activities with members of their community" (p. xv).[3] Educators should draw this information, Hirsch contends, from a "national culture." While acknowledging that what gets included as part of our national culture is sometimes arbitrary, Hirsch argues that it is precisely this culture that defines what it means to be—in our case—Americans. A crucial part of preserving this national culture is maintaining a common language: "A nation's language can be regarded as a part of its culture, or conversely, its culture can be regarded as the totality of its language" (p. 83). To undermine our national culture by encouraging multilingualism, Hirsch (1987) claims, is to increase "cultural fragmentation, civil antagonism, illiteracy, and economic-technological ineffectualness." He continues:

Tolerance of diversity is at the root of society, but encouragement of multilingualism is contrary to our traditions and extremely unrealistic. Defenders of multilingualism should not assume that our Union has been preserved once and for all by the Civil War, and that we can afford to disdain the cultural and educational vigilance exercised by other modern nations. To think so complacently is to show a fundamental misunderstanding of the role of national literacy in creating and sustaining modern civilization. (pp. 93–94)

By raising the specter of civil war if we continue to divide ourselves with "multilingualism," Hirsch underscores his view that immigrants' failing to learn English erodes our national culture and, therefore, imperils American unity and security. It is worth repeating here that I and most other advocates of bilingual education do not deny that it is important for language-minority students to learn English. The problem, however, is that many people—Jones among them—see native-language instruction in content-area classes not as a way of helping LM students succeed in their new environments, but as a practice that keeps these students from learning English and, therefore, that contributes to destructive forms of multilingualism.

As I continued to listen to Jones talk, however, it became clear to me that his fears of national disunity could not be attributed to differences in ethnicity and language alone:

"Now, it's interesting, what's most important very often isn't race. I think very often in what we can maybe call the 'White community,' there's a lot of fear right now because of crime and violence and everything else, but part of the reason for the prejudice toward minorities is that they look on minorities as not having the same value system they have. If a Mexican kid, for example, a Mexican American kid comes into a neighborhood and he's from a typical—and again your University of Michigan classes would probably throw up at this—but your typical middle-class American family, whether it's Hispanic or whatever, I think those fears are quickly alleviated. But if they come from what is considered a lower socioeconomic class, it becomes a class thing rather than an ethnic thing. Then what happens is this White neighborhood, as an example, if they perceive a difference in a value system—the old middle-class Protestant work ethic type of attitude, you know, with your basic go-to-church-on-Sunday family—if they see a difference in that, and because Blacks and Hispanics tend to come from lower economic groups, then they perceive it as a threat, and you're going to find more prejudice. So when we talk racism, I almost think it's an economic thing more than it is simply an ethnic thing—an economic thing in the sense of a value system. I think there is a value system, a middle-class value system—and I think the fear of Blacks or Hispanics is more the fear of the destruction of the value system than it is a race thing."

"What are the bases of that value system?"

"Um, of course, it's never fulfilled even in the White community; it's I would say, the old Puritan, Protestant work ethic. I think that's part of it. Um, let me see . . . God, Mom, and apple pie stuff isn't too far off. It's an ideal, but I think it's the ideal people look at. It's the 1950s TV shows. You know the Nelson family?"

"Well, sort of . . ."

"That never really existed probably, but at the same time it's perceived as the way it should be."

It crossed my mind that Jones was certainly right that the ideal of the Nelson family "never really existed," especially when one recalls Ricky's real-life struggle with drug abuse. Beyond that, however, it seems that Jones was attempting to verbalize a value-laden definition of a "national culture" that Hirsch (1987) accomplishes more articulately, though not much more precisely:

> What is common to our broad culture? Besides the English and national legal codes, American culture possesses first of all a civil religion that underlies our civil ethos. Our civil ethos treasures patriotism and loyalty as high, though perhaps not ultimate, ideals and fosters the belief that the conduct of the nation is guided by a vaguely defined God. Our tradition places importance on carrying out the rites and ceremonies of our civil ethos and religion through the national flag, the national holidays, and the national anthem, and supports the morality of tolerance and benevolence, of the Golden Rule, and communal cooperation. We believe in altruism and self-help, in equality, freedom, truth-telling, and respect for the national law. (pp. 98–99)

Despite the ironies one can point to about the way Hirsch views bilingualism as a threat to the national culture's ideals of "tolerance and benevolence," I will admit that I, too, believe that it means something to be an American. Although I'm not sure just what my definition would be, I am quite sure that it would include the notion that allowing students to learn at least temporarily in a language they understand is complementary, not contrary, to the ideals Hirsch and Jones rightfully hold in such high esteem.

As the bell calling students to first period rang, Jones began shuffling papers on his desk and concluded. "Look, I'm not saying that there aren't teachers out there or there haven't been teachers who have tended to stereotype ethnic groups like Hispanics or Blacks, but I honestly don't know of any instance of a teacher in a classroom exhibiting racist behavior. Now I'm not saying the teachers are perfect or they're not prejudiced. But as far as putting a student down or purposely giving it to a student because of his race or ethnic background, in twenty-four years, I have never seen it. And I would condemn it totally."

Paul Jones had given me a lot to think about. While I was sympathetic to his emphasis on the responsibility of language-minority students to learn English, I was troubled that from his perspective he was able to deny the existence and effects of the structures of domination that make this seemingly reasonable expectation easier said than done. Cummins (1989) has written that "minority students can become empowered only through interactions with educators who have critically examined and, where necessary, challenged the educational (and social) structure within which they operate" (p. 6). Though Jones had clearly given considerable thought to his views concerning the acculturative effects of language and schooling, I was concerned that his thinking had not reached the level of "critical examination" as Cummins defines it. In my view, Jones had essentially ignored the social and ideological forces that influenced Angela's, Claudia's, and Rosa's lives and schooling but that went beyond the ability to speak or understand English.

But what intrigued me most about my conversation with Jones was his fear of living in a nation divided against itself. Jones believes that what preserves our national unity is a shared culture based on "the old middle-class Protestant work ethic" and "God, Mom, and apple pie stuff"—which I take to mean an ideological commitment to one's family and an acceptance of personal responsibility that are grounded in fundamental, even spiritual, sensibilities, as well as on the ideals of tolerance and freedom that Hirsch specifically mentions. Insofar as he believes that a common language is essential to preserving these values, Jones is among those whom Ovando (1990) has described as having been taken in by the mistaken perception that the traditionally rapid shift to English by immigrant groups has somehow mysteriously come to a halt in the late twentieth century and that a new set of linguistic, and consequently unpatriotic, loyalties is being promoted by Washington- and state-sponsored bilingual education (p. 347). Although many people have justifiably maligned the whole notion of a "national culture" because of the oppressive and homogenizing ways the concept has been used, I nonetheless will repeat that I think it means something to be an "American," and I think that that definition has a great deal to do with ideals like freedom and tolerance and equality of opportunity.

The problem, however, is the specific ways these values are pursued on the levels of individual decision making and public policy. I have said that Jones and I share many of the same values; I will add now that we both fear living in a divided nation. Where we part ways, though, is in the type of divisions we fear. Jones looks to the "terrible problems" experienced by countries like Russia and India and emphasizes that, although a one-semester ESL program would be acceptable, schools have a responsibility to preserve national unity by acclimating students to our national culture and language as soon as possible. Thus, Jones's reverence for "middle-class" ideology becomes the rationale for educational structures in which measures to accommodate the needs of LM students are reduced or abolished. By keeping Angela in a science class where she cannot read the textbook or understand the teacher, we are—so this reasoning goes—defending the United States of America.

In contrast, the division I fear is that which Jones himself alluded to when he mentioned that racial tensions are intimately tied to issues of "socioeconomic class." We live in a time when the distance between the rich and the poor is growing rapidly and when the burden of this discrepancy is falling disproportionately on minorities. Although schools are not entirely to blame for this situation, minority student dropout rates have been shown to contribute to these students' inability to escape poverty (Secada et al., 1998), and as I have pointed out, Latino students continue to leave schools in alarming numbers—at two and three times the rate of their African American and White counterparts. Walter Secada, the head of a national committee to investigate and recommend action concerning the high dropout rate among Latino students, has asserted in the popular press that "for the social ills associated with dropping out to fall disproportionately on any one group is a recipe for social and economic disaster that will make the Watts riots look like Disney World" (quoted in "Experts Call Education Gap National Threat," *USA Today*, pp. 1–2). Moreover, Miranda and Quiroz (1990) argue that reducing inequality between Latinos and the rest of society will not be a moral preference, but an economic imperative:

> Hispanics will constitute about one-third of overall labor force growth between [1989] and the end of the century, and a growing proportion of taxpayers supporting Social Security, Medicare, and other transfer payment systems needed to support an aging society. An untrained and underemployed labor force will not only retard direct economic output, but increase demand for public assistance and diminish the tax base necessary for the support of essential government services. Improving the Hispanic community's economic standing—and the human capital characteristics of individual Hispanics—clearly services the economic interests of the nation. (p. 28)

As these writers warn, we should fear separatism, but in my view, opposing a responsiveness to LM students' needs in the name of a shared commitment to "middle-class" values ironically creates circumstances where attaining the socioeconomic status needed to participate in that type of "American dream" is impossible for a great number of LM students. Paul Jones should, indeed, fear national divisions, but not the kind that are manifest in bilingual education programs, sheltered and language-sensitive content teaching, or our neighbors' speaking Spanish. Rather, what he should fear is the prospect of students—many of them from language- and ethnic-minority groups—being denied access to an education that may help them escape cycles of poverty and hopelessness. It is in this disenfranchisement—not in students' being taught in Spanish until they can understand English—that our national unity and the democratic values that sustain it are most seriously threatened.

Building Structures

Although I already knew as much, Karen Akers later confirmed to me that Paul Jones's reservations about bilingual education and the reasons behind them were common among the Addison High staff: "Certain people think that bilingual education means not learning English, means lack of loyalty to the United States, means cultural separatism, means the former Yugoslavia."

As I have attempted to show, these assumptions emanate from an ideology which holds that preserving our national unity, that being an "American," precludes retaining one's ethnic heritage or participating in programs like bilingual education—practices that some see as a threat to the notion that diverse peoples must unite to form a "common culture." I have also argued that such an ideology is part of a structure at Addison High that encourages agency in the form of some teachers' dismissing their obligations to their language-minority students, resulting in continued failure for people like Angela and Claudia and in the likelihood that these girls will eventually be among the thousands of Latinos who drop out of our nation's schools each year and for whom the "American dream" will remain unattainable. I continued to observe the harmful effects of these conditions each time I visited Addison High.

Not long after my conversation with Jones, Martinez informed me that Claudia had tested low enough on a special education test to be classified as learning disabled. She was to be placed in Addison's special education program, though she would still be attending ESL and her sixth-period physical education class. Martinez said she hoped that the special education classes, in which there were several Latino students, would be a positive move for Claudia socially and would encourage her to remain in school. Though clearly not pleased, Martinez tried to be optimistic, saying, "If she does well, she can go to the vocational training center next year."

Angela, meanwhile, knowing that she had no chance of passing math, had pretty much given up on the course, though she politely sat through class every day. In a way, however, her assurance of failure was liberating, for because she had nothing else to lose, we left the Trans Math book in her backpack and began working through the Spanish-language text I had received from my father's acquaintance about six weeks before. After looking through the explanations and examples, Angela read the first question out loud: "*In the number 3,265 what is the value of the numeral 2?*" Angela knew the answer. "*200,*" she said.

After class, I went to Bates and showed her the pages Angela and I had worked through. Bates reminded me that the Trans Math book was designed so that even if students didn't understand something in the earlier chapters, they should be able to do subsequent material. I, in turn, again reminded Bates that Angela needed help with even basic problems, especially division. "Well," Bates said, "she can use the calculator for that." I thought for a moment, then asked her to let me know next week what she wanted to accomplish with Angela the rest of the term. "It's a shame that you're only here two days a week," she said as I headed for the door.

"I'm just one person," I complained to Akers as we stood later that day in the crowded hallway, the privacy of our conversation secured by the din of students' voices and slamming locker doors. "Claudia's in special ed; Angela's failing math, geography, and science." I went on, saying that in my view, the school's lack of flexibility had put the two girls on a path straight out of Addison High, and I felt as though I couldn't do a thing about it.

Akers lowered her voice, so I held my tape recorder up near my shoulder. "I agree, we've got to do something," she said. "You remember Rosa? Of course you do. We had Rosa here however many semesters and getting zero credits, and so she drops out. Is that a big surprise to anyone?"

"It wasn't to me," I said. Before continuing, Akers glanced around.

"And does it make life easier for people, except for Rosa?" I didn't say anything, so Akers answered her own question. "Sure. So who's gonna fight that?"

Despite the implied answer to her question, what Akers said next articulated not only her optimism but also her understanding of the connection between Addison High's structure as an institution and the individuals that make up that institution: "If you're looking at this place as a system, it looks as though the school is saying, 'Well, now we don't have to worry about that.' I don't think people are that cold-hearted, so if we can get at those individual teachers, and we get enough of them, then progress becomes systemic. I think it's all interrelated. There are a few people at this school who really support those kids; you know, you work with them. So there is this little piece, and as that piece grows to be two people and so on, the system begins to change."

As I made my way to the next class, as I watched students hurrying to maintain their schedules, carrying books, wearing clothes and speaking to teachers—all in ways that shaped and were shaped by that place, that idea, called "Addison High"—I thought hard about what Akers had said. Maybe she was right. Maybe the cumulative effect of individuals' actions might be that "the system" I saw manifested in these hallways and classrooms "begins to change." And later, as I recalled Akers's words, I thought of how clearly they echoed Dewey's thoughts (1941/1988b) about the necessity of individuality in promoting more democratic ways of living:

> Democracy is a personal way of individual life; . . . it signifies the possession and continual use of certain attitudes, forming personal character and determining desire and purpose in all the relations of life. Instead of thinking of our own dispositions and habits as accommodated to certain institutions, we have to learn to think of the latter as expressions, projections, and extensions of habitually dominant personal attitudes. (p. 226)

At Addison High I had seen some teachers giving extra time to work with LM students and reaching out to these students in other ways that went beyond their job requirements. I had seen, in other words, people who were choosing to exercise their individuality by making a positive difference in Latino students' lives. And so, even though the broader changes Akers had spoken of still seemed very far away, she—and Dewey—had renewed my hope that these changes might someday occur after all.

CHAPTER SIX

Identity, Resistance, and the Production of Persons

Bricks and mortar alone do not tell the story of educa-
tion. It is a human endeavor in which the adult genera-
tion attempts to impart to its children the knowledge,
values, and skills needed to perpetuate the community.
Thus it has been in Addison.

AN ADDISON HISTORIAN (name withheld)

Homecoming and Cultural Reproduction

"Please remember that during the Queen's Assembly, proper de-
corum must be observed."

The members of Alice Martinez's ESL class looked up and
watched Principal Dohm's voice come through the intercom
perched above the doorway. Though the summer had been over
for several weeks, the students still looked well rested. Angela
was back, along with Claudia and her brother Felipe. With his
long face, dark skin, and high cheek bones, Felipe looked very
much like his sisters, Rosa and Claudia. Five other students sat in
the classroom, though their attendance throughout the semester
would turn out to be sporadic.

The room, the third to be used by the ESL class in three years,
was more intimate than the ones we'd used in the past. This one,
used for other periods of the day as a meeting place for special
education classes, was carpeted, about half the size of a regular
classroom. Martinez had commented that it would have been
great to have had this space for our very own, a place to paint a
mural on the wall, a place to work on the computer that rested
on the corner desk, to display our work, but by now we knew

better than to expect this would happen anytime soon. This room, in fact, had been designated only at the last minute after the English teacher whose room the ESL class was going to use during her planning period had said that such an arrangement would have been "very inconvenient." In a top corner of the chalkboard was written a note: "ESL class, Please do not move the furniture."

When Principal Dohm made his announcement, the ESL students had just finished collaboratively writing a brief self-description paragraph in preparation for composing their own short individual biographies the next day. The paragraph read as follows:

> I live in Addison. Addison is a small, old town. I have lived here for three years. I came here to find work. There is work in the fields and in the factories. After work I go out with my friends to the mall. In the evenings I go out for dinner at El Conejo [the Rabbit]. When I grow up, I want to move back to where I was born.

Martinez dismissed the students to the Queen's Assembly, a part of the traditional Addison High homecoming celebration. Students and teachers crowded the hallway, dressed in green and white, the school colors. The cheerleaders wore their uniforms, the football players identifiable by their ties and sport coats. None of the ESL students or teachers had dressed for the occasion.

In the darkened gym a student band called The Bleeding Turnips blasted a pretty good Pearl Jam imitation from four-foot-high amplifiers at the front of the stage. Beth Reinstra handed me a plastic megaphone with the Addison High logo printed on the side. "Keep it," she yelled over the music. Students packed onto the bleachers passed a naked life-size inflatable doll over their heads until it was confiscated by one of the teachers. After the students were all seated, most of the teachers still lingered near the doorways, silhouetted in the light from the hallway spilling into the gym. The Bleeding Turnips finished their song with a strong final chord and a roar of approval from the crowd, and the president of the student council stepped to the microphone, tapped it twice, and introduced the nominees for Homecoming Queen. One by one, weaving slightly in their high heels, escorted by handsome, thick-necked boys in suits, the four nominees made their way down an aisle formed by strings of small white Christmas tree lights taped to the floor.

Parents and grandparents seated in folding chairs along either side of the Christmas tree runway, some with sateen "Addison High Boosters Club" jackets, snapped photos and nudged each other with elbows. They leaned together and spoke into each other's ears to be heard over the crowd, then looked back and smiled and applauded their children nominees, who now sat with legs crossed properly at the ankle and hands resting demurely on their laps, each in front of her own four-by-eight-foot plywood panel on which was painted Ariel, the Little Mermaid, and the nominee's name. The whole ceremony took about fifteen minutes.

Addison High tradition dictates that the Queen's Assembly be followed by the homecoming parade, which passes through the city's tree-lined residential streets to the football stadium across town. I followed the procession from the sidewalk, trying not to be too conspicuous with my tape recorder in hand. Hundreds of people lined the route as the Addison Band led the way, playing arrangements of a wide variety of music, including the rock and roll classic, "Smoke on the Water." The musicians were followed by cheerleaders and members of the flag team, who stepped high and tipped and spun their flags in nearly perfect unison. Police officers with caps pulled low over their eyebrows had blocked off side streets with their patrol cars, lights flashing, and fire truck sirens wailed so loudly I covered my ears. Between songs by the band, members of the group's drum corps took over, shifting from their steady, metronomic role to that of a soloist, pounding out offbeat rhythms punctuated with rim shots and no-look clicks against the sticks of the person marching alongside. Children from the elementary schools sat on the curb and waved signs offering messages like "Go Addison Eagles," "You're number one," and "Eagle Pride." Parents waved to their embarrassed children while elderly neighbors, some covering their legs with blankets and sipping coffee from thermoses, watched from lawn chairs along the parade route.

I walked quickly down the sidewalk and found a spot just past a corner where the parade took a left turn, toward the football stadium on the east side. On this corner is a Kentucky Fried Chicken. A group of about six Latinos, ranging from childhood to middle age, stood in the parking lot around a car with Texas license plates. The family had a bucket of chicken, several biscuits, and Cokes resting on the hood of the car. They ate their lunch as the parade passed them by.

The nominees for Homecoming Queen came into view. The first nominee sat atop the backseat of a red BMW 325I convertible; the next girl rode in a late model Corvette, followed by the other prospective queens in a Porsche Carrera and a white Mustang GT. "It doesn't take long for a few thousand dollars to roll by," I overheard someone say. It was a cool day, too cold for just the evening dresses the nominees wore, so some had borrowed Addison High varsity jackets to wrap around their shoulders.

It was then that I heard a strange sound—not so much unfamiliar as out of place there on the parade route. I more felt than heard it at first, a beat thumping inside my chest. A series of vehicles carrying the school's various clubs began to pass by, and when I finally located the source of the thumping, I laughed out loud, for what I heard was Latino rap music so loud that it shook the sides of the low-rider pickup truck that carried Addison High's Multicultural Awareness Club. Mexican and African flags flew from the antennae, and many of the students crammed into the bed of the truck wore green, red, and white caps with "La Raza" stitched on the front. I waved as the truck went by.

During a football game at Eagle Stadium, though there are no officially assigned seats, the people of Addison know exactly where they belong. The east bleachers are given up to the opposing team's fans, and the night of the Addison homecoming, several seats remained empty. The west bleachers, topped by the press box, are for the hometown supporters. The fifty-yard line seats are for the parents of the players and the other adults who are leaders in supporting the school, including many of the older teachers who themselves have children in the middle or high school. These loyalists dress in green and white, some with pom-poms and Addison Eagles caps or jackets. To their right sit the students who support the school but are not among its popular groups. These are the boys in the glee club, the girls who cheer on their friends in the band or on the drill team—those who after the game do not attend the parties reserved for high-status football players or cheerleaders. The left section of the bleachers is the place for the popular student crowd, often referred to by the others as the "rich kids." To their left, seated on a grassy incline which still affords a clear view of the field, the middle school students wait to assume what will be—in a year or two—their designated places in the grandstand.

Standing behind the end zone, near the main exit, by the bathrooms and the concession stands where you can't see much of the field, groups of Latino and African American students huddle in small groups, hands pushed into their pockets. These outsiders occasionally drift up into the stands in pairs, but not very often. They wear sneakers, baggy pants, caps with "La Raza" or "Homie" written across the front. Dozens of junior high students, those who don't belong on the grassy incline near the rich kids, dress like their older counterparts and take their places in the end zone. The night of the homecoming game, I wore a couple of shirts under my jacket, and I was still cold enough to go buy a cup of coffee and cradle it in my hands. People shifted back and forth on their feet to try to stay warm, little puffs of steam rising from their faces as they breathed. Some of the kids in the end zone were wearing jeans and just T-shirts.

As I stood there among the crowd at the edge of the field, glancing up at the scoreboard to find out about what I couldn't see on the field, Emilio came up and nodded. He wore a short-sleeve Chicago White Sox T-shirt and, backwards, an Oakland Raiders baseball cap. "Hey, Todd. What are you doing here?" he asked. I had first met Emilio while attending lower-track classes with Rosa, Claudia, and Angela. Very popular among Addison's Latino students, he had impressed me with his quick wit, which he often used to torment his teachers, who frequently responded by sending him to room "D-112," the discipline office. We had begun to talk quite a bit, and he had even introduced me to some of his friends as someone who could "talk Mexican." I hadn't seen him for a while, though, which he explained was because he had been locked up in the county juvenile detention facility—euphemistically known around Addison as "the center"—for fighting. Standing there in the cold, Emilio began to tell me about life at the center—the prolonged isolation, the weekend visits from his parents, the chore of waking up early each morning to clean the toilet in his room. He was glad to be out. "I'm gonna laminate my parole certificate and tape it on my bedroom wall," he said.

At halftime Addison trailed by a touchdown—a pretty good game, I guessed, even though I couldn't see much from behind the end zone. Emilio, though, said he had to go home. "There might be trouble," he said, glancing around. "Besides, I got a curfew with my probation."

I said good-bye to Emilio and wandered through the end zone crowd. The atmosphere seemed tense. Students pushed each other, grabbed each other's caps, and whispered about sneaking off for a cigarette. As I walked past a group of girls, I caught a fragment of what one of them was saying to her friends: ". . . so I went up to him, took off my jacket, told him to fuck off, and gave him a good shove."

Each year, the homecoming activities at Addison High bring together the school and its constituencies to celebrate the community and its traditions. The Queen's Assembly, the parade, and the game itself may thus be said to be a means by which Addison High reflects and promotes the values of the community where it exists. As I have suggested in these descriptions, however, a tension is at work here. For while the homecoming activities I described are supposedly meant to cultivate cooperation and a common identity of people as members of the Addison High community, these activities are also opportunities to reinforce the marginalization of certain people within that larger community. Thousands of people of different ethnicities and socioeconomic levels may all walk through the same gate at Eagle Stadium, but Emilio and others like him still stand in the end zone.

The divisive effects of the Addison High homecoming celebration are imitated in schools throughout the country (Foley, 1990). As is the case at Addison, despite the noble intentions of America's professed democratic vision of education, tension lies between the ideal and the real; that is, schools' articulated aims are often inconsistent with what they actually do. In order to understand why this gap exists, one must acknowledge that schools often function paradoxically. While they may be places that proclaim a democratic message of education as a means of affording social mobility and political and economic power to the dispossessed, what they actually do, as researchers like Martin Carnoy (1974) and Samuel Bowles and Herbert Gintis (1976) have argued, is perpetuate present cultural and social systems through the ideological preparation of young people for participation in capitalist society. In summarizing their argument about the relationship between schools and the capitalist economy, Bowles and Gintis write,

> Education in the United States plays a dual role in the process by which surplus value, i.e., profit, is created and expropriated. On the one hand, by imparting technical and social skills and appropriate motivations, education increases the productive capacity of workers. On the other hand, education helps defuse and depoliticize the potentially explosive class relations of the production process, and thus serves to perpetuate the social, political, and economic conditions through which a portion of the product of labor is expropriated in the form of profits. (p. 11)

Among the more incisive articulations of the connections between ideology, culture, and schools is that offered by Pierre Bourdieu. According to Bourdieu (1979), society is not "natural," not a "given" ontological necessity; rather, it is constructed and reproduced over time to ensure generational continuity. As a part of this process, certain people are in positions to impose definitions that are consistent with their own interests as to what will constitute the knowledge and values that are worth instilling in our children. Schools, as part of a larger system of symbolic institutions that tacitly confirm what it means to be educated, tend to perpetuate existing power relations and class control through the reproduction of a dominant culture (p. 79). In short, Bourdieu (1979) argues that pedagogical actions, which can never be defined independently of their membership in a system subjected to the effects of dominant ideologies, "reproduce the system of cultural arbitraries characteristic of that social formation, thereby contributing to the reproduction of the power relations which put that cultural arbitrary into the dominant position" (p. 26).[1]

The notion of cultural reproduction has served as a theoretical framework for several important studies of how this process is effected through schooling. For instance, in *Framing Drop-*

outs, Michelle Fine (1991) offers evidence that, far from being a democratizing force, the New York high school she studied made a priority of creating and maintaining an elaborate system of efficiently expelling or coercing into dropping out those students whom the faculty and administration deemed losers or trouble-makers. To speak specifically of Latino students, Douglas Foley's *Learning Capitalist Culture: Deep in the Heart of Tejas* (1990) documents how the high school in a small Texas town reinforces the town's values, prejudices, and, therefore, the social organization that keeps Latino students in poor barrios and low-paying jobs. Perhaps the most influential study of cultural reproduction is Paul Willis's (1981b) *Learning To Labor: How Working Class Kids Get Working Class Jobs,* which I will refer to below.

In conversations highlighting cultural reproduction, however, it is worth underscoring that Bourdieu is not talking only about one socioeconomic class exercising dominance over another. Merely to say that schools are in the business of suppressing difference and thereby reproducing existing social, political, and economic strata is to oversimplify Bourdieu's emphasis on culture and its importance within educational institutions. Cultural reproduction should not be reduced to the notion that members of the dominant classes consciously conspire to oppress (although it may include that). Rather, if we think of culture as the learned symbolic systems by which people create meaning and construct their realities, then we can begin to understand some of the complex ways in which culture mediates social relations, including those relations that result in the domination of some groups by others. If, for instance, we acknowledge that Addison High's curriculum, daily schedule, disciplinary practices, homecoming activities, and definitions of a "good student" emanate from the ideological framework of the dominant culture, then we can understand more clearly what happens when students operating within a different set of cultural assumptions are placed in that setting.[2]

Bourdieu's highlighting the mediating role of culture suggests that reproducing power relations involves more than forceful coercion; it also includes the crucial process of convincing the members of marginalized groups to embrace dominant world views. One way to think about how and why this process of "ideological transformation" occurs is to consider the notion of "hegemony" as articulated by Antonio Gramsci. In Gramsci's (1992) terms, *hegemony* refers to the process of establishing and maintaining political control by forming ideological alliances, both among ruling classes and between the ruling classes and "subaltern" groups. The key to establishing hegemony lies in the ability of those in power to make their own interests appear to be synonymous with the interests of less privileged social groups. This process involves the use of ideology to win "the spontaneous consent given by the great masses of the population to the general direction imposed on life by the dominant fundamental group" (p. 12).

Gramsci argues that this type of "consent" is accomplished through the workings of the state, which he defines as including two "superstructural levels." The first, "political society," refers to the "apparatus of government" which can effect "direct domination" over subaltern groups (p. 263). The second, "civil society," is that which consists of "the ensemble of organisms commonly called private," and includes, as Giroux (1983) has summarized, those "institutions that rely upon meanings, symbols, and ideas to universalize ruling-class ideologies, while simultaneously shaping and limiting oppositional discourse and practice" (p. 276). Taken together, these two levels of the state comprise "the entire complex of practical and theoretical activities with which the ruling class not only justifies and maintains its dominance, but manages to win the active consent of those over whom it rules" (Gramsci, p. 244). Gramsci's notion of state-effected hegemony is useful when studying educational practices because it offers us a deeper understanding of the consequences of reproducing what Bourdieu called privileged "cultural arbitraries." For if we think of schools as inherently cultural institutions that are part of the apparatus of the state as Gramsci defines it, then we can begin to see their potential as sites for establishing more effective and permanent forms of domination—the kind of domination that, ironically, is supported by the consent of the oppressed themselves.

As an institution that is shaped by dominant ideologies, Addison High may be said to promote those ideologies by means of a host of symbolic artifacts and practices: everything from textbooks to teaching methods to homecoming rituals. When these efforts fail, students whose culturally embedded values are not those of the school can be, of course, controlled to an extent by detentions or suspension. However, a complete "victory" in the school's terms can only come when Latino students and their families genuinely believe that to accept and act upon the ideologies of the dominant culture is in their best interest—that is, hegemony is achieved when students and their parents willingly participate in forms of cultural reproduction that may lead to their own subjugation.

Indeed, no school policy or program is politically innocent; they all carry meaning in a larger political and ethical sense. In this view, a football game, for instance, is no longer just a game, but a cultural event replete with meanings that support a dominant world view that in turn has social, political, and economic consequences for the people of Addison.[3] More specifically, the Addison homecoming game is part of the cultural politics of the school in that through this game and the activities that surround it, the school does not homogenize; rather, it reproduces difference in socioeconomic class. In other words, Addison High is effecting the production of persons who will have differing access to power and choice in the larger society. These differences, in turn, lead to unequal opportunities for students of various social and ethnic groups to participate in those decisions that shape their lives. From the perspective of the dominant classes, then, it's not that the Latino students don't "belong" at the game; they have a definite place there, and that place is in the end zone next to the exits and the bathrooms. In this sense, the football game is doing exactly what it is "supposed to do." From the perspective of a citizen teacher, however, this game and its accompanying rituals are cause for concern, for these activities are among the mechanisms by which some students are being prepared to tolerate, or even accept, severe limits on their ability to participate democratically in the associated activity that surrounds them.

Generally speaking, hegemony is being achieved to whatever extent Latinos participate willingly in the activities of Addison High. As I have been arguing, because the school is a cultural institution, marginalized students' participation in the activities it sponsors indicates at least a partial acceptance of the dominant ideology that guides the school—an ideology that in many ways denies the value of their experience and masks the forces at work to perpetuate their limited access to democratic forms of social participation. But students unintentionally take part in hegemony in other ways, as well, even ways that are allegedly intended to empower ethnic minority groups. One such example is the Multicultural Awareness Club (MAC).

In 1992 a group of students presented to the Addison principal a proposal to establish a Latino student organization to celebrate Latino cultures and to lobby for the school's greater attention to the particular needs of the Latino students and the communities they represent. Alejandro, cofounder and president of the MAC, said that Principal Dohm had denied the original proposal and agreed instead to "a multicultural club" that sought to acknowledge all ethnic backgrounds represented at the school. Dohm explained to me his rationale for this decision as follows:

> My personal thinking is that when you talk about different cultures that you do not exclude any culture. And in this building we have obviously an African American population that has African American culture. We have a significant Latino/Hispanic culture. But I also have a population of students from Pakistan; I have a smaller group of students from India, who maintain their cultures very much in their homes. We have a significant population of Irish, which would seem strange, but in Addison they're here. We have a larger population of, for lack of a better term, German background. We also have, more than you would think, Native Americans. So in my mind, if you have a Hispanic club, by the very nature of the club it says, "Well, you must be of Hispanic origin to join." If you have an African American club, by the very nature of it, you need to be a Black American. If you have an Irish club, you have to be Irish. If you say "multicultural," students who are interested in their culture, whatever it may be, [can participate, and so] you have honor and appropriate reverence to that culture.

During our conversation, Principal Dohm added that the Multicultural Awareness Club is part of an ongoing strategy on his part and that of the teaching staff to affirm and celebrate the ethnic diversity represented at Addison High. Citing progress in the form of language arts textbooks, the social studies curriculum, and the purchase by the school library of thousands of dollars worth of multicultural materials, Dohm underscored the school's commitment to creating a culturally inclusive environment: "I think the student population is such that we need to continue to make everyone aware of the cultural diversity in this building. And I think we've come a long way with that." Dohm's motives for deciding in favor of a club made up of students of diverse ethnicities were questioned, however, by a University of Michigan Latino student activist who had offered to help organize the proposed Addison High Latino student group. According to this activist, Dohm "basically told us that he didn't want us stirring up trouble in his school with the type of radical bullshit we have at the university."

Despite this initial controversy, Addison's Multicultural Awareness Club has now been in place for several years and is made up primarily of Latino students. The preamble to the MAC Constitution, originally printed in the ostentatious solemnity of a computer font reminiscent of medieval script, articulates the club's main goals:

> We the members of the Multicultural Awareness Club are formed to obtain and achieve the goals to overcome discrimination, to focus on education, to learn more about cultures, to form unity, and retain pride in oneself. Under the articles of the Constitution and with support from adults and students, these goals shall be achieved.
>
> As members of the club we are able to say how we feel or what we think under politeful circumstances. We are also expected to be dedicated to participate and work together on projects and activities. As members we are to follow the laws of the constitutional articles.
>
> Together we can show that we are good people and can be proud of who we are. If we can come together in peace and work together we can be looked at as someone special and can overcome discrimination. Under this club we desire to overcome the label of being just a "minority."
>
> This club is formed not only to obtain these goals, but it is also formed to show everyone, the community and ourselves included that we have pride and can work together to accomplish our goals. Through this club may members be aware that there is

a future, a dream and a reality—that we can make a difference and establish ourselves as leaders and role models for future MAC generations.

In order to work toward these objectives, Alejandro told me that he was dedicated to effecting reforms in the curriculum:

> What I'm going out for this year is to teach more multiculturalism in the classes, because in our history books, you know, we teach that the English came over to America and set up colonies and everything like that, but you never hear about Hispanic culture. The only thing I heard about Hispanic culture was Christopher Columbus. But there was nothing else.

In Alejandro's view, education that celebrates the richness and contributions of Latino culture is the first step toward different ethnic groups' cooperation in solving social ills emanating from racism: "In order for racism and discrimination to be dissolved, each of us needs to learn about everyone's culture. Like, we're all a nation, and to be a nation, we all need to come together and work toward a common goal."

The reality of the way the MAC functions, however, is considerably more limited than Alejandro's vision. At an after-school meeting of the MAC, the group's faculty advisor explained to me that Addison High practices "what you might call 'the holiday approach' to multiculturalism: We only acknowledge minority cultures by serving meals in the cafeteria twice a year." Nieto (1994) has argued that this "Holidays and Heroes" approach, which she defines as one in which "multicultural education is understood as consisting primarily of ethnic celebrations and the acknowledgment of 'great men' in the history of particular cultures" (p. 397), is repeated in schools across the country. The fundamental flaw in such practices, Nieto points out, is that they do not address the "deeper structures of cultures, including values and lifestyle differences, and an explicit emphasis on power differentials as they affect particular cultural groups" (p. 397). In the case of Addison High, Alejandro explained that on two occasions—Black History Month and Cinco de Mayo—the MAC students and their parents plan and prepare food without financial support from the school: "The work is done basically by the students, and if we need to buy things for the events it's usually us putting our money together." The school cafeteria staff adjusts by having the cafeteria make less food, but is otherwise uninvolved. The menu for the most recent Black History Month meal was barbecued ribs, fried chicken, and greens. At the MAC meeting I attended, the students were planning to serve tacos, rice, and beans on Cinco de Mayo.

The day these meals are served, the MAC also features so-called "celebrations" such as speakers and films presented in open classrooms throughout the day. Students may attend these presentations if they've signed up in advance. Alejandro's major complaint regarding these sessions, however, is that "we see a lot of the kids coming to the celebrations just to get out of class." According to Alejandro, Principal Dohm "would like to hear that Addison High School is kind of like a culture school, that we're doing a good thing by celebrating these events, these cultural events."

My intention here is not to trivialize the efforts of the MAC students and their parents. Alejandro and his other MAC members are among the most fervent advocates of multiculturalism I've met at Addison High. Rather, I think the MAC serves as an example of the ways hegemonic forces undermine efforts toward "multicultural awareness." My point here is not that serving Mexican food in the cafeteria or that offering students the opportunity to attend seminars celebrating African American or Latino cultures are in themselves bad ideas. Nonetheless, by serving tacos and fried chicken, Addison High seriously risks not only perpetuating cultural stereotypes, but also giving the impression of being a "culture school" while actually discouraging any kind of critical dialogue that might disclose and challenge the dominant ideology and the undemocratic structures this ideology maintains. When the school uses the MAC to promote cosmetic events as a substitute for more substantial changes in the curriculum and cultural life of Addison, the very people the dominant culture oppresses are contributing to their own subjugation. For in a very real sense, Alejandro and the other MAC members may be said to be participating in hegemonic practices that marginalize their culture within the school by helping to carry out such a compartmentalized and tightly controlled expression of cultural diversity.

Further, what I see as particularly troublesome about the (mis)use of the MAC is that its members represent experiences that have astounding potential for the type of inclusive, critical teaching that Alejandro envisions. Their families' migration north, the labor conditions Latinos faced (and continue to face)—these could be the points of departure for conversations which explore the relationships between cultural and economic forces and, say, the fact that so many of their Latino classmates drop out of school. As the MAC planned for Cinco de Mayo the following spring, a girl named Marta suggested that one of the scheduled speakers might be her father: "If we wanted to have somebody talk about how hard it is to move up here, like how much work it is to pick tomatoes and be poor and stuff, my dad could talk about that." The group sat silent for a moment, then moved on to another subject. At the end of the meeting, as the students were pushing their chairs back into rows, I asked a boy who had been active in the conversation whether he thought the MAC would follow through on Marta's suggestion. He looked at me and shook his head. "Aw, man, there's nothing to say about pickin' tomatoes. All's you do is just bend over and pick 'em up. Talk about that? I don't think so."

Cultural Production among "The Mexicans"

Thus far I have talked about cultural, and therefore social, reproduction as being carried out by means of cultural institutions and practices that privilege some ideologies over others, thereby maintaining the position of the dominant classes and limiting some students' democratic participation in school and society. However, another aspect of cultural reproduction operates at Addison High. Unlike Gramsci's notion of hegemony, this aspect does not depend upon members of the subordinate class ultimately accepting dominant culture; rather, it illustrates how subordinate groups manage to contribute to their own domination even as they resist ruling class ideologies.

In *Learning to Labor*, Paul Willis (1981b) has documented this process by telling the story of a group of working-class British school boys called the "lads." Willis shows how these students oppose the ideology of the school through what he calls "cultural production," the invention by groups of symbolic systems (such as styles of dress, ways of talking, behavior that violates school rules, and so on) that shape and are shaped by the group's oppositional ideology (p. 160). However, the lads' oppositional ideology is embedded in a cultural framework that values manual labor, and despite their resistance to the school and the values that sustain it, the irony of the lads' story is that their resistance ultimately perpetuates socioeconomic inequality by relegating them to a working-class life on the "shop floor." In other words, they "consent" to the status quo by engaging in behavior that maintains the division of labor that secures the privilege of the upper classes. Or, to use Willis's terms, the oppositional "cultural *production*" of the lads in the end contributes to "cultural *reproduction*," which, in turn, is an aspect of social reproduction.

In similar ways, many of Addison's Latino students resist the ideology of the school and participate in the type of oppositional cultural production described by Willis. As with Willis's lads, these students, by rejecting "the system," by behaving in ways that will get them suspended or placed in lower-track classes, often leave themselves few options but to assume "their places" in the working-class jobs that Willis warns are the frequent result of oppositional cultural production. Among many Latino students, this oppositional behavior signals an identity that separates them from other (usually White or African American) students. But as Latino students strive to retain their identity, Willis's analysis helps us see that many of them are perpetuating their own subaltern positions in school and society, thereby compelling us to ask some delicate and unpopular questions: Is there a point at which many of Addison's Latino students contribute to their own "failure"? Why do they often behave in ways that increase the likelihood of their dropping out of school and spending their adult lives relegated to low-paying jobs?[4]

As strong as a sense of identity can be among Latino students, it would be a mistake to assume that their identity can be defined categorically or permanently, for the ways in which these students seem to perceive themselves as a group are fluctuating and context-dependent. Stuart Hall (1992) has explained how contemporary conceptions of identity help us understand the complex and mutable identity(ies) of people like Addison's Latino students. Hall points out that the modern notion of identity has evolved through three different understandings of an increasingly "dislocated or de-centered subject": the "Enlightenment subject," which is based on a conception of the human person as a fully centered, unified individual; the "sociological subject," in which identity is viewed as being formed in the interaction between the self and society; and the "post-modern subject," in which identity is "formed and transformed continuously in relation to the ways we are represented or addressed in the cultural systems which surround us" (p. 277). When thinking about the Latino students at Addison High, about the ways they negotiate among the multiple lives that make up their experience, it is useful to think of their identities in this postmodern sense, as having various dimensions they must shift in and out of depending upon the context.

One example of these complexities is Addison Latino students' tendency to refer to themselves collectively as "the Mexicans," regardless of their national origin. While I suspect that this term may have originated as a homogenizing label used by non-Latino Addison residents, it nonetheless has been adopted as an emic term used not just by Mexican or Mexican American students, but also by those from Puerto Rico, Guatemala, and South Texas. Moreover, though I have heard Latino students from all socioeconomic groups refer to themselves as "Mexican," students who do well in school and otherwise seem to be accepting and acting in accordance with its dominant ideology usually identify themselves as "Hispanic" or "Latino." It is the students from lower socioeconomic groups, especially those who see themselves positioned in a contentious relationship with school authorities, who tend to refer to themselves as "Mexican." Thus, while these terms do represent ethnicity, they also connote class distinctions.

Nonetheless, no single pattern of behavior accompanies students' identifying themselves as "Mexican," and to be a Mexican in this sense (I will use the term without quotation marks from here on) is not necessarily to deny one's membership in the Addison High community. A Mexican student at Addison High is at once a Mexican and an Addison High student. But there is tension in this divided identity, for being a Mexican often involves cultural production that conflicts with the dominant culture of the school, and the ways in which students negotiate these tensions have serious consequences. Students like Alejandro, for instance, are very "successful" in the school's terms. They—along with students of all other ethnic groups—participate in the activities and practices of the school that are shaped by the dominant school culture. Such students thereby reinforce their identity as members of Addison High community. By getting good grades, obeying school rules, or participating on sports teams or in musical groups, many Mexican students benefit by emphasizing their "mainstream" identity. Praise from teachers, scholarships to college, and success within a capitalist economic structure are the frequent rewards for being a "good Addison High student"—Latino or otherwise. On the other hand, there is often a great deal at stake for those students who emphasize their identity as Mexicans. For while these students may retain benefits such as social acceptance by peers and meaningful connections with their families, their cultures, and their language, these benefits often come at the expense of the rewards enjoyed by Latino students who conform to the school's dominant culture. In sum, the question of which aspect of their identity students choose to emphasize is crucial in determining whether Mexicans will be included or excluded from the benefits of mainstream culture.

According to the official discourse of the school, Addison's Latino students are "Hispanic" as identified by criteria set down by the state of Michigan that include factors such as national origin and language use. However, among the students themselves, what it means to be a Mexican at Addison High is determined by definitions generated in the process of cultural production and conveyed symbolically.[5] Symbolic markers such as styles of dress and modes of behavior construct understandings of who these students are, and these understandings have important consequences which illustrate very well the cultural cross fires in which these students find themselves as the hegemonic forces of Addison High come into conflict with more localized conceptions of identity.

I had long ago chosen to forsake the staff lounge and spend most of my lunch periods with the students in the cafeteria. As a researcher I didn't want to be identified as a teacher, and, besides, as a break from the solitude of my Ann Arbor apartment, I enjoyed being in a room reverberating with the energy of five hundred teenagers. Many students ate their lunches in ethnically mixed groups, and it would be misleading to give the impression that Addison High is made up of racial enclaves completely disassociated from each other. Students of differing ethnicities do "hang" with each other, often as very close friends. Still, generally speaking, when school activities involve large numbers of students—at a football game, for instance, or in a cafeteria—the tendency is for students to group themselves according to ethnicity, and so it was never difficult to find the Mexicans at lunch time. Carrying their yellow Styrofoam trays and a carton of either chocolate milk or Hawaiian Punch, they always showed up at the same long linoleum table near the windows. Always the first to arrive was Zeke, a fleshy starting offensive lineman on the football team. He wore a gold crucifix around his neck and a T-shirt I had seen on several other of Addison's Mexicans. The shirt depicted two large eagles facing each other with claws and beaks poised menacingly. One of the eagles—a bald eagle—was wrapped in a United States flag, the other—a golden eagle—was draped by a Mexican flag. Beneath the two birds was a pool of blood and the caption "Mexican American." As he did every day, Zeke paused briefly in the crowded lunch room and bowed his head in a silent prayer before eating.

Zeke and I were joined by the regulars. Emilio sat down and offered me some of his French fries. Frank arrived a moment later, his hat typically askew, wearing a white sweatshirt on the front of which was depicted a young Latino with the sleeves ripped off his T-shirt to reveal muscular arms, his head encircled by a bandanna headband. The figure looked over his shoulder at an image of *La Virgen de Guadalupe*. Sergio, Mike, Carlos, and a few others arrived and sat down as they did every day. At the other end of the long table, about ten feet from us, sat the usual group of about eight to ten Latina girls. Although the conversation around this table typically was interspersed with Spanish, that day we spoke English. I asked why they always sat together.[6]

ZEKE: Hangin' out at the same table just happens. Everybody knows where their people are. Everybody knows where to belong. It's like a Mexican thing. Like, we hang around with the Mexicans, with the vatos. It's a tradition.

TODD: What's a "vato"? I know it's a Latino guy, but what's the difference between a Latino guy who's a vato and one who isn't?

EMILIO: It's like a dude, a Hispanic dude, a friend. Like, you can come up to somebody and say, "Hey, vato." A vato thinks he's pretty bad; he fights sometimes, but usually it's just someone you can joke around with. Like, with a friend, you can say something bad to him, but he's not going to get mad or anything. It just wouldn't be important.

TODD: [to Emilio] Are you a vato?

EMILIO: Well, sometimes. Like me, if I don't like something, I can smack somebody, but normally it doesn't bother me.

FRANK: "Homie" is what we sometimes say, too.

EMILIO: But every time they see us hang out together they think we have a gang or something. Like, they send us to the office and start asking us questions about each other.

ZEKE: Yeah, that always happens.

FRANK: They think something's goin' on.

EMILIO: You know like how we all go to the rest room and walk around together? They'll say, "What are you guys going to go to a fight or something?" They think we're a gang. Like, if we have a table full of Mexicans, they think we have a gang going on. They think we're a bunch of troublemakers, right? They think we're a bunch of hooligans. Mrs. Alvarez told me that one time.

FRANK: Yeah, they'll ask us questions like that, like we're going to make trouble or something.

TODD: Does that happen to other students?

EMILIO: No. No.

ZEKE: When White people hang out, they don't think they're a gang. It happens sometimes to the Blacks, but the majority to the Mexicans.

TODD: Why do you think that happens mostly to the Mexicans?

EMILIO: 'Cause they think we're trouble.

ZEKE: 'Cause we ain't wealthy. We ain't rich like all them. Just, we gotta do our stuff to be on top and stuff, you know.

TODD: If you guys hang out together, what are some of the other groups they have here at school?

EMILIO: Just the Blacks and the Whites and the Mexicans. And if you're a different race you just hang out with whoever you want to. You pick your color and it works.

TODD: You guys have a lot of Latino students here, so you'd think that a large part of what they teach here would be about Mexicans. Do you learn a lot about that? Do you learn things about Mexico?

ZEKE: They usually talk about Black slaves and Whites.

EMILIO: Yeah, and that's all.

ZEKE: We never have our chance. Like, you know Cinco de Mayo? We should have our day off. Like they have Martin Luther King day; why can't we have ours? Cinco de Mayo's a more respected day than Martin Luther King.

TODD: Why is Cinco de Mayo so important?

ZEKE: Because it was a tradition through the whole of Hispanics. Like Martin Luther was only himself. We have Pancho Villa that died; why don't we have his day off? He was more important than Martin Luther King. Pancho Villa fought for our country.

TODD: What is your country?

ZEKE: Well, our back roots are . . . I'm not ashamed to say it, but we're from back in Mexico. But see you guys can't say, "Well, Mexico is this and that." Mexico used to be mostly part of the United States right now. Like California and everything was ours.

EMILIO: But they don't teach that. You gotta learn that yourself.

ZEKE: Yeah, you gotta learn that yourself.

TODD: So, where did you learn it?

EMILIO: In the library or whatever.

FRANK: I think we got all right classes, it's just that we want to learn more about our history.

ZEKE: I went to the library, and I used to listen a lot to my mom and dad. But one thing I don't understand, they give respect to the Black people, who were slaves. We were never slaves; why can't they give us the same respect?

FRANK: We gotta earn our respect. They think we're all in gangs.

ZEKE: Yeah, like, we can't go in that group where they decide, you know, about the school activities and everything. We don't have the same chance as White people. We can't have the same chance. You know how, like, they have the pep assembly? And they design the whole assembly. And they got like these dances and everything? You know how they got their people out on their floats and stuff? They're more in the program.

TODD: If you all could change some of the things here, what might they be?

ZEKE: Well, one thing they don't got, they don't got a lot of Hispanic teachers here. I'd change that. I'd make a Mexican principal. They have three White people, why can't they have one black or one Mexican? Make it even.[7]

TODD: Why do you think that would be important?

ZEKE: It would help us out more. You know if they put a Mexican in there, he's gonna help his race out a little bit more—boost it up a little.

As this conversation suggests, among the consequences of the cultural production of a Mexican identity at Addison High is that students who foster this identity find themselves in an oppositional relationship with the dominant school culture. The cafeteria conversation further suggests that the Mexicans are well aware of their oppositional stance, as they tend to preserve their identity as a symbolic form of resistance against a school environment that systematically devalues who they are. Virginia Vogel Zanger (1993) observed a similar situation in her study of Latino students in a Boston high school, where she found that the students who decided to stay in school said that some of their peers had dropped out because of the school's attempts to "monoculture" them. In Addison, Mexican identity is established to a certain extent by the dark skin, eyes, and hair common to people of Latin America. However, merely to be of Latin American descent does not qualify a person as a Mexican in a sense that includes this identity's oppositional connotations. Several students who are listed as "Hispanic" by Addison High and who are succeeding within the mainstream culture (i.e., getting good grades, integrating socially, and so on) are considered by other Latino students to be "acting White." Thus, to be a Mexican at Addison High is not so much something determined by genetics, but something students create (or have created for them) on a daily basis.[8]

In this process, language use is among the symbolic markers of Mexican identity in that almost all of Addison's Mexican students understand at least some Spanish, which they have learned from their parents and grandparents. A person's level of Spanish fluency, however, is not crucial in determining his or her membership in the Mexican student community. These students' conversations, though sometimes interspersed with code-switching, are almost always conducted in English.[9]

At least as important as language in representing identity are Mexican students' patterns of appearance and behavior. Among the ways Mexicans represent their identity—particularly the boys—is to decorate their skin with various words and designs. Sometimes the markings are temporary, as they were when Emilio wrote "Vato Loco" in beautiful script letters with an ink pen on the inside of his forearm. Often, however, the statement is more permanent in the form of tattoos, the most common being three blue dots arranged in the form of a triangle on the side of the hand where the forefinger meets the thumb.

As important as what is on Mexican students' skin, however, is what covers it. That is to say, the ways in which students dress take on significance in indicating Mexican identity. Generally, Mexican students follow guidelines concerning how to wear certain types of clothes. Shirts with buttons in the front are attached all the way to the top, in contrast to White students' usually leaving the shirt open at the neck. Pants are worn baggy and very low on the hips—an extreme form of the loose fit popular among non-Mexicans. Though these general patterns of dress are also practiced frequently among the school's African American students, as well as by some Whites who cultivate a kind of antiestablishment identity, Mexicans have their own markers that set them apart from other groups which may be said to be assuming an oppositional stance toward the school.

One form of what might be called "rebel" imagery popular among Mexicans are the hats and jackets of the Oakland Raiders. Though Mexican students may be said to have an ethnic connection to the Raiders based on the team's California location, several Mexicans mentioned that they liked the Raiders because of the team's reputation as being the "baddest" in the NFL, a legacy put forward by the Raiders' slogan, "Just win, baby." This affinity for what might be called "lawless" athletes is also suggested by the frequency with which Mexican students wear shirts depicting former heavyweight boxing champion and convicted rapist "Iron" Mike Tyson. On Claudia's favorite shirt was an image of Tyson superimposed on the words "He'll Be Back."

Mexicans' clothing indicating a more specifically ethnic identity includes T-shirts depicting caricatured urban Latinos in a "low-rider" Chevy convertible. These cartoon figures are a self-parody: one vato with chino pants and a stocking cap, another with hair slicked back into a pompadour, wearing gold jewelry, with his arm around a Latina with "big" hair and a small dress. Beneath these figures is the caption "Homies." Also popular among the Mexican boys are hair nets or black stocking caps with the words "East Side" embroidered on the front. Felipe (Claudia's brother) explained to me that he wears his "East Side" hat because, "It's like in California there's East Los Angeles where all the Mexicans live. And here the East Side in Addison, that's where we live. It's all Mexican. They have low-rider cars and stuff like that."

Other images focus more specifically on a Mexican national identity. Caps and shirts decorated with the Mexican flag or the words *"Puro Mexicano"* are common, as are images of the Mexican-born boxing champion Julio Cesar Chavez. The fighter is usually depicted surrounded by a Mexican flag, his championship belt slung over his shoulder; he is identified as *"Nuestro Campeón,"* "Our Champion." Another means of signifying Mexican nationalism, however, is through clothing that depicts Christ and the saints, usually accompanied by a quotation from the Bible or a Catholic prayer book. Angela often wore a T-shirt that has on the back a picture of Christ praying. The caption reads, in Spanish: *"Man does not live by bread alone, but by every word that proceeds out of the mouth of God."* Emilio had a shirt featuring Simon of Cyrene, accompanied by the words,

"He carried the cross for Christ." Though various religious images appear frequently on Addison Mexicans' clothing, no figure is as important as *La Virgen de Guadalupe*. The depictions of *La Virgen* nearly always include a Mexican flag, at times wrapped around her shoulders, at others small and in the background. This constant juxtaposition of *La Virgen* and the Mexican flag suggests that these symbols are inseparable—that for the Mexicans of Addison, displaying Catholic imagery is an operation not only of faith but also of reinforcing identity. That Addison's Mexicans practice Catholicism is particularly significant given that the majority of Addison's Christian residents are Protestant. Faithful religious observation is the rule among Addison's Mexicans, with many of them attending Spanish-language masses on Sunday mornings.

Tenuous Alliances

Although the types of symbolic markers I have been describing help establish a Mexican identity for some students, it is useful, as Hall (1992) has reminded us, to view identity as flexible and context-dependent. Alejandro, we have seen, moves in and out of the roles he plays as a Mexican and as a "successful" Addison High student. Another way this flexibility is evident at Addison High is in the ways Mexicans share certain aspects of their oppositional identity with other marginalized groups like "Blacks" (an emic term used by Addison students of all ethnicities) and "poor Whites." This is not to say that Mexicans, Blacks, and poor Whites come together in a move of solidarity that obliterates all distinctions among them. It is, however, to point out that what it means to be "Mexican," "Black," and "trailer trash" (again, a disturbing but emic term used by many Addison students) are in some respects the same. I will show how these various identities sometimes overlap each other by focusing briefly on the "rules" students tend to follow for interracial dating and on the uneasy relationships Mexican students negotiate with Blacks and poor Whites. I raise these issues not to undermine notions of group identity and, by extension, cultural production, but as a way to demonstrate further complexities in the ways

Addison students seem to understand themselves and others.

Generally speaking, the boundary defining whom it is "acceptable" for Addison students to date is clear enough: they almost always date within their ethnic group. In Emilio's words, "Most of the people here stay with people of their own races." At the beginning of the 1995–96 school year, the reality of this boundary became clear when a conflict between Blacks and Mexicans arose as a Black student became angry because his former girlfriend—another Black—started dating a Mexican. Ironically, even when students date across ethnic lines, the result is often to strengthen group identity. As Emilio explained, "a lot of Mexicans go out with Mexican girls, but some go out with the White girls, and when they do, some of the White boys get mad." In Emilio's case, opposition to his being involved with his White girlfriend comes not only from the "White boys" but also from the girl's parents: "My girlfriend's name is Linda; you might know her. She looks like she's Mexican, but she's not. Her mom and dad are prejudiced. They don't really like Mexicans."

However, even though the most common type of couple at Addison High is that made up of students of the same ethnicity, and even though inter-ethnic dating often highlights the lines separating ethnic groups, some students, like Emilio and Linda, do indeed cross those lines. Felipe, for instance, said that he didn't allow race to restrict his dating: "Well, I had a girlfriend last year who was White. It depends if people like each other. I don't care if she's White or Black. If I like her, if I feel something for her, I go after her." Sometimes this interracial dating causes difficulties in very practical matters such as language use. In Felipe's case, he said, "For me goin' out with girls who don't know Spanish is pretty hard. It's like school." However, despite Felipe's difficulties with English and despite the unofficial rules discouraging students from dating outside their own ethnic group, these dating practices suggest that connections (and, as we shall see, even identification) are possible between Mexicans and other marginalized groups.

The tenuous connections we see in students' dating practices reflect broader ethnic relationships at Addison High. Blacks, Mexicans, and Whites, for instance, usually "hang" with "their own," and each group tends to have its designated cafeteria tables.

However, though Mexicans, Blacks, and Whites are recognized as distinct groups, Mexican students tend to view their Black peers as sharing in the Mexicans' marginalized status within the school. This shared identity leads to the two groups' participating in some of the same forms of cultural production, usually in the form of clothing styles. At times, however, these shared forms of representation lead to ambiguity concerning who gets "credit" for certain types of oppositional symbols. In the eyes of some Mexicans, this ambiguity threatens the integrity of their distinct identity. Emilio, for instance, has strong opinions about Mexicans' sacrificing their identity for a more generic oppositional status:

> Most of the Mexicans want to be Black. They dress Black. You know how Black people sag their pants down? I don't like seeing Mexicans doin' that. It's not right; they're their own culture and they shouldn't try to be nobody else's. It embarrasses Mexicans when you say "Look at that Mexican; he's tryin' to be Black." Like, you know how Mexicans got low-rider cars? Like, I think we invented low-rider cars. But the Blacks, now, they're rich and stuff, and they bring them out in public, and people think they made them up, but it's the Mexicans that made it up.

Thus while the Mexicans recognize that both groups have been marginalized by the "Whites," the Mexicans—as Zeke articulated in our cafeteria conversation, expressing a sentiment I had heard many times—feel that Addison High Mexicans don't get the same "respect" as do "the Blacks."[10] This perception leaves Mexicans with a dilemma: Do they unite with Blacks as partners in a struggle for "respect," or do they compete for a "more privileged" minority status?

This ambivalence gets played out most dramatically in fighting among students. Indeed, whom Latino students fight with further illustrates that identity markers are contingent upon the situation. The general rule, articulated by Emilio, is that Mexicans don't fight members of their own ethnic group: "Well, we almost always fight Black people and White people." In my three years in Addison, I never saw a fight between two Mexicans. However, as Alejandro, Zeke, and Emilio have suggested, Mexicans see themselves and the Blacks as struggling against the dominant White culture, a perception which encourages solidarity between the groups. According to Emilio:

> But we don't hardly ever fight Blacks anymore 'cause we all want to be together, you know? That's what the White people want is for Mexicans and Blacks to fight. We're just trying to get all together and trying to work things out. Like at the [Huron County] fair, when the Black people fight the White people, they, the Black people, come to us and we help them and stuff, and sometimes they help us. And sometimes at school, too. That's how we are. We work together.

However, though the unofficial "rules" of fighting suggest a certain uneasy truce between Blacks and Mexicans, these rules often give way to interracial tensions. As I mentioned earlier, such tensions recently ran high between Blacks and Mexicans when a Mexican began dating a Black girl. When the two boys originally involved in the dispute fought in school, each was joined by members of his ethnic group. The situation escalated to a point where Felipe described it as "awful. It got to where every time you turned around there was some Black kid and a Mexican going at it."

The question of Mexican identity—and the consequences of assuming that identity—get further complicated by class issues. As we have seen from the account of the homecoming football game, the terminology often used to name "successful" White students is not only "White" but also "the rich kids." Moreover, Latino students who seem to be behaving in ways that indicate they've acclimated to "mainstream" culture are sometimes said to be "acting White." However, at Addison High students don't need to be Black or Mexican in order to be marginalized or to exercise oppositional cultural production similar to that of Mexican students. I observed an example of such opposition one day in Trans Math class. I had taken a place in the back row, flanked by Alex, a Mexican, on my right and his White friend Eric on my left.

"How long since you joined this class?" Eric asked me.

"Oh, about a week and a half," I said. When Eric went to the front of the room to drop his assignment in the basket on the teacher's desk, Alex turned to me and said, "You're not a student, right?"

"No," I said. "Not here, anyway."

"Well, Eric's a nice guy, but he's not too bright." Alex is a good-looking kid. Short black hair, smooth olive skin, and eyes tinted blue from his designer contact lenses. He wore a T-shirt that said "Puro Mexicano" on the back. Below the words was an image of a man wearing a large sombrero and smoking a cigar, with a bandanna tied around his neck and an ammunition belt slung over each shoulder. Draped over the back of Alex's chair was an expensive-looking Polo jacket. He pulled his books from a leather Eddie Bauer backpack.

While the class took a quiz, Alex and Emilio managed to trade insults from across the room. "Hey, *perro* [dog]," Emilio called out.

"*What do you want, migrant?*" Alex replied. They both laughed.

"Okay, guys, let's cut out the Spanish in here," the teacher said.

"Hey, migrant," Alex then asked Emilio, "who you riding home with?" Emilio pointed to a White seated behind him. "Jesse?" Alex said. "That White trash from the trailer park?" Jesse looked up from his quiz, laughed, and gave Alex the finger.

Alex then turned to Eric and said, "Hey, you still owe me money. Where's my dollar?"

"I won't pay you a dollar," Eric said. "I'll give you some food stamps, though."

Rob, a White student sitting in the front row, slapped his pencil on his desk. "Why do we got to know this stuff? Is anyone ever going to ask us what a polygon is?"

"Whether you choose to think it's important is one thing," the substitute teacher said. "What the book thinks is important, and what the school requires us to have done is another thing. If you thought it was funny yesterday ignoring me, fine, but not today. Tomorrow we have a test."

Rob held up his hands. "Easy, big fella," he said. Two boys stood up from their seats, grabbed the bathroom pass (which is supposed to be used by only one student at a time), and walked out into the hallway.

"Why have Rene and David both left?" the teacher said, and walked out of the room to find them. The teacher returned with Rene.

"Do you know why I don't tell you I'm leaving?" Rene said. "Because you're snobby." A blonde girl sat off in the corner by the windows. I hadn't heard her say a word all semester, and that day, like every other day, she stared straight ahead, her chin in her hand, blinking once in a while, nothing else.

Tommy, who sat in front of me, was wearing around his neck a silver medallion of a marijuana leaf with the word "Legalize" carved beneath it. Mounted on the back of the medallion was a small roach clip, which Tommy used to hold the hall pass when he left the room to get a drink of water or go to the bathroom.

As the class finished the quiz, an African American student named Troy walked by and deliberately stepped on Rob's tattered vinyl backpack. Rob (a White) pushed Troy, who responded with a little return push on Rob's shoulder. "Go ahead," Rob suddenly said out loud. "Hit me, and see what happens. Just get the fuck out of here."

On the other side of the room, Eric stood up. "C'mon," he said. "Don't fight in Trans Math; fight in Algebra instead. We're all losers in here anyway."

There is a curious camaraderie being revealed in this scene. Though students are placed in Trans Math rather than algebra because of low grades in previous math classes or because they are not enrolled in the "college preparatory" track at Addison High, the practical effect of these criteria is that the students who "belong" in Trans Math come from predominantly poor and/or ethnic-minority families. In other words, the poor Whites, the Blacks, and the Mexicans in Trans Math have, in this context, a great deal in common: they are, as Eric put it, the "losers" of Addison High. Although racial tension is evident in the classroom interactions between students, when Troy and Rob began posturing for a fight, the fact that they are of different ethnic groups was not as important in Eric's mind as the solidarity they must rely upon to cope with the reality of their place on the margins of their school community.

Further complications arising from this intersection of ethnicity and class are the distinctions sometimes made within the parameters of a Mexican identity. Indeed, while the generally marginal status of Addison's Mexicans provides a tentative basis for solidarity with poor Whites, some Mexican students in Addison are similar to those studied by Romo and Falbo (1996, p. 136) in that they seem to resist an identity that associates them with either poverty or Mexican national origin. For instance, Zeke's comment that, "I'm not ashamed to say it, but we're from back in Mexico," may be read as an indication that immigrants from Mexico carry a stigma that Addison's Mexican American students prefer to avoid. Similarly, Emilio noted that not all Mexicans are quick to admit that their recent family history includes field labor:

> Mexicans are weird. I don't know. The way I see it is that all Mexicans, when they came here, wherever they came from, had to work in the fields. That's what we had to do; we had to work in the fields. Like the Blacks did with slavery, right? I know we had to work in the fields. People say "Well, my parents never had to work in the fields," but I know they did, 'cause all or most of them did. They just don't want to admit it 'cause they're embarrassed, the Mexicans are. I think every Mexican had to work in the fields, like their moms and dads or at least their grandmother or something. But they deny it. They say, "Well, my grandmother never worked and my mom didn't either," but I think they're lying.[11]

If Emilio is right, the same students who will confess to a Mexican identity will also try to distance themselves from any connotations of poverty that may accompany that identity. In my view, the reluctance of Mexicans to admit to their families' likely history of migrant labor suggests once again that there is a great deal of diversity within even apparently unifying cultural categories and that the production of persons at Addison High is a complex process that involves the constant renegotiation of identities within various contexts. As these identities fluctuate, so does the type of cultural production effected by students who assume them, as well as the boundaries that distinguish one group from another.[12] Though these fluctuations may sometimes compromise a group's ability to unite against hegemony, the types of shared and shifting identities I have discussed in this section may also be viewed as a challenge to thinking of students as occupying overly deterministic ethnic, cultural, and social categories.

The persistent problem, however, is that even if we recognize the multiple, localized, and shifting nature of students' identities, the consequences of living out these identities mirror those experienced by Willis's lads. That is, such students' identifying behavior ultimately contributes to their exclusion from the school's mainstream culture and activities, thereby perpetuating the disparity in students' opportunities for democratic participation at Addison High and beyond it. Thus, whatever potential may lie in Latino students' evolving identities for changing the ways they act and are acted upon, this potential is not being realized—it is being contained within the structure of the school. Something is needed, then, to revise this pattern. As we shall see in the following section, that "something" may be the individual agency of a citizen teacher who draws on Latino students' identities to inform and motivate a critique of discriminatory social relations.

Identity as Resistance: Felipe, Emilio, and Mr. Thompson

I sat in front of Emilio and behind his friend Sergio in science class and listened to the boys' conversation.

"I couldn't do much this weekend," Sergio said. "I had too much math homework."

"Yeah, you multiplied," said Emilio.

"I had to write an English essay, too."

"But you've been takin' French."

Don, an African American boy seated across the aisle, then asked Emilio about a test he was being allowed to postpone because of a recent absence. "Hey, Emilio, how come you don't have to take the test?"

"'Cause he's Mexican." Sergio said.

Emilio asked Ms. Palmer, the special education teacher who serves as an aide in the science class, for the answers to the review sheet.

"That's not part of my motherly duties," said Palmer.

"Don't get mouthy," Emilio replied. Palmer leveled her eyes at the boy and beckoned him out into the hallway.

"I'm sorry, Miss," Emilio said as he stood. "I didn't think you could hear me."

As Emilio returned to his seat a few moments later, he whispered to Sergio, "She tried to choke me and shit."

"It's because you're Mexican," Sergio said.

Emilio laughed, turned to me, and asked, "Really, Todd? Is that true?"

I shrugged. "What do you think?"

"Yeah, I think it is," Emilio said. "She puts me down 'cause I'm brown."

Given the many ways oppositional behavior is tied to ethnicity at Addison High, it seems that Willis (1981b) is correct when he writes of the likelihood that, for example, Emilio's behavior will result in his being denied access to the benefits that come with willing participation in the dominant culture. However, as I have suggested, to speak of cultural reproduction only as a means of exclusion is to risk the generalization that places like Addison High operate like what Willis calls a cultural "black box," where richly diverse students are subjected to unrelenting hegemonic forces until they graduate as automatons that function according to the programming of dominant ideology. Or, considering the role cultural production plays in this process, we may be led to think that even if students do create their own oppositional culture, they do so only to have this identity relegate them to the bottom of the socioeconomic ladder. Granted, Addison High is ripe with examples of such effects. We have seen how homecoming traditions symbolically represent what it means to be a proper and successful Addison High student, while Emilio's "oppositional" behavior in science class came very close to getting him sent to the office (again).

But the Latino students at Addison High are more than passive and faceless members of a subaltern group, and to speak of them only as objects or agents of symbolic mechanisms of oppression is to tell only part of their story. There is, indeed, much more to tell, for although I have seen Latino students' cultures under assault by that of the school, Giroux (1983) reminds us of something that is, I think, equally important: "Culture is . . . both the subject and object of resistance; the driving force of culture is contained not only in how it functions to dominate subordinate groups, but also in the way in which oppressed groups draw from their own cultural capital and set of experiences to develop an oppositional logic" (pp. 282–283). As Giroux suggests, because culture is not static, whatever control it mediates is always in flux, and in that fluctuation lies the potential to restructure the cultural frameworks by which Addison High operates and to renegotiate the ways in which its Latino students participate in the activities that take place there.

Educators needlessly restrict themselves, I think, when their descriptions of such "renegotiations" are limited to theoretical frameworks that remain on an exclusively structural level. As I have been arguing throughout this work, in order to describe more accurately and productively the ways in which educational institutions stray from their democratic ideals by reproducing sociocultural privilege, we must seek to understand the dialogic relationship between social structures and human agency as it occurs at the level of everyday life and—in our case—concrete school relations. In other words, looking at specific people, sites, and events highlights the complex and dialectical nature of the ways in which teachers, students, and other human agents come together within specific historical and social contexts in order both to reproduce and, potentially, to revise the conditions of their experience.

To refer again to some points I made earlier, historian George Lipsitz (1990), in a discussion of Gramsci's notion of hegemony, suggests that appeals for hegemonic legitimacy always take place within concrete historical circumstances, in contested societies with competing interests: "Even while establishing dominance, those in power must borrow from the ideas, actions, and experience of the past, all of which contain potential for informing a radical critique of the present" (pp. 67–68). Moreover, as we have seen, Willis (1981a) argues that the notion of localized cultural production underscores the agency emanating from small groups and challenges the values of the dominant culture:

> [Cultural production] insists on the active, transformative natures of cultures and on the collective ability of social agents, not only to think like theorists, but to act like activists. Life experi-

ences, individual and group projects, secret illicit and informal knowledge, private fears and fantasies, the threatening anarchic power arising from irreverent association . . . are not merely interesting additions. . . . These things are central: determined but also determining. They must occupy, fully fledged in their own right, a vital theoretical and political transformative stage in our analysis. (p. 114)

I am encouraged by Willis's words, for they suggest that although ideologically laden forms of symbolic representation can serve to oppress, they can also be used to promote democratizing social action. Or, as Willis (1981b) himself succinctly puts it, "Cultural reproduction always carries with it the possibility of producing alternative outcomes" (p. 172). As I mentioned in the introduction to this book, several writers have provided examples of the democratic potential of cultural production by emphasizing the importance of ethnic identity in the history of the American labor movement. We have seen, for instance, that Nancy Fraser (1997) and Robin Kelley (1997) contend that ethnic and gender identity have been powerful forces in motivating working-class solidarity. Similarly, Giroux (1999), in contesting the assertions of those who view cultural identity as "ornamental, a burden on class-based politics," draws on Gramsci's writings to argue that "class is always lived through modalities of race and gender" (p. 1). George Sánchez (1993) has demonstrated the value of this critical perspective by meticulously documenting the ways in which the evolving ethnic identity of Mexican Americans "engendered political radicalism" that helped fuel the progressive labor movements of the 1930s and 40s (p. 12–13). Further examples of the crucial role of ethnicity in fostering social activism include César Chávez's leadership of the United Farm Workers of America, as well the more recent efforts of the "Justice for Janitors" organization to win fair wages for the mostly Latino maintenance workers who clean high-rises in downtown Los Angeles. My point here is that by seeking to understand more thoroughly the origins and consequences of students' cultural identities, educators may position themselves to better assist students in drawing upon these identities in the interests of democratic empowerment and justice.

To be sure, we have seen that education directed toward such ambitious aims is difficult to pursue in schools where being an ethnic- and/or language-minority student is usually experienced as a barrier to success as the institution defines it. In Felipe's case, for instance, teachers' failure to revise their instruction to accommodate his limited English proficiency proved to be an ongoing problem. His head bowed, Felipe spoke slowly and at length when he described his frustration in this way:

> Sometimes here I feel like I'm in a lost world or something. It's not the kids; it's like school. Like homework that you don't understand, and if you don't turn them in you get in trouble and stuff. You just feel kinda weird. Like a story and you have to say in front of class and you don't know how to read real good, you get nervous and just feel bad. I think the people who don't know real good English, they should try to help them more. That would help a lot and make things a lot better. I had help like this in eighth grade, but that's all, not here, not in the high school. And extra time. Like people who know English real good, they can do the homework just like that 'cause they understand. But me, I don't have nobody to help me at home with my homework, so I just have trouble with that. And when I'm doin' my homework, I'm like, I don't understand, so I just don't worry about it because if I keep thinkin' about it I just get mad and I feel like not goin' to school the next day. I just feel alone, like my sister [Rosa] did. Sometimes I feel like that and feel like not comin' to school. I'm like "I don't care." I just don't care so I don't, like, get scared . . . . Like next year I can quit if I want. See, if I feel like that I just quit. Sometimes I feel like getting out of the school real quick and just going back to Puerto Rico, 'cause here, sometimes I just feel kinda . . . kinda small.

Despite Felipe's claims of a lack of English fluency, his words eloquently and powerfully attest to the painful consequences of being a Spanish-dominant Puerto Rican student at Addison High. However, while there are no easy solutions to the troubles he describes, notions of oppositional cultural production make it possible to imagine ways of teaching and learning in which an identity as an LM student need not be an educational liability. Mr. Thompson, an Addison High art and geography teacher, did just that: He highlighted the cultural identity of his Latino students, but he did so in ways that helped them critique undemocratic social relations rather than submit to them.

As I entered Mr. Thompson's classroom with Angela, Felipe, and Emilio, I was struck by how different it was from the room in which Rosa and I had struggled through geography two years before. This room looked more to me like an artist's studio than a geography classroom. No maps hung on the walls, no globes in the corner, just an expansive space with a ceiling about sixteen feet high and crisscrossed by open scaffolding. In the front corner was a door to a small bathroom, and next to the door a real traffic light that students flipped to red when the bathroom was occupied, green when available. Hooks and wires dangled from the rafters, and the walls were adorned with antique metal Coke, Pepsi, and Mobile Oil signs and a collection of tapestries from Africa and Latin America. A sombrero hung above the front bulletin board next to a street sign reading "Bobby Knight Court." Near the front wall stood a life-size cardboard figure of Ray Charles, which Thompson had dressed in a T-shirt featuring the Hard Rock Cafe, Tijuana.

Mr. Thompson is a large man, about fifty years old with long wavy gray hair and a full white beard. On one of the first days of class that fall semester, Thompson spent much of the class period playing a video (on his huge A-V system) of the previous night's ABC Evening News, which had covered the exodus of Cuban refugees to the U.S. in August and September of 1994. The segment included interviews with Cubans who had chosen to remain, and Thompson asked Felipe to ask Angela whether she understood what the people being interviewed were saying. Angela responded (via Felipe) that she did, though she added that the people spoke with an accent very different from what she was used to. Thompson asked Felipe whether the accent sounded strange to him, too. Felipe said it did, but that he had kind of gotten used to it when he had gotten to know some Cubans in Miami.

Thompson then pointed out the socioeconomic position of those Cubans who remained and were now disparaging the refugees. "Do you think," he asked, "that maybe the wealthier Cubans have options to remain that the others who set out into the ocean in those leaky rafts do not?" Several members of the class thought so. Also on the news video was a poll indicating that fewer than half of Americans would support a U.S. invasion of Haiti to restore democracy, while 57 percent would support military action to stem the flow of refugees. "What color are most Haitians?" Thompson asked. A student raised her hand and called out, "Black." "Right!" Thompson said. "Now, what does this tell you about U.S. foreign policy?" No response. "Does race have anything to do with it?" Still no response, at first. Soon, however, by leading the students with questions, Thompson made his point: "So, to sum things up, it sure seems, doesn't it, that racism may be an important factor in determining U.S. foreign policy."

About a week later, the geography class was continuing its study of the Caribbean by watching a video called *The Travel Magazine*. The video was essentially a travel brochure, showing sandy beaches, busy markets, and opulent hotels. The students had received instructions to divide their papers lengthwise by a straight line, to write the name of each country discussed on the left, and the characteristics of each on the right. Already, I had come to expect more from Thompson, so I wondered what he was doing.

Thompson grabbed the remote and pressed "pause." "You see those huge hotels?" he asked. The class nodded. "Lemme tell you a story about those hotels." Thompson went on to describe a trip he had taken with a group of students to the Bahamas, where, Thompson explained, "Blacks are not allowed at the poolsides or beaches of the tourist hotels." He then recalled an incident when his group had been at the pool of a Bahamian hotel. The hotel security guards had approached two African American boys in the group and told them to leave the pool. It wasn't until Thompson explained that the boys were with him that the guards allowed them to stay. Emilio raised his hand.

"What if Mexicans go on the beaches?"

"That depends on how dark you are," Thompson said. "Now, take you, for instance." Thompson pointed out that Emilio, by having fairly light skin, could probably get away with using a hotel-controlled beach without any trouble. "But if Felipe here—with his dark skin—tried it, the security guards would be all over him. Why do you think they do this?"

Emilio spoke up: "'Cause they think minorities are dirty."

"Perhaps they do," Thompson replied. "But why might they think that?" This time it was Felipe who answered.

"Because it's the White people who have the money, and they don't want people to think that it's a low-class hotel," Emilio said.

"That's right! They don't want to offend the tourists, and the tourists who have money are almost always White. It's an obviously racist policy, but it's done for financial reasons!" Thompson was almost yelling at this point. Emilio and Felipe were writing like crazy on their note sheets.

The next time I visited Thompson's geography class, they had been studying Mexico for several days. Thompson walked among his students and reviewed: "We've been talking about some of the stereotypes people have about Mexico. What did we say those were?" Emilio was first to speak.

"Mexicans are lazy; they're 'spics,' migrants. People make tomato jokes about them."

"All right, but what have you told me is the reality?" Again, Emilio answered.

"They're not lazy. The main reason they come here is 'cause they got no job in Mexico; they're poor."

"Okay," Thompson said, "we've also been looking at beach resorts in Mexico on the videos. If this were all we knew about Mexico, would we know a stereotype or a reality?"

"Stereotype!" Emilio hadn't even bothered to look up from his notes this time.

"Why?"

"Not all of Mexico is like that. Not everybody sits in grass huts drinking tequila while guys jump off cliffs. And not everybody goes to discotheques."

After the review session, the video resumed—a National Geographic presentation on the history and culture of Mexico. Thompson called out above the video voice-over: "What did it say was the ethnic makeup of Mexico?"

"Native American and Spanish, mostly," Felipe answered.

"Good. Make sure you write it down."

Emilio and Felipe had moved their chairs to within a few feet of the video screen and were writing steadily.

The next morning Thompson had trouble with his video equipment, and as he was busy trying to get the unit up and running, Emilio sat on his backpack on the floor in front of a White girl who parted and smoothed his hair with a large plastic comb. She then coaxed Emilio's hair into six evenly-spaced French braids that began at his forehead and weaved their way to brightly-colored rubber bands to hold them in place. Thirteen people watched the spectacle, fourteen if you included me.

When the girl finished, Emilio was curious to see what he looked like, so he went to the bathroom, flipped the switch to "red," and went inside. He was back out in only seconds. "There's no mirror in there," he said, and asked Thompson, now crawling around on the floor beneath the video equipment at the other end of the room, if he could go to the bathroom. When Thompson didn't answer, Emilio drifted toward the door leading to the hallway and stopped just inside the room. Thompson still lay busy and out of sight. I wondered whether Emilio was going to make a break for it. (I suspected that if this were math or science, he'd have been long gone by now.) He leaned further out of the room, looked around the corner into the hallway, but at last came back inside, choosing to amble around the room and ask girls if they had a pocket mirror he could borrow. A classmate said, "Hey, Emilio, you look like The Predator." Emilio finally got his mirror and decided he didn't like what he saw. He returned to his place on the floor, where, surrounded by girls, one of them undid the braids and shaped his hair into a fountain-like pony-tail. Emilio feigned protest, calling out to Thompson, "Teacher, look!"

By showing some of the ways Mr. Thompson calls attention to and critiques the ways in which people, especially his Mexican and African American students, are represented and treated, I do not wish to imply that I think Thompson is free from the ideology that dominates Addison High and society at large. One day, for instance, the class watched a movie called *Rudy*, in which the protagonist, a boy from a steel mill family of Gary, Indiana, devotes himself to his dream of playing football for Notre Dame. The film is filled with images of Rudy running alone through empty stadium tunnels and falling asleep in the library after studying long hours. Finally Rudy gets his acceptance letter, which he reads while sitting on a park bench, looking across a pond at Notre Dame's famous golden dome, accompanied by the inspirational swell of an orchestra string section. Given the fact that Thompson didn't lead students in a critique of the film, the viewing of this modern Horatio Alger story, with its "work hard and you'll get ahead" message, in some ways downplays the broader sociocultural barriers faced by many of Addison's poor and ethnic minority students.

Moreover, we should not discount considerable evidence that Thompson is working within a profession that often creates its own barriers for Latino students. Parsons (1965), for instance, found that in the school of a small California community, teachers routinely demonstrated preference for Whites over Chicanos by selecting Whites for classroom leadership roles and by negatively stereotyping Chicano students as lazy or slow. Similarly, Valencia (1991b) has noted that a study by the U.S. Commission on Civil Rights (1973) based on observation of over four hundred classrooms in Southwestern U.S. states found that compared to Whites, Chicano students received significantly less praise and encouragement from teachers. This study concludes that "the discovered disparities in teacher behavior toward Mexican-Americans and Anglos are likely to hinder seriously the educational opportunities and achievement of Chicano pupils" (p. 43, cited in Valencia, 1991b, p. 11). As Erickson (1987) and Gibson (1991) have argued, the effects of these types of teacher-student interactions are exacerbated by many teachers' tendencies to coerce students into using an unfamiliar language or otherwise assimilating into schools' cultural mainstream. Faced with such pressure, Latino students often become, to use Erickson's (1987) words, "increasingly alienated from school" and either grow to be "actively resistant—seen as alienated and incorrigible or passively resistant—or fade into the woodwork as a well-behaved, low-achieving student" (p. 348).

Nonetheless, despite harmful collective habits such as these, and despite instances (like showing the *Rudy* film) of failing to acknowledge the range of sociocultural forces constraining poor and ethnic minority students, I believe Thompson demonstrated that even if teachers can't escape the culturally mediated dominant ideology of most schools, they (and their students) can sometimes maneuver within it. For in his geography lessons, Thompson was, I think, going beyond platitudes about tolerance or cultural sensitivity that sound noble enough but fail to address the structures that reflect and perpetuate societal power disparities. In his own way, then, Thompson was engaged in what Susan Hynds (1997) calls "critical constructivist" pedagogy, which underscores not just the social nature of learning but also the cultural politics that influence it. Hynds argues that as part of this critical constructivist approach, teachers should deliberately initiate classroom conversations on social and cultural issues such as race, gender, and social class, conversations that Hynds believes are unlikely to happen if students are left entirely to their own designs. In other words, she contends that teachers' responsibilities include "stepping in the way of bigotry" and inequality (p. 269) by initiating discussions in which students can explicitly interrogate cultural and political realities. I believe that this is the kind of teaching Thompson was engaged in as he led his students through conversations that uncovered the racial and ethnic prejudices implicit in U.S. immigration policies and some travel companies' marketing schemes.

Hynds's "critical constructivism" and Thompson's teaching also illustrate, I think, the value of Dewey's argument against the myth that progressive, democratizing education requires that teachers leave students "free" to do whatever they are led to do by their "natural" impulses (Hirsch, 1996, p. 7). On the contrary, Dewey (1926/1989) strenuously objects to the notion that educators should merely "surround pupils with certain tools, materials, appliances, etc., and then let pupils respond to these according to their desires." Indeed, to those who would falsely caricature democratic education by saying that teachers' suggesting any end or plan to students represents an "unwarranted trespass" on their intellectual freedom, Dewey's response is uncharacteristically direct: "Such a method is really stupid" (p. 56). Such teaching is "stupid," Dewey goes on to explain, for at least two reasons. First, he points out that whatever "spontaneous activity" students would allegedly be engaged in would not be spontaneous at all, but would derive from the classroom environment and from students' previous social experience. In other words, Dewey makes clear that to think of teaching as something other than a kind of intervention in students' lives is absurd. Second, and perhaps more important to his conception of democratic education, Dewey argues that teacher intervention is essential to direct students in activities in which "ends" or "purposes" arise in conjunction with the activities themselves. That is, Dewey stresses that the means or methods used in a classroom are the ways in which worthwhile aims become evident and articulated. Dewey puts it this way: "Each step forward, each 'means' used, is a partial attainment of an 'end.' It makes clear the character of that end and suggests ways people can, with original and independent thinking, take the next step. The 'end' is not, in other words, an end or finality in the literal sense, but is in turn the starting point of new desires, aims, and plans" (p. 60).

In my view, this inseparability of means and ends is precisely what we have seen demonstrated in Mr. Thompson's geography class. For in Thompson's teaching, his "means" are themselves democratizing in the sense that they are responsive to students' present knowledge and abilities, they encourage students to participate in a critical examination of the messages they receive through various media, and they make clear the connections between what is being taught in school and the world beyond it. At the same time, however, these means are also directed toward the future; they are developing in students those habits of thought and conduct that students might bring to bear on their activities in as-yet-unforeseen circumstances. Thus, as is suggested in Emilio and Felipe's positive response to these lessons, Thompson stirred in at least some of his students an astute, potentially oppositional awareness that affirmed their ethnic identities, but not at the cost of a self-destructive form of cultural production as described by Willis.

Though it's hard to say exactly what effect Thompson's teaching had on his Latino students, it was influential enough to prompt Emilio to follow Thompson's suggestion that he remain after school one day to speak with visiting members of the University of Michigan's Latino student organization. As the meeting broke into small groups, Emilio ended up talking to a university student named Mario. We sat around a table in the cafeteria, still able to smell the institutional lunch served earlier that day. Mario, a big guy who grew up on the Gulf coast plain of Texas, leaned forward on his elbows and looked at Emilio and the others around him. "The key for you is self-esteem," he said. "And that's what learning more about your heritage will give you." Mario then talked about the revolutionary history of Mexico, especially the Zapatistas and other groups' struggles for independence and justice.

"We never learned that stuff in school," one of the Addison students said.

Mario went on, shifting his focus from the past to the futures of the students whose eyes were fixed on his earnest expression: "Would you rather own your own company or be in some dead-end job? For that you need an education, and in order to get that education, you need a high self-esteem." The janitor began moving tables around in the cafeteria, making it harder to hear. "But you gotta be careful," Mario continued. "That shit about you work for what you get? My dad was a bus driver for years; he worked all the time, and it didn't get him much. What counts is having the attitude, knowing people. You come to me when I got my own company, you got a job. I know just 'cause you're here that you're interested in making something of yourself. That's what a Chicano is—someone who takes pride in his heritage, someone who wants to know more about himself."

"So, what am I called?" Emilio asked.

"You wanna learn more about your past? About yourself?"

"Yeah."

"Then that's what you are."

The buses had left long before the after-school meeting ended, so I gave Emilio a lift home. As we drove through the neighborhoods of Addison's East Side, I thought about Mario's encouraging, even inspirational words about the importance of Latino students' valuing their cultural heritage. But I thought, too, of his father, a proud man who had worked hard all his life but who, according to Mario, didn't have much to show for it. This story of high hopes weighed down by socioeconomic realities reminded me of what Emilio had told me about his family just a few weeks before. He recalled that when he was a child, his family had lived in Florida, where they made a living, in Emilio's words, "picking cucumbers and stuff." While there, Emilio's young sister died of a burst appendix, which Emilio said was

brought on when she "ate a pickle with poison fertilizer on it."
"Her name was Nora," Emilio told me. "She was only like two
years old. We were only a year apart; we were like twins. We looked
alike, too." Though he doesn't remember his sister well, Emilio
explained that he keeps a photo of her on a shelf in his room:

> There's a guy, my dad's friend, he knows how to make these
> things out of wood, and you put a picture inside of it and some
> glass on it. He designs it himself. It's real nice. It's me and Nora
> put together. My name's on the side and it gots her name on the
> bottom. It's really cool; like she's wearing a dress. I don't know,
> we used to be good friends. We loved each other, but now I don't
> really think about it.

Since those days when poverty had caused Emilio's family to
have access only to health care that was tragically inadequate,
Emilio explained that their situation has improved only slightly.
Though his father had secured a job when they first arrived in
Addison, he was disabled by an accident at work in which, according to Emilio, "something went into his toe and made a hole
in it." Emilio said that since the accident, his father's health has
steadily declined: "After that his back started hurting and his
arms, and some days he can't feel them, and now he's got to give
himself shots." Presently, the family's financial burden rests on
the shoulders of Emilio's mother, who he said has begun to show
the effects of a grueling work schedule at the local Kmart: "My
mom, she's always working. She's only about fifty, but she looks
really old. She works too much."

As I turned my Honda onto Emilio's block and pulled into
his driveway, he amended this history he had begun in our earlier
conversation. Despite his family's past struggles, Emilio remained
hopeful about the future, saying that he saw their experiences as
similar to those of many other of Addison's Latino residents:

> Like, if you're a Mexican, and you work in the fields all your life,
> you just come to Addison and start from the beginning. You can
> get a part-time job and then you get a regular job where you start
> making pretty good money. And then you don't need help no
> more, and the great-grandsons or whatever can get rich. That's
> the way we are; that's where I see Mexicans at. The migrants

come here to get help and find jobs, but they don't want their kids working out in the fields.

Planning to follow this pattern, Emilio explained that he had no intention of "working out in the fields" all his life. Instead, he said, "I want to be the first in my family to graduate from high school, maybe go to college, and be a good example to my little brothers." As we sat in my car, the engine idling, I asked Emilio if he knew what he wanted to do when he got older. He turned in the passenger seat and faced me. "You know the people that work in like, AAA? You know, like insurance guys? I want to be one of those. My dad said if I finish high school I could do that, and I don't want to mess it up." I told him I thought he'd be very good at it.

Before leaving, Emilio asked if he could come to Ann Arbor some time to see a wrestling match.

"Sure," I said. "I have a wrestler in my class at Michigan. He told me they have a home meet next week."

"Is he Mexican?"

"No, he's African American."

"Yeah? That's cool."

We said good-bye, and Emilio stepped out of the car and shut the door. He slung his backpack over his shoulder, climbed the steps to his front door, waved once more, and went inside. That was the last time I ever saw him.

The following week at school, when Emilio didn't show up for geography class, I asked some of his friends if they had seen him and learned that he had been "locked up" again in the juvenile detention center for violating his parole by getting into another fight. I called the center but was told I couldn't visit Emilio because I was neither a family member nor an attorney. The man I spoke with did say, though, that I was welcome to write.

A couple days later I wrote Emilio a letter in which I tried to be encouraging, telling him innocuous things like "hang in there" and "study hard." I also asked him some questions about what his days in the center were like and mentioned what was going on in my classes at the university. Before folding the page and stuffing it and an extra stamp into an envelop, I reread what I had written and couldn't help thinking that it sounded tepid and futile.

In less than a week I received a reply, part of which goes like this:[13]

> Hey man what's up? not much in this detention but doing my time probably for a couple of months or weeks. Hey man thanks for looking out other words thanks for writing me. Thanks for still standing around and putting positive things in this mix up head of mine.
>
> I'm not going to give up. My Dad finally came in here and visited me Sunday he told me he would never come and see me but he did for the first time I was happy to see him but he started to cry I wish I never would of let him down. So I got a lot of thinking to do, but I don't want to do nothing stupid things will just get worse. Yes we go to school here but stay in the same building every day and all day. Yes we take classes we get to outside for gym. We get up at about 6:30 am get out of school about 3 pm. Yes, its different here you can't laugh there to serious about things. No roomates your in a cell all alone. . . . Thanks for the stamp. But I could of use one of mine. . . . Take care homie and stay true. Your friend, Emilio Mendez.

At school the next week, Thompson's geography students worked in groups of four on a project in which they used clay and plywood to construct raised relief maps of various Caribbean countries. The assignment also required that each group research their particular country and write a report which they were to share with the rest of the class. Thompson's students worked well together, shaping mountains and beaches, taking notes on books he had collected as resources for their written reports. Angela and Felipe sat beside each other at a table with the other members of their group, with Felipe translating into Spanish the information about Cuba that they read from an encyclopedia. Thompson circulated around the room, answered questions, and from time to time raised his hands and his voice to give further instructions. This and the video analyses of the previous week were examples of good teaching, I thought: rigorous, relevant to contemporary concerns, attentive to a variety of learning styles, and—with Felipe and Angela assigned to the same group—relatively accessible to all students. Still, that day, even Thompson's creative and energetic teaching seemed strangely inadequate as I thought of Emilio sitting alone in his cell or playing basketball in a gym class surrounded by a tall chain-link fence. Feeling pretty useless, I did the only thing I could think of: I wrote Emilio back. Again, his reply came soon after:

> Todd
> Hey Man what's up Loco. Thanks for looking out again I got your letter I'm glad to hear you got mine. My P.O. [parole officer] came in today and told me I will get out on my birthday June 6 [three months from then], I thought I was going to get out next week guess not. But nothing I can do but do my time. As days go by they get worst o-well.
> Hey Loco I got a question for you, you think I can make it to college? So man I going to let you go until you right again. Take it easy homie
> Your friend Emilio Mendez.
> P.S. I hope you can understand my writing.

As I finished reading Emilio's letter, it occurred to me that while I could, in a literal sense, understand his writing well enough, I would never really comprehend what it was like to live through the complex and painful experiences that had led Emilio back to the center. The poverty that had taken his sister from him and that gnawed at the health of his parents, the unlikelihood that Emilio would ever "make it to college," the anger that drew him time after time into fights. These were part of Emilio's world, but not mine, and to work toward solutions to such immense problems required, I knew, more than the efforts of Mr. Thompson and me.

I found out from Emilio's friends that immediately after his release from the center, his parents had moved the family back to Florida. I wondered how much of their decision was based on their desire to take Emilio away from the circumstances that had been so troublesome to him in Addison. But whatever the reason, none of the boys I talked to knew exactly where he had gone. The school office, too, said he had left no forwarding address or phone number. Though it's now been years since I've seen or spoken with Emilio, I think of him often and consider sometimes what I'd say to him if we were ever to meet again. I think I'd ask about his parents and whether he was in school or working. I'd tell him that I thought he was a gifted, intelligent, and funny person. I'd tell him, too, that I am grateful to him for being so friendly to me in school and for all he gave to me, and that I'm sorry I wasn't much help to him in Addison. And though I know it's unlikely he'll ever read this book, it's nice to dream that some day he might and that in this way I can say to him, I miss you and hope you are safe and happy.

CHAPTER SEVEN

The Tesoros *Literacy Project:* An *Experiment in Democratic* Communities

We lie, as Emerson said, in the lap of an immense intelligence. But that intelligence is dormant and its communications are broken, inarticulate, and faint until it possesses the local community as its medium.

JOHN DEWEY, *The Public and Its Problems*

From Determinism to Democracy

It was just past noon, and I was on my way to the cafeteria to eat with Felipe, Zeke, and the rest of the Mexicans when I passed the large reception area of the Addison High counseling office and saw that staff members were holding a luncheon commemorating the retirement of Martha, a secretary who had worked for the Addison Schools for over thirty years. Long tables were covered with white paper cloths, and Beth Reinstra called me over to join her in a line of teachers who waited to fill plastic plates with pasta salad and sections of a six-foot-long submarine sandwich. Reinstra introduced me to an English teacher named Laura Vedder, who was in line behind us. I shook her hand, and the three of us found seats next to Martinez and Soto.

I mentioned to the ESL teachers that I was surprised to see them there, that I thought they would be busy with their classes in one of the middle schools.

"We made a special point to be here," Martinez said. "We've known Martha for a long time."

Soto nodded. I noticed that on her lapel she wore a button depicting a rose alongside her name, "Mrs. Soto." I asked her about it.

"It's for the other staff members here," she said. "The other teachers don't know our names. One of them calls me Mrs. Hernandez, just because it's a Spanish name, I guess. They think Alice and I are speech teachers, or Spanish teachers. And they think we're the same; they confuse us. I don't know, maybe it's because we both have dark skin and short hair."

Vedder laughed. "That's terrible," she said.

As we chatted Vedder began to ask about my work, why I bothered to make the drive from Ann Arbor, what I had learned so far. I responded by talking about Rosa's alienation from her teachers and fellow students, about the ESL students' struggles in their content-area classes, and about the cultural differences that separate me and most other teachers from people like Claudia and Emilio and that make understanding and responding to them complicated and difficult for us.

Vedder looked up from her dish of fruit. "Sounds interesting," she said. "Now, what are you gonna do about it."

That was a question I had been thinking about for a long time.

As the months went by I came to respect Vedder as a person and as a teacher, especially the way she reached out to students who seemed to have little success or interest in school. I spoke with students who said they had never liked school, but who were challenged in Vedder's class to value themselves, to use literature to reflect on their experiences and issues that were important to them, and (in Vedder's words) to "express who they are." A girl in one of Vedder's classes summed up many students' feelings toward Vedder by saying, "She listens to you."

The more I spoke with Vedder about her work, the more I knew that she, Martinez, and I shared an interest in groups of students who were disenfranchised at Addison High. During one of our conversations in an empty classroom after school, Vedder expressed our common interest by saying, "It's not just the Latino kids; a lot of my White students who are poor face the same kinds of problems around here. They feel like there's no place for them here, like they don't belong here, and you know what the sad thing is? They're right."

Our shared concern for students who were situated on the margins of what I have earlier called the school's dominant culture eventually led Martinez, Vedder, and me to initiate what came to be called the *Tesoros* (Treasures) literacy project, which we hoped would help address for a small number of students what we understood to be some of the challenges that come along with being either poor or Mexican at Addison High. The framework for the *Tesoros* project was to have Martinez's ESL students work collaboratively once each week for ten weeks with counterparts from Vedder's section of eleventh-grade American Literature. The specific reading and writing activities we included in the project centered on the notion that students should search for and value the "treasures" of their own experience. Our plan was that students would come together to read Spanish- and English-language texts, translate these texts for those in the group who could not understand them, write in response to their own and each others' stories, and assist each other in revising and editing their work. We hoped that these activities would help us work toward two mutually dependent objectives: first, to help students succeed by providing them with opportunities to read and write in ways that built upon the literacies they already possessed; and second, to create a space where they might participate in conversations that enabled them to establish relationships with people from whom they were normally separated. We hoped, in sum, that the *Tesoros* project might be useful to the students who agreed to participate—the start of a change at Addison High, a change that would represent progress toward the kind of meaningful and productive connections that might help students like these feel like they actually belonged in the classes they attended.

Given the extent to which the *Tesoros* participants were typically excluded from participation in the academic and social life of Addison High, Dewey's tenets of democratizing pedagogy seemed to me like a useful framework to lend some sort of patterned integrity to the project. Dewey (1916/1985) argues that the principal aim of education should be to enable individuals to develop a "capacity for growth" that occurs through the freedom, creativity, and dialogue of a democratically constituted society (p. 107). Such a society, Dewey insists, must be a way of life, a continuous process by which people come together to establish and preserve all individuals' abilities to participate in the activities of the communities in which they live:

> A democracy is more than a form of government; it is primarily a mode of associated living, of conjoint, communicated experience. The extension in space of the number of individuals who participate in an interest so that each has to refer his own action to that of others, and to consider the action of others to give point and direction to his own, is equivalent to the breaking down of those barriers of class, race, and national territory which kept men from perceiving the full import of their activity. (p. 93)

In order to work toward growth through democracy, Dewey (1916/1985) further contends that aims in education must represent "a freeing of activities," which involves creating circumstances in which people might reflectively plan and implement flexible courses of action to achieve specific goals (p. 112). As I considered which courses of action might be useful to the *Tesoros* students, I found especially compelling Dewey's notion that the freeing of activities depends upon thinking of the general aims of growth and democracy not as static goals but as "ends in view" (p. 112). Similar to what I had seen demonstrated in Mr. Thompson's geography class, understanding an aim as an end in view means that people should think of going through the process of working toward a desirable end as part of the end itself. Or, to use Dewey's words, "The aim is as definitely a means of action as is any other portion of the activity" (p. 113). Thus, ends in view, as Dewey (1930) defines them, are not goals lying beyond activity; rather, they are "foreseen consequences which arise in the course of activity and which are employed to give activity added meaning and to direct its further course" (p. 225). People must first engage in some sort of activity, and as they do so, ends in view arise insofar as these agents begin to think of the activity in terms of its outcome, thereby defining and deepening the meaning of what they do and why they are doing it. In Dewey's view, then, an end and the processes of achieving that end become essentially indistinguishable. In working with the *Tesoros* students, the notion of ends in view seemed to me to be especially important because, as I have suggested, our primary goal for the project was to counteract the alienation that Latino and poor White students endured in school. To think of this aim as an end in view meant that the activities in which the group participated needed to be characterized by the democratic inclusion that we hoped would be the result of the project. As ends in view, students' writing, reading, talking, and listening would—we hoped—be experiences that would themselves provide students with motive and direction to join in future undertakings of reflective and purposeful engagement with themselves and others.

In the context of this discussion of the *Tesoros* project, it is worth underscoring that, to Dewey (1927/1988), enacting an end in view of democracy necessarily includes fostering those habits of mind and action that contribute to communities where inclusive participation is possible. As Dewey contends, "Democracy is not an alternative to other principles of associated life. It is the idea of community itself" (p. 328). This vision of democracy and community as interdependent—Dewey's notion that each, in effect, constitutes the other—is difficult to bring about due to the realities of actual classrooms and the constraints that societies and cultures place on students like those who would soon participate in the *Tesoros* project. Nonetheless, Dewey calls for democracy as it develops from individual sites and localized practices, and to conceive of the *Tesoros* activities as ends in view created the possibility that a group of students sitting in a classroom in the middle of a Michigan winter could actually be a part of Dewey's broader democratic vision.

In what follows, I will describe how the *Tesoros* project may be understood as the participants' enacting, as a collective end in view, Dewey's notions of what should (and does) happen in democratic communities. While taking into account the cautions that recent theorists have set forth regarding the homogenizing and exclusionary potential of communities (Noddings, 1996; Sennett, 1977; Young, 1990), I will argue that we might work toward avoiding such pitfalls by focusing on what Dewey (1916/1985) describes as two criteria of a democracy: that it enable, first, "numerous and varied" interests shared by members within a society, and, second, "full and free . . . interplay with other forms of association" (p. 89). These two traits, the first emphasizing common ground within groups, and the second, the interactive difference within and among them, are, to Dewey, "precisely what characterize the democratically constituted society" (p. 92). I believe that what emerged during the *Tesoros* project was just this dialectical tension between unity and separation—a tentatively empathetic "togetherness" made possible by the Latino and the poor White students' shared marginalized status at Addison High, but also complicated (and enriched) by the Latino students' assertion of a separate identity that caused a disruption in what Dewey calls our "habits" of thought and conduct. By presenting the *Tesoros* project within the framework of these criteria, I will argue for a reading of Dewey that places greater emphasis on affective relationships than is usually attributed to his work— relationships that I believe enable members of a community to encounter difference as complementary and socially productive rather than threatening. Through this reading I seek again to encourage teachers to understand schooling and its effects not as predetermined but as open to revision. Also, I hope that this account might serve as an example to teachers that collaborative reading and writing has the potential not only to bring people together but also to allow for and value difference within communities as essential to individual and social growth.

Affection As an End in View

It was just before nine on a February morning as I made my way through the halls of Addison High with five students in tow. Vedder had warned me that these were "extreme cases," students who had "checked out" of her American Literature class and had already lost course credit because of their absences or failure to turn in assignments. Passing rows of lockers and open classroom doors, I chatted quietly with each student in the group, mostly because I was genuinely interested to learn a bit about them, but also at least in part to heed Vedder's warning to keep them from drifting off to a bathroom for a smoke. The first of these students I spoke with, Lisa, told me that she hated school but that things had gotten better for her after leaving home and moving in with her boyfriend's family. Aaron, wearing a Georgetown Hoyas baseball cap backwards, said he enjoyed watching college basketball on cable TV. Katie, a pale girl with flaky skin and dark eye shadow, admitted that she liked to write poetry but that she was probably going to fail Vedder's class because of her truancy. "I have to work a lot," she explained. Jaime, a Chicano born and raised in Addison, had his right hand and arm heavily bandaged nearly to the elbow. A couple of days before, he said, he had "gotten mad" and punched his fist through his bedroom window. Susan, Vedder had told me, hadn't volunteered a word in class the entire first semester. As we walked, she didn't say anything but chewed on the cuff of her Mickey Mouse sweatshirt.

In the Addison High teachers' lounge and counselors' offices, these students and dozens like them are called "underachievers" or "at-risk." But in the hallways and cafeteria, where euphemism is rare, they are the "burnouts," "losers," and "trailer trash." Though I was nearly twice their age, to me this group of young people looked tired and old. When I checked over my shoulder to see them shuffle through the hallway, I felt like a boy dragging behind him a bunch of slightly deflated balloons.

We reached the top of the steps leading to the second floor and entered the small classroom where Martinez met with her ESL students during second period each day. The American Lit students settled into seats near the door, facing but at a safe distance of about ten feet from the Latinos, who sat quietly near the windows at the other side of the room. Some of these ESL students—Angela, Claudia, and Felipe—I knew fairly well, while others had been in Martinez's class for only a short time. George, a tall, thin boy, had arrived from Mexico just a few weeks before, about the same time that two brothers named Hector and Manuel had come from Brownsville, Texas. Though George seemed to be making a relatively smooth adjustment to his new environment, Hector and Manuel had experienced some trouble. Before class began, I had asked Manuel how his first days at Addison High were going. "Not so good," he said:

> When I got the first day here people were discriminating, 'cause I was going to get in a fight with this kid 'cause he was calling me

a wetback. And I didn't know anybody, just me and Hector. I was getting out of gym, and I was walking down to my class, and this guy was with a couple of his friends, and he just called me a wetback. I just kept on walking, but then I thought to myself, Well, how come he's telling me that? I'm not even bothering him. And I came back, and I said, "How come you said that?" And the security he saw me and followed me, and I said, "Hey, that guy was calling me stuff." And the security guard got me instead of him. And he was holding me, and I was like, "Hey, let me go." And he called the other security, and the security came with the principal and the three of them got me.

I felt really bad. I just got home and I was like, "Damn, I have to go to school tomorrow again." My parents got home, my dad got home from work. I told my dad, "Hey, I don't wanna go to school no more." And he goes, "Why not?" "Because this guy was calling me a wetback and I don't like it. I don't wanna go back to school." And he was like, "Well, you have to go."

Though Manuel and Hector continued to come to school, Martinez told me that they had been causing problems in class. "They're so disrespectful," Martinez complained. "They're a bad influence on the other kids." I could understand her concern. Hector rarely completed the work Martinez assigned, preferring instead to draw in his notebook. The previous week, Manuel had stormed out of the room, cursing Martinez for having scolded him for using a phone on the teachers' desk. Both boys had already been in trouble with the assistant principal for skipping school and smoking cigarettes on campus. They also frequently harassed another new ESL student named Lucia, calling her *"mamacita,"* and they often used slang I didn't understand but which Angela assured me were *"bad words."* Lucia spoke almost no English and had also been attending Addison High for only a couple of weeks. The only ESL student in the class from a middle-class family, she had shown me photos of herself and a maid standing in the courtyard of her home near Mexico City.

Martinez and I occupied the gulf separating the American Lit and ESL students as the two groups glanced at each other in embarrassed silence, apparently wondering how all this would turn out. A few days earlier, Vedder, Martinez, and I had asked participants to present themselves to members of the other class either by writing a letter of introduction or by drawing pictures that, as Vedder had put it in her written instructions, "communicate five to seven ideas about who you are." We teachers then exchanged these materials between the American Lit and ESL students and asked that they use them to prepare questions to ask their counterparts when the two groups finally met. We planned to use these drawings, letters of introduction, and response questions as a way to encourage the participants to revise and expand upon what they had already written.

As I've suggested above, Martinez, Vedder, and I hoped that these initial activities would be the first steps in the group's enacting the aim of a democratic community as an "end in view." We were particularly interested, at this point, in having students share information about themselves that might help them establish some kinds of personal connections with each other—to establish a sense of "belonging" in an environment where they often experienced alienation. The time had come. And so at that first meeting we formed groups that included students from both classes, we retrieved our materials from our notebooks, and, when everything was ready, the students sat and stared at each other.

Angela leaned over to Claudia and whispered, "*I don't want to do this.*"

Angela had good reason for her reluctance. As a result of her limited English-speaking ability and, as described earlier, the interruptions in her schooling, she had continued to fail all of her classes except ESL and gym. Just a few days before, I had watched Angela stare blankly at an assignment that asked her write about whether she would like to have lived in Elizabethan England. (When I translated the question, Angela had shrugged and said, "*I don't know. I wasn't there.*") For Angela, as for the other language-minority (LM) students, most of such work continued to be divorced not only from her culture, but also from her strengths and needs as a learner of both language and content-area material.

I tried to be encouraging, saying to Angela, "*I know you wrote some good questions for Aaron. Why don't you share them with us?*" After a bit of prodding, Angela agreed. She read her questions to Aaron as she had written them, in Spanish, with Claudia acting as her translator: "*Where did you live before you came to Addison?*" "*Do you live with your brothers and sisters?*"

FIGURE 1: *Aaron's sketches to introduce himself.*

"Why are you afraid that you won't be able to pay your bills?"
"Why do you like to help people you don't know? Is it because
you feel sorry for them?" With each question Aaron talked about
what he had drawn, while Claudia translated his words back to
Angela and the other LM students. For the most part, Aaron's
answers were brief, and after he had finished and the others had
taken their turns, the students rewrote their original introductions. Figure 1 shows Aaron's sketches. The following letter is
his explanation of them:

Dear Friend,
I'm glad you know a little bit about me. In my drawings I started
out with where I live. I live in Addison, Michigan. I didn't always
live in Addison. I've lived in Florida, Texas, and Alabama, too. I
drew a fear of mine, which is one of failure. I don't want to
struggle through life and have a lot of bills to pay. I drew one of
my successes. That was one of a first-place trophy in karate. I've
been practicing for seven years. Another picture I drew was a
goal. My goal in life is to get a good job. Right now I plan to be
an electrical engineer. The last picture I drew is one about the
people I live with. They are a nice family. I'm living there because
I was kicked out of my house.

Im 17 years old
Im from México I have lived
here for 3 years. I came to UsA
with my family to work and learn
English. Nosotros vinimos alos
Estados unidos para estar con
mis abuelos y mis tios. porque
mi abuelita esta mala del riñon
y tambien porque vinimos a trabajar
en el campo porque aya en México
no hay mucho trabajo y todo aya
esta muy caro poreso nosuinimos
para aca para progresar y salir
adelante aunque esta un poco
dificil aqui pero uno comoquiera
sela pasa bien aqui.

FIGURE 2: *Angela's self-introduction.*

Angela contributed more than questions; in spite of having originally written only two sentences, she developed her own introduction in response to her conversation with the other members of her group. Figure 2 shows her text, which shifts from English to Spanish after a few sentences, and a fully English version is given below:

> My name is [Angela Muñiz.] I'm 17 years old. I'm from Mexico. I have lived here for three years. I came to USA with my family to work and learn English. *We came to the United States to be with my grandparents and my aunt and uncle because my grandmother has bad kidneys and also because we came to work in the fields because there in Mexico there isn't much work and everything is very expensive. And so we came here to progress and to get ahead. Although it's a little difficult here, things are going well.*

Claudia's original introduction had mentioned that she was from Puerto Rico and that she had left school after having bitten her teacher. Jaime had written response questions to Claudia's work; he and several others in the group wanted to know more

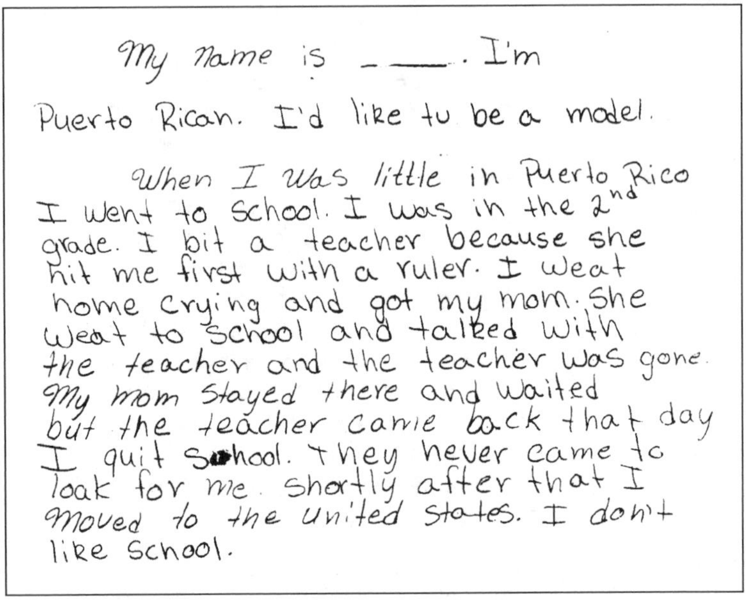

My name is ___. I'm
Puerto Rican. I'd like to be a model.

    When I was little in Puerto Rico
I went to school. I was in the 2nd
grade. I bit a teacher because she
hit me first with a ruler. I weat
home crying and got my mom. She
weat to school and talked with
the teacher and the teacher was gone.
My mom stayed there and waited
but the teacher came back that day
I quit school. They never came to
look for me. Shortly after that I
moved to the United States. I don't
like school.

FIGURE 3: *Claudia's self-introduction.*

about the incident. Figure 3 presents Claudia's final draft, translated and transcribed with help from Jaime, in which she gave
her audience several of the details they had asked for.

As we have seen, in Dewey's (1916/1985) view, democratic
communities depend in part on a "shared interest" among their
members, a sense of working together, which Dewey asserts is
made possible by a "free play back and forth among the members of the social group." Members of such a group, Dewey continues, "must have an equable opportunity to receive and take
from others. There must be a large variety of shared undertakings and experiences" (p. 90). Through this "shared undertak-
ing" of introducing themselves, the *Tesoros* students had learned
a fair amount of information about each other. In addition to
what they heard from Aaron, Angela, and Claudia, for instance,
the group now knew that Jaime's goal was to become a para-
medic and that Lucia considered herself a pretty good volleyball
player. Also emerging from our initial conversations was that
nearly all of these students shared experiences of their families'
having been uprooted by poverty. Insofar as our aim was to make

Addison High a more inclusive community, to create circumstances where Latino students and poor students of any ethnicity could both feel and know that they belonged there, I believe that these examples of *Tesoros* introductions may be read as evidence that we had taken modest steps in enacting an "end in view" resembling an aspect of Dewey's notion of democratic communities—that is, that we were participating in the communication of experiences and interests that is central to Dewey's accounts of community and democratic formation. "Democracy," Dewey (1927/1988) contends, "will have its consummation when free social inquiry is indissolubly wedded to the art of full and moving communication" (p. 350).

In order to enable students to make their reading and writing connect more clearly to their own and each other's lives, and to encourage the "free social inquiry" that Dewey argues must be a part of such conversations, Vedder, Martinez, and I designed the next *Tesoros* activity to focus even more explicitly than the first on students' families and personal histories. We hoped that by telling their stories, students might recognize more clearly the experiences they had in common and thus discover a new and better way of being at school and being with each other. The potential of narrative to help us move toward these goals has been suggested by Jerome Bruner (1986), who writes that because we account for our actions and for the human events that occur around us principally in terms of narrative, "[I]t is conceivable that our sensitivity to narrative provides the major link between our own sense of self and our sense of others in the social world around us" (p. 69). Building upon Bruner's argument, David Schaafsma (1993) emphasizes storytelling as a way of establishing the type of community advocated by Dewey. Stories, Schaafsma has written, "may be seen as selves, provisional representations of our struggle to define ourselves in the world. But in the process of shaping those selves, stories may also become one means of shaping relationships with others in community" (p. 48).

Students in the *Tesoros* project seemed to move further toward forging these links between themselves and between their social worlds when they participated in responding to a story by Jesús Colón entitled "Little Things Are Big" from Vedder's American Literature anthology. In the story, a Puerto Rican man sees a young White woman in a subway station at night, struggling to hold her child's hand and carry several packages. Though the man wants to help the woman, he decides not to, for he knows that she would be frightened if he were to approach and speak to her. After Hector, Manuel, and Katie read the story out loud in class, I asked the students to volunteer their own verbal accounts of a time when they felt the effects of racial and/or class-based prejudice—or, as I then put it more generally, a time when they "felt as though they didn't belong." Suddenly, nearly everyone had something to say.

"I got a story about me and my friends at the mall," Jaime said. Hector, Manuel, and Felipe sat up and nodded at each other as if they already knew what Jaime was about to tell us. As Martinez whispered translations to Angela and Lucia, Jaime recalled that recently he and some of his "Mexican friends" had been kicked out of the Addison mall by a security guard even though, according to Jaime, they were "just standing there talking." What particularly upset Jaime, however, was that the guard had said nothing to a group of Whites who Jaime claimed "were doing the same thing as us—just standing there."

Katie spoke next, first noting that the harassment Jaime described was typical, but then pointing out that such treatment extends to poor Whites like herself and her friends:

> There's a bunch of us who will sometimes go to our little hang-out at the mall parking lot, and people will sometimes talk about me and my friends and say, "Well, they're stupid," and stuff like that. It doesn't matter who you are or where you go, you're going to get it somewhere. It doesn't matter if you're black, white, green, yellow, or orange. People at school here, they talk about people who hang out in parking lots. They say we're scum or that we're drug addicts, y'know. I just don't need that. All's we are is a bunch of friends, and there's nothing else to do in this town. When you do find something to do, you either get chased out by the cops or you get dogged by people at school. I guess it's just who you hang out with.

The *Tesoros* participants knew that Katie was right—that, as she had put it, "who you hang out with" makes a great deal of difference at Addison High and in the surrounding community.

That is, the identities that students create, or that are created for them, based on ethnicity, language, and/or socioeconomic class, are among the complex sociocultural forces that can have harmful consequences for those who are outside of privileged groups like the wealthy Addison High students who would call Katie "scum" or those who can hang out at the mall without being asked to leave. I had seen the consequences of these identities at the homecoming football game and in the lower-track math classes that were filled almost exclusively with poor and minority students. I had seen the consequences, too, as I had walked through the poverty-stricken neighborhoods of Addison's East side, an area that most of these students called home.

During moments such as these, I believe that these students were constructing a community in ways that probably never would have occurred had we not acted to carve out this alternative space in the schedule and curriculum of Addison High. Specifically, students were finding in these marginalized identities the basis for a solidarity which enabled a dialogue that helped them articulate and assess the social realities in which they lived. They were highlighting their own experiences with racial and class prejudices, and in doing so they were reflecting upon their lives in ways that allowed them to understand more clearly their places in their school and community. Put another way, they were developing a greater consciousness of the world in which they lived and naming the forces within that world that constrained them.

What was particularly encouraging to me, however, was that as the students spent more time reading and writing together, they seemed to be increasingly willing to assume the risks involved in sharing with each other some of the more personal aspects of their lives. In the context of Dewey's thought, this type of interpersonal connection is important because, as Jim Garrison (1996) notes, an affective sense of connection motivates action in the democratic communities Dewey envisions (p. 440). To Dewey (1930), all "habits"—those dispositions which at once demand and include certain types of activity—"are affections": "all have projectile power," and "a predisposition formed by a number of specific acts is an immensely more intimate and fundamental part of ourselves than are vague general, conscious choices" (p. 25). Indeed, to Dewey (1916/1985), meaningful and consequential participation for all members of a community requires "nothing less than that socialization of mind which is actively concerned in breaking down the barriers of social stratification which make individuals impervious to the interests of others" (p. 127). Dewey (1916/1985) adds that the chief constituent in this socialization process is "intelligent sympathy," which he defines as "a cultivated imagination for what men have in common and a rebellion against what unnecessarily divides them" (p. 128).

In what I see as a significant step in that process of fostering "intelligent sympathy," Aaron launched his own "rebellion against" the *fronteras* that "unnecessarily divide" people who seek to establish communities as Dewey defines them. Near the end of our discussion of "Little Things Are Big," Aaron produced photographs of his family and said that he wanted to share them with his classmates. I believe that Aaron's comments about the photos, along with our reactions to his story, illustrate a willingness to become vulnerable in a way that contributed to the community these students were at once working toward and experiencing. As I think Aaron's words show, such a community is most likely to develop as an end in view in a space of trust established through honesty that may, at times, be risky. As Aaron passed around his photographs, our conversation went like this:

AARON: This is the only picture I got of my whole family together. My mom's in this one, but that was a long time ago.

KATIE: That's you? With the little dimples?

AARON: Yeah, that's when I lived in Alabama. The guy that took that picture, he has a friend that's in the movie business out there. He took another picture, a single of me, that he sent into a contest down there. And my picture won, so I got to be in a movie.

SUSAN: You were in a movie?

KATIE: I'm gonna rent that movie so I can see you.

AARON: I was the main actress's son. They paid me $200 a day.

KATIE: Yeah? So where's the money now?

AARON: My dad spent it on Christmas gifts, 'cause we were really poor down there. But, it was great because when we were shooting the film, I got my own trailer and stuff.

GEORGE: Did you get a limousine, too?

AARON: No, I was only about four or five. All I had to do was sit on the actress's lap and draw and stuff. She'd come over and feed me and stuff. Like, she just had me in her lap; I didn't really talk or anything.

MARTINEZ: And did you have any opportunity to continue with this?

AARON: No, we left our mom down there, 'cause my mom used to go around with other guys. My dad just took me and my brother and just left.

KATIE: Was your brother jealous 'cause you were an actor and everything?

AARON: Not really. We were all in it as extras. Like my mom was a waitress, and my dad in one scene had to walk through the background. That's my little brother and my half brother and my dad and his girlfriend now. He loves posing for pictures and stuff. This is my older brother with his girlfriend—well, his wife now. He's got his own corporation now. And this is another half brother from my mom's side.

TODD: So you and your brother and your dad left Alabama?

AARON: Yeah, yeah. Like, we lived down the street from this trailer place, so he took me and my brother and put us down there, while my dad and my mom's dad went over to get the car while she was over with some other guy. They got there and there was this other guy, this guy that my mom was foolin' around with, so my mom's dad went in there and beat him up. Then we just took the car and left for up here where my grandma lives.

TODD: Wow.

AARON: The guy that she was with, um, when my dad took the car and stuff, that guy ended up giving her sixty-two stitches—from her neck all the way down—and broke her legs with a baseball bat.

PAUSE

HECTOR: Have you seen your mom since?

AARON: I seen her about two years ago. But my dad found out she was up here. She tried sneaking up here to see me and my brother, but my dad sent her to jail 'cause she didn't pay child support. She owes, like, $25,000 in child support for me and my brother. So they sent her to jail; they stuck her in there for three months.

CLAUDIA: And you saw her in jail? You went to see her in jail?

AARON: Yeah, she was all happy; she's always happy. She's got a real nice personality. She thinks life is a big party.

TODD: Your folks are really good-looking people.

AARON: My dad still looks like that. He hasn't changed a bit.

MARTINEZ: Aaron, do you still correspond with your mom?

AARON: Not much. I'm not even sure where she is. She ran off with some biker gang.

SUSAN: How old is she now?

AARON: She's about twenty-six, twenty-seven.

FELIPE: Holy cow.

KATIE: A lot of my friends are twenty-six.

AARON: Well, maybe she's like, twenty-eight. I'm nineteen.

FELIPE: You're nineteen?

CLAUDIA: But you have an older brother, right?

AARON: Yeah, but she was pregnant with him when she was, like, thirteen. She had my brother on her fourteenth birthday. And she had me on my aunt and uncle's wedding day. Yeah, my mom, she's fun to be around.

As I listened to Aaron's story, I understood why he had waited to bring his photos to class and talk about them: his honesty, his willingness to risk opening those personal spaces where he might connect with others in ways that didn't normally happen in school, requires time for people to move beyond the awkwardness that accompanies unfamiliarity. Nonetheless, by taking this step, Aaron had allowed the other *Tesoros* students to exercise "intelligent sympathy" by creating a level of solidarity that had not existed before that moment. Thus, Aaron also helped me understand what Dewey (1927/1988) meant when he wrote that if a society is to be transformed into a truly democratic community, "there is no substitute for the vitality and depth of close and direct intercourse and attachment" (p. 368). In other words, I began to see more clearly the personal investment required by Dewey's notions of community—that such notions imply that we consciously and deliberately seek to foster relationships that reflect what Nel Noddings (1984) describes as "caring": an "engrossment" in the other, a commitment to "consider their natures, ways of life, needs, and desires" (p. 17). In an argument that I see as consistent with Dewey's position, Noddings contends that the capacity and will to care for others—an ethical sentiment—cannot be developed without "memories" of the initial, enabling sentiment of caring and being cared for that is aroused through activity. A learned, ethical sentiment, Noddings writes, "occurs in response to a remembrance of the first" (p. 79). By arguing that people must draw upon lived experiences of caring relationships in order to care deliberately, she is describing what I see as an end in view of the "attachment" that Dewey contends is necessary for the formation and nurturing of democratic communities. Such memories are, I think, precisely what were created as a result of the conversation Aaron initiated.

In order to head off any possible misunderstanding of my present emphasis on relationships, I should point out that Dewey does not argue for something as sentimental (or potentially limiting) as isolated, individual friendships. To be sure, among the more consistent themes of Dewey's work is that societal relations must be guided by the evaluative scrutiny of scientific intelligence that reveals the consequences of associated activity (1930, pp. 172–180; 1957, p. 237; 1916/1985, pp. 196–199; 1927/1988, pp. 356–362). Dewey would concur, I suspect, with Richard Sennett's (1976) assertion that a society's emphasis on intimacy can be immobilizing if the "open expression of feeling" supplants individuals' desire and ability to act together as a public (p. 11). At the same time, however, Aaron's decision to bring his photos to class and to talk about them with such candor demonstrated why affective relationships are important in Dewey's conception of democratic communities: namely, because these relationships inform and motivate people to act in ways that promote their own and each others' growth. "Intelligence," Dewey (1935) tells us, "does not generate action except as it is enkindled by feeling" (p. 51). Dewey (1927/1988) clarifies the connection between "intelligence" and "feeling" when he writes that democratizing growth of both individuals and society is best accomplished through "the perfecting of the means and ways of communication of meanings so that genuinely shared interest in the consequences of interdependent activities may inform desire and effort and thereby direct social action" (p. 332). As Dewey uses the term, "interest" certainly implies more than an empathetic connection, an alleged understanding of others through shared experience. Rather, to Dewey, people have a "common interest" insofar as they acknowledge a shared stake in the consequences of what they choose to do or what is done to them. As I read Dewey, however, this "common interest" is not discovered solely by reason; rather, it is developed at least in part by affective relationships that inspire the "feeling" that prompts intelligence to action. In Dewey's (1927/1988) view, then, the concepts of "self," "other," and "action" are mutually dependent in working toward his democratic ideals: "A distinctive way of behaving in conjunction and connection with other distinctive ways of acting, not a self-enclosed way of acting, independent of everything else, is that toward which we are pointed" (pp. 352–353).

In the context of the *Tesoros* project, this mutually dependent character of affective relationships and social action meant that, as part of pursuing our ends in view, we were attempting to encourage uses of language that recognize speakers and listeners as agents with the power to expand the boundaries of their discourses and to revise the circumstances in which they live. Aaron had changed a small part of his world by contributing to a class discussion in a way that, as he later confirmed to me, he had never done before. Though surrounded by a broader school environment that normally affords no legitimacy to such conversations, Aaron had used his voice to confirm the *Tesoros* classroom as a space where he belonged, where people would listen to him and show that they cared about what happened to him and his family—at least enough to listen intently and to ask questions about his experiences. He had, in other words, taken a step toward exercising control over what the contexts of his schooling would look like and how he and others would participate in those contexts.

Moreover, though these alternative ways of acting in school aren't easy to encourage among students who have had little experience in doing so, Aaron enabled me to hope that the *Tesoros* project could foster habits that might carry over into broader contexts like the Addison High campus. Indeed, I hoped, if at-risk students were presented with opportunities to interact as Aaron and his *Tesoros* classmates had, then this sense of community, this experience of connectedness to other people with whom we share our selves and our interests, might contribute to a school environment that worked against the isolating cultural and class structures that made Addison High alienating and irrelevant to so many of its students. After the class period during which Aaron shared his family story, I thought hard about several Addison students I had come to know during my time there but who had since dropped out of school. I remembered Eric, the boy from the trailer park who had announced in what he called his "dummy" math class that "We're all losers in here." I thought, too, of Claudia's sister Rosa, who had left school and was working as a maid in a local motel. I wondered whether these and many other students might have been with us in that room, whether they might have chosen to remain at Addison High, if they had had the opportunity to be heard as we had heard Aaron.

Difference within Community

By now I hope it is clear that as I read Dewey, his ideal of democratic communities requires creating opportunities for people to establish with each other meaningful, empathetic connections that inform and motivate social action. Further, I have been offering what I see as evidence that those of us involved in the *Tesoros* project were making modest progress toward that ideal, that we were enacting an "end in view" of creating a community that would meet the first of Dewey's criteria for democracy by, in our case, bringing people together in relationships that would enable them to recognize their "shared interest."

In what follows, however, I will emphasize the second of Dewey's (1916/1985) criteria: that democracy depends upon a "full and free interplay with other forms of association." Here I wish to describe how, while these students had established connections with each other based on their status as outsiders, at times our project served a somewhat paradoxical yet equally important purpose: namely, to provide a forum for the assertion of a distinctly Latino identity. In this sense, these students demonstrated what Joseph Harris (1989) describes as the importance of making a provision in our discussions of community for "a sense of overlap, of tense plurality, of being at once part of several communities and yet never wholly a member of one" (p. 11). By designating themselves as the "Mexicans," the Latino *Tesoros* participants may be said to have established a community within a community, an alternative "form of association" with the White *Tesoros* students, and I believe that the presence of this Latino identity within the *Tesoros* group provided the opportunity for the dialogue that Dewey contends is necessary for growth. To Dewey (1916/1985), the "free and equitable intercourse" that enables people to recognize their common interest must at the same time promote changes in people's thought, changes brought on by exposure to difference, and these "various and more varied points of contact" denote "a liberation of powers which remain suppressed as long as the incitations to action are partial, as they must be in a group which in its exclusiveness shuts out many interests" (p. 93). Thus, in Dewey's view, this interaction between social groups fosters a "change in social habit—its continuous readjustment through meeting the new situations produced by varied intercourse" (p. 92). In other words, people who see themselves standing on ground that is completely common remain inert, while the "full and free interplay" with difference creates what Harris calls "a useful dissonance as students are confronted with ways of talking about the world with which they are not yet wholly familiar" (p. 17). Such dissonance, I think, is a necessary constituent of the "rich and manifold association with others" (p. 329) that Dewey (1927/1988) argues enables individuals to strengthen community by complementing one another's unique functions. In sum, then, if the first part of my description of the *Tesoros* project was about coming together, this second part is about the importance of how the White and the Latino students remained apart.

As we have seen earlier, in the larger school setting, Addison's

Latino students signified their ethnic distinction in several ways, such as how they used language, whom they associated with, and how they dressed. This assertion of difference was reinforced by the specific ways in which the ESL students chose to participate in the *Tesoros* project. The activity following our reading and discussion of "Little Things Are Big" called for students to bring to school a tape or CD of their favorite song to play for the class. They then talked and wrote about how that song had some kind of special significance for them. Lucia chose a song entitled *"Las Piedras Rodandas"* ("Rolling Stones") by the Mexican group *El Tri*, which she explained made her think of her best friend in Mexico. The song, she wrote, *"makes me sad because I remember what we shared when we were together, when we were angry with each other, when she or I had a problem, when I was angry with my boyfriend and she made us happy."* Lucia is an enthusiastic and knowledgeable fan of Spanish- and English-language groups. She could have brought in anything that was played on Addison radio stations. That Lucia chose to share this song with her White counterparts suggests, I think, that what was significant to her, what mattered even as she was currently living in *El Norte*, was the strength of her friendships she had made in her home country.

The Latina identity that Lucia had highlighted in her choice of music was also evident in the next phase of the project, which began with our reading of a short story entitled "Martinez' Treasure." This story is an account of a poor, elderly Mexican couple who one day discover a treasure chest, which they bring into their home but are unable to open. Thinking that the chest contains gold, the aging husband and wife find renewed joy in their lives and great respect from their families and the villagers. After living their final years in happiness, the old man and woman die, but when the chest is at last opened by their children, it is found to contain only *santos*—paintings of "saints" on flat pieces of wood. Because the story was printed in English, Vedder's students were able to read it on their own in preparation for our next *Tesoros* meeting. Martinez's ESL students, however, read in class, with one of the group's bilingual students translating summaries of each paragraph for Angela and Lucia—the two students who had the most difficulty understanding English.

During our next meeting of all *Tesoros* participants, we discussed "Martinez' Treasure" and asked students to think about people who were important to them and whom they considered to be positive influences in their lives—their personal *santos*. The assignment, then, was for each student to represent his or her *santo* in an art project using materials I had bought from a scrap store for $3.50. When the *santos* were finished, students were to describe in writing the person they had chosen to represent and why that person was important to them. I thought it unlikely that students would be able to finish their *santos* in the forty-five minutes of second hour, so I had arranged to have the class meet in a conference room adjacent to the counseling office, where the students could return throughout the day during their study halls to work on their projects.

We gathered around the large conference room table, which was soon cluttered with piles of materials: blocks of Styrofoam and foam rubber, lengths of cardboard tubing, crayons and markers, bottles of Elmer's glue, swatches of fabric, shiny white envelopes, sections of poster board in various colors and shapes. With Lucia's cassette tape of the Mexican pop star Luis Miguel playing in the background, Katie sat thinking, unable to decide who her *santo* would be. When I suggested she choose one of her parents, she thought for only a moment and said, "I don't think so. They're not worthy." She considered her boyfriend but decided that he would be embarrassed to be the subject of an art project. At last she made her decision and got to work. I checked in with her after several minutes. She was constructing a cardboard figure of her cat.

While the White students tended to make *santos* of friends or, in Katie's case, her pet, the ESL students underscored the traditional Latino emphasis on the family by choosing almost exclusively to represent parents and grandparents. Manuel, for instance, made a figure of his *abuelito*, his grandfather. After carving a torso from a block of Styrofoam, Manuel attached arms made of cardboard tubing and then began work on a foam rubber sombrero and a pancho he cut from a patch of blue cloth. "That's what he wears sometimes," Manuel explained. As he worked, Manuel kidded Claudia about her project. Seated next to him, Claudia wove yarn through her figure's head.

"Hey, Claudia," Manuel said. "How come you're so dressed up today."

"I gotta meet with my probation officer," she said.

"Um." Manuel said. "Hey, what's that thing on your *santo*'s head."

"*That's hair.*"

"It looks like spaghetti to me."

"Boy, you better shut up. That's just the way my mama's hair is, white and kind of like strings. *But you don't talk about my mother.*"

"Okay, okay. I didn't say I didn't like it."

Despite making what Manuel thought to be stringy hair, Claudia finished her *santo* and described it in this way:

> My saint is my mom. She is important to me because she loves us. She wants us to do right and be a better person. She takes care of us by giving us advice, cooks for us, cleans our house, and washes our clothes. So when we come back from school everything will be clean. She understands what we do. And I love my mom. When I have a family I'm going to be like my mom in some ways like caring for my family when they're little. And when they grow up I'll teach them to be responsible by doing things for themselves.

Angela, too, constructed a cardboard image of her mother, praising her for, among other things, being *"very kind to me and my other siblings"* and for *"always being there to care for my grandparents."*

Although Lucia also chose to focus on her mother as her *santo*, she represented her mother more abstractly than did the others by drawing and coloring a picture of a red rose. When the bell rang, I explained that I was going to remain there with the projects throughout the day and that students could come to work on their *santos* if they could get permission from their study hall supervisor. Lucia, the only student who had finished, handed me her drawing.

"*Will you write this in English?*" she asked. I told her I would. After the students had left, I glanced at Lucia's writing. It was short, so I figured I could take care of it in the few minutes between classes. I was doing fine until I got to a phrase I didn't recognize, *se marchita*. Just then George walked into the room with a permission slip.

"*Hey, George. How do you say this word in English?*" I asked. He leaned over the page.

"It's like, 'wilts.' *She's talking about a flower.* The flower wilts." I thanked George and finished Lucia's paragraph:

My Santo, by Lucia
To me a rose is like a saint that represents my mom because she is a very important person in my life. She is fresh like a rose and pretty, and she wilts when she is sad. She is like a pretty rose.

The only Latino student who did not depict a family member as his *santo* was George. Instead, he began by cutting from the label of an onion sack a cartoon image of a Mexican wearing a large sombrero, leaning against a cactus. He then used the figure as the centerpiece of a three-dimensional relief, complete with cardboard desert plants and mountains in the background. His hands moved swiftly and skillfully as he worked and chatted with me, his Atlanta Braves baseball cap pulled low over his eyes. Although George spoke to me in English, what he told me further emphasized the Latino identity evident in his *santo*. I asked him whether he thought he and his family would be staying in Addison much longer. "Prob'ly not too long," George said. He went on to explain:

> At first my mom first came over here to Los Angeles to work, and she met my dad. She worked in tapes, like, you sell tapes, you know? She begin working there and then she met my dad. And he said that he couldn't find no job no more so they came over here to Michigan and found a job. My dad and mom came here just to work. My dad, he works in Ohio for a White man; my dad makes flowers and picks pickles. That White man is helping my dad bring more Mexicans to America. He puts a lot of money to bring Mexicans here to work for him. He like too much Mexicans. And he's really nice, too. We make money. A lot of money.

George continued to talk as he worked, eventually shifting the conversation to what he saw as the major differences between living in Addison and in Mexico:

I kind of like it here because we can work and make money and go to school. It's different because in Mexico you don't have to go to school if you don't want to. In high school you have to pay over there, so it's hard for me to go to school. Here it's nice because we can find jobs and learn English. I wanna be a mechanic. My dad says if I learn here I could have my own garage in Mexico and make money. It's really poor over there, so we're gonna learn here and then go back over there. And that will be good because my sister's still in Mexico. She's fifteen.

George was just finishing as the period ended. His final touch was to tape across the top of the highest mountain of his desert scene the word "Mexico," which he had spelled out in letters he had cut from a sheet of aluminum foil.

"I gotta go to lunch now," he said, and disappeared in the direction of the cafeteria.

As I have been suggesting, George's *santo* and what he said to me as he worked on it make a strong statement concerning his ties to his native country and culture, as well as his intention to return there. Similarly, his ESL classmates, with their *santos* focusing on their families and, in Manuel's case, depicting traditional Mexican clothing, underscored their ethnic distinctiveness within the *Tesoros* group.

Hector, however, never made a *santo*. Rather, he continued working on a drawing he had begun a couple of weeks earlier. While the other *Tesoros* students had busied themselves by cutting and pasting pieces of foam rubber, cardboard, and cloth, Hector kept drawing, pausing only to get up and sharpen his pencil. Later in the day, he returned to finish his work (see Figure 4), which he said he wanted to show to the class. "It's just a bunch of stuff that tells about my life," he said.

To accompany his artwork, Hector had written "A Prayer from the Barrio," part of which goes like this:

I know that once I open my eyes for the first time of the day there's always a chance for my *vida* coming to an end. After having my picture in the Sunday paper for doing *males*, people always seem to be staring at me. I feel like telling them *Que quieres?* or yelling out at my *barrio*. But I don't. I'm supposedly out of the gang now. . . . It used to feel good when my homies treated me like their brother, always watching out for me. I just feel more

FIGURE 4: *Hector's drawing.*

obligated. Now that I'm older it seems like everyone's in prison or dead or getting high on *tecatos*. . . . All I can think about is whose funeral will I have to attend next or will people be coming to my funeral next! *CHALE*, I made it through another day. I guess I can kick back and pray for forgiveness tomorrow.

As with much of the work done by his Latino classmates, I think Hector's "prayer" and his illustration of *La Vida Loca* in-dicate that these students were using their participation in the

Tesoros project to make eloquent statements underscoring their sense of themselves as Mexicans. When Hector punctuates his writing with words and phrases in Spanish, when he includes in his drawing a Chevy low-rider and *La Virgen de Guadalupe* beside a Mexican flag, he is asserting an identity that is very different from that of the White students and the teachers of the *Tesoros* project. This is not to say that Hector's work is not subject to more complicated, even disturbing readings. By depicting his central figure with a gang insignia tattooed on his hand, by framing his illustration with a prison wall laced with razor wire and a young Latino man brooding behind the bars of a jail cell, he is laying claim to a world distant from even the other *Tesoros* Latinos by identifying himself with stereotypes that reinforce his own marginalization. This type of behavior resembles that which Gramsci (1992) describes when he writes of the ways in which subaltern groups may inadvertently contribute to their own oppression by participating in practices that, although they appear resistant of the dominant culture's values, ultimately contribute to hegemony (p. 244). Operating from an identity reflected in Hector's work, many of Addison's Latino students also resist the White-dominated school by cutting classes or dropping out, but the result is these students' further distancing themselves from the potential benefits of an education.

Despite these very real dangers, however, I had observed enough of Hector's interactions with the other *Tesoros* participants to see his drawing and his "prayer" in a more positive light. Given Hector's faithful attendance in this particular class, his willingness to assist others in their work, and the friendly conversations he seemed to enjoy with his fellow students in the group, I interpret his drawing and writing not as a rejection of his membership in the *Tesoros* community, but as a demonstration that communities need not be based solely on common experience or understanding. Thus, it may be said that Hector's work represents an apt response to the concerns that some writers have raised regarding the menacing potential of communities that downplay or reject difference among their members. Iris Marion Young (1990), for instance, has warned that, "whether expressed as shared subjectivity or common consciousness, on one hand, or as relations of mutuality and reciprocity, the ideal of community denies, devalues, or represses the ontological difference of subjects, and seeks to dissolve social inexhaustibility into the comfort of a self-enclosed whole" (p. 230) Similarly, Noddings (1996) has argued that educators should view the ideal of community with intelligence and caution, recognizing that "community" has a "dark side"—its tendencies toward "parochialism, conformity, exclusion, assimilation, distrust (or hatred) of others, and coercion" (p. 258). In light of these cautionary words, Hector provides us with a powerful example of the notion that truly democratic communities not only must allow for dissent, but also they depend upon it. To speak specifically of how such dissent might be viewed as productive in educational settings, I believe that although Hector's work may be a part of a social dialogue, a conversation with Whites who share his marginalized status, his drawing and writing, by asserting a self that remains distinctly Latino, even individualistic, deconstructs the notion of collaborative learning activities as a purely unifying enterprise. Rather, he helps us understand the value of John Trimbur's (1989) argument that collaborative educational practices should not be viewed as merely consensus-making, but as "a process of identifying differences in relation to each other" with the goal of seeking to understand "how people differ, where these differences come from, and whether they can live and work together with these differences" (p. 610). Hector thus enriches our understandings of the role of collaboration in community formation by representing reading and writing as a model of the difficult negotiations that occur when diverse peoples seek to understand each other and then to struggle collectively to establish and maintain the types of communities Dewey envisions.

The *Tesoros* project may, therefore, be seen as a space where the Latino students could engage in such a struggle, where they could acknowledge that they were writing as part of a class that was not free from the physical and ideological constraints of Addison High, but where they nonetheless could resist the homogenizing or marginalizing tendencies of school-based literacy practices—even those operating in an alternative setting like the *Tesoros* project. To be sure, Hector's prayer and the Latino students' *santos* gave their White counterparts the chance to share a glimpse of a world that is very different from their own, but at the same time these narratives preserve—or even constitute—a designation of a self that can participate in but not be subsumed by the communities in which they participate. I believe that this process of distinctive participation is precisely what Dewey hopes to encourage when he emphasizes the "interplay of association" as an essential activity not only between but also within democratic communities.

If "community" as Dewey tends to define it (and as I have been using the word) depends upon dialogue, then I think it is important to ask what we should expect from bringing people together as we did in the *Tesoros* project and sharing each others' stories. The White students and I learned a great deal about what it is like to be uprooted from one's home and forced by poverty to relocate in a region where one is viewed as part of an alien invasion that threatens the social, economic, and even moral well-being of this country. The Latino students, on the other hand, heard powerful examples of the consequences of class prejudice and the struggles of coping with estrangement and violence within families. However, while these stories may have opened our eyes to a new understanding of the world, should we have been troubled that this understanding was not necessarily a common one? Or, to put it another way, Hector could spend months telling me about life in a Brownsville *barrio*, but did the fact that I never completely understood what he was talking about jeopardize the possibility that he and I could share membership in the same community? As I have argued, I believe that the short answer to this question is "no." For the "full and free interplay with other forms of association" that Dewey sets forth as a criterion of democracy is possible only if we are willing to give up the notion that democratic communities depend upon our "being or feeling like" the others who inhabit them. Hector, George, and the other Latino *Tesoros* students helped me understand that by encountering difference, by "not connecting," individuals may discover that the habits that encourage democracy are provisional, that they must be continuously renegotiated, and that they may mean different things for different people.

This importance of difference to Dewey's conception of democratic communities has been noted by Stephen Fishman (1993), who argues that to Dewey, healthy communities "possess members whose unique functions . . . complement one another" (p. 319). Fishman reminds us that Dewey's metaphor for this process is that of a well-functioning body, an organic whole whose unique parts communicate freely with one another to achieve common ends. In order for such communities to be formed, Fishman continues, "Occasions must be provided for people to share their differences. When people understand enough about their differences in their lives, according to Dewey, they will find their common interests" (p. 320).

While I certainly see the legitimacy of Fishman's understanding of the ways in which sharing difference can lead to complementarity, I think that the *Tesoros* project suggests an alternative reading of the circumstances in which acknowledging and negotiating difference can be most productive. For all the value of Dewey's metaphor and of Fishman's interpretation of it, communities are not bodies made up of insentient parts. Rather, they consist of people who must be motivated to think and act with others despite their differences. Thus, as my experiences with the *Tesoros* students have led me to reread Dewey, I believe that his discussions of difference, of the "full and free interplay with other forms of association," must be understood in the context of his emphasis on affective connections with other human beings. While Fishman's reading begins with difference and moves toward finding commonalties, the *Tesoros* project suggested to me that if people can begin by emphasizing their connections with each other, they will be more likely to develop the motivation and disposition required to encounter difference as complementary rather than divisive. Hector's drawing, George's and Claudia's *santos*, represented experiences and perspectives that were indeed distinct from mine and from those of the other White participants in the group, but these expressions of difference were enriching because they were presented in the context of a dialogue that had included Aaron's story and various students' descriptions of shared marginalization. Thus, as an alternative to Fishman's understanding that Dewey views community members as moving from difference to complementarity, I am arguing that we may read Dewey as emphasizing an initial attentiveness to those affective, empathetic relationships that, in turn, make such complementarity possible.

Finding Room for Maneuver

We had far too much food for the party on the last day of the *Tesoros* project, especially considering that it was only nine o'clock in the morning. Susan had brought a dozen donuts; Angela showed up with a plastic container filled with *chorizo* wrapped in *tortillas*. George had contributed a half-gallon of chocolate milk, and Martinez took care of the plastic plates and cups. Vedder, who had arranged for a substitute to cover her American Literature class, had supplied a large bowl of apples and oranges. I arrived with bagels and the toaster my dad had given me for Christmas years before. Nearly everyone had brought something.

In the corner, talking to his brother, Hector ate a donut and drank a cup of orange juice. I was surprised to see him, for he had been absent most of the previous week, and Martinez had told me that he had been suspended again. I walked over to him and sat down.

"*Hey, Hector, it's good to see you. I thought you were suspended*," I said.

"*Sí-mon.* I'm not supposed to be here today."

"You'd better be careful. You could get in trouble for trespassing. "*Why were you suspended?*"

"Skipping."

"You mean you got suspended for skipping and then snuck past the hallway security to be here?"

"*Sí.*"

I shook my head and smiled at the irony. Martinez later told me that since his suspension, Hector had secretly visited the school three times, for second-period ESL only.

After we all had plenty to eat, our last act as a group was to arrange the students' work in the glass display case across the hall from the ESL room. Standing side by side, leaning over each other, the *Tesoros* students taped their writings to the narrow walls and set their other artwork on the shelves against the backdrop of a large Mexican flag. After placing his desert scene in the case next to Aaron's family photo, George took a step back, turned to me, and said, "*Now everybody can see who we are.*"

I don't pretend that the *Tesoros* project was a momentous event. The needs of poor and/or minority students demand changes in our schools and society that go far beyond temporarily altering the ways they read and write. Hector, for instance, reads well and writes beautifully in two languages. He still works ten-hour days in the tomato fields. (I don't wish to deny that there is dignity in agricultural field work or that many people find such work rewarding. However, given the fact that laborers such as Hector and his family work under harsh, even hazardous conditions and that the life expectancy of men who do such work is only forty-eight years, I am arguing that, ideally, these workers should be able to improve or choose to leave these circumstances.) To ask how students like Hector might participate in a community like those that Dewey envisions, a community whose members exercise a situated freedom to act together to improve their worlds, is to raise a question that complicates not only my description of the *Tesoros* project specifically but also Dewey's thoughts about community more generally: How do we work toward Dewey's democratic ideals in groups that are larger than those that permit the "vital, steady, and deep relationships" that Dewey (1927/1988) acknowledges are present only in immediate, localized communities (p. 369). As we have seen, the *Tesoros* project involved only about a dozen people, many of whom I considered to be my friends. We had the opportunity to meet at regular intervals and to engage in direct conversations among the members of our small group. I knew, however, that such interaction would be impossible to duplicate among the roughly thirteen hundred students enrolled at Addison High, not to mention among the faculty, school board members, and surrounding community.

Nonetheless, on that last day of the *Tesoros* project, I believed, and I still believe, that we had done well to attempt a beginning of change in and around Addison High by encouraging and celebrating localized conceptions of identity and community despite the cultural differences and ideological structures that made it difficult for us to do so. Ross Chambers (1991) acknowledges the reality of the structures that constrain how we think and live, but he also writes of "oppositional behavior" that we may effect on a daily basis. "Oppositional behavior," while not immediately threatening to social structures, nonetheless enables us to act in ways that are not in accordance with them and that may eventually revise them. Chambers calls the space for such agency "room for maneuver":

> Between the possibility of disturbance in the system and the system's power to recuperate that disturbance there is "room for maneuver," and that is that space of "play" or "leeway" in the system that oppositionality arises and change can occur. But not radical, universal, or immediate change; only changes local and scattered that might one day take collective shape and work socially significant transformations. (p. xi)

Similarly, Kurt Spellmeyer (1996) urges those of us who study and write about literacy and schooling to move beyond description and deterministic thinking and to acknowledge "the spaciousness of everyday life" and "the openness of that life to change and multiplicity, even within institutions that sometimes appear colossally inert." "Culture," Spellmeyer reminds us, "is not destiny, institutions are not destiny, economics is not destiny, because the subject is always more than an 'effect'" (p. 912).

If we believe, with Chambers, that oppositional behavior is possible (even inevitable), if we share Spellmeyer's view that we need not accept the world as we now know it, then we may also share Dewey's conviction that education is one of the means available to us to effect changes that begin in localized settings and eventually extend to the larger society. This type of education, for Dewey, is one characterized by participation in communities that at once enact and further his democratic vision. Though the conversations that lead to this vision will differ from site to site, they will have in common what Dewey so emphatically sought: the opportunity for all members of a society to participate in and act upon consequential dialogue.

As I mentioned at the outset of this chapter, this type of inclusive and meaningful dialogue was our end in view for the *Tesoros* project. That is to say, we were attempting to create circumstances where students might establish a community that not only was significant in the context of our second-period meetings, but also might enable students to shape habits of being with others that would influence the sociocultural realities found in the hallways and classrooms of Addison High and beyond. Dewey (1927/1988) helps us define what such a way of living would look like and suggests what the role of education might be in moving toward it:

> Unless local communal life can be restored, the public cannot adequately resolve its most urgent problem: to find and identify itself. But if it be reestablished, it will manifest a fullness, variety, and freedom of possession and enjoyment of meanings and goods unknown in the contiguous associations of the past. For it will be alive and flexible as well as stable, responsive to the complex and world-wide scene in which it is enmeshed. While local, it will not be isolated. (p. 370)

In order to progress toward the type of society Dewey envisions, educational ends in view must help students like the *Tesoros* participants become active and influential members of the schools they attend. Beyond that, however, these classroom associations must point the way toward the broader social action necessary to keep Claudia from dropping out of school as did her sister, to help George realize his dream of becoming an auto mechanic, or to enable students to avoid painful family circumstances such as those Aaron described. These goals depend upon people's learning how to communicate and act together in ways that reach beyond localized settings and that extend the habits of democratic communities to, for instance, district school boards, state legislatures, and federal courts—those broader institutions that exercise a great deal of influence over how students will be taught and what sorts of opportunities they will have later in life. In my more optimistic moments, I think that the *Tesoros* students— and their teachers—learned a bit about how these aims depend upon discovering and valuing our common interests and then using these commonalities as points of departure for encountering difference in ways that stimulate our imaginations toward alternative ways of being and acting together. These, in my view, are not separate objectives. Rather, I am convinced that in order to know how—or even to desire—to effect broader change, we must strive to create circumstances where humane relationships among individual people can help us forge the kind of communities that are worthy of being called "democratic."

CHAPTER EIGHT

Good Deeds: A Citizen Teacher's Reflections on Usefulness

We have in America a fast-growing number of cultivated young people who have no recognized outlet for their active faculties. They hear constantly of the great social maladjustment, but no way is provided for them to change it, and their uselessness hangs about them heavily. Huxley declares that this sense of uselessness is the severest shock which the human system can sustain, and that if persistently sustained, it results in atrophy of function.

JANE ADDAMS, *Twenty Years at Hull-House*

There is no substitute for the vitality and depth of close and direct intercourse and attachment.

JOHN DEWEY, *The Public and Its Problems*

The Problems of Usefulness

Since my first trip through the fog several years before, I had become comfortable with the drive from Ann Arbor to Addison. I had exchanged my good shoes and sport coat for sneakers and a cotton shirt, the tails of which I sometimes left hanging out of my jeans. Each morning, as I slowed to an intersection adjacent to an abandoned church, its windows covered by sheets of weather-stained plywood, I glanced at my watch. (If I was there by 8:15, I knew I'd be on time for school.) I would then turn right and, after crossing a small bridge, wave to the old man in the bright orange hunting cap who took his morning walk along the gravel shoulder. He recognized me and waved back. Where the two-lane blacktop straightened out, I pushed the Honda into its fifth and final gear, remembering to drift to the center of the road to avoid the pot holes I knew waited just beyond the big white house where I always found three children in blue jackets standing in their unpaved driveway, lunch boxes in hand, waiting for the school bus. I especially enjoyed the mornings in early fall, when, if I turned up the heater and rolled down the window, I could smell the crops lying heavy and ripe in their rows. I turned into the school driveway just in time to hear the bell calling the students to class. Downshift and swerve to the left so as to hit the speed bump with only my right wheels. Pull into the space to the left of the science teacher's Toyota. Grab my green and white Addison High School parking permit from the glove compartment and toss it onto the dashboard. I had grown accustomed to this ritual. It was—in the words of another language teacher, Professor Henry Higgins—second nature to me now.

But as comfortable as I had become with some aspects of my visits to Addison, other things about my work there had kept me uneasy. Among these was the fact that I was never convinced that I had sufficiently managed the complexities and ambiguities of trying to define how I might be useful to the ESL students. That's not to say that I viewed my efforts as completely futile. Given my background, I had reason to be optimistic about the potential of the *Tesoros* project to be the start of a trend at Addison High in which literacy teaching and learning would evolve to be an "empowering" enterprise for the school's poor and Latino students. As a student I had read books that had led me to question the values of the conservative middle-class town where I grew up. As a high school teacher I had seen students move beyond their comfortable suburban experience and be challenged by the critical reflection made possible by certain forms of reading and writing. And, for a long time, I had been encouraged by the words of learned people in the field of composition and literacy studies. I read my textbooks and professional journals and was inspired by the zeal of these social revolutionaries thinly disguised as English teachers, for they seemed to argue that if we could only teach reading and writing better, if we could empower students with the written word, if we could use literacy as a means of liberation rather than oppression, then we could transform our wretched and hateful society into a world of opportunity and justice. They suggested we could read and write our way to Eden, and, for a while, I believed them.

But if the *Tesoros* project taught me a bit about the possibilities of literacy, that project and some of the other ways in which Addison High students read and wrote taught me at least as much about the limitations of literacy—especially if we define it narrowly as a basic "tool" or "skill" assumed to be a means of socioeconomic security. As writers like Harvey Graff (1979) and Paulo Freire (1990) have argued, to define "literacy" only as a basic ability to read and write is not at all empowering; on the contrary, it is to risk sanctioning its use to socialize students to accept present injustices. Cummins (1994), too, reminds us that "a remedial focus only on technical aspects of functional illiteracy is inadequate because the causes of educational underachievement and 'illiteracy' among subordinated groups are rooted in the systematic devaluation of their culture and denial of access to power and resources by the dominant group" (pp. 307–308). Expanded definitions of literacy, such as this one from UNESCO (the United Nations Educational, Scientific and Cultural Organization) in 1962, have gone beyond merely "functional" goals to underscore the importance of critical thinking and adaptability:

> A person is literate when he [sic] has acquired the essential knowledge and skills which enable him to engage in all those activities in which literacy is required for effective functioning in his group and community and whose attainments in reading, writing, and arithmetic make it possible for him to continue to use these skills toward his own and the community's development. (cited in Robinson, 1990, p. 15)

This emphasis on "essential knowledge and skills" implies that in order to be considered "literate," people must possess the capability of assessing their environment and of knowing how to change it for their own and their community's "development." However, as Jay Robinson (1990) points out, even if we thus define "literacy" as including the *ability* to participate fully in a set of intellectual and social practices, such a literacy will not necessarily be empowering because its definition presumes "access not merely to the means for acquiring literacy but to *oppor-*

tunities for practicing its competencies in specific responses to concrete situations" (p. 18). As Robinson reminds us, and as my time in Addison had shown me, these opportunities, for many people, do not exist.

Indeed, among the things I had learned from the ESL students is that to possess the knowledge and skills to do something is not the same as having the chance to do it. Barriers such as those based upon ethnicity, gender, and social class ensure that even if reading and writing contribute to the ability to envision and articulate a possible world, such a vision will remain just that as long as people remain powerless to act. Put another way, in order to speak of being literate as "empowering," we must conceive of readers and writers as enacting social roles in which they have the opportunity not only to imagine an alternative world but also to participate in making that world a reality and then to choose to live there. Thus, as vital as it is to encourage and value students' voices in our classrooms as an aspect of democratizing education, I also think that citizen teachers must resist the temptation to believe that if we can teach our students to read critically and write compellingly to a variety of audiences and for various purposes, we will soon see an end to unemployment, poverty, neglect, and loneliness. Such an expectation is not just unrealistic: it is dangerous, for it enables educators (and the public) to wash their hands of the social conditions that can make a person's ability to read and write relatively inconsequential.

As I had repeatedly seen, Addison High's literacy practices often served as specific manifestations of a pervasive school culture that marginalized Latino and poor White students. The fact that ESL students were asked to read stories in English or write answers to questions they did not understand did not, *in itself,* encompass or cause this marginalization. Rather, particular instances of reading and writing reflect (as well as perpetuate) a larger discourse of privilege and neglect. Conversely, no single literacy project—or even a revised language arts curriculum—could by itself rectify the alienation and poverty that students like Angela and Manuel were forced to endure. What can make a difference, I think, is to view the types of reading and writing we and our students do as one of the many forms of associated activities that Dewey has described as essential to a democratic society.

This potential of our literate relationships with others to contribute to broader democratic aims is articulated compellingly by Jay Robinson. "The greatest promise of literacy," Robinson (1998) writes, "is to offer means for students to connect what is deeply personal with what can be made deeply and meaningfully public in attempts to make and remake public spaces of dialogue and possibility—places where we can meet one another, perhaps, as friends, even as we act out in words and actions our own peculiar identities, obligations, and responsibilities" (p. 5). To do this, Robinson calls for "*civic* literacy," those ways with words whereby people might engage in publicly consequential acts of citizenship that "are adequate to the complexities of collective living and problem solving" (p. 14). Such agency is possible, Robinson adds, only if it is complemented and sustained by "*civil* literacy," which "has to do with the character of the relations we seek to establish with our words and in our engagements with other members of our literate communities." The essence of civil literacy, Robinson writes, is "a willingness to listen—especially to listen to others whose voices so often go unattended" (p. 15). As Robinson reminds us, literacy can legitimately be called "empowering" only if people like Hector and Claudia can speak and if someone is there to listen to them and act with them to improve their lives as they choose. In sum, what I am calling "empowering" literacy is not so much the *cause*, but the *result* of equitable and humane social relationships.

It is difficult to write what I just did without being misunderstood. I don't wish to imply that working to rectify society's ills must be sanctioned by those in privileged positions, that the ESL students have to wait around for people like me to listen to and help them act in their interests. To be sure, revolutionaries like Che Guevara and Martin Luther King have shown otherwise. What I am saying, however, is that efforts to change the realities that constrain people's lives and literacies can in many cases be strengthened when people of diverse ethnicities, languages, and socioeconomic circumstances speak, listen, and act together. Again, to refuse to turn away from others and to strive to establish the relationships that Dewey argues are essential to democracy is a complex process made difficult by the *fronteras* of class and culture that keep people apart. Such relationships are also, however, both the means of creating and the consequences of communities which come into being when diverse peoples decide to join in humanizing praxis.

Nonetheless, as I had learned well at Addison High, merely to make such a decision did not eliminate the vast cultural distances that separated me from the Latino students I had presumed to work with. On the contrary, every day brought a new struggle to find ways to negotiate such distances in ways that might enable me to be modestly useful in helping Addison's Latino students improve the quality of their lives. Because the growing number of Latino students in American schools are most often taught by White teachers, and because teachers of all ethnicities must negotiate racial, socioeconomic, or generational boundaries, this challenge of defining usefulness in cross-cultural contexts is likely to be encountered by most of our nation's educators. And so, in this closing chapter, I'll discuss a few experiences and ideas that have contributed to my understanding of what it means to be useful as an aspiring citizen teacher. More specifically, I'll explain how I have come to think that my responsibility as a teacher committed to democracy goes beyond (though it certainly includes) planning and implementing sound pedagogical practices. Instead, I suggest that we ought to view democratizing education as a relationship—a way of being with other people—in which we teachers continually seek to understand and critique the ways in which our relatively privileged positions threaten to undermine our efforts to enhance students' opportunities to participate more fully in shaping and maintaining the lives they choose. Thus, my project here is not to explicate a method but to suggest ways in which citizen teachers might foster a disposition in themselves that I hope will enable us to make our work more attuned to the democratic ideals we profess.

The ESL students knew I came to Addison High every Tuesday and Thursday, and, as usual, as I walked from the parking lot toward the school, I looked up to see the smiling faces of Claudia, Angela, and Felipe framed by a second-story window, like a photograph in which someone had tried to include too many people. I had made my way up the crowded stairs and to the door of that semester's ESL room when Fran Soto caught me out in the hallway.

"I just want to let you know before you go in there that yesterday Claudia kind of went berserk."

"What did I miss?"

Soto explained that Claudia had been called to an administrator's office and told that if she continued to skip school, truant officers would take her and her mother to court. Claudia responded by running into the ESL room, grabbing a pair of scissors from its place on the shelf next to the crayons, and threatening to "cut" anyone who said anything more about her attendance. "I don't know why I did it," Claudia later told me. "I just got mad. Them people are always botherin' me."

When Soto and I walked into the room, Martinez looked at me through narrowed eyes and jerked her thumb toward a message—which I had seen before—written in bold letters on the chalkboard: "ESL Class, Do Not Move The Furniture." I shook my head. The note seemed so predictable, so consistent, so unequivocal in its restatement of the message to the Latino students that this space did not belong to them—that *they* did not belong at Addison High. Just then the special education teacher who "loaned" the room to the ESL class stopped in to pick up some books from her desk. She noticed our noticing her message.

"It's as much for my kids as for yours," she said.

Martinez looked away and mumbled, "I'm sure."

"There we go again," Martinez said after the special ed. teacher had gathered her things and left. "*Your* kids. They're not just *my* kids!"

Martinez was giving a test that day, but before Claudia would focus on her work, she insisted on passing around photos of her recent birthday party. The first was of Claudia herself, wearing a Mickey Mouse T-shirt, smiling beside her Mickey Mouse cake. Other pictures showed her sisters with arms slung over each other's shoulders, her brother dancing with her aunt, and her mother holding a dish of ice cream.

Felipe came in late, as he had been doing for the past several days. He was wearing a wrestling T-shirt, so I asked him how his conditioning was going. "Bad. I'm up to 110. I eat way too much on the weekends; my mom tells me that I'm going to get fat. I gotta lose ten pounds to wrestle at 100. If I can do that, I might win state this year." But Martinez interrupted.

"Listen, *mi'jo,* you know how important wrestling is, that it can be your ticket to college, but you're not going to stay eligible if you don't show up on time for class. Why have you been late so much these past couple of weeks?"

The room was quiet for a moment, with everyone looking at Felipe, waiting for an answer. When he spoke, his voice was softer than usual.

"This is the same room where they teach some of them special classes, you know, to the kids who can't learn good. And a bunch of my friends walk by here on the way to their next class. Ms. Martinez, I don't want them to think I'm stupid."

Martinez did not say anything for a moment. Then, "Well, we can talk about it later." She passed out the test, the first section of which asked the students to answer some basic biographical questions. Claudia slid the photos back into the inside pocket of her notebook and asked me to read her first question: "Where do you live?" Claudia paused, then opened her backpack, pulled out an Addison High sweatshirt, and laid it on her lap. Slowly, with a pencil that long ago had had its eraser end rubbed flat, Claudia copied the letters from the sweatshirt to the blank space on her paper.

The rest of the test required students to label parts of the human body. Although Soto assisted Felipe, he didn't want to write, saying, "*No, I already know.* That's mouth, ears, hair, neck . . . ."

Soto, however, was persistent. "Do it. I know you know how to say them in English, but you've got to practice your spelling."

Martinez circulated among the other students, making sure they were recording the lists correctly. From two rows away, Martinez noticed that Angela was chewing gum. "*You have to throw that gum away when you leave this room, mi'ja,*" Martinez said. "And chew with your mouth closed."

Within fifteen minutes, Hector sat quietly drawing a picture of his girlfriend back in Texas. "You finished?" I asked. He nodded. I wasn't surprised; as I had learned from the *Tesoros* project, Hector is very bright. He had completed his test despite having missed the last two weeks of school after having been suspended for skipping school in order to help his family harvest pumpkins. "Hey, how do you say 'pumpkin' in Spanish?" I asked.

"*Calabaza*," he said.

Near the end of the hour, the students turned in their tests. Martinez skimmed through the stack and looked up at Angela.

"*Mi'ja, what are you waiting for? You've got to study. You had those words several days ago. Why didn't you learn them?*" We try to help, but you've got to do something, too. If you don't try, you're never going to learn English. What's the matter with you?"

Though Angela stared down at her desk, I could see the corners of her eyes begin to glisten with tears.

"*In my house*," Angela said quietly, "*We almost always speak Spanish. Well, every once in a while my brother and I will speak a little English. But my brother, he learned from a friend, and my parents won't let me go out and hang out with my friends.*"

Martinez shot a quick look my way. "There are a lot of cultural influences going on here, aren't there?"

Martinez then turned her attention to the whole group and announced that she suggested the students all try to get into sixth-period study hall together so they could receive help on their assignments from me, a Spanish major from a nearby college, and some bilingual students who already were assigned to that particular period. Principal Dohm had given permission to change the schedules immediately.

Claudia responded first: "Ms. Martinez, I don't wanna change. *I don't like that teacher in that class.*"

Felipe said he didn't want to change because he would miss the lunch hour with his friends. Hector looked up from his drawing. "*I don't care.*"

"*Me neither*," Manuel said.

By then Martinez's frustration was clear. "You know, this is something we need to talk about: Some of you are missing way too much school. We get the opportunity to help you, but you don't take it. You kids have got to put forth some effort of your own."

With just a few minutes remaining in the period, we chatted. Angela asked whether we had heard the story of a teenaged girl who had arrived from Mexico several weeks before. It seems that a former school district administrator (a Chicana and resident of Addison) arranged to have this girl come to Addison and live with her, promising to pay the girl's travel expenses and to provide living accommodations in exchange for help around the house. Though the girl did have an uncle and aunt living nearby, she didn't originally stay with her relatives because they lived in a trailer with their two children. What I heard next made me wonder whether my Spanish was fading sooner than I had expected. For Angela explained that the woman hadn't allowed the girl to go to school, but forced her to remain in the house, cooking and cleaning like—to use Martinez's words—an "indentured servant." This "arrangement," Martinez confirmed, was one the woman had previously made with at least two other girls. When the girl managed to call her uncle and aunt, the two "rescued" her, but the woman had refused to turn over the girl's visa papers and clothes. The girl ended up attending school in a neighboring district, and although she was fifteen years old, was placed in a seventh-grade classroom because of her inability to speak English.

"Can you imagine," Martinez said. "That poor girl sitting in that room with all those little kids?"

Manuel looked up and muttered, "Prejudiced bastards."

"*Mi'jo,* watch your language," Martinez said, but rested her fingertips lightly on his shoulder.

In classes like these, as Martinez took on the challenge of attending to students' many and diverse needs, one her of gifts, as I had seen for several years now, was her ability to negotiate the apparent tension between, on one hand, the pressure to acquire the skills required to participate in the Addison High curriculum and, on the other, to value her students' identities and to appreciate their particular struggles. In second-period ESL, it didn't seem odd to me that within ten minutes, Claudia could be allowed to take class time to pass around her birthday pictures and describe them in Spanish, while Angela could be scolded for failing to study her English vocabulary.

While it seemed to me that Martinez had the personal history and, hence, the authority to recognize and attend to the complexities of her ESL students' experiences, I worried that I lacked the background to understand what these students were going through. Without this insight, I was afraid that my role at Addison High had become too narrowly defined—almost crudely utilitarian and too closely aligned with what the school as an ideological institution deemed "useful." For a long time now, at the end of each ESL class period, I had arranged my schedule for the rest of the day according to which students were in the most immediate (and often desperate) need of assistance. I usually attended geography class with Felipe, then science with Angela. Claudia frequently needed help in fifth period Trans Math. After a break for lunch, I circulated among English, math, and study halls—again, depending on who had an assignment due or a quiz or test that needed translating.

Before I had grown accustomed to my work in Addison, I had fancied myself in the role of a teacher-researcher dedicated to understanding and critiquing the structures and practices that disenfranchised students like those in Martinez's ESL class. I had intended to help make Addison High a place where these students genuinely belonged, where teachers were responsive to their particular abilities and needs. I had wanted to speak and work in opposition to a dominant discourse that kept ESL students from developing their abilities and choosing how they wanted to live their lives. I had wanted, in other words, to play a role in a praxis that would change the circumstances in which these students lived. Instead, as it had turned out, I seemed to spend most of my time tutoring Claudia, Angela, and the others in the same classes that I had come to suspect contributed to these students' troubles at school. Sitting through another introductory lecture on complementary angles or trying to explain in Spanish the anatomy of a cell, I often wondered what possible good I was doing there. In particular, without the benefit of the life experiences of someone like Martinez, I wondered whether I was even able to interpret with any sort of accuracy what the needs of these students really were. Moreover, I wondered whether my relatively privileged position as a White educator was getting in the way of my understanding what might be the most appropriate response to these needs. I wondered, in short, whether I was—reflectively and responsibly—being useful.

In my view, this sense of urgency, this keenly felt desire to do some good in this world, may serve as a prompt for citizen teachers to adopt an expanded notion of their work, especially when that work takes place in contexts where students represent a diversity of cultures and languages. That is, teachers must cultivate an identity not just as instructors of academic content or even as activists dedicated to promoting democracy. Rather, citizen teachers must also think of themselves as social scientists striving to be more attuned to how their students view the world and how their culturally situated values shape the ways they think and live. For it is only by complementing our own knowledge and training with such understandings that we educators can hope to be useful to students in associated activities guided by their priorities rather than our own. In taking on what might be called this broadened professional sensibility, citizen teachers have much to learn from cultural anthropologists, for whom encountering and representing difference is a constant focus of their work. In particular, I believe that citizen teachers would do well to join the conversations of educational ethnographers, whose basic methods of long-term participant observation reflect the circumstances of teachers who interact with students over extended periods of time. Thus, by thinking like ethnographers, by familiarizing ourselves with their past and present concerns, teachers stand to gain a heightened sense of the complexities of teaching and learning in cross-cultural contexts, as well as some insight into how these complexities might be negotiated in useful ways.

As John Ogbu (1985) has documented, the history of anthropology as it relates to education dates back to the final decades of the nineteenth century. During this time, researchers worked toward making available to educators and policymakers knowledge about culture and its transmission that would refute false and prejudicial ideas concerning the intellectual and learning capabilities of non-Western peoples and of minorities, immigrants, and working-class people in Western societies (p. 276). Ogbu goes on to note that in the 1960s and 1970s, the researcher's role was honed to refute the notion of "cultural deprivation" and to revise what then constituted conventional education research by encouraging investigation that does not divorce educational processes from their sociocultural contexts. Ogbu concludes that, complemented by a refinement of methods and the increasing popularity of ethnographic fieldwork, the purpose of anthropological description of educational settings has been to provide a "database for analysis aimed at the understanding of specific problems, including those pertaining to cognition, language and communication, roles and identities, school-community relations, and the like" (p. 282).

More recently, Steven Z. Athanases and Shirley Brice Heath (1995) have written specifically of the contributions ethnography has made to research in the teaching and learning of English. Athanases and Heath argue that ethnographers have provided valuable descriptions of readers and writers as embedded within specifics of time and place. Such descriptions, the authors continue, help account for the role that language plays in cultural representation and, hence, contribute to our understandings of how "individuals become cultural carriers, transmitting and transforming ways of behaving, believing, and valuing within their social group" (p. 267). In sum, educational ethnographers have often been seen as useful in that they contextualize language use: they help teachers think of speaking, listening, reading, and writing as aspects of and situated within broader cultural forces, thereby affording enriched understandings of the causes and consequences of different ways with words.

Working from this kind of analytical framework, I have viewed Addison High's officially sanctioned literacy practices as just one part of the larger symbolic discourse the school uses to reinforce the marginal status of its Latino students. I have, for instance, described Angela's unsuccessful attempts to answer questions in response to a chapter in a science textbook she cannot read; I have shown some of the ways in which events like Addison's homecoming football game reflect and help perpetuate hierarchical social identities within the school community; I have documented and critiqued teachers' beliefs in the importance of Latino students' acclimating to an allegedly unifying United States "national culture." I hope that these findings may be useful in that they may eventually lead to teachers' viewing their pedagogy as a cultural practice that they can revise to be more responsive to the unique abilities and needs of their Latino students. However, despite the potential of such research done well, at least two problems lead me to question whether the study and analysis of educational sites will be useful to citizen teachers in helping them promote democratic social and political change on a scale that extends beyond classroom walls. The first problem, by now familiar, is epistemological. The second, closely related to the first but often left out of our professional conversations, is ethical.

By now the argument is common that teacher-researchers should be at least as concerned with *how* they are going about their work as with the results and content of cultural description and analysis itself. That is, teacher-researchers and other ethnographers have, for the most part, rejected the notion that they can describe social phenomena as though there existed an empirical reality that is authoritatively "knowable" within a stable epistemological paradigm.

By acknowledging that culture is not only something teacher-researchers study but also something *from* which they study—that is, a medium which is going to influence what they see, how they see it, and how they talk about what they see—several writers have highlighted the role of hermeneutics, the process of reality-constructing interpretation, and have thereby introduced what some have referred to as the postmodern "crisis of representation." Essentially, this "crisis" has resulted from what Jean-Francois Lyotard (1984) called the contemporary "incredulity towards metanarratives" and the ensuing "uncertainty about adequate means of describing social reality" (xxv). But if our ways of knowing have been complicated by postmodern thought, this "crisis" is especially acute among those who attempt cross-cultural representation of the type I was pursuing in Addison. Indeed, people like me must confront the notion that if the ways we make sense of our worlds are so different from those of "the other," then any efforts to represent one culture in terms of another are at best problematic, perhaps futile.

As the anthropologists George Marcus and Michael Fischer (1986) have argued, one of the greatest promises of ethnography is that it enables more productive and culturally sensitive representations than can be achieved from alleged "totalizing visions of reality" (p. 8), for it is a method which demands that researchers—to use the words of Clifford Geertz (1973)—"hover closely" over the sites they are studying and employ "thick description" to represent other people's words and actions within the cultural contexts that give them meaning. But even if we teacher-researchers do our best to situate what we observe, even if we strive for what Geertz (1983) calls "local knowledge," the basic theoretical problem—our "crisis"—persists. James Clifford (1986) puts it this way:

> If ethnography produces cultural interpretations through intense research experiences, how is unruly experience transformed into an authoritative written account? How, precisely, is a garrulous, over-determined cross-cultural encounter shot through with power relations and personal cross purposes circumscribed as an adequate version of a more or less discrete "other world" composed by an individual author? (p. 25)

By posing this question as he does, Clifford, too, suggests what I have mentioned above—that the "crisis of representation" involves at least two issues: first, the fact that critiques of dominant paradigms have raised questions concerning whether we can "know" and represent others, and second, the ethical implications of attempting to do so. If Geertz (1988) is right when he talks about ethnography as "putting words down onto paper" (p. 1), then any educational research complicated by a social conscience will inevitably involve questions of rhetoric concerning how we will interpret and then "compose" ourselves and "the other" honestly and responsibly. Further, if, as Robinson (1990) suggests, we understand rhetoric as an interpretive *act*, then we must take seriously the notion that the way we represent our students and ourselves is not politically or ethically benign, either to them or to us.

Especially in recent years, writers have suggested that, too often, such representations amount to forms of imperialism and erasure. Edward Said (1978), for instance, has argued in *Orientalism* that the genres of writing developed in the West to represent non-Western societies have included rhetorical devices which make Western authors active, while leaving their subjects passive. Eva Hoffman (1989), in *Lost in Translation*, gives us this warning: "For all our sophisticated deftness at cross-cultural encounters, fundamental difference, when it's staring at you across the table from within the close-up face of a fellow human being, always contains an element of violation" (p. 94). Thus, any cross-cultural "translation"—and I include my own in Addison—includes potentially oppressive self-representation—that is, usurping the ownership of another person's experience and putting it into one's own terms. In effect, as teacher-researchers, we "hang" the other on our own rhetorical frameworks, and, even though we may have the noblest of intentions, our efforts to do right by our students may thus be thwarted by the possibility that what we think is best for them and what they themselves desire are very different things.

Given his insightful characterization of ethnography as fiction, it is ironic that the tendency to separate the epistemological from the ethical is illustrated in Geertz's own discussion of the posthumous publication of Bronislaw Malinowski's *A Diary in the Strict Sense of the Term*, in which Malinowski writes candidly and disparagingly about the "natives" with whom he lived and worked. Geertz (1983) claims that the outcry and hand-wringing this publication prompted among anthropologists was made "to come down to Malinowski's moral character or lack of it" (p. 56). That is, people were upset that Malinowski turned out not to be as kind or gracious a person as everyone had assumed him to be. In Geertz's view, however, this focus on Malinowski's morality obscured the real question raised by the *Diary:* whether or not "anthropological knowledge of the way natives think, feel, and perceive" (p. 56) is even possible. Thus, the issue, Geertz summarizes, is not moral, but strictly epistemological. However, as Geertz himself elsewhere acknowledges (1988), because ethnography is, in fact, writing (the act of representing another person with our words), the point that Geertz downplays in his discussion of Malinowski is precisely the one I believe needs to be underscored in the professional conversations of citizen teachers: namely, that the process of constructing our understandings of students (especially understandings that I have been calling the "useful" kind) is not just about epistemology. It is also about ethics—if by "ethics" we mean something like a system of ideas guiding our conduct toward others. In short, I think there exists an intimate and dialectical relationship between how we *know* "the other" and how we *are with* "the other."

This is not to say that we should disregard the epistemological issues that so concern Geertz. As I have suggested, there are serious consequences of failing to see things from, to use Geertz's (1988) parlance, "the native's point of view" (p. 56). Indeed, Athanases and Heath (1995) have done well to remind us that in recent years, "educational research labeled ethnography has shown little evidence of being guided by what scholars in cultural anthropology and the ethnography of communication have articulated as sound principles to guide the conduct of ethnographic research" (p. 263). To encourage teacher-researchers to adhere more closely to these "sound principles," Athanases and Heath rightly call for increased attention to the methodological features of anthropological research models and then provide a guide for negotiating the dilemmas an ethnographer is likely to encounter—dilemmas such as selecting research sites and informants, identifying which data to analyze, and insuring the credibility of what an ethnographer claims to know by enhancing a study's validity and reliability. To repeat, I share these writers' concern with the epistemological legitimacy of our work. We teacher-researchers owe it to our students and our colleagues to make our accounts—however imperfect and subject to our inevitable cultural filtering—as valid as possible in terms of the contexts that give them meaning.

My hope, however, is that these important conversations regarding methodological rigor will take place within a broader context that includes scrutiny of the relationships we teacher-researchers initiate when we go beyond studying our students and begin acting with them. For if we strive to be useful, that is, if we use our research to inform a praxis characterized by direct and overt intervention in others' lives in order to effect positive change, then we are engaged in activities that give the ethical issues surrounding teacher-research new urgency. In Addison, I began my work by observing classroom activities, recording conversations, and writing descriptions and analyses of what I saw and heard. Eventually, though, I found that what I was learning enabled (even compelled) me to involve myself in the lives of Claudia, Felipe, and the other ESL students more assertively than I had before. I began tutoring these students, acting as their advocate in their interactions with teachers, lobbying counselors and administrators to make changes in school policies that I thought would help language-minority students succeed. As my role as an ethnographer began to change to that of a teacher-researcher, I grew more aware that acting for, or in the interest of, others has its own, and different, ethical dimensions.

Most acutely, my concern with treating education and educational research as forms of social activism is that the sociocultural privilege most teacher-researchers possess may lead us to import notions from our own cultural perspectives about what actions constitute positive change and then to impose these notions on our students. Given this danger, teacher-researchers must be circumspect concerning the ways in which the changes we help bring about will influence (and be influenced by) the relationships we establish with the people to whom we are trying to be useful. Indeed, if we presume to act with our students to change their worlds, then it seems to me that we are obligated to ask hard questions about who determines what those changes will be, whose cultural values they represent, and—ultimately—whom such changes will benefit. Teacher-researchers who ignore these questions risk obscuring the colonialist potential of their work. If, however, we acknowledge that what we do in our classrooms is a complex process that requires reflection and negotiation with our students regarding how we should understand them and act with them, then we move toward making schools places where people can encounter each other in relationships of mutual influence. The kind of teaching and teacher-research I'm advocating, then, is guided by a theoretical framework which includes an ethical sensibility that keeps us from making our work essentially a one-way transfer of values and ways of thinking and living.

This way of understanding the work I was committed to in Addison was, in some ways, threatening, for it implied that *I* may have needed to change, to remove the blinders that allowed me to see the world only from my own privileged position, to rethink the assumption that Angela, Claudia, and Juan wanted more than anything else to be like me. But even though a mutually influential exchange between teacher-researchers and their students introduces yet another dimension of complexity and uncertainty to our work, Giles Gunn (1992) reminds us that this uncertainty brings with it new possibilities: "Unless there is reciprocal modification of each category by the opposite . . . there can be no increase in self-knowledge, no challenge to prior conceptions, no risk of personal confusion or disruption" (p. 11). To be open to such disruption is, I have found, more difficult than we teachers often realize, for we live and work immersed in a history of imperialism that spans from the conquistadors to the manufacturing and marketing departments at Nike and that constantly sets forth the notion that what is worthwhile is imported from *El Norte:* as the ubiquitous slogan says, *"siempre Coca Cola."*

This colonial spirit—which encourages us to assume that we know what is in our students' interest and that spurs our inclination to act upon this assumption—is certainly a banner I admit to having carried with me to Addison. Sometimes I marvel at the mobility I enjoyed there, the opportunities I had to accomplish what I was tempted to see uncritically as so many constructive things. On one fairly typical day, I sat through fourth-period science class with Angela. At the end of the period, as the students filed out of the room, Angela's teacher, the next day's substitute, and the special education teacher who worked as an aid in the class all gathered around me as I stashed my notebook and tape recorder into my backpack. They talked to me for almost half an hour of their lunch period: "It's so hard to teach the Latino students," they said. "What can we do? We don't speak Spanish." What interested me most about that conversation is not so much what was said, but the teachers' admission that, despite Angela's having attended Addison High for over a year, this conversation took place only when I, the White teacher from the university, came calling.

But propelled by a kind of self-righteous zeal, I had to tear myself away, had to make a phone call to Steve, the Prentice-Hall sales representative, to see about getting Angela another copy of a textbook in Spanish. "Sure, Todd," he said, "it should arrive within a week." Next, on to the physical education office, where I explained to the gym teacher that Hector and Manuel had refused to wear shorts in gym class not because they were challenging his authority, but because they were cold. "But, sir," I argued quietly, "They're freezing out there; they just arrived from Brownsville a few weeks ago, and down there it's eighty degrees." "I'll talk to them," the gym teacher said. (By now, I felt Kipling's burden resting comfortably on my shoulders.) But no time to gloat; I had to run to the middle school for a meeting with Martinez about my plan to form writing groups among Latino students. After that, back to the high school to translate Angela's computer test. You know, sometimes I would get on a roll; I dashed around Addison High doing so many good deeds that I surprised even myself, and at the end of the day when I climbed into my white Honda and drove off toward the horizon, I could imagine those Latino students to whose aid I had rushed looking after me in astonishment and gratitude and wondering out loud: "Who was that blue-eyed man?"

And then I would drive home, reflecting on what a splendid adventure the day had been, recalling the words of Melville's Ishmael: "I love to sail forbidden seas, and land on barbarous coasts" (p. 26). Still, my day was not over, for I knew then I must write, and as the voices of the choir of King's College in Cambridge, England, rose from a compact disc and filled my apartment like perfume, I fed my field notes into a Macintosh, translating my and Angela's experiences into a form that fits rather handsomely into a book chapter or conference paper. By and by, though, I couldn't help thinking that those good deeds, all the attention I enjoyed, that act of writing, represent—more than anything—power. And even though I'm pleased that Angela had a new Spanish-language textbook and that she was able to pass her computer test, even now I can't help wondering whether that power has done to me what it tends to do to everyone else.

Perhaps I'm overly concerned; after all, we're only talking about teacher-research—research that carries the possibility of so many fruitful connections. Indeed, as Stephen North (1987) has written of educational ethnography, "[its] power as a mode of inquiry . . . derives from its ability to keep one imaginative universe bumping into another" (p. 284). Still, what concerns me is that if, in Addison, one imaginative universe bumped into another, I had a pretty good idea which one would be eclipsed, and chances were it was not going to be mine. bell hooks (1990), caricaturing a privileged voice, has described the potential consequences of such "bumping" in this way:

> No need to hear your voice when I can talk about you better than you can speak about yourself. No need to hear your voice. Only tell me about your pain. I want to know your story. And then I will tell it back to you in a new way. Tell it back to you in such a way that it has become mine, my own. Re-writing you I write myself anew. I am still author, authority. I am still colo-

nizer, the speaking subject, and you are now at the center of my talk. (p. 151)

As hooks reminds us, there is great power in the language that teachers use to conceptualize their students. For insofar as our representations of students influence the institutions we construct and our agency within those institutions, the ways in which we compose ourselves, the "other," and the relationship between us do have consequences that are very real. In March 1995, I had a conversation in the Addison High staff lounge with Ms. Alvarez, one of the school's counseling staff. As I ate my sandwich, I mentioned that Claudia, who had become notorious for her truancy, was not in school that day. Alvarez grew strangely pensive and said in a quiet voice, "I worry about that girl." Thinking of the likelihood of Claudia's again failing most of her classes, I nodded as I chewed. But Alvarez continued: "Todd, I'm afraid she won't live very long. I've seen it before; girls like Claudia just get lost. Their families are poor; they drop out of school; and they wind up on the streets of Detroit or Toledo. I'm afraid that she'll die of AIDS or a drug overdose, or that someone, a pimp or a drug dealer, will kill her."

My lunch went heavy in my hand. For it had suddenly become clear to me that if we citizen teachers interpret what we see in our classrooms inadvertently, if we write impoverished stories leading only to cosmetic changes in the ways we teach while failing to critique and revise the structures of domination in which we are comfortably situated, if we—in other words—neglect our democratizing mission, then we are implicated in policies that are, quite literally, deadly serious. At that moment, questions of Claudia's schooling and of what she and I could do to improve it were granted new urgency as my mind fixed on the image of a full body bag lying in a Detroit morgue.

Usefulness Revisited: Contingency, Locality, and Critical Empathy

By now I hope it is clear that among my concerns regarding citizen teachers' inquiries into the lives of their students is that in the course of such inquiries the epistemological and the ethical inevitably converge—that there is no legitimate way to dismiss the difficulties and consequences of negotiating the kinds of cultural and socioeconomic boundaries we often cross when we enter our classrooms. In Addison, because of factors like my age, ethnicity, and education, I was undoubtedly "other" to Angela, Claudia, and Felipe. And ours was a relationship fraught with the danger that our interactions would be in no significant way "reciprocal," that I would be "useful" only in terms of my own understandings and aspirations.

At no time did I feel these dangers more acutely than late one night when I received a call from a Chicana friend of mine. This was a close friend; we had taken several classes together and spoke on the phone at least a couple of times a week. When my daughter, Kaitlin, had visited on Halloween, this friend had invited us to use her house as a "home base" for trick or treating, as she lived in a residential neighborhood much better for collecting candy than was my apartment complex. On this particular night, my friend and I began our conversation by chatting for a while about things I don't remember. I'll never forget, though, what happened next. She apologized in advance, then said she was no longer going to be my friend because of the work I was presuming to do with Latino students. She explained, using words like "colonialism" and "imperialistic." When I hung up the phone, I remained for a long time sitting on the floor between my living room and kitchen, my back leaning against the frame of the doorway. I thought hard about Manuel, Claudia, Felipe, and Angela. I wondered whether my inability to understand completely these students' experience might cause me to impose upon them my own values, whether by my tutoring and research I was encouraging them to act and think in ways that are legitimated by my own sociocultural perspective rather than theirs, whether my professional goals were leading me to exploit them despite my good intentions. I wondered whether it would be better if I just stayed away.

Though it wasn't an easy decision, I chose to keep driving to Addison, for I am convinced that to stay away is itself a form of action. To ignore is to neglect, and while George Bernard Shaw (1952) was right when he cautioned us against the objectifying arrogance displayed by Henry Higgins, he was equally astute to remind us that "the worst sin towards our fellow creatures is not to hate them, but to be indifferent to them; that is the essence of inhumanity." It is good that we hesitate at *fronteras* of ethnicity, gender, language, and social class. We have ample reason to pause and wonder whether we should take that next step and presume to participate in the lives of others, as I was participating in the education of Addison's ESL students. But eventually, I think, we citizen teachers must ask ourselves this: What kind of world do we want to live in? Is it one where, because of the potentially exploitative complexities of encountering "the other," we despair altogether of attempting such connections? Is it one where we resolve to live and work only in enclaves with our "own kind" (whoever that may be)? In my view, such isolationism is not only undesirable but also impossible, for the real question is not *whether* we will interact with those who are "different" from us, but *how* we will do so. Thus, despite—or, perhaps, because of—the high stakes, I have dared to hope that my education, my native language, and the color of my skin do not necessarily disqualify me from the work I was attempting to do. The fact that I am a White teacher does not, in my mind, afford me the comfort of a hermeneutic and ethical paralysis that would absolve me from what I see as a responsibility to address some very pressing needs.

What my position of privilege does require is that I make that privilege a central part of the framework from which I view my work, that I constantly ask what that power means and how my own culturally embedded assumptions may influence what I see (or don't see), what I do (or don't do). We must try, in other words, to understand what Maxine Greene (1988) calls the "layers of determinateness"—those "effects of class membership, economic status, physical limitations, as well as the impacts of exclusion and ideology" (pp. 8–9)—that lead us to assume that we know what is best for others and that allow us mistakenly to define "success" in our terms rather than theirs.

I should note here that my own priorities and those of the students with whom I have worked were not always at odds. Usually, for instance, we agreed that education is valuable. However, what keeps me from being completely sure that my own conclusions were consistent with the plans and desires of Addison High's Latino students is my memory of people situated in authoritative positions—teachers, administrators, tutors from the university—who confidently (and often incorrectly) told these students what they needed. I had heard, for instance, Latino students being informed that they would benefit from being submerged in all-English content-area classes, from assimilating to the "American" cultural norms, and from quitting their after-school jobs so that they could spend more time on their homework. The fact that Latino students saw these admonitions as contrary to their interests suggests, I think, that once we base our understandings of what we should do in our classrooms not solely on our own social and cultural perspectives but also on those of the young people with whom we work, then we open the possibility that we may contribute to our students' acquiring greater social and political freedom in the form of increased opportunities to participate in their worlds on their own terms. This freedom, as Greene (1988) argues, should not be understood as the "negative freedom" of deregulation, self-dependence, and unreflective consumerism (p. 7). Rather, it is a freedom that must be "an achievement within the concreteness of lived social situations," a purposeful activity in which people are able to name the causes of their oppression, "imagine a better state of things," and "share with others a project of change" (p. 9).

To think of our work as an attempt not just to understand others but also to strive with them to rectify real problems is to conceive of the role of the teacher-researcher as going beyond, for instance, my documenting what Angela does in class or conducting interviews with her. Rather, such a revision challenges the prescriptive nature of research and teaching rooted in colonialism and places a new emphasis on how I am to *be together* with her in a relationship that encourages the type of freedom Greene describes.

Just what this relationship entails and, specifically, what the role of the researcher should be within it is a subject Dewey (1927/1988) takes up in the final pages of *The Public and Its Problems*. In *Public*, Dewey is primarily concerned with describing the "conditions which must be fulfilled if the Great Society is to become a Great Community; a society in which the ever-expanding and intricately ramifying consequences of associated activities shall be known in the full sense of the word, so that an organized, articulate Public comes into being" (p. 350). Because the "articulate Public" depends upon bringing people together to participate equitably in activities that improve their society, Dewey's explanation of the role of the social scientist in this process provides several useful guidelines to citizen teachers who seek to ground their work in more thorough understandings of their students' lives.

First, Dewey contends that social scientists serving the interests of democracy must deny absolutist notions of desirable social action. To Dewey, whatever recommendations researchers offer as a result of our investigations must be appropriate to the particular contexts of our inquiry; that is, we must acknowledge the *contingency* of possible courses of action: "A solution, or distributive adjustment, needed at one time is totally unfitted to another situation" (p. 356). Once these possible solutions are implemented, Dewey argues for flexibility and adaptability—for policies and proposals to be treated "as working hypotheses, not as programs to be rigidly adhered to and exhausted." These programs, he contends "will be experimental in the sense that they will be entertained subject to constant and well-equipped observation of the consequences they entail when acted upon, and subject to ready and flexible revision in the light of observed consequences" (pp. 361–362).

Shortly after I first arrived in Addison, I had what I thought was a wonderful plan. I hoped to work with teachers to form writing and tutorial groups among Latino students—those who were fully bilingual and those who were considered "limited English proficient." These groups, I reasoned, would enable the non-English-speakers to learn the language of Addison High more efficiently; to receive assistance in math, geography, and science while they learned English; and eventually to pass their classes, graduate, and move on to college or a comfortable career. What I discovered by and by, however, was that my best-laid plans were based on my own assumptions about what those students needed—assumptions based on some ideologically foundationalist notions of what was worth learning and what type of life was worth living. I was planning for their "success" as it is defined within a cultural/educational system that legitimates who *I* am, the maintenance of which is certainly in *my* best interests.

It's not that my original plan was terribly misguided. Again, like almost all ESL teachers I know, I still think that, in most cases, it's a good idea for Latino students to learn English and to further their education—especially if they plan to remain in the United States. Nonetheless, what I learned from observing and listening to Addison High's Latino students was that any project designed to promote their interests must respond to a wide range of academic and sociocultural issues that may have been left unattended by my initial plan. For instance, because students like Angela and Claudia had an immediate need to pass their classes, I spent much of my time relearning and tutoring in basic math and science. One afternoon I found Felipe, an all-state wrestler, crying in a corner of the library because he was unable to read "The Cask of Amontillado," which was printed in English. He was especially upset because he had to pass sophomore English in order to remain eligible to wrestle. We spent the next several weeks working together during his study hall, reading his assignments, writing his essays—first in Spanish, then in English.

But the particular "solutions" in which I participated, those contingent responses, were not limited strictly to schoolwork. With Felipe, my being useful included helping him write a letter to his new girlfriend, who lived in Chicago. With George, I worked on filling out his application to work at the local Red Lobster restaurant. With Angela, I learned that I could be most useful by not bothering her, but by sitting across the room and waiting— simply being available. I don't wish to suggest here that these somewhat eclectic efforts are all that is required of those who wish to work toward Dewey's Great Community. Indeed, the type of collective action Dewey advocates is more reflective, more deliberate, and broader in scope than these examples imply. Still, the point here is that what I initially thought would be useful, and what Felipe, Juan, and Angela found useful, were often very different, and I needed to revise my actions accordingly.

Dewey's argument that social action should be a response that is contingent upon specific circumstances suggests a second guideline for teachers who also see themselves as researchers: namely, that because decisions regarding social action should be determined locally within communities characterized by democratic participation, the social scientist must assume no special prominence in planning and implementing social policy. As James Gouinlock (1988) has noted, Dewey is emphatic that social scientists in a democratic society would have no authority to prescribe solutions to social problems. "Instead, they would devote themselves to determining how the complex and powerful forces in society actually function. . . . In this way the knowledge needed by the public would be provided" (p. xxxii). Indeed, Dewey's crucial innovation regarding the "knowledge" generated by the social sciences comes in the way this knowledge is used and by whom, for while he concedes that the processes of inquiry and the dissemination of conclusions "is a work which devolves upon experts," the framing and executing of policies is the business of communities operating in "face-to-face intercourse" (1927/1988, p. 367).

This call for the social scientist to inform rather than to persuade (or coerce) an articulate public suggests that, here in these local spaces, the role of the teacher-researcher is to enter with others into relationships in which all participants share information and decision-making power. Insofar as I was able to view my work as approximating this process of forming equitable relationships with "the other," my time in Addison became not just a means to an end, but in itself a form of social activism—an ongoing enterprise of working with others on terms and toward goals that were mutually determined. Thus, my "real work," my genuine opportunity to be useful, did not begin when I wrote a book or delivered a conference paper. Rather, it was already occurring when I recommended to Felipe's study hall monitor that he be allowed to work with a bilingual friend, when Manuel called me over to help him summarize a story for English homework, when I asked Claudia for advice on how I might help my daughter resolve a conflict with a friend, or even when I sat in the back row of science class and waited for Angela to ask me a question. According to this understanding, teachers' careful observations of and responses to their students are not preparatory acts, but are themselves—to use Dewey's (1927/1988) words— "a distinctive way of behaving in conjunction and connection with other distinctive ways of acting" (pp. 352–353) that constitute democratic activity.

As we have seen, Dewey's aims extend beyond such localized relationships. Dewey's goal is a broad, systematized, society-wide transformation—a collective establishment and nurturing of a Great Community. Nonetheless, when we consider how this process must begin at the local level, definitions of "usefulness" previously thought of strictly in terms of sociopolitical policy tend to be recast to include questions of personal disposition. In other words, the question asked by, say, a citizen teacher desiring to be useful becomes not so much "What can I do to/for others?" but "What is the nature of my relationship with this person? How can/should we *be together?*"

It seems to me that in order to ask these questions and to use them not only to help ourselves negotiate cultural boundaries in the interests of democracy but also to desire to do so, citizen teachers must strive toward exercising what Jay Robinson, speaking in classroom conversations, has called "critical empathy." This term refers to the process of establishing informed connections with other human beings, of thinking and feeling with them at some emotionally, intellectually, and socially significant level, while always remembering that such connections are complicated by sociohistorical forces that hinder the equitable, just relationships that Dewey (and, presumably, we) desire. Critical empathy is a hopeful but cautious concept. It is a disposition which urges us to understand the powerful structures and ideologies that constrain people to think and act in prescribed (often exploitative) ways; it demands that I acknowledge the risk that what I take to be empathetic understanding is merely another type of construction of the other according to my view of the world. Critical empathy compels me to admit that I don't understand what it's like to be forced by poverty to move to an area where many people—politicians in their campaign speeches, administrators and teachers in the schools, other young people who live on my street—view my family and me as part of an unwashed tide eroding the nation's economic and moral foundations. Further, in the context of the kind of work I do, critical empathy makes me keenly aware that when I delivered my last conference paper in a hotel ballroom filled mostly with White academics and graced by the light of chandeliers—a paper that discussed how literacy might serve the interests of democracy and justice—almost all of the people busily refilling water pitchers and making the beds upstairs were Latino.

At the same time, critical empathy holds out the hope that I, a White teacher from a small, West Michigan town, can have some kind of meaningful and productive relationship with Latino students whose cultures and experiences differ so dramatically from my own. This hope lies in critical empathy's refusal to admit the conception that human beings encounter each other as unified, essentialized selves. Rather, critical empathy relies on an understanding of the self as characterized by multiple, shifting, and highly contextualized identities. And so while I will never completely understand what it is like to be one of the Latino students of Addison High, I may, nonetheless, be able to connect with these students in partial and mutable ways. With Angela, for instance, we both brought to our early conversations the challenges and surprises involved in caring for young children—her siblings and my daughter. George and I began our relationship by sharing our mutual interest in sports. When Felipe showed me a wallet-sized picture of his grandmother and told me how much he missed her, the affection he described felt familiar to me as I thought of the members of my own family who live far away. I mention these examples not to be glib or sentimental, but to suggest that these initial and tentative connections, these diverse and shifting points of contact, marked the beginnings of relationships that have democratizing potential. For by resisting metanarratives that reify cultural difference and that make the boundaries between people completely impermeable, the notion of critical empathy opened the possibility that the second-period ESL students and I might understand each other just enough to be able to work together toward making Addison Public High more responsive to the public it serves.

Turning the Glass on Ourselves

As I have suggested, working toward the kind of community-building empathy Dewey and Robinson encourage requires that we citizen teachers scrutinize ourselves as a part of the process of understanding our relationships with others. We must peel back the "layers of determinateness," not expecting to find a "real self" underneath, but to understand more clearly how those layers themselves constitute who we are in that they influence our interactions (i.e., *how* we are) with others. Cornel West (1993) points out the need for this type of self-reflection in his definition of "prophetic criticism," which, in my view, is closely aligned with ideals of democratic communities and the critical empathy that I believe is necessary to work toward achieving them. "Prophetic criticism," West writes, "is first and foremost an intellectual inquiry constitutive of existential democracy—*a self-critical and self-corrective enterprise* of human 'sense-making' for the preserving and expanding of human empathy and compassion" (p. xi, my italics).

Indeed, for West, "sense-making" that fosters "human empathy and compassion" relies not on a general criticism of society in a depersonalized, generic sense; rather, prophetic criticism demands a self-criticism which must be exactly that—a critique of the self, of "me," and of the nature of my connections with others. To exercise such scrutiny is a difficult step, for to ask these questions is, for many of us, to critique our own positions as educators whose privilege is grounded in our sociocultural status and in the assumption of our expertise. It follows, I believe, that to engage in this kind of self-criticism honestly, we must stop clutching our degrees and our supposedly detached methodologies to ourselves like fig leaves and, instead, confront the frailties—and even the pain—that our privilege conceals. James Baldwin (1963/1993) in *The Fire Next Time* articulates what that self-reflection demands:

> [A] vast amount of the white anguish is rooted in the white man's . . . profound need to be seen as he is, to be released from the tyranny of his mirror. All of us know, whether or not we are able to admit it, that mirrors can only lie, that death by drowning is all that awaits one there. It is for this reason that love is so desperately sought and so cunningly avoided. Love takes off the masks that we fear we cannot live without and know we cannot live within. I use the word "love" here . . . in the tough and universal sense of quest and daring and growth. (p. 95)

To be sure, Baldwin understands that, in his own words, "what we do not know about the other reveals, precisely and inexorably, what we do not know about ourselves." He sees the connection between our own well-being and a "tough," "daring," transforming love for others. Such a "quest" is uncertain; it demands a breaking free from the familiar, the comfortable. But there is hope, for, as we wander, afraid to remove our masks and to heal, bell hooks (1990) steps into our path, holds up her hand, and speaks as a voice of the "other" who must—for all our sakes— be heard: "Stop. We greet you as liberators. This 'we' is that 'us' in the margins, that 'we' who inhabit marginal space that is not a site of domination but a place of resistance. This is an intervention. I am writing to you" (p. 152).

Me, bell? Me, Angela? Liberation from what? hooks is talking, I think, about liberation in terms of a fundamental change in the way we teachers see our role in the world. She is talking about encountering others within a space of "recognition and understanding, where we know one another so well, our histories, that we can take the bits and pieces, the fragments of who we are, and put them back together, re-member them" (p. 214). In sites where this type of re-membering can occur, teaching in cross-cultural contexts becomes not a prescriptive, potentially colonialistic enterprise, but a chance for us to grow through our connections with others—interactions that keep us challenging ourselves and seeing ourselves in new ways. hooks urges the transformation of what was once our offering our hand in a gesture of assumed generosity into a grasping for emotional and spiritual freedom—a self-knowledge enabling us to understand more completely the parameters that restrict our acting in ways that help us realize our potential as human beings.

Though this type of "re-membering" may be accomplished only through struggle, through an unsettling disclosure of assumptions and power matrices that shape potentially exploitative relationships, I believe hooks's and Baldwin's (and Dewey's) words articulate an opportunity to be more than I am now, for, as the Peruvian theologian Gustavo Gutierrez (1984) has argued, an awareness of the need for self-liberation is essential to a correct understanding of the liberation that accompanies the creation of a more democratic society:

[Liberation] is not a matter of "struggling for others," which suggests paternalism and reformist objectives, but rather of becoming aware of oneself as not completely fulfilled and as living in an alienated society. And thus one can identify radically and militantly with those—the people and the social class—who bear the brunt of oppression. (p. 146)

Similarly, Jane Addams (1910/1990), herself a person of considerable privilege who nonetheless joined with those less fortunate than she to struggle against the excesses and injustices of an emerging industrial society, argues that such joint activity fosters benefits for all those involved in it:

Nothing so deadens the sympathies and shrivels the power of enjoyment, as the persistent keeping away from the great opportunities for helpfulness and a continual ignoring of the starvation struggle which makes up the life of at least half of the race. To shut one's self away from that half of the race life is to shut one's self away from the most vital part of it; it is to live out but half the humanity to which we have been born heir and to use but half our faculties. (p. 69)

I am convinced that the possibility of such liberation and human fulfillment—for "the other" and for ourselves—depends upon the type of reciprocal modification called for by Baldwin and hooks, which is to say that the "fundamental, structural overhaul" of oppressive institutions Dewey advocates needs to begin, and end, in some very private spaces. But if a commitment to changing society requires a commitment to changing our selves, it seems to me that citizen teachers must ask additional questions: How far are we willing to go in this crusade for democratization? What is the extent of the sacrifices we are truly willing to make in our efforts to establish a Great Community as Dewey describes it? I continue to ask these questions because, even after many years, I struggle with whether I can (or even want to) "identify radically and militantly" with people like Addison's ESL students and whether I need to do so in order to engage in collective action with them.

And so I continue to assess the ethical validity of my work, especially since the personal investment I have made is so tentative, so dependent upon my own schedule and priorities. While doing the fieldwork for this project, I could get behind the wheel of my car and be back to the comfortable books and scholarly conversations of Ann Arbor in an hour. One summer I was thinking about giving up my apartment near the University and moving to Addison, where rents are lower and where I could involve myself more completely in the world of Addison High's LM students. A professor, however, cautioned me: "Be careful; you may need to get away sometimes." I thought of my friends nearby, the swimming pool at my apartment complex, the schedule of interesting films coming through town. I renewed my lease.

After my experiences in Addison, I honestly don't know whether my having pursued a terminal degree, and now tenure, by working with Latino students is a socially sanctioned form of hypocrisy—whether I should feel guilty that I could drop Emilio off at his house in the *barrio*, watch him walk up the warped steps of his sagging front porch, and then rush home in order to catch *La Traviata* at the University's performing arts center; whether, in order to be able to think of myself as "truly committed" to students like Claudia, I would need to sell everything I have and follow a selfless life not often modeled or rewarded in academic circles.

For now, I can only repeat what I have already said: that in order to be "useful," I must rely on a disposition, a way of participating in a dialogical relationship with others in which we are somehow able to struggle together to identify and overcome forces that hinder our joint participation in efforts to make this a better world—though these forces are very different for Angela than they are for me. Again, I don't wish to suggest that the expertise we citizen teachers gain from rigorous professional training and study has no value. My way of understanding what goes on at Addison High is something useful that I can bring to my relationships with the teachers and students there, and if I don't have anything more substantial to offer to people like Claudia and Felipe than my own good will, then I shouldn't have thought about traveling to Addison to encourage mutual action with them. Nonetheless, even though students may benefit from our experience and advocacy, we should be cautious about assuming that we can easily know about such students' needs and how we can be useful to them. Such caution is like the chafing seams of an ill-fitting shirt, keeping us uncomfortable, keeping us aware of our every move.

Thus, my view of what constitutes "good deeds" has changed since I began driving to Addison several years ago. I find that I am now more patient, more humble in the sense of being unsure of what is the right thing to do. In our interactions with those whom we teach, I argue, then, for a provisional and restless peace. My hope is that citizen teachers, invigorated by a desire to be useful in the pursuit of democracy, may learn to live with this paradox, may seek to establish relationships characterized by an ethical attentiveness which forsakes self-serving, isolating ideologies in favor of those that strive to effect justice through informed and affective human connections. For I have come to believe that in order to change the world for the better, our actions should begin and end face-to-face, *cara-a-cara*, with others. In communities such as these, people could no longer be forgotten.

Epilogue

The year following the *Tesoros* project, I saw much less of Alice Martinez and her students than I had during the previous three years. I had warned them (and myself) that continuing the frequency of my visits would soon be impossible, that the need to write a dissertation and find a job demanded that I slowly but very surely withdraw from my immediate relationship with them. I drove to Addison when I could, usually not more than once every two or three weeks. Since then, from my new home in Chicago, my communication with Martinez and the ESL students has dwindled to an occasional card or phone call—not a lot of contact but enough for me to know that most of the people introduced in this story still lived in the area. In June 1998, I returned to Addison to see how they were doing.

When Angela emerged from the East Side bungalow where she lived with seven other members of her immediate and extended family, I was glad to see that her broad smile hadn't changed since I had last seen her. She told me that by and by she had begun to like school more than she had during her first two years at Addison High and that she was proud she had graduated with her class. As she explained, however, this accomplishment came only after considerable difficulty:

> The classes that were the hardest were government, American history, and math because I had to read a lot. Well, I could read the books for those classes, but I couldn't understand the words even though I could pronounce them. And I don't think I was prepared to do the math here. It's harder here because when I was in primaria the things they taught us were basic, like addition, subtraction, multiplication. . . . But here we had to do harder things like fractions, and I didn't understand that.

After having failed the American history and government courses required for graduation, Angela made up these credits by enrolling in evening adult education classes during her senior year. She was able to pass these courses, she said, in large part because her teacher spoke both English and Spanish, assistance she wished she had received in her classes at Addison High. *"If I could have changed some things about high school, I'd have teachers who could speak two languages,"* she said. After graduating, Angela was employed at a local tortilla factory and in a restaurant, places where she had begun working while she was still in school. One day at the *totilleria*, Angela slipped and fell, straining some ligaments in her back. As a result of the accident, she was no longer able to endure long hours on her feet and was forced to quit both her jobs. She was now spending her days at home caring for her young cousins and several neighbor children—a situation which, to Angela, had grown tiresome: *"I don't like it because I don't like being at home all the time."* Her dream, she said, was *"to study in college to be a translator, maybe in Mexico or here."* Keeping her from this goal, however, was the glacially slow process of achieving legal residency status. *"I want to go to college, but I need papers to do that,"* she said. *"We have a lawyer who's helping us, but I need to get my papers soon, before I turn 21, or I have to start all over again."* As of this writing, Angela was within a few months of her twenty-first birthday, and she was still waiting for her papers from the INS.

At first I barely recognized George. He had grown at least two inches and had put on about twenty pounds, mostly in his chest and shoulders. In his thick forearms, veins bulged under the skin. We sat in the back yard at a picnic table near a red, white, and blue swing set. When I mentioned the flowers encircling the yard, he smiled and said that he had planted most of them himself.

I asked him how school had gone since I'd left. "Sometimes kids would say things that would make you feel bad," he said. "They be talking about Mexicans a lot, and they'd say like, 'You a Mexican, you ain't supposed to be here,' and 'Go back to Mexico, to Taco Bell.' And just stuff like that, stupid stuff." Despite the sometimes hostile environment, George, too, had remained at Addison High long enough to graduate. Since then, he'd been working and living with his father in a small rented house in Ohio. Most weekends they drove up to Michigan to see his family: "I work in the refrigerators, electronic stuff," he said. "And scooters, electric scooters. I just sit down and work on the little motor; we make them." George spoke casually but positively about his work, saying, "It's nice, fresh. I make about three hundred dollars a week." I asked George if he wanted to continue in this job or whether he had other plans. "I just wanna get money and buy me a new car," he said. "I don't care what kind, just get me to somewhere else. I just don't like it here. I don't like Michigan winters. I just wanna be a mechanic. Ms. Martinez, she's gonna hook me up with a college, a free college to learn to be a mechanic."

"Are you pretty excited about that?" I asked.

George shrugged his shoulders. "Not really. If I get excited, it's just to get me a car. I be going to college, but if it didn't get me a car I won't go to college. Because I just want a car to go cruising somewhere else, 'cause it's boring. I don't want to ride bike going somewhere else. I just wanna work, start living, start a family."

Start a family. That surprised me, and so I asked him, "You got a girlfriend?"

"Nah," he said, then laughed. "I'm gonna go find me one right now." Then, taking advantage of a brief pause, George made a connection between his desire to "start living" and broader issues that influence whether or not that might be possible: "I wish the United States beginning to bring Mexican people over here to work. I want Mexico and the United States to get along together. And they could make good money, a lot of money. They can trade a lot and stuff."

"How do you think people could make that happen?" I asked.

He thought for a moment, then said:

Talk to the President, and the person who really into that stuff, like teachers who are into it, where it's really important for them to have Mexican and American people together. It's much better that way. A lot of people get hurt right now, with Mexicans, got beat up in immigration; they get raped and stuff. Like the cops who beat up the Mexicans in the green truck. You see that on TV? Remember? That's not right. Just get along together, that's it. 'Cause if we wasn't here, who pick the fields? Who do all that stuff? No one. Because in the summer, we don't care about the sun and stuff, we just wanna work and make money. Like I worked in the corn, pickles, tomatoes, watermelon, apples. I didn't like it very much, though. It was pretty hard work, but I have to do it 'cause I gotta help my family, too.

When I entered Manuel's house, the first thing he did was to introduce me to his fiancée, who shook my hand and then went to the kitchen to get us some sodas. "You got a place to stay?" he asked. "'Cause if you don't you can stay here." I thanked him but said I had a motel room on the outskirts of town.

Manuel said that he had dropped out of school shortly after I left and had begun working at a small factory making brake lines for GM sport utility vehicles. Though Manuel liked the job and was "making pretty good money," he was fired after eleven months when his employer discovered that he was not yet eighteen. After working intermittently at several different jobs and being unemployed at one point for about seven months, Manuel turned eighteen and found work that he said he liked very much:

It's a new company here in Addison. They make gas tanks for Chrysler. I go in at seven at night to seven in the morning. But it's cool because I worked like yesterday, and I work today, and I get my weekend off. Then I go in Monday and Tuesday, and I get Wednesday and Thursday off, and then I work my other weekend. I run a machine called a gun drill. I run that machine. And we ship the stuff to a lot of places, to Monterey, Mexico, and Europe, and one is in Michigan, I think.

At that time, Manuel was living with his parents, his two younger siblings, and his fiancée. Planning to marry within a year, he emphasized his determination to keep working: "Yeah, I wanna keep my job," he said. "I wanna keep it steady, 'cause my girlfriend and I are living together here for about a year, and we're going to want to get a new place."

While Manuel seemed happy and relatively secure in his job, Hector had missed out on the good fortune of his younger brother. Like Manuel, Hector dropped out of school in 1996 and started working at the brake line factory, where he had apparently impressed his employer with his skills and work ethic: "I was 17 years old, and I was a supervisor. I just knew how to do every-thing on the line and all the paperwork and everything. I did a really good job; me and my brother were the best people work-ing on the line. Everybody said we were the best workers there. I mean, everybody else was older than us, me and brother, but I got promoted past all those people." Also like Manuel, however, Hector had been fired when, according to Hector, a fellow em-ployee who had been passed up for the promotion given to Hec-tor told the employer that he and Manuel had falsified their ages on their applications. Since then, in Hector's words, "Everything went downhill." Though he worked a number of jobs, he said he had lost them all for the same reason: "I just started partying every day, and every time I had to go to work I was partying the night before, so I wouldn't go to work the next day 'cause I'd be all hung over and I wasn't getting enough sleep."

Things hit bottom for Hector in early 1998, when he was arrested for drunk driving and sentenced to ninety days in the county jail. While there, Hector passed much of the time pursu-ing his interest in art. "I did some good artwork in there. I made a picture frame. It's bad, man. It's all Mexican colors. And I made some baby shoes, and a heart picture frame. The picture frames I sold for, like, thirty dollars a piece." Hector said that he had fashioned a crude blade for his projects by filing the edge of a metal strip taken from the headset of a personal stereo. His pri-mary materials were empty potato chip bags, which he explained have "a chrome color on the inside and lots of different colors on the outside."

By the time I spoke with him, Hector had been out of jail for a little over two months and, at age twenty, had recently begun a new job as a machinist. He said he was relieved to have found work, especially considering what he described as his current obligations: "I got a girlfriend now that I'm living with, but she's a lot older than me, man. She's, like, thirty-six years old, and she's got a thirteen-year old daughter. Actually, I got a family now, and so now I gotta be responsible. My mom can't take care of me no more. I'm not a little boy any more."

Of all the students in the ESL class, Felipe was the one who, it seemed to me, was the most likely to stay in school. As a gifted wrestler, someone who could contribute to the life of Addison

High in a way that was sanctioned by his coaches, his teachers, and his mainstream peers, he had been encouraged in ways that most other LM students would never experience. Still, despite the ribbons and medals, despite the pats on the back and the admonitions to "study hard" so he would remain eligible for athletics, Felipe had dropped out by the end of his junior year. His principal reason for leaving, he explained, was truancy brought on by frustration with his schoolwork: "I liked school at first. My freshman year was easy, but as soon as you get up in tenth grade, with higher books and stuff and government and history, there's a lot of words that are really confusing. And so I was almost always home; that's why I lost a lot of credits. That's what happened to me pretty much."

Upon leaving Addison High, Felipe was directed by a counselor to a nearby alternative school called "Oak Village," which is intended to accommodate students who have been "unsuccessful" in regular high school settings. Felipe said that at Oak Village, he liked the small classes, the teachers (who he said are "smart, pretty much"), and particularly the individualized approach to learning: "You know how you always be behind at the high school? But with this place, you go on your own pace. It's not like they move on and leave you behind; you do your own work. You sit there with a book, and they tell you what you gotta do. If you got any questions the teacher will just help you out, and that stuff stays in your head." Though Felipe seemed pleased with his experience at Oak Village, after about two months he was again expelled for truancy. He struggled to explain why he had stopped going to school. "I don't know," he said. "I just didn't want to go no more."

Felipe stressed that he hoped to return to Oak Village in the fall and added that, in the meantime, he planned to pursue a money-making strategy that he had recently become involved in. He handed me a glossy catalogue, then sat on the edge of the couch as he explained to me what he saw as a promising future:

> Well, right now I'm in this business, sales person, marketing. It like sells products and stuff like that. . . . I started for about a month already. It's pretty good. I sold a couple of stuff. Every

month it's like you sell at least five hundred dollars every month, you get a check back every month from them and the profit which you make out of it. And I start my own down line; it's like my own business. My down line, they sell too, and I get some percentage off that. There's this guy who makes like a hundred thousand dollars every month, and they pay for his gas that he spends to go to places and stuff. And they pay for his dinner. He keeps his receipt, he sends it back, and he gets all that money back. And they pay for your house and your car. It's pretty nice; it's real nice.

Though reluctant to dampen his enthusiasm, I asked Felipe as delicately as I could what he might do if the "business" didn't work out. He answered without hesitation:

Me? I'm gonna be boxing. That's pretty much what I wanna become, a boxer. If it doesn't work out I'm still gonna be in that business. Or I can have another job. But I probably won't even need it after I move up in this 'cause, you know, a hundred thousand dollars every month. If I move up that high, it'll probably take me year, that's it, to move up to that level. And it's going to be a lot easier for my life, 'cause a hundred grand every month, and plus they pay for my house and they pay for all that stuff. I'll be set.

During most of my conversation with Claudia, she cradled in her lap her one-year-old daughter, Maria. Claudia said that she had continued in school for nearly a year after I left Addison and that for a while, things had gone "pretty okay." Claudia spoke with particular fondness of her special education class and the teacher, Mr. Ferris, who she said "would be calling on me and separating me to the class, so he could help me a lot." She added that because Ferris doesn't speak Spanish, "I was teaching him Spanish, and he was teaching me more English. And that was good." In addition to offering Claudia individualized attention with her schoolwork and an environment that affirmed her native language, Ferris went out of his way to improve Claudia's attendance. "If I didn't come to the class, he'd get mad," she said. "He'd be looking for me to take me to his class. Like, he'd find me in the lunch room or in the gym. But with him my attendance was pretty good."

In spite of the relatively positive experience of her special education class, Claudia explained that, by and by, school became harder because "I had to speak English all the time." As she explained, these persistent difficulties in trying to learn content-area material in English were compounded by tensions that arose between Claudia and her peers:

> I had problems with the students. 'Cause I was going dressed up not like them. 'Cause they dressed up like hippies, and they be talking 'cause I was dressed up nice and all that. So they got a problem with that. And then when I started wearing baggy pants and T-shirts like them, then they were talking, like, "Oh, look how she looks now." And these were friends and friends of my friends. I never got in a fight with them, but they were trying to get in a fight with me 'cause I liked to talk to my other friend—he's black—and his friend, by the library. So they were getting jealous 'cause I was more with them. So that's why they were talking bad stuff about me.

Tired of her academic and social troubles, Claudia eventually followed the lead of her siblings and dropped out of school. Several months later, she became pregnant with Maria, and though she confirmed that her responsibilities as a mother "take a lot of time," she nonetheless had completed two adult education courses the previous term. Claudia said that she enjoyed these classes "'cause I met more people" and "because they be helping me more there in reading and writing. And some words I never heard in English, but I'm hearing them there, and that helps me 'cause the teacher I got, she speaks Spanish and English. And they have books in Spanish and English." Claudia said that she planned to continue taking classes in the fall: "I can get my diploma there. I already went this year, and I think I gotta be there, like, two more years." Looking ahead, Claudia said, "I want to get my diploma and probably go to college. I think I probably want to work on computers 'cause that's what I did a lot with Mr. Ferris."

Before I left, I asked Claudia about her older sister, Rosa. I had been trying to reach her since arriving in town, but she hadn't returned my calls, and, during my visits with Felipe and Claudia, as well as the several other times I had stopped by, she wasn't at home. Claudia had told me that since leaving school and working for a short time at a nearby motel, Rosa had given birth to a boy and had been unemployed. Claudia added that she didn't think her sister had any plans to find a job or return to school.

Back in my motel room I sat at the desk and paged through the glossy catalogue Felipe had given me. It said that the products inside "promote healthy bodies and minds" and that "the opportunity to share these products with others promotes financial health." Page eight advertised a back roller designed to "combat the abnormal body tension which can cause discomfort along the spine, neck, and limbs." On page eleven was a photo of a pair of metal balls with "specially designed nodules" that promised to "stimulate and relax any part of your body when rolled between your palms." A later page featured an "anti-cellulite gel" which, according to the description, "may help the skin achieve a smoother, firmer, more youthful appearance when applied in firm, circular, motions on affected areas." The next day I picked up George as I had promised and took him over to visit Martinez. As we drove through the streets of Addison, I asked him whether he thought Felipe could make a living as a boxer. Staring out the open window of my car, George laughed and said, "I don't know."

When I think about the young people whose stories I've presumed to tell in this book, I know that the blame for whatever difficulties they have endured in the past and are likely to encounter in the future cannot be laid solely on the steps of Addison High. As we have seen, to expand the limited options available to these students is a complex challenge that can be met only through a transformation that extends beyond schools and into the broader society: Angela was kept from attending college because of federal immigration policies; George and Manuel were tied to sustenance-level jobs that form a necessary part of this country's present, and relatively unquestioned, economic system; Hector struggled with potentially destructive dependencies for which he could afford no treatment; Claudia was likely to be hindered in her attempts to earn a high school diploma, attend college, and get a job working "on computers" in the absence of affordable day care for Maria; Felipe, faced with the likelihood that he would be unable to find work that would pay a livable wage, had resorted to bravado and dreams that he could build a secure future for himself through marketing schemes and professional sports. To be sure, all of these are obstacles that require responses on far-reaching levels of public policy. Still, I can't help wondering whether these students might have more life choices available to them if they had attended a school that consistently valued who they were and that drew upon the knowledge and literacies they brought to their classes in ways that would have helped them to realize their diverse potentials.

As I've suggested, these kinds of structural changes are possible only through the agency of individuals who commit themselves to working with others toward a vision of a world in which all people can more democratically participate in shaping the courses and conditions of their lives. Sadly, however, one need not look far for evidence that people can be surprisingly inert and uncaring even in the face of clear evidence of measures that could be taken to rectify inequities such as those that many Latino students face in schools. As I've discussed in this book, there is growing consensus among teachers and researchers working with LM students that such students benefit from well-staffed bilingual programs, that they respond positively to the individual attention made possible by small classes and peer tutors, and that they rise to the challenge of a rigorous but comprehensible curriculum. We know, too, that through sheltered content and language-sensitive teaching methods, content-area teachers—despite their language limitations—can offer effective instruction to LM students. What is lacking, then, is not the knowledge of how to teach LM students well, but the collective political and moral will to do so. When I reflect on our country's general disregard of LM and other disenfranchised students, when I consider our willingness to forget them, I worry, for at times like these I also recall the words of Thomas Jefferson: "I tremble for my nation when I think that God is just."

Nonetheless, I continue to be what Cornel West (1999) has called "a prisoner of hope." That is, I continue to believe that critically empathetic connections with people like Angela, Claudia, and Felipe can prompt what may be our strongest motivation to engage in the praxis necessary to do what we can to address their diverse and urgent needs. For as West reminds us, "empathy is not simply a matter of trying to imagine what others are going through, but having the will to muster enough courage to do something about it" (p. 12). Put another way, it is relatively easy to read another article or watch another news broadcast about the struggles of language-minority students and to say, "They just need to learn English." It is more difficult, I think, to turn our back on someone we know.

The last evening I could stay in Addison before returning to Chicago, I stopped by one last time to see if I could catch Rosa at home. She was out, but Claudia and I sat for a while on the front steps of the family's two-story house. "It's so hot inside, but it's cooler out here," Claudia said. We sat in the twilight, next to the flower bushes alongside the steps, staring across the street at an abandoned grain elevator complex surrounded by a sagging barbed-wire fence. Behind us on the porch, Claudia's daughter, Maria, crawled on white plastic patio furniture. Claudia told me that Maria usually slept through the night now, but that in the recent heat she would sometimes wake up at one or two in the morning. Claudia described how she would then get the child a drink and bathe her in cool water. "After that," Claudia said, "she goes right back to sleep."

I asked her how she liked being a mother. "I like it," she said, "but it's hard." She explained that she didn't get out much any more. "A couple days ago a Mexican guy came to see me. He's a friend, and he knows that sometimes I just need something to happen. . . . I just gotta get out of here." When I asked her where she might go, she couldn't say.

Maria climbed down from her chair, came up behind her mother, and put her arms around Claudia's neck. "Are you hungry, honey?" Claudia said. The child nodded. We stood up, shook hands, and said good-bye, promising to stay in touch. Claudia took Maria by the hand and went inside. I walked out to my car, started it up, and cranked the air conditioner to "high." I sat there idling for a while on the street, writing these things in my notebook so I wouldn't forget them.

Appendix

Transcript of the Teachers' Meeting

ALVAREZ: Maybe we should hear from each of you as to where you think she's at and also from Ms. Martinez in terms of her reading ability. You've tested her and you have an idea about where she is and maybe start from that point and see what we can do to help her. We just heard from Mrs. Schaffer [Angela's typing teacher] and she said that she was doing a whole lot better this semester; she's really opened up, she's really trying harder, and she doesn't seem to think that there will be a problem   10
with second semester.

PEARSON: So she was here first semester?

ALVAREZ: Yeah.

BATES: I think she understands a lot.

MARTINEZ: Well, yeah, but I don't think she reads much, though. She doesn't understand that much—enough to get by but a lot of it will just go right over her head. She'll pick out a word here or there but then she doesn't really understand what's it's about. Like, I talk in English to her as much as possible.   20
You know, like, "What did you do last night?" and a lot of the time she really can't understand.

TODD: Yeah, and I know from personal experience in trying to learn Spanish that that's a very dangerous thing to do because you can generally figure out what the conversation is about, but it's very easy— because you don't want to feel stupid—to make the next step and assume you're following the conver- sation when you're really not. I remember times when I thought I knew what was going on and it   30
turned out I had barely a clue.

ALVAREZ: [To Martinez] Do you know how much education she had prior to coming here?

MARTINEZ: She went to the sixth grade. In Mexico, that was as far as she got. And then when she came here they put her in the ninth grade. But I guess she had to pay in Mexico and couldn't afford it.

ALVAREZ: And she's living with . . .

MARTINEZ: Her mother and step father. And two older brothers and an older girl.   40

PEARSON: And it's all Spanish?

MARTINEZ: And it's all Spanish. I try to get her to watch some television to practice her English in some way, but her mother does not speak any English and her father a little bit. Her brothers, too, just a bit.

PEARSON: That's two strikes right there on us.

MARTINEZ: Also, she does not socialize other than church, and that's all Spanish. She goes to the Spanish church, and all Spanish functions.

BATES: Okay, well then what *can* we do for her? She doesn't   50
go to the movies; she doesn't hang out with friends.

PEARSON: If I was going to go to Mexico, going to try and be immersed, I think that I would learn the language. But if she's coming here with no intention of being immersed in English, it's like we're beating our head against the wall.

MARTINEZ: But she has really made great strides.

BATES: I tested her when she first came—just her math skills. Because the Transition [Math] book we use was written for the average seventh grader, which   60
would, if she quit in sixth grade, would be right where she belongs. But she came in second semester last year, so was at a disadvantage then, which was to be expected. And I couldn't communicate at all with her; she's talked to me a little bit this year, and she's got a few things down. She has the basic skills; that's all you're supposed to need to know: whole numbers, addition, subtraction, multiplication, and division, and if she needs to she can use a calculator. She knows how to run the calculator,   70
not a lot but enough to get by. So she should be able to get by in Transition Math.

MARTINEZ: Yeah, but she wouldn't, for instance, be able to do any story problems.

PEARSON: See, I equate this to what I saw about four years ago, when we had a Japanese student come. But that girl that we had in Japanese we were doing very similar things that we're doing in computers. You know, you copy, you try and make it look like what it says in the workbook. I saw her with her   80 Japanese dictionary translating every word in the exercise to find out even what it was about. At the end of the semester this girl was really speaking.

MARTINEZ: I'm sure she had a higher ability in her own language.

PEARSON: Oh, yeah, plus she was also immersed in an English home.

MARTINEZ: Yeah, the same thing happened with our Arabic kids. They caught on like that. [She snaps her fingers.] As soon as they heard a word they didn't   90 know it was like, "Say that again," and they'd write it down. But Angela is much more limited in her own language.

TODD: I think, too, the fact that her family speaks all Spanish has a lot to do with this.

MARTINEZ: Right, it's a male-dominated society where she's from, and the female is expected just to get married and have kids. But her brother does encourage her to go on and do something with her life.

BATES: Let's see, is she sixteen? Will she be quitting school   100 when she turns sixteen?

MARTINEZ: No, she won't quit; she is sixteen. Yes, she took driver's training. Fran Soto took her to driver's training and tutored her all summer, sat in class, translated all the exams, rode in the car.

BATES: If she can pass driver's ed she's capable. We have a lot of kids who can't pass the driver's ed.

MARTINEZ: But there everything was translated for her. And Fran was actually in the car with her in the backseat, and whatever was said to her by the   110 instructor, like "Turn here," Fran would say in Spanish.

PEARSON: [To Martinez] Aren't we validating the wrong

response by you being there all the time? I don't
know; that's what I'm worried about.

MARTINEZ: You mean like a crutch?

PEARSON: Yeah.

MARTINEZ: I don't think so. If someone is interested in her and
giving her assistance and her comfort level is high,
it's very good for her. 120

ALVAREZ: See that would be true for foreign exchange
students we have because they have completed
eleven years in their own home school.

PEARSON: Whereas she's way behind.

ALVAREZ: Right. And the more you talk Spanish with these
girls the more they want to talk Spanish with you.
But it's not the same with Angela.

PEARSON: Yeah, it seems that we're looking at a whole
different ball game here, and I just wonder how I'm
gonna be able to communicate with her. 130

BATES: Well, they were thinking in the fall of moving her
to Jim Weaver's Trans Math just because he teaches
Spanish too, but he doesn't think that would be any
advantage for her when I talked to him about it.

MARTINEZ: I don't know why he doesn't think that would be a
good idea.

BATES: Well, he didn't think that he would have time to
talk to her in Spanish because his class is full; he's
got thirty-four kids in there.

PEARSON: I don't know; I think that would be a positive start. 140

MARTINEZ: So do I.

ALVAREZ: The reason she wasn't changed was that she was getting help with science and now that didn't work out.
Sara decided that she didn't want to do it anymore.

BATES: Sara thought that she was doing all the work for her.

TODD: Angela, though, said that one of the things she
appreciated in that class is just . . .

BATES: Having someone she could talk to?

TODD: Exactly. It ties in with what you were saying earlier,
Alice, about whether we're doing her a disservice 150
by giving her this instruction in Spanish, and my
feeling is that it's good for her to have someone
around who's her age and who she can talk to

because she does try very hard, and I've seen a couple of these kids already, in just the time I've been here, dropping out of school, and here you have a kid who at least tries. You just hate to see her continue to fail all the time.

MARTINEZ: Well, a large part of the first part of first semester, before Sara, she would go in, she'd try to smile at the other girls in the class. I'd ask her, "Mi'ja, do you try to smile at the other girls?" They didn't talk back to her; they wouldn't associate with her; they wouldn't speak Spanish, even the Mexican girls. 160

BATES: I know, I tried that last year. Didn't work.

MARTINEZ: Right, so there was not a buddy for her. I says, "Who do you eat lunch with?" She says, "*No-body.*" Now can you imagine going through six hours a day, alone . . .

PEARSON: Not talking to anybody. 170

MARTINEZ: Yes, not talking to anyone, except one or two teachers.

PEARSON: That would be hard.

BATES: Yeah.

MARTINEZ: And then when she came to me, and I was pushing English, really pushing English, and then I just said to myself, "this is ridiculous; this child needs some Spanish, too." Just to be able to communicate and get rid of this frustration; she was just ready to explode. So now we use both languages. In my 180 class she does all her writing in Spanish. Whenever we do any journals, any story writing, it's all in Spanish. Then we translate it, and then she reads that, shares that. And half the time I have to make her read out loud. And that alone has been very hard for her.

BATES: She's very shy.

MARTINEZ: Very shy, to read that out loud. For her that's a major accomplishment.

ALVAREZ: So, in terms of Angela in math, though, I heard you 190 say that she has the basic skills down . . .

BATES: She has the basic skills she needs.

MARTINEZ: Where I see she needs more help, too, is in social studies.

TODD: I'm not sure where Mr. Marx is today.

PEARSON: Oh, yeah, now there's just a plain lot of reading, and he lectures a lot, probably.

MARTINEZ: Yes, and it goes right over her head and then she'll bring the test down for me to help her. And I can't translate a whole test to her and expect her to 200 understand what the teacher has been teaching her in that hour. The expectations just have to be changed there. Yeah, and in science, too. There have got to be some real changes, somehow. And I understand where the teachers are coming from: How can we give our test to them when she's not doing what everyone else is doing?

PEARSON: Does she have to take six hours, do you think?

MARTINEZ: Yeah, but what about pass/fail?

PEARSON: That would be fine with me if she'd like to take 210 computers on a pass/fail. Then all she's got to do is do half the work and she'd be able to pass.

MARTINEZ: That's a good idea, I think. She *is* doing her best; she's here all the time, so we have to give her something for trying. She's doing the best she can with what she has.

PEARSON: I'm just wondering with some of these academic classes whether she could take them twice. Take two sessions of it.

ALVAREZ: Well, I think that's what she was already doing 220 from last year.

MARTINEZ: She didn't get any credit last year for them.

PEARSON: Well, I'm saying like two hours a day.

MARTINEZ: No, if she didn't understand it the first time, she's not going to understand it the second time unless somebody's there to translate for her.

BATES: Well, what can we do? Other than put her in Mr. Weaver's class because he does speak Spanish.

MARTINEZ: I like that idea.

ALVAREZ: But Mr. Weaver doesn't have any more room. 230

BATES: But he team-teaches that class; so shouldn't there be room for one more?

PEARSON: What's the class where they help kids . . . ?

ALVAREZ: Study skills?

PEARSON: Yeah, how about study skills?

MARTINEZ: No, that's for special ed kids, and she's not special ed.

TODD: Yeah, special ed is reserved for kids with pretty serious learning disabilities.

PEARSON: And her disability is no English. That's a pretty serious disability.   240

BATES: Well, I just got a new student in my class; maybe somebody will drop out of Weaver's class.

MARTINEZ: A buddy system works.

BATES: We tried that last year, and it really didn't work.

PEARSON: Well, we noticed the other day she kind of put herself in the corner where nobody could sit near her. She chose the only computer where nobody could get near her.

TODD: But there's another girl in the class who speaks Spanish, and if we could get her to sit next to this   250 other girl when I'm not there, that would probably help quite a bit.

PEARSON: Okay, if we could maybe talk to the other girl and see what she says. I'm willing to give her some incentive or extra credit or whatever if she would be willing to answer questions and help Angela. I don't want to make a deal with every kid in class, but maybe if she's willing, this could work out. And in my class, the kids work on these projects at their own pace, so as long as she's got the notes,   260 she should be okay.

ALVAREZ: Do you write them on the board?

PEARSON: Well, they're not always 100 percent written, but . . .

BATES: Angela is able to copy things from the board. We've started that in my class for her, so that's good practice in writing English.

PEARSON: Some days I'll go ahead and demo everything right there on the screen.

TODD: Is it possible to get that math book in Spanish?

BATES: When we had books from the other publisher, we   270 had books in Spanish, but I don't know if this one's available in Spanish. I haven't seen anything to show that it is. This one was written in Chicago, so you'd think it would have a Spanish translation.

MARTINEZ: I'll ask the Chapter One people if we can get that in Spanish.

PEARSON: You know that wouldn't be a bad idea just to order a half a dozen or so, or one of each of those texts if they're available. I don't know if it's available, but there's no harm in asking.   280

MARTINEZ: You know what else they have? They have a lot of these units on cassette.

TODD: Well let's call these publishers and find out what they've got.

MARTINEZ: If I knew what they needed, if I could get a list from Mr. Marx, of what he's covering, like oceans, or whatever, I'd see what I could find.

TODD: Okay, Alice, but is that really your job to do that? It seems to me that it's not. It's your job to teach English.   290

BATES: Whose job is it?

PEARSON: Yeah, [to Martinez] your job is to teach them English as their second language, and that's why I say these sources in Spanish would be really helpful.

MARTINEZ: That's the job of the Chapter One people, to find out alternative methods to teach a student.

BATES: Yeah, not us. When I taught at the middle school, we had these Spanish textbooks, and the Chapter One people got them for us. I never got them.   300

PEARSON: Well, to tell you the truth, I haven't looked.

BATES: Yeah, I didn't do the ordering for these. You haven't seem them in Spanish?

PEARSON: My book is an English book. What you have to do is contact Scott Foresman.

TODD: Aside from looking into a different math book, can you think of anything else we might be able to do? When I'm there, I can take Claudia and Angela over to the next room and work with them, but it's still very hard 'cause even in Spanish we have to go   310 very slowly. We can make it through like the first five or ten problems.

BATES: It's something. Whatever little bit you do helps. And honest, it does, it helps a lot.

TODD: Are there any suggestions as to what you might be able to do on the days I'm not there?

BATES: Um, I have suggested that Claudia and Angela work together. Sometimes they do, but Claudia's into socializing more than a lot of the other kids. Not that she was out of line.   320

MARTINEZ: Angela is staying for tutoring help from that group of tutors that comes after school [from the University of Michigan]. She asked me to write a note that says, "I need a ride to the high school." So she hasn't missed a session with those people yet.

PEARSON: I'll talk to that girl and see what I can come up with.

TODD: Thanks so much.

MARTINEZ: [to Bates] You seem to have a good relationship with her; she's commented to me that you try to talk to her.   330

BATES: Yeah, she seems to understand most of what I say to her when I get a chance to talk to her, which I don't very often anymore. She was in a better class for that last year, but this year I don't have time for that at all in that class, literally, I don't have time.

MARTINEZ: So then we'll look into books.

BATES: Right.

ALVAREZ: But we'll keep her with you?

BATES: I guess so, if Weaver is full. It's good for her that she's with Claudia, I think, although in class I don't   340 see much interaction between them even when they sit together. I have to suggest they work together.

ALVAREZ: In evaluating them, who do you think is better, I mean between her and Claudia?

BATES: Well, Claudia could do a lot better but she's not there very often. [to me] Since you've been coming, she's been there more often. As far as ability?

ALVAREZ: Yeah, when they turn in their papers, who gets better grades?

BATES: Well, Claudia I think has more to work with up   350 here [pointing to her head]. She catches on quicker than Angela does.

ALVAREZ: But I got the impression that Claudia doesn't have a lot of math skills.

MARTINEZ: Claudia might actually be LD, but she understands more English, and she's not shy.

BATES: No, the last quiz, Claudia had a C and Angela had a D. So I see the opposite in class. [To Todd] When you work with them individually, do you see a difference?   360

TODD: Well, I'm not sure about that. But one of the things that worries me is that once we get past any language problems, it still seems they don't have much of a background in math.

MARTINEZ: I think so.

TODD: For example, sometimes even with pretty basic subtraction of, say, one angle from 180 degrees. Angela today finally figured it out, but Claudia didn't.

BATES: But Claudia wasn't here when we did that chapter, the first geometry chapter.   370

ALVAREZ: Okay, back to Angela. Okay, Todd, you'll continue to come twice a week? And, Alice, in your class, you work more on the English and not on any other homework she has in any other class, right?

TODD: And she's getting help in the tutoring group?

ALVAREZ: Yup, she's been my faithful one; she's had perfect attendance. So between what you're helping her with and what they're helping her with, I think the main thing was we were wondering where she was math-wise. And I think we know that she can do it. 380 And Mr. Pearson said he was going to have a student help her in his class. And she's doing okay in her typing class. And we're missing, then, science and geography.

TODD: [to Bates] But you know, it sounds like you're a little more optimistic about Angela's math skills than I am. I really think that she struggles. I think that you could put a Spanish text in front of her and that she would still be pretty clueless.

BATES: I'm sure she is going to struggle to some degree,   390 but if you look around, most of the kids in that class are struggling. But the basic skills she needs to handle the work in that book is supposed to be what she has. And I did have her do some papers. I tested her this summer. She has the skills, she really does. She doesn't know much about decimals or fractions, but that's supposed to be okay in that textbook. Now whether she is learning it or not because of the language barrier, I don't know. I really don't know. But I see some improvements from last year. She couldn't answer any of the questions 'cause she was totally overwhelmed.

400

MARTINEZ: Would it help, do you think, to reduce the number of questions she has to do for homework?

BATES: Except that half the answers are in the back of the book and you know she's starting to copy the back of the book. So she really only had to do the other half, right? I assign all of them.

ALVAREZ: Do the students have to show their work?

BATES: Well, most of them don't, because seventh grade math should be done in their heads. And I don't hold them to showing all their work.

410

ALVAREZ: Well, the thing is that for you to find out where she's missing steps you almost need to see her work.

BATES: Well on some things but not on everything, and whatever Angela can do I'll accept. But look, I don't know what else to do. I have thirty-three in that class, and I have about thirteen stinkers in there and another thirteen are lost.

ALVAREZ: What happens when Todd's not there?

420

BATES: I really don't have time to notice this year. I could have told you last year. I mean, some things, like today she didn't want to leave the class until she had the notes, so she must be understanding a little better.

MARTINEZ: Sometimes I see Claudia and Angela not eating lunch and going to the library and working on math or social studies. Because once in a while they have to do a project and research on a country or something, and they would just copy from a bunch of books and encyclopedias and nothing went with anything and they would show it to me but they were so proud because they were doing something.

430

BATES: They both passed their last quiz. [to Todd] You were here and helped them, right.

TODD: Yeah, but I did a lot of it.

Notes

1. "Addison High" is not the school's real name. Throughout this work, I have also changed all names of the school's students, faculty, and staff, as well as the names of streets, businesses, and other landmarks that would compromise the anonymity of the people who appear in the book.

2. Miranda and Quiroz (1989) report that of the 20.1 million Latino residents in the US in 1989, the largest segment was the Mexican American population (12.6 million, or about 63 percent of the total). Other segments of this overall Latino population include Central and South American (2.5 million, or about 12 percent), Puerto Rican (2.3 million, or about 11 percent), and Spanish or other Latino (1.6 million, or about 8 percent).

3. Students whose lack of facility in English may have negative consequences for their academic achievement in monolingual English classrooms are also often referred to as "limited English proficient" (LEP). Because I think this term may be read to imply deficiency, I prefer and will use "language-minority" (LM) to refer to such students. I should note, however, that some writers do not use these terms synonymously, but consider LEP students to be a subgroup within the broader LM designation.

4. Though Alvarez used the term *Hispanic* in this conversation, and while the Addison Public Schools and many state and federal organizations also use this term to refer to persons of Mexican, Puerto Rican, Cuban, Central or South American, or other Spanish-speaking culture of origin, regardless of race, I am using *Latino* to refer to such people for two principal reasons. First, while *Hispanic* literally means "belonging to" or "derived from" Spain, *Latino* more accurately implies a recognition of the diversity of Spanish-speaking cultures and identities that are distinct from Europe and that include an acknowledgment of the Native American contributions to these cultures. Second, *Hispanic* may be considered a bureaucratic, categorical term imposed on people by governments and other institutions in support of marginalizing, even op-

pressive, policies, while *Latino* tends to be the term of choice of persons of Spanish-language origins in naming themselves. Even having said this, however, I wish to emphasize that my use of *Latino* should in no way be read as an attempt to conflate or downplay the richly diverse cultural and national identities of the people introduced in this book and the striking differences in their unique histories, demeanors, and desires. On the contrary, while I think it would be wrong to discount the importance and consequences of the students' collective identity as Latinos, it is crucial that readers view these students as people who cannot be defined merely in collective terms. Indeed, the more time I spent in Addison, the clearer it became to me that these students embody differences resulting from many complex forces such as nationality, socioeconomic status, gender, family circumstances, and even those personality traits (shy, friendly, nervous, and so on) that are hard to define but are nonetheless among the variables that combine (and recombine) to determine who they are in their own and in others' eyes.

Chapter Two

1. These statistics are misleading due to the way they are defined. In the high school's report, the dropout rate is defined as "the percentage of students who leave school in any one year, adjusting for those who move in and out of the district." The retention rate, in turn, is defined as "the percentage of ninth graders who graduate from high school within four years, adjusting for the students who move in and out of the district and to alternative programs." The problem with these data is that the retention and dropout rates, as they are calculated in the report, are measuring student retention and attrition over two different time periods. To calculate the percentage of students who leave school in any one year and then subtract that from 100 percent is not going to indicate accurately the percentage of students in a given class who graduate after four years. Rather, the retention rate—again, as it is defined in the report—should be based on a *cumulative* dropout rate; that is, the retention rate could be determined by subtracting from 100 percent the cumulative percentage of students in a class who left school between grades nine and twelve.

2. I have withheld this administrator's name in order to ensure confidentiality.

3. This 28 percent dropout rate accords with the 1990 census data for the City of Addison, which indicate that 71 percent of Addison residents aged twenty-five years and over had completed high school.

4. This quotation is taken from a history of Huron County published in 1990. I have withheld the title and author's name to preserve anonymity.

5. This number compares with 22.8 percent at the state level and 13 percent at the national level. (Source: Michigan Database Census Track Information, 1994.)

6. This quotation is taken from the source referred to in Note 4 above. It is worth noting that this history of the area was "produced in coop-eration with the Huron County Chamber of Commerce." Because this collaboration may have required that the author depict the county's development in the most positive possible light, references to the nega-tive experiences of Latino workers and their families have been largely ignored. Also, despite the significant number of Latino residents in the area and the important role they have played in the county's develop-ment, this 216-page book mentions Latino individuals only three times— once in the actual text and twice in photograph captions.

7. Source: Addison's daily newspaper, October 24, 1994 (I am with-holding the newspaper's name to protect the anonymity of people de-picted in my account of Addison).

8. The 1990 Census reveals a correlation between poverty and educa-tional attainment. In Huron County, 60 percent of the families living below the poverty line had heads of the household who had not gradu-ated from high school.

Chapter Three

1. In this study, the reason cited most frequently by Latino students for dropping out was that the student was experiencing a "school disci-pline problem" (17 percent). As I will argue, such "reasons" are often better understood as results rather than causes of Latino students' nega-tive experiences at school.

2. Elizabeth's belief that learning English here in the United States would lead to economic prosperity for her and her family was a notion I heard repeated frequently among Addison's staff and Latino students. Eliza-beth, however, fell short of her goal. She failed three of her classes that semester and permanently returned to Mexico at the end of the school year.

Chapter Five

1. Please recall that "Chapter One" was the name Karen Akers used to refer to the federal funding the district received to provide extra assis-tance to "at-risk" students.

2. The contrast Akers points to between attitudes toward language-minority students and attitudes toward special education students ap-

parently extends to decisions about how the district funds its programs for LM students. Akers mentioned that LM students compete—usually unsuccessfully—with special education students for funding: "You're fighting for funding against the special ed kids, and who's got the greater advocacy in terms of parents? Think about it. Now this is making generalizations here, but if you think about these kids we're working with, their parents might be in the fields; they might not speak English well themselves; they don't know how the bureaucracy in this country works, and they don't fight city hall. But you got some middle-class parents whose kid has some kind of disability and needs special education, they're in Lansing and Washington advocating those programs. And the Latino parents just traditionally don't. There just aren't a lot of advocates for these kids in these programs."

3. While I am, I believe, representing Hirsch's argument accurately, I am obliged to point out that he is not extending the same courtesy to Dewey. To imply that Dewey considered teaching specific information useless or—worse yet—that he was not concerned with access to participation in democratic communities is to ignore what I see as the unifying theme of Dewey's work.

Chapter Six

1. Henry Giroux (1983) has pointed out that this understanding of schools as important sites of cultural reproduction is based on Karl Marx's (1969) notion that "every social process of production is, at the same time, a process of reproduction" (pp. 531–532).

2. Central to Bourdieu's analysis of how the mechanisms of cultural reproduction function within schools is the notion of "cultural capital," which Giroux (1983) describes as including the "different sets of linguistic and cultural competencies that individuals inherit by way of the class-located boundaries of their family" (p. 268). Bourdieu argues that children inherit from their families those "sets of meanings, qualities of style, modes of thinking, and types of dispositions that are assigned a certain social value and status in accordance with what the dominant class(es) label as the most valued cultural capital." Schools, Bourdieu claims, play a particularly important role in legitimating and reproducing dominant cultural capital. They tend to legitimize certain forms of knowledge, ways of speaking, and ways of relating to the world that capitalize on the type of familiarity and skills that only certain students have received from their family backgrounds and class relations. Students whose families have only a tenuous connection to the dominant cultural capital are at a decided disadvantage" (Giroux, 1983, p. 268). The way Bourdieu understands culture is consistent with the

work of Clifford Geertz. In *The Interpretation of Cultures* (1973) Geertz proposes a semiotic concept of culture—that is, viewing culture as consisting of systems of signs by which humans construct meaning: "man is an animal suspended in webs of significance he himself has spun. I take culture to be those webs" (p. 5). Culture then is a system of practices and ideologies and values that groups draw upon to make sense of the world, or, in Geertz's terms, to make things *mean*. The point Bourdieu makes is that the ruling classes manipulate these meanings for their own benefit.

3. One way to underscore the creative nature of cultural events like the Addison homecoming game is to view them using anthropologist Zdzislaw Mach's (1993) distinction between "ritual" and "ceremony," a difference Mach argues lies primarily in structural and functional concerns. "Ceremony," he suggests, reflects social order rather than creates it: "Ceremony merely represents the social relationships and does not itself constitute them" (p. 75). "Ritual," in contrast, "creates social order, acts out the symbolic world and transforms it" (p. 72). Ritual, then, is functional in that it makes possible and initiates action, a dynamic and constantly regenerative process of social order and of the identity of individuals in that order. I should point out here that Mach sees the agency implied in his notion of "ritual" not just as an instrument of hegemony. Though Mach contends that ritual creates social order, this creation, "if organized by the group opposing the existing balance of power, also [creates] social disorder or an alternative order" (78).

4. Such questions are, to be sure, difficult to raise. Nonetheless, Willis's *Learning To Labor* is an important contribution to the literature of educational ethnography precisely because his concept of "cultural production" underscores the troubling reality that the "lads" consciously choose to participate in behavior that leads only to a grueling life on the "shop floor." To acknowledge this reality is not to blame the victim; it is to strive toward a more complete understanding of the diverse forms of agency within schools as we seek ways of creating circumstances where students will not "choose" to leave.

5. Mach (1993) has underscored the importance of the symbolic construction of group identity: "By constructing definitions of others and of one's own group, of 'they' as opposed to 'we,' the model of the world encompasses the whole social universe perceived by members of a particular community. Social order, therefore, has its internal and external aspect that refers to the structure of the group itself and to its relations with other groups. Symbols of identification, of exclusion and inclusion, symbolic labels attached to people, are the cultural substance of which the model of the social world is created" (p. 38).

6. As I've indicated, during this conversation several other Latino boys were seated around the table. Though they listened and often nodded in agreement with what was said, their voices do not appear in this transcript because Zeke, Emilio, and Frank did all the talking. I have not included the entire conversation, opting instead to focus on the main issues raised.

7. The administrative structure of Addison High is such that Principal Dohm is assisted by two vice principals, one in charge of discipline, the other responsible primarily for curriculum development. As Zeke indicates, all three of these positions at that time were occupied by White men.

8. Again, I don't wish to imply here that Latino students who earn high grades or are otherwise successful in the school's terms have no Mexican identity. I have heard Emilio, for instance, refer to these students as Mexican. However, this comment is usually followed by a qualification like "but she acts White" or "but he kisses the teachers' butts." My point here is that at Addison High ethnic identity does not depend solely on heredity; rather, it depends largely upon the continuous acting out of symbolic representation that includes an oppositional stance to dominant school ideology.

9. Douglas Foley, in *Learning Capitalist Culture: Deep in the Heart of Tejas* (1990) offers what to me have been useful insights as to how we might better understand the role of symbolic representation—specifically, language use—in perpetuating social strata. Foley sets forth what he calls his "performance theory" that emerged from his research on class reproduction and resistance in schools. This performance theory, Foley explains, is based on Marx's discussion of self-objectification through alienated labor and on the work of Habermas, who defined "labor" in the broader sense of communication and thus revised Marx's notion of "alienating labor" by emphasizing the role of language, rather than solely economics, in reproducing class distinctions. Foley then draws on the work of Erving Goffman to argue that all human communication has a dramaturgical quality. Foley (citing Goffman) argues that people generally manage the flow of language in ways that shape the impression or image they wish to convey to others concerning their social identity. According to Foley, the advantage of synthesizing these theoretical perspectives is that together they provide researchers with a way of understanding how history and social class dynamics influence the ways in which people create (or recreate) themselves through language.

10. A frequent specific complaint regarding this issue is that African Americans "have a whole month" to celebrate their heritage, while

Mexican students perceive their culture as receiving recognition only on Cinco de Mayo.

11. Carl Husemoller Nightingale, in *On the Edge: A History of Poor Black Children and Their American Dreams* (1993), documents a situation similar to what Emilio suggests here: namely, that poor minorities embrace mainstream American values and beliefs. Nightingale argues that the tragedy of poverty and violence he witnessed in Philadelphia derives from minorities' being excluded from the promise of prosperity that is a cornerstone of our "American dreams."

12. Though I'm reluctant to speculate, I wonder about the extent to which Mexicans' hesitation to admit that they or their parents have worked in the fields results from what might be called "self-loathing." I raise the issue not only because of Emilio's words cited above, but also in response to what he told me regarding his dating preferences: "I can't stand Mexican girls, man; I think they're ugly. I like White girls. I love 'em to death. But like I said, Linda, she's White. She's cool." Mainstream culture constantly tells Emilio that Mexicans are second-class. Perhaps he's starting to believe as much.

I should add, too, that this ambiguity regarding identity is not limited to students. Alice Martinez and Fran Soto may be said to "walk the line" between oppositional and mainstream practices. On one hand, Martinez and Soto are, in many ways, very Mexican. They provide a safe haven for students in the ESL classroom, where they can speak Spanish. These teachers also frequently call attention to the oppressive forces acting upon Latinos. One day in ESL, for instance, the conversation turned to an agricultural region in California—populated by large numbers of Latinos and, more recently, Whites—found to have an unusually high rate of cancer due to the pesticides used on the area's farms. Martinez said, "The Anglos who live in the area are now starting to get the cancer, so now they're doing something about it." She repeated her words in Spanish, making sure that the students knew what she was saying. In this sense, Martinez and Soto are orchestrating an unofficial, even subversive, enterprise. On the other hand, because of their position on the school faculty, their permanent residency in Addison, and their age, Martinez and Soto are sometimes seen as operatives in support of Addison High's definitions of success. One day, after Martinez had confiscated Felipe's portable stereo, he complained that his ESL teachers were "working for the system."

13. In a later correspondence, Emilio gave me permission to include his letters in this work. Still, I've included only parts of them here, deleting things that I think it appropriate to keep from public view.

REFERENCES

Abi-Nader, J. (1993). Meeting the needs of multicultural classrooms: Family values and the motivation of minority students. In M. J. O'Hair & S. Odell (Eds.), *Diversity and teaching: Teacher education yearbook 1* (pp. 212–236). Fort Worth, TX: Harcourt Brace Jovanovich.

Abu-Lughod, L. (1991). Writing against culture. In R. Fox (Ed.), *Recapturing anthropology: Working in the present* (pp. 137–162). Santa Fe, NM: School of American Research Press.

Addams, J. (1990). *Twenty years at Hull-House.* Urbana, IL: University of Illinois Press. (Original work published 1910)

Ammon, M. S. (1987). Patterns of performance among bilingual children who score low in reading. In S. Goldman & H. T. Trueba, (Eds.), *Becoming literate in English as a second language* (pp. 71–105). Norwood, NJ: Ablex Publishing Corp.

Anzaldúa, G. (1987). *Borderlands: La frontera = The new mestiza.* San Francisco: Spinsters/Aunt Lute Book Company.

Arreaga-Mayer, C., & Perdomo-Rivera, C. (1996). Ecobehavioral analysis of instruction for at-risk language-minority students. *The Elementary School Journal, 96*(3), 245–258.

Athanases, S., & Heath, S. B. (1995). Ethnography in the study of the teaching and learning of English. *Research in the Teaching of English, 29*(3), 263–287.

August, D., & Hakuta, K. (Eds.). (1997). *Improving schooling for language minority children.* Washington, DC: National Academy Press.

Baldwin, J. (1993). *The fire next time.* New York: Vintage International. (Original work published 1963)

Barton, P. E. (1991). *The state of inequality.* Princeton, NJ: Educational Testing Service.

Behar, R. (1993). *Translated woman: Crossing the border with Esperanza's story*. Boston: Beacon.

Bennett, W. (1988/1992). The bilingual act: A failed path. In J. Crawford (Ed.), *Language loyalties: A source book for the official English controversy* (pp. 358–363). Chicago: University of Chicago Press, 1992. (Reprinted from *Our children and our country: Improving America's schools*, by W. Bennett, 1988, New York: Simon & Schuster)

Berlin, I. (1969). *Four essays on liberty*. New York: Oxford University Press.

Bonhoeffer, D. (1955/1971). *Ethics*. (E. Bethge, Ed., & N. H. Smith, Trans.). London: SCM Press.

Bourdieu, P. (1979). Symbolic power. *Critique of Anthropology 4*(2), 73–116.

Bowles, S., & Gintis, H. (1976). *Schooling in capitalist America: Educational reform and the contradictions of economic life*. New York: Basic Books.

Brozo, W. G. (1990). Hiding out in secondary content classrooms: Coping strategies of unsuccessful readers. *Journal of Reading, 33*(5), 324–328.

Bruner, J. (1986). *Actual minds, possible worlds*. Cambridge, MA: Harvard University Press.

Carger, C. (1996). *Of borders and dreams: A Mexican-American experience of urban education*. New York: Teachers College Press.

Carnoy, M. (1974). *Education as cultural imperialism*. New York: McKay.

Chambers, R. (1991). *Room for maneuver: Reading the oppositional in narrative*. Chicago: University of Chicago Press.

Chamot, A. U., & O'Malley, J. M. (1986). *A cognitive academic language learning approach: An ESL content-based curriculum*. Wheaton, MD: National Clearinghouse for Bilingual Education.

Chesterfield R., Chesterfield, K., Hayes-Latimer, K., & Chavez, R. (1983). The influence of teachers and peers on second language acquisition in bilingual preschool programs. *TESOL Quarterly, 17*(3), 401–419.

Clifford, J. (1986). Introduction: Partial truths. In J. Clifford & G. E. Marcus (Eds.), *Writing culture: The poetics and politics of ethnography* (pp. 1–26). Berkeley: University of California Press.

Clifford, J., & Marcus, G. E. (Eds.) (1986). *Writing culture: The poetics and politics of ethnography*. Berkeley: University of California Press.

Clough, P. (1992). *The end(s) of ethnography: From realism to social criticism*. Newbury Park, CA: Sage Publications.

Cohen, J. (1993). Constructing race at an urban high school: In their minds, their mouths, their hearts. In L. Weis & M. Fine (Eds.), *Beyond silenced voices: Class, race, and gender in United States schools* (pp. 289–308). Albany: State University of New York Press.

Collier, V. (1989). How long? A synthesis of research on academic achievement in a second language. *TESOL Quarterly, 23*(3), 509–531.

Colón, J. (1994). Little things are big. In B. Bernstein (Ed.), *Language and literacy: American literature* (pp. 525–528). New York: McDougal, Littell, & Co.

Crawford, J. (1989). *Bilingual education: History, politics, theory, and practice*. Trenton, NJ: Crane.

Crosno, M. (1994). Martinez' treasure. In B. Bernstein (Ed.), *Language and literacy: American literature* (pp. 991–997). New York: McDougal, Littell, & Co.

Cummins, J. (1981). The role of primary language development in promoting educational success for language minority students. In California State Department of Education (Ed.), *Schooling and language minority students: A theoretical framework*. Los Angeles: Evaluation, Dissemination, and Assessment Center, California State University, Los Angeles.

Cummins, J. (1984). *Bilingualism and special education: Issues in assessment and pedagogy*. San Diego: College Hill Press.

Cummins, J. (1989). *Empowering minority students*. Sacramento: California Association of Bilingual Education.

Cummins, J. (1994). From coercive to collaborative relations of power in the teaching of literacy. In B. M. Ferdman, R. Weber, & A. G. Ramírez (Eds.), *Literacy across languages and cultures* (pp. 295–331). Albany: State University of New York Press.

Damico, A. (1978). *Individuality and community: The social and political thought of John Dewey*. Gainesville: University Presses of Florida.

Darling-Hammond, L. (1995). Teacher knowledge and student learning: Implications for literacy development. In V. Gadsden & D.

Wagner (Eds.), *Literacy among African-American youth: Issues in learning, teaching, and schooling* (pp. 177–200). Cresskill, NJ: Hampton Press.

Delgado-Gaitan, C. (1987). Traditions and transitions in the learning process of Mexican children: An ethnographic view. In G. Spindler & L. Spindler (Eds.), *Interpretive ethnography of education: At home and abroad* (pp. 333–359). Hillsdale, NJ: Lawrence Erlbaum Associates.

Delgado-Gaitan, C. (1988). The value of conformity: Learning to stay in school. *Anthropology and Education Quarterly, 19*(4), 354–381.

Delgado-Gaitan, C. (1990). *Literacy for empowerment: The role of parents in children's education.* New York: Falmer Press.

Detlefsen, K. (1998). Diversity and the individual in Dewey's philosophy of education. *Educational Theory, 48*(3), 309–329.

Dewey, J. (1916/1985). *Democracy and education: An introduction to the philosophy of education.* New York: Macmillan.

Dewey, J. (1922/1988). Education as politics. In J. Boydston (Ed.), *John Dewey: The middle works, 1899–1924* (Vol. 13, pp. 331–334). Carbondale: Southern Illinois University Press.

Dewey, J. (1926/1988). Individuality and experience. In J. Boydston (Ed.), *John Dewey: The later works, 1925–1953* (Vol. 14, pp. 55–61). Carbondale: Southern Illinois University Press.

Dewey, J. (1927/1988). The public and its problems. In J. Boydston (Ed.), *John Dewey: The later works, 1925–1953* (Vol. 2, pp. 235–372). Carbondale: Southern Illinois University Press.

Dewey, J. (1929/1962). *Individualism old and new.* New York: Capricorn Books.

Dewey, J. (1930). *Human nature and conduct: An introduction to social psychology.* New York: The Modern Library.

Dewey, J. (1935). *Liberalism and social action.* New York: G. P. Putnam's Sons.

Dewey, J. (1938/1963). *Experience and education.* New York: Collier Books.

Dewey, J. (1939). *Freedom and culture.* New York: G. P. Putnam's Sons.

References

Dewey, J. (1941/1988a). The basic values and loyalties of democracy. In J. Boydston (Ed.), *John Dewey: The later works, 1925–1953* (Vol. 14, pp. 275–277). Carbondale: Southern Illinois University Press.

Dewey, J. (1941/1988b).Creative democracy: The task before us. In J. Boydston (Ed.), *John Dewey: The later works, 1925–1953* (Vol. 14, pp. 224–230). Carbondale: Southern Illinois University Press.

Dewey, J. (1957). *Outline of a critical theory of ethics.* New York: Hillary House.

Durán, R. (1987). Factors affecting development of second language literacy. In S. Goldman & T. Trueba (Eds.), *Becoming literate in English as a second language* (pp. 33–55). Norwood, NJ: Ablex.

Dwyer, M. (1998). Creating and sustaining change for immigrant learners in secondary schools. *TESOL Journal, 7*(5), 6–10.

Eckert, P. (1989). *Jocks and burnouts: Social categories and identity in the high school.* New York: Teachers College Press.

Eisenhart, M. (in press). Changing conceptions of culture and ethnographic methodology: Recent thematic shifts and their implications for research on teaching. In V. Richardson (Ed.), *The handbook of research on teaching (4th ed.)*

Ellison, R. (1989). *Invisible man.* New York: Vintage Books. (Original work published 1952)

Erickson, F. (1987). Transformation and school success: The politics and culture of educational achievement. *Anthropology and Education Quarterly, 18*(4), 335–356.

Experts call educational gap national threat. (1995, September 6). *USA Today,* pp. 1–2.

Faltis, C. (1993). *Joinfostering: Adapting teaching strategies for the multilingual classroom.* New York: Merrill Press.

Faltis, C. (1994). *Cultural diversity in schools: From rhetoric to practice.* Albany: State University of New York Press.

Feinberg, J. (1973). *Social philosophy.* Englewood Cliffs, NJ: Prentice Hall.

Feistritzer, Emily C. (1986). Educational vital signs: Teachers. *American School Board Journal, 173*(10), A12–A16.

Fern, V., Anstrom, K., & Silcox, B. (1997). *Active student learning and the LEP student, 1*(2). Washington, DC: National Clearinghouse for Bilingual Education. Available at http://128.164.90.197/ncbepubs/directions/02.htm.

Fillmore, L. W. (1985). When does teacher talk work as input? In S. Gass & C. Madden (Eds.), *Input in second language acquisition,* (pp. 17–50). Rowley, MA: Newbury House.

Fillmore, L. W. (1992). Against our best interest: The attempt to sabotage bilingual education. In J. Crawford (Ed.), *Language loyalties: A source book in the official English controversy* (pp. 367–377). Chicago: University of Chicago Press.

Fillmore, L. W., & Valadez, C. (1986). Teaching bilingual learners. In M. S. Wittrock (Ed.), *Handbook of research on teaching* (3rd ed.) (pp. 648–685). New York: Macmillan.

Fine, M. (1991). *Framing dropouts: Notes on the politics of an urban high school.* Albany: State University of New York Press.

Finn, J., & Resnick, L. (1984). Issues in the instruction of mentally retarded children. *Educational Researcher 13*(3), 9–11.

Fishman, S. M. (1993). Explicating our tacit tradition: John Dewey and composition studies. *College Composition and Communication, 44*(3), 315–330.

Fishman, S. M., & McCarthy, L. P. (1998). *John Dewey and the challenge of classroom practice.* New York: Teachers College Press; Urbana, IL: National Council of Teachers of English.

Fleischer, C. (1995). *Composing teacher-research: A prosaic history.* Albany: State University of New York Press.

Fleischman, H., & Hopstock, P. (1993). *Descriptive study of services to limited English proficient students: Summary of findings and conclusions* (Vol. 1). Washington DC: Office of the Undersecretary, U.S. Department of Education.

Foley, D. (1990). *Learning capitalist culture: Deep in the heart of Tejas.* Philadelphia: University of Pennsylvania Press.

Fraser, N. (1997). *Justice interruptus: Critical reflections on the "postsocialist" condition.* New York: Routledge.

Freire, P. (1990). *Pedagogy of the oppressed.* (M. Bergman Ramos, Trans.). New York: Continuum.

Fueyo, V. (1997). Teaching language-minority students: Using research to inform practice. *Equity and Excellence in Education, 30*(1), 16–26.

Garcia, E. E. (1991). Bilingualism, second language acquisition, and the education of Chicano language minority students. In R. Valencia (Ed.), *Chicano school failure and success: Research and policy agendas for the 1990s* (pp. 93–118). New York: Falmer Press.

Garrison, J. (1996). A Deweyan theory of democratic listening. *Educational Theory, 46*(4), 429–451.

Geertz, C. (1973). *The interpretation of cultures: Selected essays.* New York: Basic Books.

Geertz, C. (1983). *Local knowledge: Further essays in interpretive anthropology.* New York: Basic Books.

Geertz, C. (1988). *Works and lives: The anthropologist as author.* Stanford: Stanford University Press.

Gersten, R. M., and Jiménez, R. T. (1998). *Promoting learning for culturally and linguistically diverse students: Classroom applications from contemporary research.* Belmont, CA: Wadsworth Publishing Company.

Gibson, M. A., & Ogbu, J. U. (1991). Minorities and schooling: Some implications. In M. Gibson & J. Ogbu (Eds.), *Minority status and schooling: A comparative study of immigrant and involuntary minorities* (pp. 357–381). New York: Garland.

Giroux, H. (1983). Theories of reproduction and resistance in the new sociology of education: A critical analysis. *Harvard Educational Review, 53*(3), 257–293.

Giroux, H. (1999). Rethinking cultural politics and radical pedagogy in the work of Antonio Gramsci. *Educational Theory, 49*(1), 1–19.

Gitlin, T. (1995). *The twilight of our common dreams: Why America is wracked by culture wars.* New York: Metropolitan Books.

Glaser, B. G., & Strauss, A. L. (1967). *The discovery of grounded theory: Strategies for qualitative research.* Chicago: Aldine Publishing Co.

Goodlad, J. I. (1985). The great American schooling experiment. *Phi Delta Kappan, 67*(4), 266–271.

Gouinlock, J. (1988). Introduction. In J. Boydston (Ed.), *John Dewey, the later works, 1925–1953* (Vol. 2, pp. ix–xxxiv). Carbondale: Southern Illinois University Press.

Graff, H. J. (1979). *The literacy myth: Literacy and social structure in the nineteenth-century city.* New York: Academic Press.

Gramsci, A. (1992). *Selections from the prison notebooks of Antonio Gramsci.* (Q. Hoare & G. Nowell-Smith, Eds. and Trans.). New York: International Publishers.

Greene, M. (1988). *The dialectic of freedom.* New York: Teachers College Press.

Gunn, G. B. (1992). *Thinking across the American grain: Ideology, intellect, and the new pragmatism.* Chicago: University of Chicago Press.

Gutierrez, G. (1984). *A theology of liberation: History, politics and salvation.* Maryknoll, NY: Orbis Books.

Gutmann, A. (1999). *Democratic education.* Princeton: Princeton University Press.

Hakuta, K., & Gould, L. J. (1987). Synthesis of research on bilingual education. *Educational Leadership, 44*(6), 38–45.

Hall, S. (1992). The question of cultural identity. In S. Hall, D. Held, & T. McGrew, (Eds.), *Modernity and its futures* (pp. 274–322). Cambridge: Polity Press in association with the Open University.

Harper, C., & Platt, E. (1998). Full inclusion for secondary school ESOL students: Some concerns from Florida. *TESOL Journal, 7*(5), 30–36.

Harris, J. (1989). The idea of community in the study of writing. *College Composition and Communication, 40*(1), 11–22.

Hemmings, A. (1996). Conflicting images? Being Black and a model high school student. *Anthropology and Education Quarterly 27*(1), 20–50.

Henze, R., & Lucas, T. (1993). Shaping instruction to promote the success of language minority students: An analysis of four high school classes. *Peabody Journal of Education, 69*(1), 54–81.

Hirsch, E. D. (1987). *Cultural literacy: What every American needs to know.* New York: Vintage.

Hirsch, E. D. (1996). *The schools we need and why we don't have them.* New York: Doubleday.

Hoffman, E. (1989). *Lost in translation: A life in a new language.* New York: E. P. Dutton.

Hondagneu-Sotelo, P. (1994). *Gendered transitions: Mexican experiences of immigration*. Berkeley, CA: University of California Press.

hooks, b. (1990). *Yearning: Race, gender, and cultural politics*. Boston: South End Press.

Hudelson, S. (1987). The role of native language literacy in the education of language minority children. *Language Arts, 64*(8), 827–841.

Hynds, S. (1997). *On the brink: Negotiating literature and life with adolescents*. New York: Teachers College Press.

Jiménez, M. (1992). The educational rights of minority children. In J. Crawford (Ed.), *Language loyalties: A source book on the official English controversy* (pp. 243–250). Chicago: University of Chicago Press.

Jiménez, R., Gersten, R., & Rivera, A. (1996). Conversations with a Chicana teacher: Supporting students' transition from native to English language instruction. *Elementary School Journal, 96*(3), 333–341.

Kelley, R. D. G. (1997). *Yo' mama's disfunktional!: Fighting the culture wars in urban America*. Boston: Beacon Press.

Kondo, D. K. (1990). *Crafting selves: Power, gender, and discourses of identity in a Japanese workplace*. Chicago: University of Chicago Press.

Kozol, J. (1991). *Savage inequalities: Children in America's schools*. New York: Harper/Perennial.

Krashen, S. D. (1982). *Principles and practice in second language acquisition*. New York: Pergamon.

Lara-Alecio, R., & Parker, R. (1994). A pedagogical model for transitional English bilingual classrooms. *Bilingual Research Journal, 18*(3–4), 119–133.

Lather, P. (1998). Critical pedagogy and its complicities: A praxis of stuck places. *Educational Theory, 48*(4), 487–497.

Lau v. Nichols. (U.S. Supreme Court, 1974). In J. Crawford (Ed.), *Language loyalties: A source book on the official English controversy* (pp. 251–254). Chicago: University of Chicago Press.

Lessow-Hurley, J. (1996). *The foundations of dual language instruction*. White Plains, NY: Longman.

Lippmann, W. (1922/1965). *Public opinion*. New York: Free Press.

Lipsitz, G. (1990). *Time passages: Collective memory and popular culture*. Minneapolis: University of Minnesota Press.

Lucas, T. (1996, December). Promoting secondary school transitions for immigrant adolescents. *ERIC Digest*. Washington, DC: ERIC Clearinghouse on Languages and Linguistics.

Lucas, T., Henze, R., & Donato, R. (1990). Promoting the success of Latino language-minority students: An exploratory study of six high schools. *Harvard Educational Review, 60*(3), 315–340.

Lyon, J. (1992). Secretary Bennett *versus* equal educational opportunity. In J. Crawford (Ed.), *Language loyalties: A source book on the official English controversy* (pp. 363–366). Chicago: University of Chicago Press.

Lyotard, J. F. (1984). *The postmodern condition: A report on knowledge*. Minneapolis, University of Minnesota Press.

Mach, Z. (1993). The symbolic construction of identity. In J. Rollwagen (Ed.), *Symbols, conflict, and ideology: Essays on political anthropology* (pp. 22–92). New York: State University of New York Press.

Marcus, G. E., & Fisher, M. J. (1986). *Anthropology as cultural critique: An experimental moment in the human sciences*. Chicago: University of Chicago Press.

Marx, K. (1969). *Progress of capital*. Moscow: Progress Publishers.

McCracken, G. D. (1988). *The long interview*. Qualitative Research Methods Series, Vol. 13. Newbury Park, CA: Sage Publications.

McDermott, R. P., & Gospodinoff, K. (1981). Social contexts for ethnic borders and school failures. In H. T. Trueba & K. H-P. Au (Eds.), *Culture and the bilingual classroom: Studies in classroom ethnography* (pp. 213–230). Rowley, MA: Newbury House.

McLaren, P. (1995). *Critical pedagogy and predatory culture: Oppositional politics in a postmodern era*. New York: Routledge.

McLaughlin, B. (1992). *Myths and misconceptions about second language learning: What every teacher needs to unlearn*. Santa Cruz, CA: National Center for Research on Cultural Diversity and Second Language. (ERIC Document Reproduction Service No. ED 352806)

McMillen, M. M. (1993). *Dropout rates in the United States, 1992*. Berkeley, CA: MRP Associates, sponsored by the National Center for Educational Statistics, Washington, DC.

Mehan, H., & Villanueva, I. (1992). Untracking low achieving students: Academic and social consequences. In *Focus on Diversity*. Santa Cruz: National Center for Research on Cultural Diversity and Second Language Learning, University of California, Santa Cruz.

Melville, H. (1967). *Moby-Dick: An authoritative text*. New York: W. W. Norton & Co.

Mercer, J. R. (1973). *Labeling the mentally retarded: Clinical and social systems perspectives on mental retardation*. Berkeley: University of California Press.

Merino, B. J. (1991). Promoting school success for Chicanos: The view from inside the bilingual classroom. In R. Valencia (Ed.), *Chicano school failure and success: Research and policy agendas for the 1990s* (pp. 119–148). New York: Falmer Press.

Michigan database census track information, 1994. Lansing, MI: Department of Human Services.

Michigan State Board of Education. (1986). *Hispanic school dropouts and Hispanic student performance on the MEAP tests: Closing the gap*. Lansing, MI: Author.

Milk, R., Mercado, C., & Sapiens, A. (1992). Re-thinking the education of teachers of language minority children (Focus number 6). Washington, DC: National Clearinghouse for Bilingual Education.

Miranda, L., & Quiroz, J. T. (1990). *The decade of the Hispanic: An economic retrospective*. Washington DC, National Council of La Raza.

Moll, L. C. (1988). Some key issues in teaching Latino students. *Language Arts, 65*(5), 465–472.

Moll, L. C. (1992). Bilingual classroom studies and community analysis: Some recent trends. *Educational Researcher: Special Issue on Bilingual Education, 21*(2), 20–24.

Moll, L., and Diaz, S. (1987). Change as the goal of educational research. *Anthropology and Education Quarterly, 18*(4), 300–311.

Natriello, G., McDill, E. L., & Pallas, A. M. (1990). *Schooling disadvantaged children: Racing against catastrophe*. New York: Teachers College Press.

Necochea, J., & Cline, Z. (1993). Building capacity in the education of minority students. *Educational Forum, 57*(4), 402–412.

Niebuhr, R. (1941). The *nature and destiny of man: A Christian interpretation*. New York: Scribner.

Nieto, S. (1992). *Affirming diversity: The sociopolitical context of multicultural education*. New York: Longman.

Nieto, S. (1994). Lessons from students on creating a chance to dream. *Harvard Educational Review, 64*(4), 392–426.

Nightingale, C. H. (1993). *On the edge: A history of poor black children and their American dreams*. New York: Basic Books.

Noddings, N. (1984). *Caring: A feminine approach to ethics and moral education*. Berkeley: University of California Press.

Noddings, N. (1996). On caring. *Educational Theory, 45*(3), 254–271.

North, S. M. (1987). *The making of knowledge in composition: Portrait of an emerging field*. Upper Montclair, NJ: Boynton/Cook.

Northcutt, L., & Watson, D. (1986). *Sheltered English teaching handbook*. San Marcos, CA: AM Graphics and Printing.

Oakes, J. (1985). *Keeping track: How schools structure inequality*. New Haven, CT: Yale University Press.

Ogbu, J. (1985). Anthropology of education. In T. Husén & T. N. Postlethwaite (Eds.), *The international encyclopedia of education: Research and studies* (pp. 276–298). Oxford: Pergamon Press.

Ovando, C. (1990). Politics and pedagogy: The case of bilingual education. *Harvard Educational Review, 60*, 341–356.

Pallas, A. M., Natriello, G., and McDill, E. L. (1988, April). *Who falls behind: Defining the "at risk" population—current dimensions and future trends*. Paper presented at the meeting of the American Educational Research Association, New Orleans, LA.

Parsons, T. W. (1965). *Ethnic cleavage in a California school*. Unpublished doctoral dissertation, Stanford University.

Pérez, B., & Guzmán-Torres, M. E. (1996). *Learning in two worlds: An integrated Spanish/English biliteracy approach* (2nd ed.). White Plains, NY: Longman.

Poplin, M., and Weeres, J. (1992). *Voices from the inside: A report on schooling from inside the classroom*. Claremont, CA: Claremont Graduate School, Institute for Education in Transformation.

Ramirez, J. D. (1991). *Final report: Longitudinal study of structured English immersion strategy, early-exit, and late-exit transitional bilingual education programs for language minority children.* San Mateo, CA: Aguirre International; United States Department of Education.

Reed, L. (1989). Dirty boulevard. On *New York* [CD]. New York: Warner Brothers Records.

Richard-Amato, P. A., & Snow, M. A. (1992). Strategies for content-area teachers. In P. A. Richard-Amato & M. A. Snow (Eds.), *The multicultural classroom: Readings for content-area teachers* (pp. 145–163). New York: Longman.

Robinson, J. (1990). *Conversations on the written word: Essays on language and literacy.* Portsmouth, NH: Boynton/Cook.

Robinson, J. (1998). Literacy and lived lives: Reflections on the responsibilities of teachers. In C. Fleischer & D. Schaafsma (Eds.), *Literacy and democracy: Teacher research and composition studies in pursuit of habitable spaces: Further conversations from the students of Jay Robinson* (1–27). Urbana, IL: National Council of Teachers of English.

Rodríguez, C. (1989). *Puerto Ricans: Born in the U.S.A.* Boston: Unwin Hyman.

Romo, H. (1996). The newest outsiders: Educating Mexican migrant and immigrant youth. In J. L. Flores (Ed.), *Children of la frontera: Binational efforts to serve Mexican migrant and immigrant students* (pp. 165–182). Charleston, WV: ERIC Clearinghouse on Rural Education and Small Schools. (ED 393631).

Romo, H., & Falbo, T. (1996). *Latino high school graduation: Defying the odds.* Austin: University of Texas Press.

Ronda, M. A., & Valencia, R. R. (1994). "At-risk" Chicano students: The institutional and communicative life of a category. *Hispanic Journal of Behavioral Sciences, 16*(4), 363–395.

Roosevelt, T. (1986). The children of the crucible. In S. Brumberg, *Going to America, going to school: The Jewish immigrant public school encounter in turn-of-the-century New York City.* New York: Praeger. (Original work published 1917)

Rosaldo, R. (1989). *Culture & truth: The remaking of social analysis.* Boston: Beacon Press.

Rose, M. (1989). *Lives on the boundary: A moving account of the struggles and achievements of America's educational underclass.* New York: Penguin Books.

Rossell, C. H., & Baker, K. (1996). The educational effectiveness of bilingual education. *Research in the Teaching of English, 30*(1), 7–74.

Rueda, R. (1991). An analysis of special education as a response to the diminished academic achievement of Chicano students. In R. Valencia (Ed.), *Chicano school failure and success: Research and policy agendas for the 1990s* (pp. 252–270). New York: Falmer Press.

Ryan, A. (1995). *John Dewey and the high tide of American liberalism.* New York: W. W. Norton & Co.

Said, E. W. (1978). *Orientalism.* New York: Pantheon Books.

Sánchez, G. (1993). *Becoming Mexican American: Ethnicity, culture, and identity in Chicano Los Angeles, 1900–1945.* New York: Oxford University Press.

Schaafsma, D. (1993). *Eating on the street: Teaching literacy in a multicultural society.* Pittsburgh: University of Pittsburgh Press.

Schatzman, L., & Strauss, A. L. (1973). *Field research: Strategies for a natural sociology.* Englewood Cliffs, NJ: Prentice-Hall.

Secada, W. G., et al. (1998). *No more excuses: The final report of the Hispanic dropout report.* Washington, DC: United States Department of Education, Office of Bilingual and Minority Languages Affairs.

Sennett, R. (1977). *The fall of public man.* New York: Alfred A. Knopf.

Shaw, G. B. (1952). The devil's disciple (Act III). In G. B. Shaw, *Three plays for Puritans: The devil's disciple, Caesar and Cleopatra, & Captain Brassbound's conversion* (pp. 1–82). London: Constable and Co.

Sleeter, C. E., & Grant, C. A. (1991). Mapping terrains of power: Student cultural knowledge versus classroom knowledge. In C. E. Sleeter (Ed.), *Empowerment through multicultural education* (pp. 49–67). Albany: State University of New York Press.

Solzhenitsyn, A. (1980). *Détente: Prospects for democracy and dictatorship.* New Brunswick, NJ: Translation, Inc.

Spellmeyer, K. (1996). After theory: From textuality to attunement with the world. *College English, 58*(8), 893–913.

Street, B. V. (1984). *Literacy in theory and practice.* New York: Cambridge University Press.

Strong, M. (1983). Social styles and the second language acquisition of Spanish-speaking kindergartners. *TESOL Quarterly, 17(2),* 241–258.

Tchudi, S., & Mitchell, D. (1999). Exploring and teaching the English language arts (4th ed.). New York: Longman.

Tierney, W. (1993). The cedar closet. *Qualitative Studies in Education, 6,* 303–314.

Tippens, D., & Dana, N. (1992, March). Culturally relevant alternative assessment. *Science Scope,* 50–53.

Tomasky, M. (1996). *Left for dead: The life, death, and possible resurrection of progressive politics in America.* New York: The Free Press.

Toruellas, R. (1991). The failure of the New York Public Educational System to retain Hispanic and other minority students (statement submitted to the New York State Black and Puerto Rican Legislative Caucus, March 24). In C. E. Rodríguez (Ed.), *Puerto Ricans: Born in the U.S.A.* (pp. 121–157). Boulder, CO: Westview Press.

Trimbur, J. (1989). Consensus and difference in collaborative learning. *College English, 51*(6), 602–616.

Unger, R. M., & West, C. (1998). *The future of American progressivism: An initiative for political and economic reform.* Boston: Beacon Press.

University of California Linguistic Minority Research Institute Education Policy Center. (1997). Review of the research on instruction of limited English proficient students. Davis, CA: University of California–Davis.

U.S. Bureau of the Census. (1994). *County and city data book.* Washington, DC: Bureau of the Census.

U.S. Bureau of the Census. (1990). *United States census.* Washington, DC: Author.

U.S. Commission on Civil Rights. (1973). *Teachers and students: Differences in teacher interaction with Mexican American and Anglo students.* (Mexican American education study, Report 5.) Washington DC: U.S. Government Printing Office.

Valdés, G. (1996). *Con respeto: Bridging the differences between culturally diverse families and schools: An ethnographic portrait.* New York: Teachers College Press.

Valencia, R. (Ed.). (1991a). *Chicano school failure and success: Research and policy agendas for the 1990s.* New York: Falmer Press.

Valencia, R. (1991b). The plight of Chicano students: An overview of schooling conditions and outcomes. In R. Valencia (Ed.), *Chicano school failure and success: Research and policy agendas for the 1990s* (pp. 3–26). New York: Falmer Press.

Vasquez, O., Pease-Alvarez, L., & Shannon, S. M. (1994). *Pushing boundaries: Language and culture in a Mexicano community.* New York: Cambridge University Press.

Verplaetse, L. (1998). How content teachers interact with English language learners. *TESOL Journal, 7*(5), 24–28.

Vinz, R. (1997). Capturing a moving form: "Becoming" as English teachers. *English Education, 29*(2), 137–146.

Walberg, H. J. (1987). Letter dissenting from the majority opinion: Bilingual education: A new look at the research evidence. (Briefing report to the Chairman, Committee on Education and Labor, U.S. House of Representatives). Washington, DC: U.S. Government Printing Office.

Walberg, H. J. (1989, April 13). *Promoting English literacy.* Paper presented at the Public Policy Conference on Bilingual Education, Washington DC.

Weis, L. (1995). Identity formation and the process of "othering": Unraveling sexual threads. *Educational Foundations, 9*(1), 17–33.

West, C. (1993). *Keeping faith: Philosophy and race in America.* New York: Routledge.

West, C. (1999). The moral obligations of living in a democratic society. In D. Bateston & E. Mendieta (Eds.), *The good citizen* (pp. 5–12). New York: Routledge.

Westbrook, R. B. (1991). *John Dewey and American democracy.* Ithaca: Cornell University Press.

Wilhelm, J. (1997). *"You Gotta BE the Book: Teaching engaged and reflective reading with adolescents.* Urbana, IL: National Council of Teachers of English; and New York: Teachers College Press.

Willis, P. (1981a). Cultural production is different from cultural reproduction is different from social reproduction is different from reproduction. *Interchange on Educational Policy, 12(2–3)*, 48–67.

Willis, P. (1981b). *Learning to labor: How working class kids get working class jobs.* New York: Columbia University Press.

Wolf, M. (1992). *A thrice told tale: Feminism, postmodernism, and ethnographic responsibility.* Stanford: Stanford University Press.

Wolterstorff, N. (1983). *Until justice and peace embrace: The Kuyper
lectures for 1981 delivered at the Free University of Amsterdam.*
Grand Rapids, MI: William B. Eerdmans.

Young, I. M. (1990). *Justice and the politics of difference.* Princeton:
Princeton University Press.

Zanger, V. V. (1993). Academic costs and social marginalization: An
analysis of Latino students' perceptions at a Boston high school. In
R. Rivera & S. Nieto (Eds.), *The education of Latino students in
Massachusetts: Issues, research, and policy implications* (pp. 167–
187). Boston: Mauricio Gastón Institute for Latino Community
Development and Public Policy, University of Massachusetts.

INDEX

Author

After teaching high school English and social studies for six years, **Todd DeStigter** received his Ph.D. in English education from the University of Michigan in 1996. He is currently assistant professor of English at the University of Illinois at Chicago, where he teaches classes in methods of teaching English and in the interrelations between literacy, pedagogy, and democracy.

This book was typeset in Adobe Sabon by Electronic Imaging.
Typefaces used on the cover were Futura, Goudy, and Optima.
The book was printed on 50-lb. Williamsburg Offset
by Versa Press, Inc.